PICTURES ON A PAGE

Photo-journalism, Graphics and Picture Editing

DAILY NEWS

NEW YORK'S PICTURE NEWSPAPER ®

10¢

Vol. 52. No. 38 Copr. 1973 New York News Inc. New York, N.Y. 10017, Saturday, August 8, 1970★ WEATHER: Sunny, breezy and warm.

JUDGE AND 3 DIE IN GUN BATTLE

Verdict: Death. Convict James McLain holds shotgun and pistol on Superior Court Judge Harold J. Haley as he tries escape from San Rafael, Calif., court. A gunman invaded McLain's trial, passed guns to him and three convict witnesses, then took Haley and three others hostage. Judge, McLain and two others died in battle. —*Story p. 3; other pics. centerfold*

PICTURES ON A PAGE

Photo-journalism, Graphics and Picture Editing

Harold Evans
Editor, The Sunday Times, London

in association with Edwin Taylor,
Director Design, Sunday Times

Holt, Rinehart and Winston
New York

EDITING AND DESIGN

BOOK ONE Newsman's English
BOOK TWO Handling Newspaper Text
BOOK THREE News Headlines
BOOK FOUR Pictures on a Page
BOOK FIVE Newspaper Design

Library of Congress Cataloging in Publication Data Revised
Evans, Harold.
Editing and design.
Vol. 2 lacks ed. statement.
Includes bibliographies.
CONTENTS: book 1. Newsman's English.—book 2. Handling newspaper text.—book 3. News headlines.—book 4. Pictures on a page.—book 5. Newspaper design.
1. Journalism. 2. Newspaper layout and typography.
I. Title.
PN4775.E9 070.4'1 77-15201
ISBN 0-03-013131-6 (V.4)

Production team: Victor Shreeve, Adrian Williams
George Darby

First published in the United States in 1978
Printed in Great Britain

Contents

Photographs are arranged clockwise on the page

To Kate Evans

These are the pictures which open—and end—this book

Covering all angles: Photographers on scaffolding adjacent to St. Paul's Cathedral cover the funeral of Sir Winston Churchill. The picture was taken from the portico of St. Paul's by Alan Ballard (Topix). Some of the results are seen in Chapter 2, pages 27–30.

DAILY NEWS 10¢

JUDGE AND 3 DIE IN GUN BATTLE

Verdict: Death.

'Take lots of pictures, we are the revolutionaries', escaping prisoners shouted at Jim Keane, of the *San Rafael Independent Journal*. They led Judge Haley from his courtroom at the point of a shotgun; the judge and two of the prisoners died in a gun battle.

Hope in a New Land: Jewish immigrants arrive at Haifa, Israel in 1948. By Robert Capa, courtesy International Center of Photography, New York.

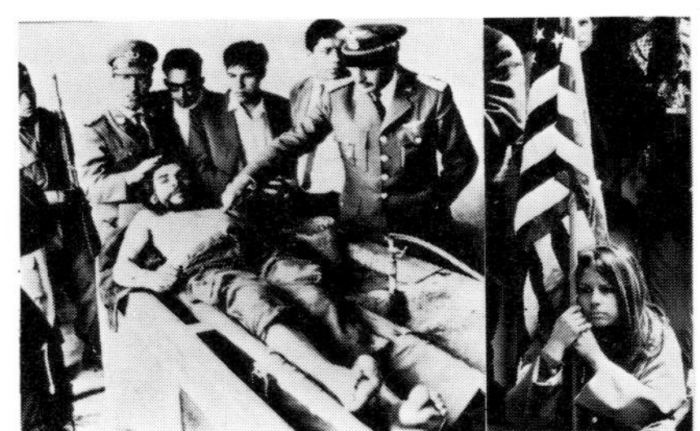

Che Guevara, the guerrilla, is dead, but nobody believes it until Bolivia puts his body on display—UPI.

A girl student holds the American flag during a protest. AP reported that readers could not decide whether it was an insult or homage.

Yasser Arafat, head of the Palestine Liberation Organisation. Picture by Graeme Baker of S.I.P.A. and Rex Features.
Framing. A tall ship caught between Manhattan tower skyscrapers by Eddie Adams of Associated Press, a World Press Photo Award.
Scale. Lips with microfilm, by Michael Ward, *The Sunday Times*.

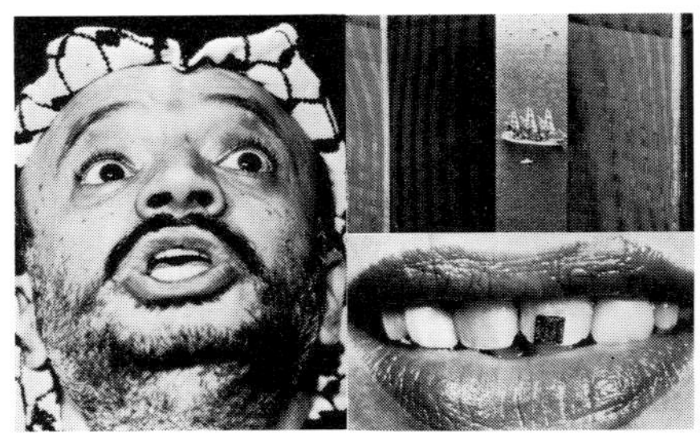

South African police put down a riot at Cato Manor. Photographer—Laurie Bloomfield, copyright Argus Printing and Publishing Company, Durban.

Bengali guerrillas bayonet Biharis on a polo field, photograph by Horst Faas and Michel Laurent of Associated Press, Pulitzer prize winner, 1972.

Robert Kennedy lies dying of a bullet wound in a Los Angeles hotel, 1968 and Mrs. Ethel Kennedy holds up a hand of protest—Harry Benson, Time-Life.

The Wedding Group by Robert Doisneau-Rapho.

Preface

This is a book for the people who put pictures on pages; and for all of us who look at them in newspapers and magazines. I hope it will stimulate the professionals and entertain the ordinary reader. He will become aware that he is the subject of manipulation, but his curiosity may be excited by the processes from assignment to cropping that lie behind the images he takes for granted. To enable the newspaper reader to glance at pictures of an earthquake in Sicily in 1976, Bryan Wharton left London at 1.15 p.m. on a Friday, took two flights, drove 700 miles, took his photographs, drove 700 miles back to the airport, arriving in his office at 2 p.m. on Saturday, two hours before deadline. One big photograph was used on the front page—but was it the best use of his work? See chapter nine. Many photographs in this book are evocative of great events, but it is not an attempt to identify the all-time best. There are some pictures that are familiar and will last forever and others that have never been published. Some of these were outright rejects but they have value here because they cast light on what it is that makes some photographs survive the photographers.

For my professional colleagues this volume is intended to be a companion to the books on editing and design, and particularly volume five, *Newspaper Design*. It is sustained by a belief that there is too little discussion of the principles of selection and editing and by a deepening depression at what passes for photojournalism. The still photograph is not to be supplanted by the ephemera of the night's television. It can provide a permanent visual experience. But photography is a wasted medium on so many newspapers, a mere token tribute to a technical capacity. There is even less realisation of the possibilities of graphics and drawing and the final section is devoted to some straightforward propaganda.

This book could never have been completed without the collaboration of Edwin Taylor, an Associate Editor and Design Director at *The Sunday Times*. To say that I am responsible for the content and Taylor for the layout is to understate his role. Every photograph and almost every idea was discussed between us and he often made me see. George Darby edited the manuscript with consistent skill and zeal. After these I must acknowledge a debt to the photographers and not simply those whose work appears here. Famous and unknown they have all—without exception— entered into the spirit of the enterprise with enthusiasm, generous with their time and their work. I am grateful for their prints and for their insights. I have been sustained throughout by the support of the National Council for the Training of Journalists and its Director Alec Newman who first asked me to undertake this work more years ago than any of us care to remember.

I owe thanks for innumerable courtesies to many newspaper librarians, though specially to *The Sunday Times*, and to the great picture agencies of Associated Press, United Press International, and Keystone, Camera Press, Topix, Magnum, Rex Features, Gamma, and personally to Hal Buell, A.P.'s Vice President.

I share with everyone who cares for photojournalism a debt to Cornell Capa and the International Center for Concerned Photography in New York, Vincent Jones, formerly Executive Editor of Gannett Newspapers, who first showed me what cropping could do, and to the organisers of the main photojournalism contests, especially World Press Photo, Ilford, Rank and Midland Bank. A number of *The Sunday Times* people made particular contributions. Laurie Zimmerman in New York was Holmes to my Watson in the search for vaguely identified photographs and elusive photographers. Vincent Page, Frank Herrmann and Jack Hallam, and on the Magazine, Bruce Bernard and Mike Rand, were helpful. Five people were indispensable: Jacqueline Pyle who typed most of the manuscript, and Joan Thomas, Doris Bryen, picture researcher extraordinary, and the designers Victor Shreeve and Adrian Williams, who made it all come together.

H.M.E.

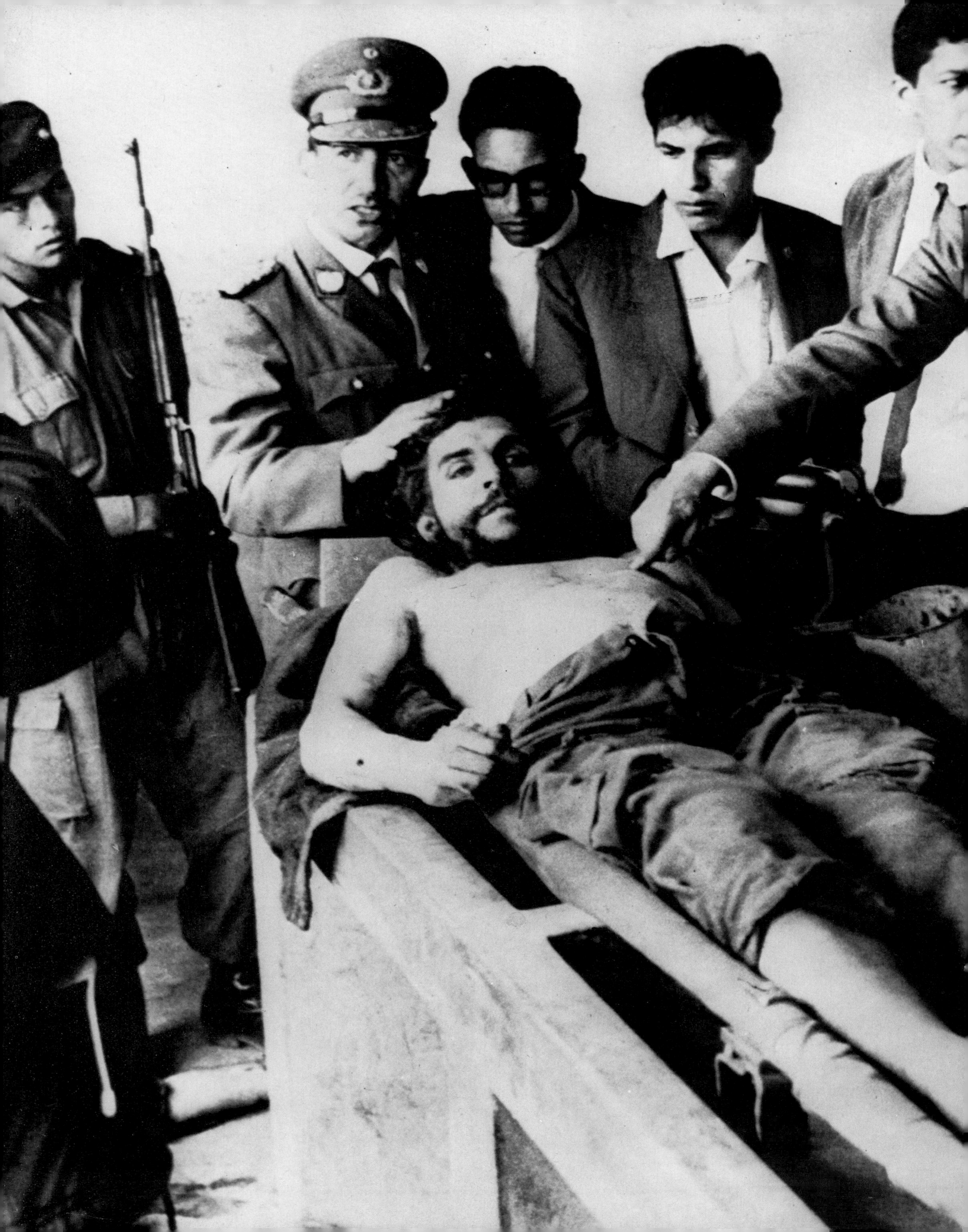

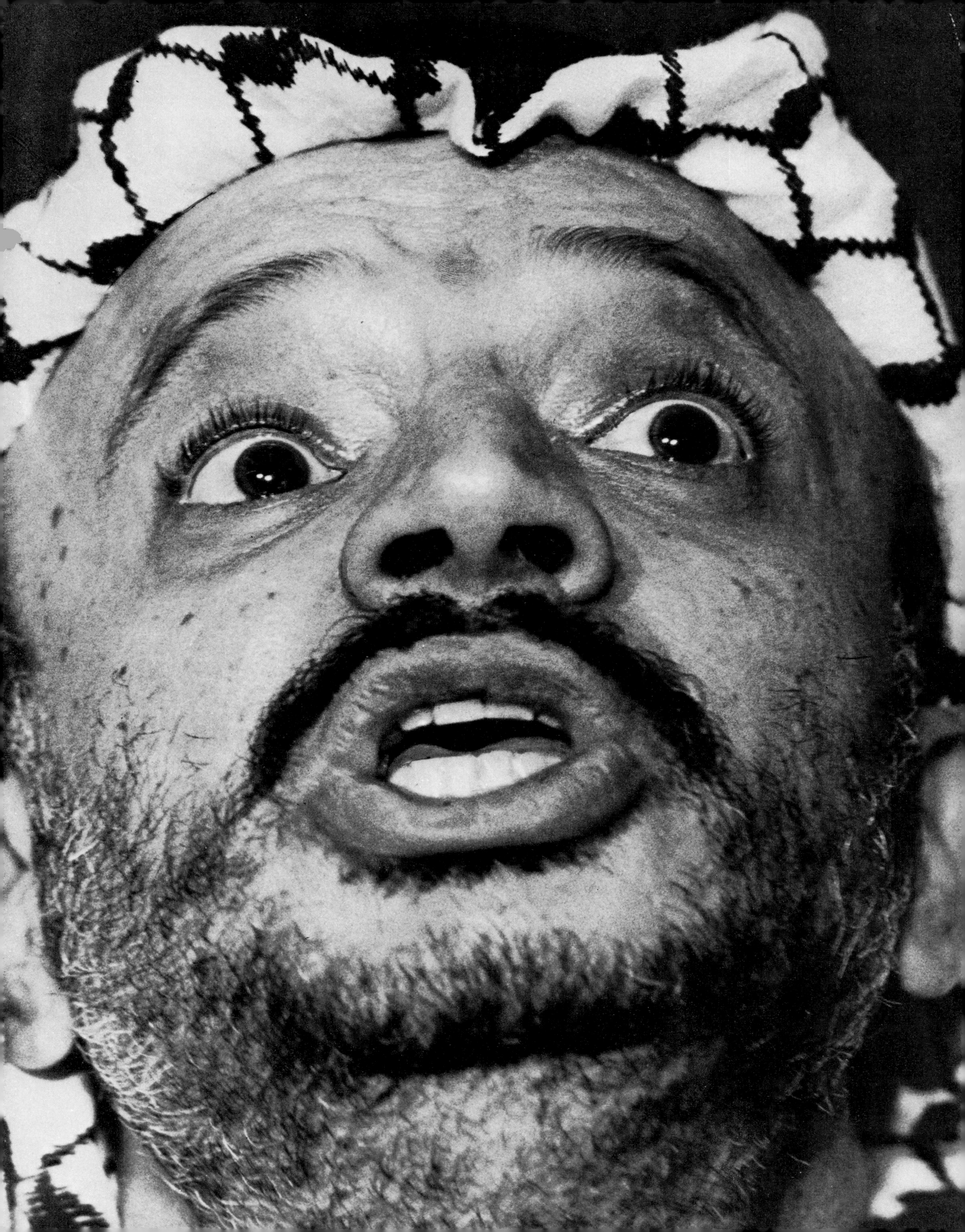

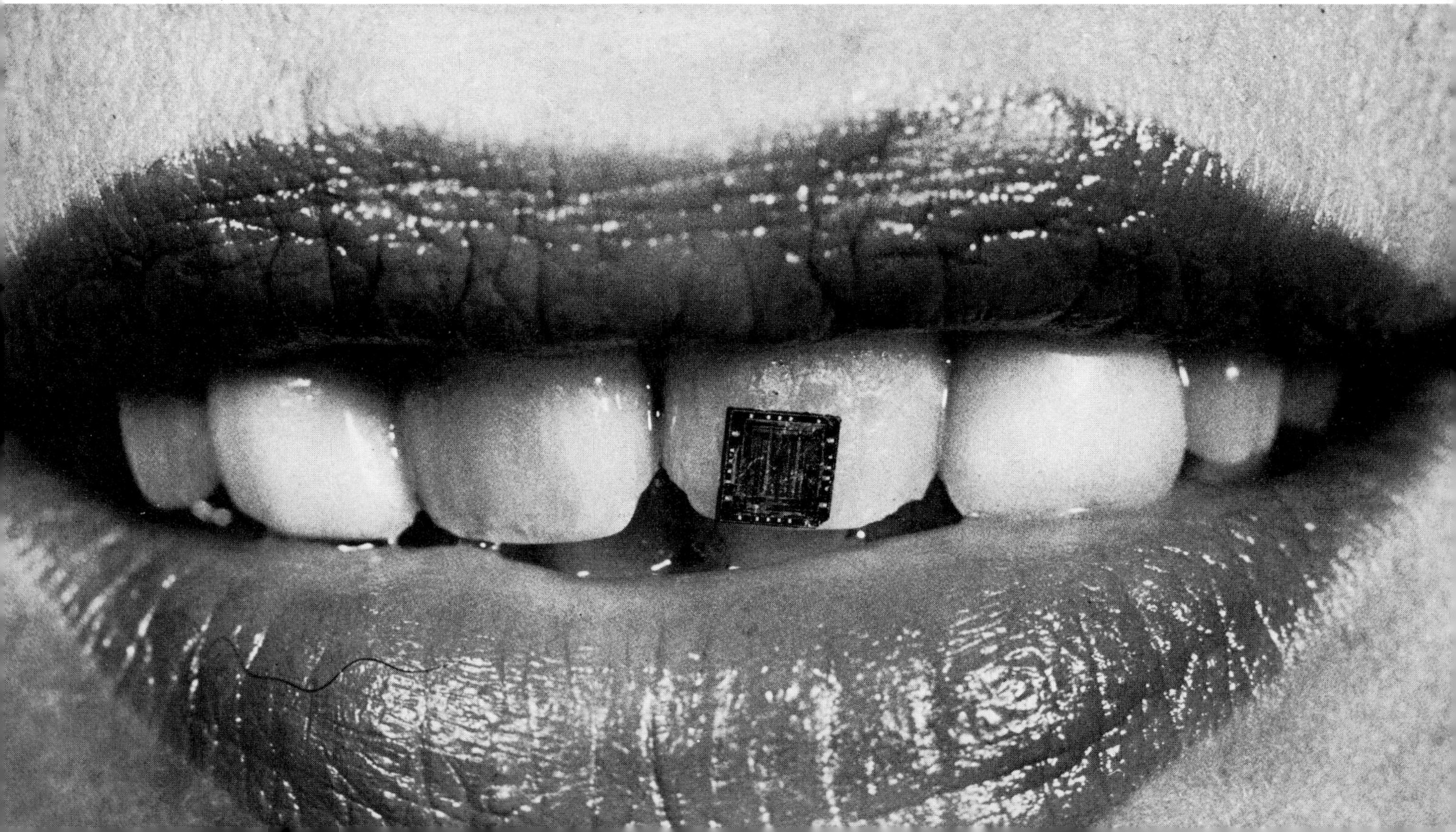

Introduction

The camera cannot lie; but it can be an accessory to untruth. Political enemies smile at each other for a hundredth of a second and the next day the newspaper reader absorbs the warmth of their friendship. Bullies can be shown as men of charity; the pompous as folksy; and honest girls as tarts. Mountains are moved with the effort it takes to fit a 500mm lens, a backyard swimming pool instantly enlarged to Olympic standards, and, thanks to photographic montage or editing, we can ponder events, irrefutably down in black and white, that never happened. In such everyday illusions there may be benevolence or malign conspiracy, but chance always affects the final perception for no single person controls the process.

The photographer may begin it, selecting the moment and the composition which fit his belief, or his ignorance. There is a set of pictures of Presidents Truman and Eisenhower, meeting for a hand-over ceremony, which faithfully records their mutual animosity. One photographer finally and momentarily coaxed the smiles he had expected at the event; and that was the picture which went round the world. From the Korean war the world saw an appealing picture of an American soldier 'sharing his last drops of water with a dying peasant'. Bert Hardy, the famous *Picture Post* photographer, told me: 'I set it up. Everybody was walking past but I had the idea and asked a GI to give the old man some water for the sake of the picture. He said he would if I was quick—and if we used my water ration.' Was the photograph truth or fiction? Hardy, who won prizes for his brave photographs of the landing at Inchon under fire, can recall scores of 'news' photographs he staged. His candour nibbles at the credibility of photojournalism, but it cannot be any more corrosive of our confidence in the truth of what we see than the assertion of some of today's photographers, hand on innocuous heart, that they take pictures to change the world.

Next there is the unseen influence of the picture editor. He can decide what is photographed. He can select, suppress, distort. He can juxtapose images to provoke derision. He can blow up a single frame in a hundred and crop it to give a tiny detail the greatest significance: the yawn in a crowded political meeting rather than the candidate in the centre of a warming crowd. He can, by selection from the picture library, manufacture stereotypes of heroes and villains—Castro is, depending on the editor's whim, a scowling belligerent or the idol of his people. Mark Godfrey has said: 'I would send my film in from Vietnam and a picture editor in Saigon would pick the frame he felt dramatic enough to transmit. Often I was horrified to find that the photographs made high drama out of field situations which were boring and tedious.' Gloria Emerson testifies, from her research for a book on Vietnam, that picture desks preferred even the ersatz excitement of the test firing of a gun to photographs which told a great deal about the exhaustion, isolation and despair of the war. The newspaper reader is unaware of the judgements that open and shut his eyes. Everyone can remember the sensational photograph (see 5A) of a police chief shooting a prisoner on a Saigon street because it was front-paged round the world. But nobody was allowed to see a similar picture, taken six years earlier in 1962 by Dickey Chapelle, again showing a Vietcong prisoner about to be executed by his captor, a South Vietnamese soldier with a drawn gun. It was universally rejected and published only in an obscure little magazine. In 1963 Malcolm Browne photographed a Buddhist monk setting himself on fire (7B) but John G Morris, picture editor of the *New York Times* has recorded that the paper's editors thought it 'unfit for the breakfast table', and a great many other newspapers would not run it. If these pictures were part of the truth about the war, part of the truth was concealed for years. Almost every photographer can tell such stories, significant or absurd. Stuart Heydinger photographed Prince Philip spreadeagled in the mud under the belly of his polo pony. For fear of royal disapproval it was kept out of circulation by the agency, INP; now it is lost.

There are two more layers in the sieve of reality. The photographer often does not write the caption which goes with the picture and never the headline. Words can turn images on their heads: the photograph of a couple locked in embrace may be captioned Love or it may be captioned Rape. Time and again in war both sides have used one and the same photograph to attribute crimes to the enemy; and that yawn in the political meeting can be attributed as the response not to the candidate but to an opponent. Finally, there is the honest reader who can make a monkey out of all this analysis by seeing what he wants to see. His mind is a blank, ready to absorb the image only in the sense that photographic printing paper in the chemical bath is blank in the seconds before the outlines of the picture emerge. The reader imposes on the photographers' work a matrix of memory, appetite, prejudice and sophistication; and when his emotions are strong he can see the opposite of what was intended. Hundreds of people wrote to the Associated Press about the picture of the girl war protester with the American flag (frontispiece of this book); but they had formed contrary impressions. Some saw it as a moving demonstration of patriotism by a young American; others as an insult to the flag.

THESE opening observations may strike a peevish note in a book celebrating photojournalism. They are not intended to supply a single live round of ammunition to the critics who maintain that photojournalism is dead: that, in the words of Susan Sontag, it deludes the mind and deadens the emotions, posing as an accurate 'miniature' of reality when it is only a symbol. On the contrary, it is because photojournalism is so very potent that I fire cautionary blanks to remind practitioners of the responsibilities and to alert victims to the risks. Written journalism can delude the mind and deaden the emotions. It is not redundant because it requires intelligence, knowledge, sensitivity and scepticism; and neither is photojournalism. It is just that photojournalism requires more of these qualities than it has had. It requires more critical analysis, more awareness in the man who simply looks at a picture on a page. The opening qualifications on the photograph as truth are important qualifications; but qualifications are all they are. To warn the risks of being deceived by a photograph is not to admit that photography permanently deludes. To acknowledge that photography is symbolic is not to deny its uniqueness as a contribution to understanding the world we cannot see for ourselves. How better can we appreciate the reality of the mercury poisoning of Japanese families at Minamata (123A) than by looking at W Eugene Smith's pictures of the pollution and the crippled children? Those other symbols, words, are not enough to depict our invisible environment. It is more than a coincidence that the Vietnam war was at once the most unpopular in American history and the most photographed.

Certainly there are limits to photography: the final section in this book, on information graphics, demonstrates that. But photographs such as Smith's at Minamata have a value that is both cognitive and emotional, and if our emotions today are deadened by a surfeit of shock then the photograph is all the more remarkable for the response it can arouse. The shock produced in different generations by Matthew Brady in the Civil War, or Roger Fenton in the Crimean War, or by the 12 photographers hired by the Farms Security Administration poignantly to portray the deprivation of the dust-bowl Okies, may all be written off as parts of a pre-television past. But most editors today would testify that for causing them anxiety and provoking the readers there is still enormous power in a single still photograph. Hundreds of newspapers published photographs by the *Boston Herald American*'s Stanley Forman of a woman and two-year-old child plunging to their deaths from a fire escape, in 1975; and thousands of readers reacted angrily against 'cheap journalism, voyeurism, irresponsibility, poor taste and invasion of privacy . . . giving our kids a nightmare.' The power of the news photograph is such that it brings difficult judgements for all of us. At the conclusion of the Bangladesh war, photographers in Dacca were invited to a 'photo opportunity' in a polo field. It turned out to be the bayoneting of Biharis who were alleged to have collaborated with the Pakistan army; that is one of the pictures in the frontispiece section of this book. People were to be murdered for the camera; and some photographers and a television camera crew departed without taking a picture in the hope that in the absence of cameramen the acts might not be committed. Others felt that the mob was beyond the appeal to mercy. They stayed and won Pulitzer prizes. Were they right?

None of this is to suggest that photojournalism is vulnerable only in its credibility. At both the crude and the sophisticated level it has visual problems, and part of this book's purpose is to explore them. They exist in the blindness and insularity of many newspapers, especially in the United States, and, among the better practitioners, the risks in emulation and subjectivity which rate what a photographer can create higher than what he can report. We have been so moved by photographers' concern—as Cornell Capa calls men like his brother, Werner Bischof, David Seymour, Bruce Davidson, Gordon Parks, and others—that imitation and exclusion may impoverish the medium. Lewis W. Hine, the pioneer humanist photographer, did say he wanted to show the things that had to be corrected, but he also said: 'I want to show the things that had to be appreciated.'

It is, perhaps, the proliferation of cliche, the death of *Life* and *Look*, and the necessary scepticism about what we see which is leading to a disturbing passion for 'creativity' in photography. Is photography art? Nowhere in this book, the reader will be despondent to learn, will we land in this marmalade. Cartier Bresson said: 'I don't know if photography is an art or not an art'. Edward Steichen, who did not give a hoot in hell about the photograph as art, wanted it to explain man to man. That was, he recognised, the most complicated thing on earth 'and also as naive as a tender plant'. It has not been brought nearer, and photojournalism has certainly been set back, by the idea that what matters is the soul of the photographer. John Szarkowski, at the Museum of Modern Art, New York, told us recently, that the more public kind of statement has been replaced: 'Many photographers now are working with their private understandings, observations and sensibilities.' And Gerald Rosenkrantz, librarian of the great Magnum agency, comments: 'Photography has shifted from the external to the internal environment'. Photographers are suckers for this kind of narcotic. Some of them may be inspired to imaginative explorations; but it will be a pity if concern with technique and the externalisation of inner fantasies suborns the value of content.

For ordinary mortals, the final word on this subject should have been spoken 25 years ago by Berenice Abbott: 'I have yet to see a fine photograph which is not a good document.' There are many good documents in this book, by many fine photographers; I hope that, together with words, they renew the case for photojournalism.

London *Harold Evans*

Chapter 1

The Unbeatable News Photograph

It is one of the peculiar characteristics of the photograph that it isolates single moments in time.

Marshall McLuhan

1A Astronaut photographed on the moon

1B Automatic camera catches bank raider

It is a fashionable fallacy that the arrival of television has rendered the still news picture obsolete. It has, on the contrary, enduring vitality and in this chapter we discuss some of the reasons; but first the reader is invited to glance at the five news photographs which open this chapter. What is their common characteristic? The answer is on the next page and the only clue is that it supports the contention that the still news photograph has a special quality.

The doubt about the vitality of the news picture is as odd as the torpor newspapers exhibited when first confronted with the opportunities of photography. There had been news photographers from 1840, daguerrotypes of the Hamburg Fire. Roger Fenton photographed the Crimean War in the 1850s, Matthew Brady and Alexander Gardner photographed the American Civil War in the 1860s and unknown photographers have left us news pictures of Communards in their coffins after the 1860 Paris insurrections. The Klondike gold rush, the Boxer Rebellion and the Boer War were photographed. But the pictures appeared in albums and exhibitions, not newspapers. Even when the feasibility of reproducing photographs in newspapers was demonstrated in 1880, newspapers remained unexcited. Photographers will maintain, with some justice, that the sloth of the fathers has been visited on the sons and the toils of invention certainly seem ill-rewarded by reproduction in their thousands of funereal group photographs. Yet even mediocre photographs attract an audience and a good news picture, even on an inside page, may attract 80 per cent of the paper's readership. It is a phenomenal figure. Let us delve into the reasons for it.

2A Amateur photographer, historic picture; Sherpa Tensing on Everest, 1953, photographed by Edmund Hillary.

3A John Gilpin, amateur, hoped to catch a DC-8 at take off, Sydney, Australia, February 1971. Then his view was blocked, and he caught the plane at 200ft. He did not see the stowaway boy of 14 falling to his death as the jet's wheel housing was opened—but it was on his film

Being there

The common factor in the five photographs which begin this chapter is that not one of them was taken by a professional photo journalist. Two of them were taken by machines. One would be hard pressed to find in them the virtues of texture, line and form that justify inclusion in an art book on photography. The first picture (1A) is by an astronaut photographing his colleague on the moon; (1B) is the work of an automatic camera recording the kidnapped Patty Hearst reappearing with a gun in a bank raid. It is an amateur again in (2A), Edmund Hillary photographing his climbing companion Tensing when the first men set foot on the summit of Everest.

The historic photograph ushering in the atomic era was taken by an automatic camera on Bikini Atoll (4A). The picture of a stowaway falling 200 ft to his death (3A) was taken by an amateur who did not even realise he had it on his film.

I do not start in this way with amateurs and automatic cameras to suggest that professional photojournalists are unnecessary or overpaid; on the contrary their skills, cunning and courage permeate this book. Nor am I suggesting that composition and tone are values too esoteric for newspapers and magazines. On the contrary, we could do with more of them and we examine in this volume how technique can give meaning to photographs. I start this way because the flood of books and exhibitions and essays threatens to obscure what needs to be emphasised: the primacy in photo journalism of content, especially news content. A day or so before I wrote this five gunmen had been photographed scrambling away with their loot after holding up a security truck on the highway and shooting the guard. The photographer was a passing motorist and the prints were inevitably ill-composed and fuzzy, but every newspaper was glad to publish them.

What comes first, in short, is satisfying the public's appetite for news—for the sensation of being there and for an image the mind can hold. That has to be said right at the beginning because there is so much fancy talk. But of course a good photographer can present us with a superior vision of a similar story, just as Ernest Hemingway was a better bullfight reporter than the local agency man. There is certainly nothing to be said for the nihilism, rampant in some American circles, that one news picture of an event must always be very much like another and composition can only weaken its raw honesty. This mostly amounts to one bum awarding another a doctorate in philosophy.

4A An atomic bomb is exploded underwater in a test, near Bikini Atoll, 1946

5A Brig. General Nguyen Ngoc Loan, police chief of Saigon, summarily executes a Vietcong prisoner in the 1968 Tet offensive

The power of the single image

Those five opening photographs satisfy one need we seem to have midway between intellect and emotion: an ache for visual confirmation. This goes beyond the corroborative value of the photograph in disputed stories like the death of Che Guevara, the My Lai massacre, or the curious fascination of seeing Mao-Tse Tung's health affirmed by the photograph of him swimming in the Yangtse, one head bobbing happily among the others. Some stories are beyond doubt but the event is not complete without the final photograph. Everest is undeniably climbed, but we want to see the photograph of the man standing on top. Sir Francis Chichester is back from sailing round the world; we know because we have heard him on the radio. But we want to see him stepping triumphantly ashore. Television has impinged on the newspaper and magazine, but it has not killed the still news photograph because it has a different function.

It informs and excites, but it cannot easily be recalled by the mind, and it cannot be pondered. By contrast the still news picture, isolating a moment of time, has affinity with the way we remember. It is easier for us, most of the time, to recall an event or a person by summoning up a single image. In our mind's eye we can concentrate on a single image more easily than a sequence of images. And the single image can be rich in meaning because it is a trigger image of all the emotions aroused by the subject. If you think of major news events, the likelihood is that you will visualise not a cine-sequence but a single scene from a single still news photograph which has been absorbed in the mind.

For me, the Vietnam war is remembered by the moment of the street execution of a Vietcong officer in civilian clothing (5A). The picture is not before me as I write but I can see vividly in my mind the despair of the victim as the Saigon officer, Nguyen Loan, points his revolver at the man's temple. (He blew his brains out, then turned to the watchers and said: 'Buddha will understand'.) It is another photograph, like the opening five, which is sustained by raw news value. Eddie Adams of the Associated Press, says: 'I made the picture by instinct. Any idiot could have taken it'. The police chief gave no indication he was going to shoot the prisoner until he did it: 'As his hand came up with the revolver, so did my camera, but I still didn't expect him to shoot'. Curiously, Tom Hopkinson, in countering the idea that television killed the famous British magazine *Picture Post*, which he edited, used the same Adams picture to make his point: 'The still picture which made the biggest impact in recent years, that of the Saigon police chief shooting his

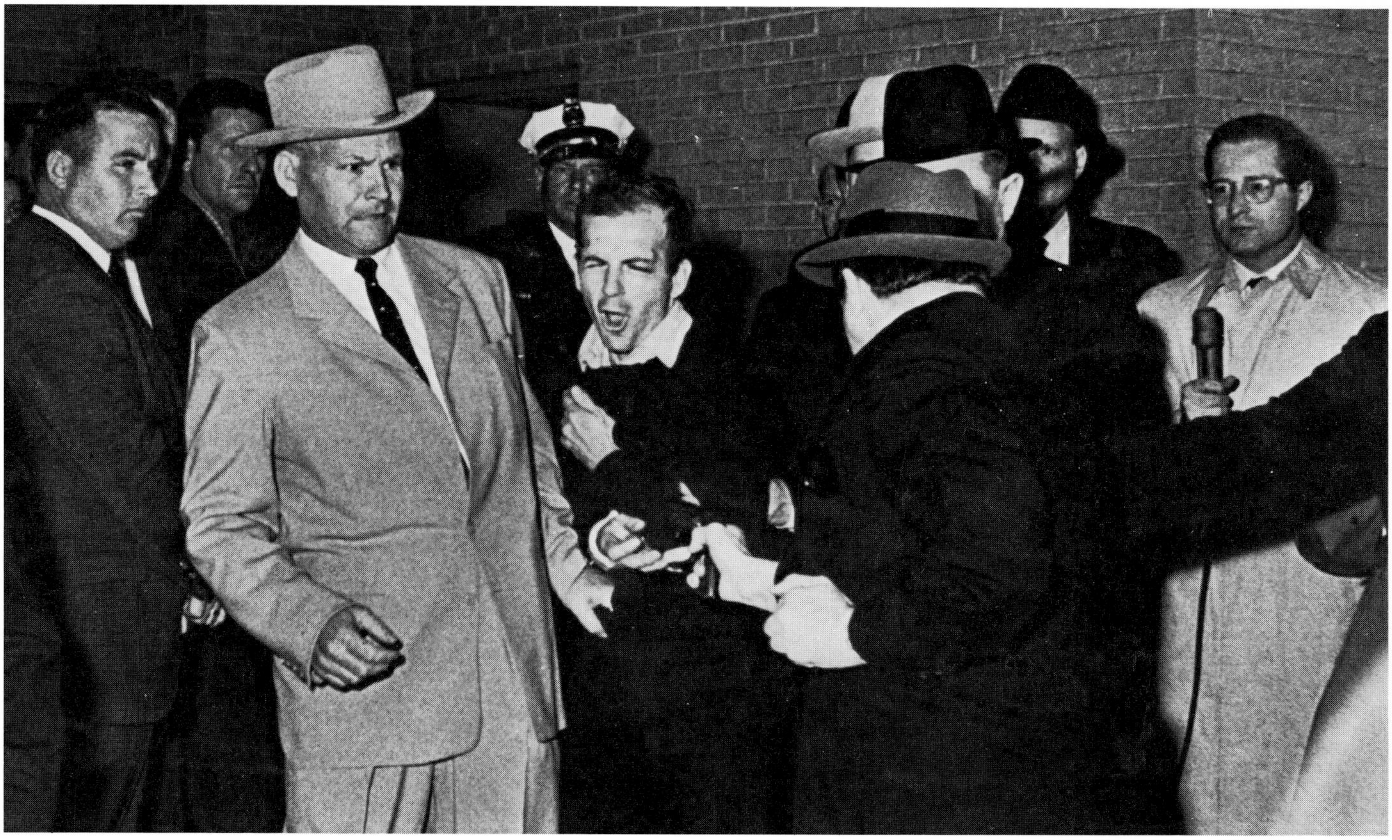

6A Jack Ruby shoots John Kennedy's assassin, Lee Harvey Oswald, during his transfer to the county jail, Dallas, 1964

Herald Tribune

THE CITY

A Nation Appalled

Nightclub Owner Silences Assassin

MOURNING IN CAPITAL

B

Vietcong prisoner in the head, would have been lost on a television film. It was precisely its "stillness"—the sense of the moment frozen in time—that made its impact'.

Of course, this is an important photograph. As the Associated Press recognised in distributing the photograph widely, the gunshot may have been one of the most important of the war not because it was heard round the world but because it was *seen*.

But it is not so much for this photograph's effect that I am using it to demonstrate the unbeatable power of the news photograph: the execution was also filmed and the effect of seeing it on TV was considerable. It is rather for the capacity of the single image to lodge itself permanently in the memory, etched in deeply here by horrified study of the print and its reproduction across the world a thousand times.

This may be a good example, but it is not rare. There are innumerable other occasions—great and small—that we remember by means of the still photograph and which provide multitudinous evidence of its endurance. Bob Jackson's photograph of Ruby shooting Oswald (6A) is another example of a famous scene which was filmed by television but remembered by the still image, brilliantly presented (6B) by the *New York Herald Tribune*.

It is another example, incidentally, of the reflex nature of some celebrated photojournalism. Jackson says: 'Oswald appeared. I raised my camera and became aware of someone moving out of the crowd. He took three steps. I pressed the button. I was not aware of what was happening until I heard the shot'. The good photographer will cultivate his instinct for the subtle moment of tension which precedes explosive action, and he will learn to use his camera blind.

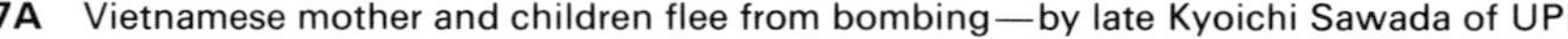

7A Vietnamese mother and children flee from bombing—by late Kyoichi Sawada of UPI

7B Buddhist self immolation: Vietnam, 1963

Still memories

Any great story like Vietnam may yield several lasting images, and some may be superior to others as photo-journalism: the defiance of the Czechs after the Russian subjugation of 1968 is better symbolised by the Prague youth impudently baring his chest to the gun (8B) than by the tank in (7C) but it would not disprove the point if the reader remembers this good but less emotional picture of Russian tankmen. It will be a test of the argument of this section if the reader recalls his own memory of Vietnam, say, and tries to elucidate whether it was indeed a single news photograph or a succession of them. It may be that the reader will recall one of the other memorable Vietnamese pictures (7A, B, 8A) or all of them. It does not matter. The point is whether he is able to determine that he is remembering by means of a single news photograph which appeared in print in newspaper or magazine. The same exercise can be tried, of course, for any memorable event.

7C Russian tanks in Prague, One of winning portfolio, Rank contest, by Kent Gavin

8A Burned by a misdirected fire bomb, children flee down a road in South Vietnam 1972

8B Prague youth, in pyjamas, defies a Russian tank following the invasion of Czechoslovakia, August, 1968

Symbolism

The examples given so far, to argue the value of the still photograph, have been of hot news events. They are sustained by the drama of the moment. But most photographs justify themselves without portraying a sensational event. There are milder photographs which can have meaning at several levels and others which can become a symbol for an era. The photograph of Eton boys standing aloof from the town boys (9A) will no doubt have different resonances for different people, but it does say something piquant about Britain in the thirties. Then recall the bragging and bluster of Benito Mussolini and his Fascist movement in Italy. The Italian dictator (10A) is addressing a crowd in the boots and swaggering uniform of the Fascist militia. He is raised above us ordinary mortals, a permanent symbol, through this photograph, of the insolence and bravado of dictatorship.

Lesser events still can yield riches. The ceremonials which are inevitably the routine of much news photography—everything from flower shows and weddings to funerals and political junkets—are not to be despised by newspapers. The press has this area largely to itself; television has to concentrate its resources because it is less flexible and more costly in time and equipment. The Museum of Modern Art, New York, staged, in 1972, a fascinating exhibition which was nothing more than a collection of photographs of such minor events. Their significance has long since passed, but the photographs, in the words of the catalogue, responded 'to issues which are not ephemeral but permanent; catastrophe and progress, pleasure and pain, victory and defeat, villainy and altruism'.

9A Two Eton boys outside Lords cricket ground in 1937 aloof from giggle and gawp. Originally published in *Picture Post*

10A The photographer is unknown. The figure is Italian dictator Benito Mussolini addressing a crowd in 1938 in Fascist militia uniform

11A Victory: The Israeli Golan Brigade after an epic battle to recapture Mount Hermon on the Golan Heights. By Kelvin Brodie

11B Defeat: Prisoners, roped together, in the Korean War. By Bert Hardy

Gestures and grimaces

Photojournalism has this rich capacity for symbolism, for representing a decade, a war, victory, hope, greed; and very satisfying it is. We expect the victors (11A) to strike certain postures and the defeated to be acknowledging that they have had it (11B). There is nothing quite so economical and effective in this as what the trade calls the mug-shot: the carefree style of the jet-setter in (12A); Mrs. Onassis, bluster in the fist of Mr. Khrushchev (12B), and so on. Quite often a still mug-shot exposes a character or common foible as well as would a half-hour television interview. But there is a danger in this. We risk the inducement of cliché in the subject, the imposition of a fixed character on an individual. This is an area where photojournalism can slide into propaganda (see chapter 8). The giveaway is the frequent use of an unflattering picture taken at one time.

12A Style: Mrs. Jacqueline Onassis en route London to Paris 1971

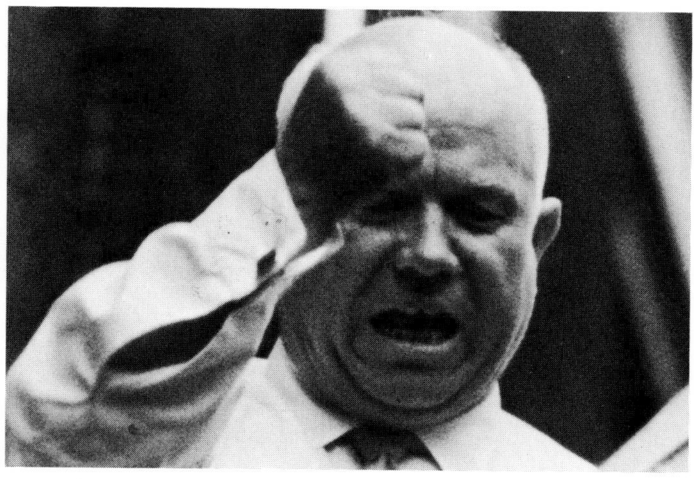

12B Nikita Khrushchev as bully in 1959 on visit to New York

12C Charles the Great, De Gaulle in 1967. By Leon Herschtritt.

12D More role playing. Marilyn Monroe conforms with a kiss for the cameraman, 1954

12E Down, nearly out: President Nixon recovering from pneumonia

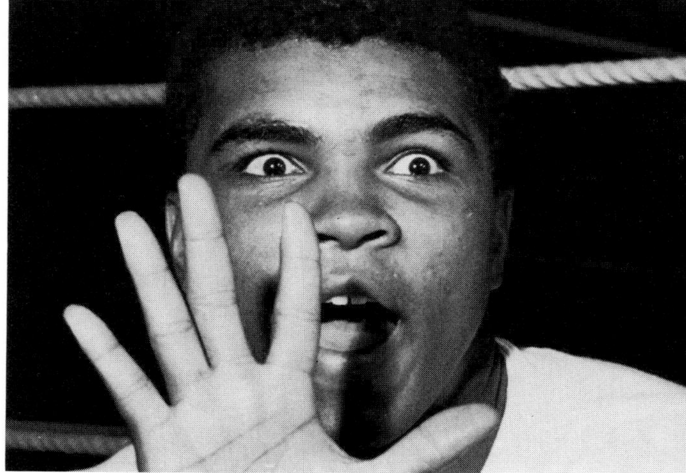

12F Mohammed Ali, alias Cassius Clay, in 1963, alias the Louisville Lip

12G Defiance, determination: Golda Meir, Prime Minister of Israel

The value of black and white

There is a second stream of defeatism about photojournalism. Newspapers which print black-and-white photographs must inevitably, it is said, be weak by comparison with colour TV or magazines and papers with colour printing. There are several reasons why this is a wrong view; and it is a fair guess that in looking at the pictures in the preceding pages you will already have demonstrated one to yourself. We have learned to 'read' black and white photographs so effectively that you are unlikely to have been actively aware that the pictures were not in colour. W. D. Wright, Professor of Applied Optics at the Imperial College of Science and Technology, has suggested, even, that the black and white picture may appear more real than the colour picture. We have learned to supply our own colour information to a black and white picture: 'You may get closer to reality with colour but the closer you get the more obvious it becomes that it is a picture not the real thing'. It would be absurd to pretend that colour is not essential to an article discussing, say, Turner's paintings, but equally there are areas where black and white is preferable. Many photographers prefer to work in black and white—more truly black to white photography with all the greys—for any social documentary. Andreas Feininger (*see bibliography*) believes a black to white photograph 'can create impressions of roundness, volume and depth, and nuances of mood that are difficult to achieve and impossible to surpass in any other medium'.

The capacity of the black and white photograph for subtlety, rich sensitivity of detail and graphic urgency is suggested on these two pages by four examples. Black-grey-white are the essential 'colours' of the frost-encrusted explorer (14A) and the comically bleak bowlers who continued playing in the wet (13A). And polychromatic colour could only weaken the other two examples, especially Arthur Rothstein's famous 1936 photograph 'Dust Storm in Oklahoma' (14C): Rothstein's picture is the visual counterpart to John Steinbeck's classic description in *The Grapes of Wrath* of the effects of the Midwest drought which turned farms into dustbowls and farmers into migrants. In black-to-white you can taste the dust as the father and two sons hunch towards a partly buried building.

13A Black and white shivers at the Scottish bowling championships. A Rank prizewinner for Gordon Rule of the *Scotsman*

14A The face of the Arctic, Allan Gill, British Trans-Arctic explorer. By Frank Herrmann

14B Drama in black and white as Australians 'storm a German strong-point'. Evocative—but one of the many war pictures staged (with home-made smoke)

14C Colour could only prettify and ruin. One of the most celebrated photographs from the Farm Security Administration publicity programme

15A What it feels like to be under the scrutiny of the 'hanging judges' of the Royal Academy. By Stanley Devon

The descriptive photograph

So much for the value of the black and white photograph in isolating a meaningful moment of time. There is a second class of photograph whose appeal is less obvious and which is consequently neglected. This is the descriptive or information photograph.

It does not have dramatic action or symbolism. It may at a glance look dull (17A), or it may catch the eye easily (15A) but the essence is that the descriptive photograph offers secondary as well as primary signals, detailed observation which appeals to the intellect rather than to the emotions, so that the picture is full of interest rather than excitement. In (15A), Stanley Devon's study of Royal Academicians selecting works for the summer exhibition, every face and posture repays a second look. (He stood just beside the painting under inspection.)

The detail must, of course, be relevant to the observation the picture is making, not just clutter. All the figures play a part in (16A) whose centrepoint is two American visitors to London among the loungers around the Eros statue, stranded like whales on an alien shore. Their expressions, summing up one generation's glum assessment of another, are intriguingly framed.

The neglect of the descriptive photograph has been roundly criticised by John Szarkowski, the Director of the Department of Photography at the Museum of Modern Art in New York, as giving us images whose simplicity verges on vacuity. It is partly due to disappointment when detail is lost by under-sized reproduction on blotchy newsprint, but in the absence of hot news too much 'photojournalism' has got into a rut of monotonously smiling bathing beauties, winsome children, talking heads and cuddly pets.

16A Two generations sit out August Bank Holiday in Piccadilly. By Chris Smith, *The Sun*

17

17A A true descriptive photograph of a fourteenth century waterfront uncovered in London. Contrast with 17B

17B Same waterfront excavation, but there is no information in the picture

Telling a story

Here is a revealing contrast between two photographs taken at the same scene: the excavation of a timber waterfront of the mid fourteenth century, built entirely of oak and discovered during redevelopment of the site. What is happening in (17B)? A girl throws a safety helmet of water at something. It is 'lively' but irrelevant. The other picture (17A) is 'dull' but full of detail about the size of the discovery, its structure, the relationship of later building. Because the context is clear, the action of the workers makes sense. They are damping the timbers that have been exposed because they are over-brittle. For this, of course, they use a hose pipe and not the useless helmet of the souped-up picture. The descriptive photograph will still have interest in 50 years.

The unique eye

There is a final group of pictures to justify faith in photojournalism. We are able to see at a scale and speed what the eye can never see, with comic or cosmic significance. The photomicrograph makes pictures of subjects you cannot see at all, reproducing the magnification produced by the electron microscope. But even the ordinary camera can yield enlargements which are astonishing and often beautiful: one thinks of Helmut Gernsheim's photograph of the seed of a dandelion, magnified a mere 35 times. Electron optical shutter systems can take individual exposures in a matter of nanoseconds (100 millionths of a second) so that we can see 'empty spaces between the thinnest slice of time'. Dr. Harold E. Edgerton showed us what happens the very instant a boot hits a football or a marble drops in milk, producing, at 1/100,000 second, a perfect coronet of splashes.

But again even an ordinary camera can, with patience and skill, show us the simple crunch of leather on bone (18B). And by sequence we can compare one moment of time with another, revealing the crucial mistake of the boxer or the slow opening of a plant. Then there is viewpoint, the camera enabling us to see in ways the eyes does not see, making us look again at the world. What is (18A)? A sea monster, a spaceship? It is in fact a commonplace—one of the 'cat's eye' rubber reflecting studs used on road surfaces. The photograph was taken in evidence in a court dispute—a motor-cyclist claimed it was dangerously high—but the photographer noticed that when he knelt down to take it 'the eye seemed to be staring out'.

The photographs so far are only a few examples of the possibilities. They will outlive the visual ephemera of the night's television newscast. They will also, I hope, sustain us as we begin to discuss the principles of commissioning, selecting and editing.

18A Guessing game for a photograph by Ford Jenkins. The title is 'Seen between Lowestoft and Yarmouth' (two seaside resorts)

18B We may flinch when the blow lands but we can see it only with the help of the camera

Chapter 2

Assignment

People are inclined to think of the photographer as a gross fellow, with a press card in the band of his battered 'newspaperman's' hat and a big cigar in his big mouth, who drives nice folks to distraction by his bedeviling insistence on 'just one more,' and embarrasses them with his near-simian behaviour.

Wilson Hicks

19A Early news photograph of a London street accident, from the archives of the Victoria and Albert Museum, London

All the photographer has to do, as Alfred Eisenstaedt defined it, is 'find and catch the story-telling moment'. This calculated understatement neatly defines the two areas of photojournalism. Finding is more the province of the picture editor these days, partly because few photographers think editorially and come up with their own ideas. Catching the moment requires fretful energy, technique, luck, and three eyes. But there are moments and moments. The early news photograph (19A) tells the 'story' of a vehicle upturned, willing hands to the rescue. A second, or even a minute's delay would not matter, nor would a change of camera angle. The other picture (20A) is also of an accident but the 'story' is different, and it lies in the composition and the fraction of a second which shows an injured woman reaching out to a policeman, a touching if puzzling gesture. Moments like these, lost forever if the photographer is not trigger-happy, are why professionals carry loaded 35mm cameras set at 12 ft, and 1/250 at f.5.6 (average daylight exposure). Shoot first and worry about focusing on the second picture. Snowdon put it well: 'It's no good saying "hold it" to a moment of real life'.

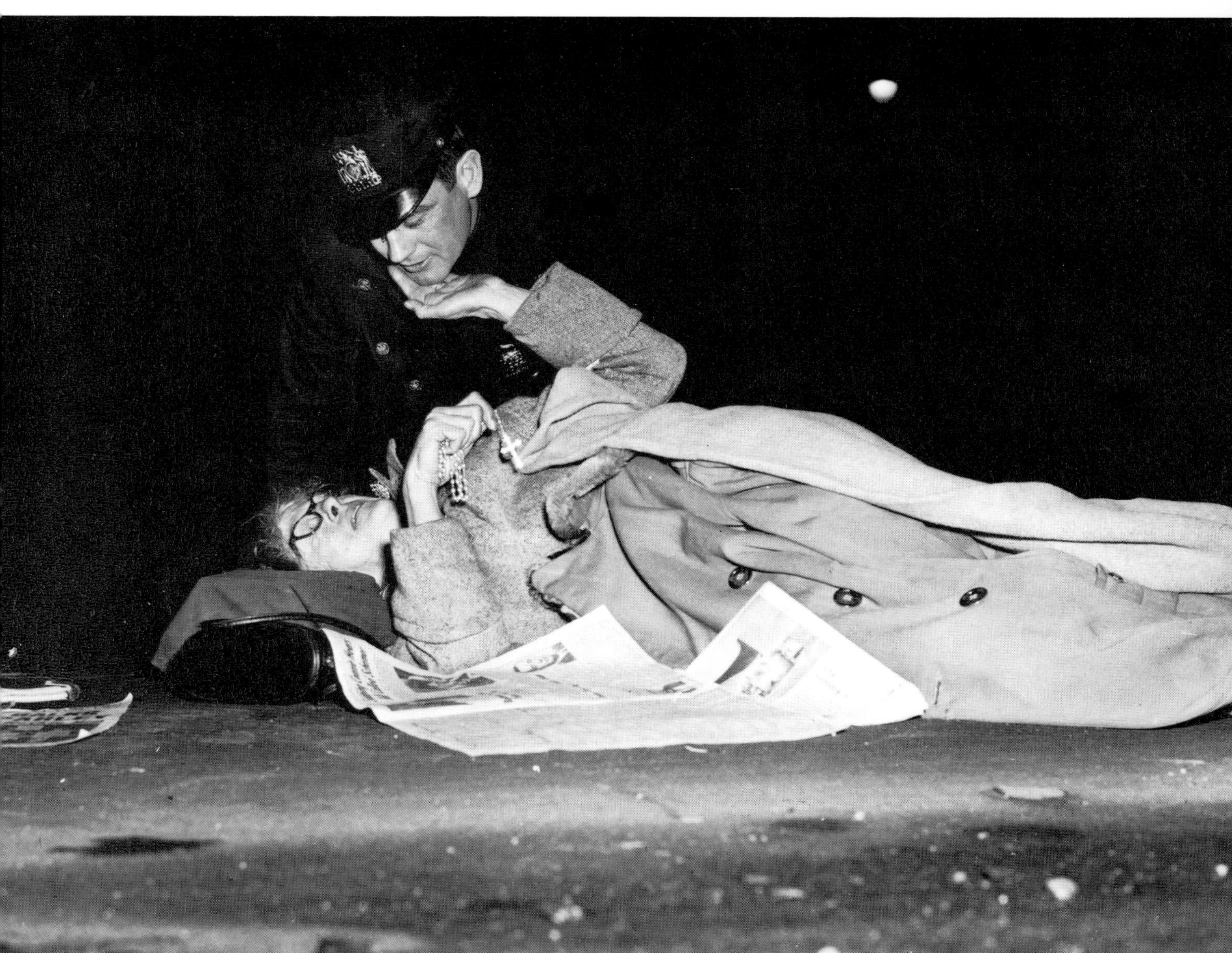

20A Patrolman comforts car victim—by Gary Kagan of the *New York Daily News*. Compare decisive moments in chapters 6 & 7

The only chance

A group of photographers sits in the front row at the photo call of a musical. There is a swirl of dance, a glitter of lights, a flurry of entrances. Not a hand moves in the front row, not a camera clicks to record the synthesis of skills. Then the male lead meets (and clutches) the female lead in stage, centre. The photographers rise as one man, and every newspaper prints the same result, captioned 'Joe Bloggs and Josephine Bloom in Look Down My Throat at the Cliché Theatre'. That is my hypothesis for the mystery of the recurring twosome and the crime must begin with editors who declare that a good picture is worth a thousand words but believe in their hearts that this refers to famous pictures in albums and not to what they themselves might inspire today and tomorrow. Photographs to them are mere decoration, flying geese to stick on the grey wall of text. Photographers not unnaturally respond by producing set pieces, especially when the briefing consists of the inspiring words: 'We want a deepish double out of that theatre job'. We must do better.

The beginning must be with editors and writers showing a better appreciation of both the possibilities of photography and the difficulties of the photographer. The writer has a second chance, the photographer rarely. If the writer forgets a question, he can telephone or search the clippings. If he misses an event he can reconstruct it by interview. The photographer, to catch the story-telling moment, has to worry about light and angles and lenses, and reconcile the need to be unobtrusive with changing his camera position. Photographers find it helps to have a companion writer on stories. 'Many pictures would have eluded me, if I had not had a companion to draw the subject's attention from me', says Thurston Hopkins. Bert Hardy's picture of Nehru (right) on the cover of *Picture Post* is an example. 'I got the journalist to talk to him', he says, 'and to tell the truth the interview was rather dull and it was nearly finished and I was a bit worried I'd got nothing striking out of it. Then by chance Nehru, while talking, leaned to pick a rose and smell it and put it down. In that moment I had my picture. It has been used all over the world. It is a picture that looks as if it had the whole of India's history behind it away back to the Mogul emperors.'

On *Picture Post* the photographer's problems were understood so much that writers were instructed to put the photographer's need before their own. In an interview the writer might get more out of his subject by a soft approach and polite questioning, but if the pictures were likely to result from stirring with argument then, in the words of the editor, Tom Hopkinson, 'he had to stir'.

21ABC Nehru with rose: Three misses (*above*) and the winner (*right*)

February 8, 1947

"We want to be friends with Britain"—
PANDIT JAWAHARLAL NEHRU

HULTON'S NATIONAL WEEKLY

WE VISIT INDIA

HISTORIC PICTURES

4D

FEBRUARY 8, 1947 Vol. 34. No. 6

23A Try and describe it in words

Setting it up

Most published photographs do not represent a moment caught on the wing in the way those on pages 19–22 do. Many have to be set up; many have to be thought up in the first place so that the photographer follows the idea of a deskman.

A picture editor may not be able to tell an aperture from an orifice, but he must have the talent for 'seeing' possible photographs in text. It is an under-rated skill. It means cultivating a sense of the inadequacy of words—imagine, for instance, trying to write what (23A) shows us—and then enthusing the photographer. Sometimes the picture editor becomes an art director, drawing the photograph in advance—(24B) is from a Mercedes advertisement which must have taken careful planning. It works. Picture editors, dare one say it, can often find refreshment in the pictorial ads.

The photographer may be able to take an unposed photograph; he may have to group his subjects and pray that a rude joke will unfreeze their faces; he may even have to ask them to re-enact some drama. There are practical and ethical problems here. I agree with W. Eugene Smith that the photographer should not attempt to make people re-create the moods and happenings of great emotional upheavals, such as bereavement, famine, fire, or the death of a leader. But Smith rightly recognised that the majority of photographic stories require some stage direction 'to bring pictorial and editorial coherency to the pictures'. There is nothing unethical in this if the picture is true to the spirit of the story and the reader is not deceived.

Normally we are not. We recognise that the newspaper conceived the idea of having an American-Chinese grin at the news of America bombing Tokio (23B): the obvious posing is part of the nudge in the ribs. There is more artifice about (24A): Mr. Shimon Peres, then Israel's Minister of Defence, sits in the garden of his London hotel calmly reading his paper, but flanked on four sides by bodyguards, whose placing directs attention to the subject (see Chap. 5). It was published on the front page of *The Sunday Times*, but it was not something that happened quite like that. Sally Soames, the photographer, and her picture editor, Kelvin Brodie, first planned the picture as a drawing, two days before the assignment. She showed the drawing to Peres and his security men and they agreed. There was a short walk to the garden, with Sally Soames anxious that she had not exposed the Minister to any risk: 'I stayed as close to him as I could so that if a pot shot was taken I could never be accused of "setting something up" which could harm this man who is always a possible target'. Mr. Peres and the guards took the positions indicated in the drawing, then everybody returned to the hotel. The picture was therefore unreal—but it had a symbolic truth.

23B Obvious but cheerful piece of posing by the *New York Daily News*

24A Security for Israeli Minister. Compare with 103C the way in which the eye is directed

24B As a spot news photograph, sensational. But arresting nonetheless as an advertisement for Mercedes. Note blur to suggest movement

Ideas

There are not enough diary events to satisfy the public appetite for photographs; and scheduled events have their own problems. There are ways of enlivening the routine, of which more later, but even on the dullest day there is more to photograph than the mayor making his 369th speech. What?

Children and animals for a start. We are all hams for the camera, but children are more so. As infants they are marvellous subjects but by five or six they grimace and pose endlessly and they need to be caught off-guard, perhaps with a long lens. The unposed nature of children at prayer (26A) is one of the reasons for its success. The simple advice about photographing animals is to do them in pairs; their relationships are often more appealing to our anthropomorphic tastes. Knowing something about the subjects' feeding, courtship and mating considerably enhances the chances of success. Sea birds following a ship, for instance, or circling a rock, usually maintain a constant distance, making focusing easier than birds flying free. Photographing fish is more dramatic when done at fish-eye level through an aquarium tank or underwater, rather than by looking down through the water (mainly because of surface glare though this can be reduced by a polarising filter). But nature photography is a subject in itself and anyone who hopes for the front page should begin by reading Heather Angel's *Nature Photography: Its Art and Techniques* (*see bibliography*).

There are other savers: ports with comings and goings, building sites, the seaside. David McEnery, who has made a living out of comic photographs, observes 'holiday makers are so relaxed they don't care how silly they look'. For picture editors still with empty diaries, no zoos, open schools, or ships or seaside, I commend the diligence of the picture editor of *The Scotsman*, Edinburgh, Mr. Stewart J. Boyd, who when I asked how he coped with the dog days replied in part:

❛ I check the papers, including the advertisements, e.g. archaeological digs have volunteers; the Lithuanians in the United Kingdom celebrate Christmas in January. Chinese and Jews celebrate their own New Year, etc. Every university town has someone involved in some project which can be made interesting. Colleges and schools too are worth a check. Teams—football, rugby *et al*—train, hold functions or build pavilions. Service bases are only too happy to help—mock rescue exercises, tanks being recovered; foreign seamen in unusual uniforms with their UK counterparts.

Ring the local MP(s). He/they are bound to be uptight about something worth a picture—state of the town hall, a road that needs an overpass/underpass. If he/they are at home get them at their hobby or play. The usually immaculate figure in gum boots makes a welcome change. There has still to be formed the tenants' association or community council that is completely happy. One of their moans must be worth illustrating.

If I cannot advance the dates of local photocalls, I get the producer choosing material for the costumes, or the stagehands building the main spectacle. There is still an on-stage picture to be had later. The same can be done with out-of-town shows due to come. I get a freelance in the town where they are playing now. Circuses ditto. Local museums/historical societies have "finds" that can be aired. Antique dealers ditto. Local hoteliers, taxi-men, coach hirers, and the local British Rail booking office can be persuaded to ring if they are extremely busy on any given day. The traffic is going somewhere. If it attracts a large number of people there must be something of interest at the end of the trail. ❜

The picture editor should never forget either that there are battalions of photographers at his command in the readers of the paper. They can be encouraged to bring in spot news snaps, enter photo contests and rummage in the attics for curiosities.

25A Success from grouping and a succinct sequence. Squirrel monkeys at Blackpool

26A Stanley Devon had finished the assignment (slum school buildings) when he caught sight of the children in close of day prayers

26D Pandas: It is the pairing which produces the interest

26C Young fox and goose. By John Randle

26B Heavy comedy. An American circus begins to unload. By Jill Freedman

27A Of the 5,000 exposures made by *Sunday Times* photographers, one of the first and most meaningful was Bryan Wharton's picture of Churchill's coffin in Parliament Square. **27B** Sir Winston's farewell to Fleet Street, seen by Tom Dixon

The big event

The state funeral of Sir Winston Churchill (pp. 27–30) is an example of the set piece event when the picture editor has to combine the skills of casting director, diplomat, and time and motion engineer. The first thing is to visit the battlefield to spot and acquire camera positions. This must begin as soon as the event is scheduled, perhaps months ahead. Picture editors who put faith in the camera positions worked out by ceremony organisers deserve what is coming to them. The organisers know nothing about photography and these days are likely to assume that what the TV man tells them is fine will suit still cameramen too. If it is a multiple-location event, such as a parade, the picture editor must walk the route and imagine the photographers at work. For the 1969 investiture of the Prince of Wales at Caernarvon Castle, the Press Association Picture Manager, Eric Pothecary, had photographs taken from every conceivable position to assess the backcloth to pictures of the pageant. For the Churchill funeral *The Sunday Times* picture editors, Jack Hallam and Chris Angeloglou, had negotiated shooting positions from a church tower, and bank and office windows, even before the death. A photographer and picture researcher checked the choices and advised on lenses. It helps to know what a lens will do; it is essential to know what a particular photographer can do. Angeloglou and Hallam had to produce a spectacular picture coverage for *The Sunday Times*, plus colour for a later magazine. They assigned these 21 photographers to 25 positions:

Malcolm Aird, Alan Ballard, David Beal, Peter Boyce (2 sites), Cartier Bresson, Kelvin Brodie, Romanu Cagnoni, Stanley Devon, Tom Dixon, Bruce Fleming, Alfred Harris, John Hopkins, Neil Libbert, Frank Martin, Sally Soames, Mike Taylor (2), Chris Thornton, Horace Tonge (2), Bryan Wharton (2), Bernard Zimmerman.

Mobility and aptitude decided the casting. To convey the ordinary people's feelings for Churchill: Cartier-Bresson (Trafalgar Square). To respond on Tower Pier to any unexpected news picture: Kelvin Brodie (he caught the surprise dipping of cranes by London dockers). To portray the last moving moments in the churchyard: Neil Libbert. Someone who knew London had to nip from Fleet Street and find his way against traffic and closed streets to Waterloo Bridge: Mike Taylor on his motorbike. Press times required pictures of famous mourners even before they arrived at St. Paul's: Peter Boyce caught them at the Carlton Club, in time to go up by helicopter and cover the journey to Blaydon churchyard.

The haul justified everyone's efforts: a rich variety of angles, positions, subjects, which enabled the newspaper to produce a striking issue the next day and a permanent record of a memorable event.

A Still Fleet Street but a closer view of
ople and a Churchill portrait on the
ndow. By Michael Taylor

28C Mourners enter St. Paul's, seen from a top-storey window overlooking Cathedral

28B Dramatically different perspective at St. Paul's. Allan Ballard, perched above the west portico, catches the concentrated effort of guardsmen pall-bearers

29A *above*: Coverage inside St. Paul's was restricted to officially allocated positions. Malcolm Aird took this from the Gallery, easily one of the best vantage points, but where every sound seemed to be amplified a million times

29B *right*: Alfred Harris took this long lens shot as the Royal Family and Heads of State watched the departure of the gun carriage. He was positioned on the south side of St. Paul's Churchyard, with 100 other photographers on a specially-built, five-tier viewing scaffold (See endpaper of this volume)

29C *below*: Ground level interior from plinth position in the south aisle, contrasting with 29A

30A *above*: Michael Taylor's motorcycle dash to Waterloo Bridge paid off with this front-page picture. **30B** *below*: Pay-off from airborne David Beal, following the funeral train

70mm Hulcher
Motorised
35mm Nikon
Hasselblad synchronised with
four strobe lights
70mm Hulcher
synchronised with strobe lights
Three cameras operated
by remote control
Motorised 35mm
with natural light
Mamiyaflex
with strobe light
70mm Hulcher

32A *top* and **32B** *bottom*: The same moment in the Liston–Patterson fight, emphasising the value of different camera positions. **32A** An overhead 70mm Hulcher, and **32B** A ringside 70mm Hulcher synchronised with strobe lights

Every angle

The single-location event invites, and often gets, a set of repetitious pictures from the same position. If there is only one camera spot, the obvious first essential is to have a change of lens, or better still two cameras, a 35mm with a wide angle 28mm lens, say, and another with a medium telephoto, say, 135mm, with 200mm also available. Or a second photographer can be assigned, one with a 50mm lens and one with a 500mm. The equipment today does not excuse monotony. Motorised cameras can be operated from great distances by radio control. When Murray Becker reported a moonshot at Cape Kennedy for AP, he operated three cameras simultaneously, and none was on a tripod. Becker says any camera will illustrate but only one will tell a story.

The agency's coverage of a big fight lives out the slogan. The AP's camera arrangement for the Liston-Patterson fight (31A) was three remotely controlled overheads, two of them 70mm Hulchers which produce fast-action sequences taking as many as 75 frames a second at speeds from 1/25 to 1/34,000th. Four ringside cameramen also shot from different angles with different cameras and lighting. AP also installed four strobe lights over the ring which were triggered by a ringside Hasselblad. For the run of sports events, two things count: a knowledge of the game and freedom to move around. Mark Kaufman was assigned to cover the race between Roger Bannister and Australia's John Landy, the first two men who had broken four minutes for the mile. He worked out beforehand where Bannister might make his final burst (116A). In cricket, it's not enough just to photograph falling wickets; only one in ten makes a picture by itself. Patrick Eager, who produces superb pictures, does it by concentrating as intensely as the players, anticipating the action as ball goes to slip, or a batsman shaping up for a big hit.

Getting in

The best picture editor can enable a photographer to do well. He cannot guarantee it. Initiative and passion are as important as artistic skill. Robert Capa obtained his first published photograph in 1931 because (a) he got into Denmark from Germany at short notice without a visa by bamboozling a Danish ticket inspector with impressive papers, one of them a menu card from a restaurant; (b) got into a meeting Leon Trotsky was addressing by walking in (Leica in his pocket) with some workers carrying steel pipes into the building. Trotsky never wanted to be photographed. The other photographers from all over the world were barred because their big box cameras made them obvious.

When Queen Elizabeth set foot on French soil for the first time in 1957 Bert Hardy had a similar problem to Capa. He was refused admission to the glittering scene inside the Paris Opera. The guards did, however, let through one group of dignitaries talking French, in full evening dress with decorations, without apparently remarking on the fact that the silent one in the group wore brown shoes and had a bulge in the pocket of his oversize dinner jacket. Hardy, like Capa, had tagged along; and made brilliant use with his Leica of the time available before the Queen arrived. He had no wide-angle lens (and regards them as unacceptable because of the distorting effect), so he took consecutive photographs of different sections of the scene from the top of the staircase, and ended it with several shots of the Queen coming up the stairs. These separate photographs were printed and joined up in a jigsaw to create the picture on these pages (the mechanics of the jigsaw are shown at the foot of page 35).

Champagne for Stockton punters

35A What happened to the bubbles? A picture-story idea that went badly wrong

How the Paris Opera join-up worked

This is Bert Hardy's photograph of Queen Elizabeth at the Paris Opera, produced by joining up 15 different sections as outlined on page 33. Smaller newspapers and magazines, without expensive equipment, can produce similar panoramas with almost any camera by simply cutting and pasting. On very wide shots the photographer would allow 50 per cent overlap; slight overlap will not work because there is distortion on the edges with most lenses, and secondly, straight lines tend to 'bulge' in the middle when the big picture is stuck together. The photographer need not worry about a tripod and precise alignment during photography—that can be done during assembly—but lighting and exposure must be identical. Picture editors should select the centre half or third of each print for assembling the finished panorama.

Briefing

It sounded like a front page picture. Stockton-on-Tees race course had been reprieved and the management was celebrating with champagne for punters. But the result (35A) was a disappointment. It could have been any bar, any dreary night. What we at the editorial conference, had envisaged in assigning a photographer was punters and champagne bubbles (foreground) with horse and winning post (background), but we had failed to suggest this and on a hectic afternoon the photographer did not come up with them himself. Briefing, then, before button pressing. Verbal discussion can be reinforced by written assignment notes. They are thought to be formal these days but Leslie Hoffman made the *Straits Times* of Singapore one of the best picture newspapers with written chits like this:

Accompany Chandran to interview Somerset Maugham, arriving BA 7 23, 18.00 hours. Chandran will try to interview at Raffles Hotel because of its association with his novel. Somerset Maugham has a good face to photograph (see library stock). Get close ups. We want pictures of Maugham seated, in rattan chair, Raffles Hotel lounge, looking rather wistful.

There may be nothing inspired about this except that many metropolitan newspapers which are full of electronic gadgetry send photographers on assignments without asking them to talk to the writer and without any briefing beyond time and place. The photographer who is kept in the dark about the story that has to be told cannot be expected to come back with the story-telling moment. There is no reason why briefings should be a strait-jacket. Photographers should shoot to the brief, secure the picture requested and then try out their own ideas. This does sometimes, admittedly, lead to different views about the photograph that merits publication and a fair example is the set of pictures below illustrating a flood story. The photographer, Frank Herrmann, regards the bottom picture as the best (see comments below) and this was the one published, but Edwin Taylor, *The Sunday Times* director of design, regards the one above it as best for newspaper publication, and says: 'Herrmann's favourite is the best composed, a photographers' photograph, but it leaves the viewer guessing. Is the object coming or going? And is it a piano? And what are the farm labourers doing with a piano in a farmyard? My selection is news; it is a demonstration picture in which the flood victim is keen to show the participating reader the height to which the water rose. It is less well composed than the third picture here. It is corny/old/often seen, and very effective.'

The photographer's view

‘ I was sent to photograph floods in Wales. I arrived only after the water had receded again and was left photographing water marks, damaged premises and unhappy people. It was unsatisfactory until I noticed dustmen gathered at the bottom of the hill. I joined them and somehow this picture of a piano being thrown away sums up the waste and futility of the floods better than all the pictures of peeling wallpaper. ’

Angles and opportunities

Picture editors must encourage photographers to regard every assignment as different. The challenge must be 'Yes, it is a run-of-the-mill job, but surprise us.' There is the chance of something unique in every job, some fleeting permutation in the scale of emotion, some juxtaposition, some symbolic comment, some concentration of detail, some new perspective.

The photographers on these and succeeding pages in this chapter did not simply point their cameras in the general direction of activity. They thought about the story, seized chances and exploited the camera. The photographer can do that by changing the focal length of his lens to get a view different from the rest of us: even bending the knees will do it since the rest of us see things at eye level. The photographer can also add contrast and drama by changing filters; he can throw the central object into relief by using a large aperture so that distracting background is blurred; he can try panning (see chapter four); he can change speed. But most of all he can move himself. The good pressman sneaks about looking for a fresh viewpoint and unposed moments.

Opinions differ on how close you can get to people. Snowdon says: 'A telephoto lens is all right for animals or sport but too intrusive for people who are unaware. If you want a close-up view you should move yourself if it is possible. The trouble is that so many photographers seem afraid to move in.' But Mark Godfrey of Magnum believes people have invisible zones of defence, that when a photographer violates the zone he will distract the subject. At the Watergate hearings, he said, the witnesses got used to photographers in fixed positions and in the breaks some good pictures came when witnesses relaxed. But when some photographer switched to wide angle and moved in closer 'the effect was to end whatever was happening'.

37A Nine faces compactly presented in this overhead shot of the Dutch Royal Family

37B Vertiginous overhead, **37C** Dramatic symbolism to celebrate America's Thanksgiving holiday, a close-up of a harvest field. By Ron Ernst of the *Detroit News*

38A Telephoto lens bunches the divers' angle and emphasises the competitive starts. The long lens is useful to simulate excitement in sports

38C The railway lines are used to focus on the story point: another photographer prepared to bend his knees

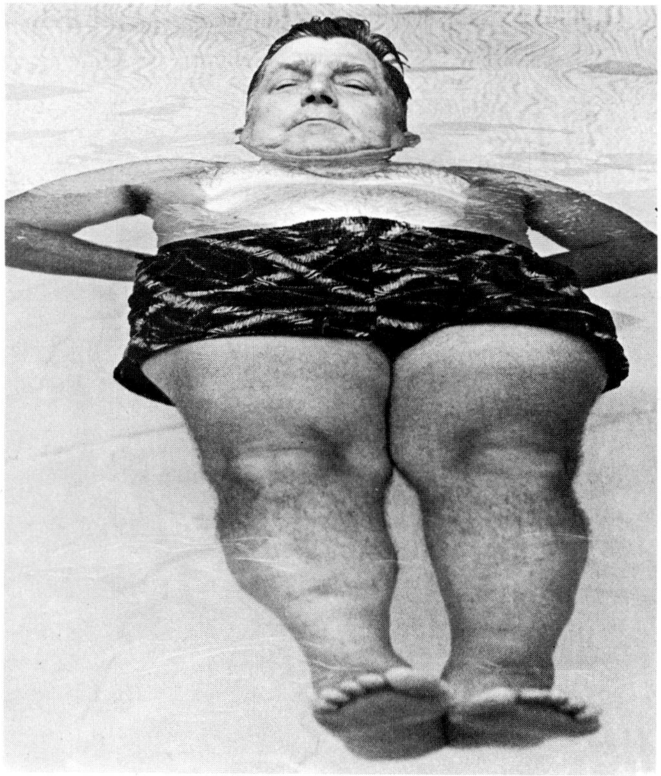

38B Man in pool: An economically distorted view by use of long lens makes a publishable picture out of nothing

39A Poodle takes a spin in the Rolls with chauffeur. A picture that was missed first time but legitimately recreated by Thurston Hopkins

High-speed thinking

To say photographers should think about the story and the camera is not to say they can afford to take a fastidious age (nor on ordinary newspapers can they afford, as the big magazines can, to spend 100 frames for the sake of a single print). Time was against Frank Herrmann in the theatre assignment described on page 40; it invariably is on this kind of work. Former *Picture Post* staff man Thurston Hopkins who captured the intriguing photograph of the chauffeur with poodle (39A) still wonders, 20 years on, whether he ought to have made the exposure while the car was moving so that the background was seen to be blurred (see chapter 4)—but concludes, rightly I think, that the rough power that adds to the memorable quality of so much of the best press photography can come about only as a result of the cameraman working under pressure.

The poodle? Hopkins was waiting at a bus stop when he saw the car going past with the dog severely poised. He did not have his camera with him but instantly he hailed a taxi, pursuing the car as eagerly as another photographer might if he had spotted an irresistible girl. The man at the wheel, it turned out, owned a hire car firm and whenever he had a little spare time he would take the grateful poodle for a spin round Hyde Park in the Rolls. He was happy to agree to the photocall the next day.

'Several of my old colleagues remain convinced that I set up the whole picture but this is something I hardly ever did while working on stories which were to be presented as observed actuality. What I did do quite frequently was recreate a picture; that is, I set people in motion in a particular situation, drawing from them a brief performance rather in the manner of a film director controlling a short scene, but never allowing or persuading my actors to behave other than they would *normally behave* in that particular situation. It is, as all professional photographers know only too well, easy to be carried away by the excitement of improvisation, and to falsify truth grossly in the eagerness to produce a more dramatic, or aesthetically pleasing picture.'

40A

40B

Just one more, please

The time of performers is often limited. Frank Herrmann says: 'When Kurt Joos put on a performance of his famous ballet *The Green Table* I was asked to take a picture of Joos that would also convey something of the ballet. I was given five minutes after the full dress rehearsal and the dancers were so tired and obviously irritated that I needed more than one exposure to get my picture: **40B.** Then one of the dancers took off his mask and placed it on the table. To my relief I saw here the possibility of a better picture, **40C**, minus the dancers, which certainly made them happy. Kurt Joos himself couldn't have been more obliging.'

Viewpoints

The commonest picture assignment is probably the meeting or hearing. How many times does the photographer arrive, point his camera frontally at the group and depart, and how many times is the subsequent print discarded? The wide-angle front view of a man on a platform produces grey gaps, and foreground/background clutter, yet if the photographer will move around and try a shot with a longer lens he can often produce a concentrated picture with high impact. I emphasise: just moving—never mind the gadgets—is the secret of photojournalism.

The camera is a wonderful tool, said D. A. Spencer, but nine-tenths of people using it are simply button pushers, who 'let off their cameras as one lets off a firework'.

There were 25 photographers to record the famous day when Babe Ruth, a dying man, made his farewell after 22 years of heroic baseball. It had been decided that his No. 3 shirt would never be used again. Thousands of fans jammed the Yankee stadium to pay tribute, the band played and the cameras clicked in front of Babe, attempting to catch his expression as he stood on the homeplate. Nat Fein of the *New York Herald Tribune* and Harry Harris of AP took the picture with the others but did not feel they told the story: somehow the fact that Babe's uniform and his No. 3 would never be used again had to be included. They walked around behind Babe Ruth and both took celebrated photographs. Fein's won a Pulitzer prize (Harris did not enter) and he scored additionally because he remembered the preaching of his picture editor Richard Crandell: 'When you can, make your picture without flash bulbs. Natural light catches the mood of the occasion'. Most photographers were using flash because the light was dull, but Fein opened the aperture to f5.6 and slowed the shutter on the Speed Graphic to 1/25th. Seeing the stadium from Babe Ruth's viewpoint we get a sense of the great man's feelings and the emotions of the crowd.

41 A Traditional but boring photograph taken with 55mm lens

41 B Same meeting as **41 A** but more impact, 105mm lens from the side

Babe Ruth retires: Both **42A** and **42B** show Babe Ruth at the Yankee stadium on the day he stood by the homeplate to acknowledge the crowd's tribute. Two months later he was dead. They are clear enough statements but they do not tell the story or recapture the mood of the occasion. Contrast with **42C** below

42C Nat Fein's prizewinning picture, taken from behind, includes Ruth's No. 3 uniform and members of the Yankees

The soft focus

Two awkward assignments rescued by fresh viewpoints. Bryan Wharton (43A) had to illustrate an article on alcoholism. There were two obvious solutions: a bleary tramp with meths bottle (overdone) or a man pouring himself a drink (dull). He went to a meeting of Alcoholics Anonymous, an unpromising subject, but focused his camera so that three reforming alcoholics were blurred in the background with their three redeeming cups of tea sharply in the foreground. It made the point. Kelvin Brodie (43B), on a routine parade, makes a joke about army bull and tickles the eye by juxtaposing a small object (boot) made big and a big object (Guardsman) made small.

43A How to photograph alcoholics trying to dry themselves out without unhelpfully revealing their identities. Similar problems arise for features on divorce, probation, suicide

43B Boot and bull: An inspection of the Scots Guards which is also drill book example of composition devices discussed in chapter 5

Case History The elephant and a chick

An idea, a viewpoint, and an eagerness to experiment: All three qualities for a successful assignment are evident in the case of Ian Tyas, the chick, and the elephant.

Tyas, a young photographer with Keystone Press, had to take an Easter photograph. First, he thought of a newly hatched chick and then he thought of an elephant, not everyone's association of ideas but a large and small juxtaposition that had been in his memory from admiring a well-known picture of an elephant and mouse. He immediately had the idea that made a startling and comic

picture—can you guess it?—but he tried other possibilities first, with the help of the zoo's curator at the Sherwood (Notts) Zoo. He took shots of chick on the trunk, rough skin and knowing eye of the elephant Emily contrasting with soft chick; and then he photographed the chick nestling in the big flappy ears.

The ultimate picture (page 46) made more of the weight of the elephant. The foot must weigh the better part of a ton . . . what would the great weight do to an innocent little chick? The curator used a walking stick to get the elephant into the idea, the chick was very trusting and Tyas got down on the ground to produce his intriguing shot.

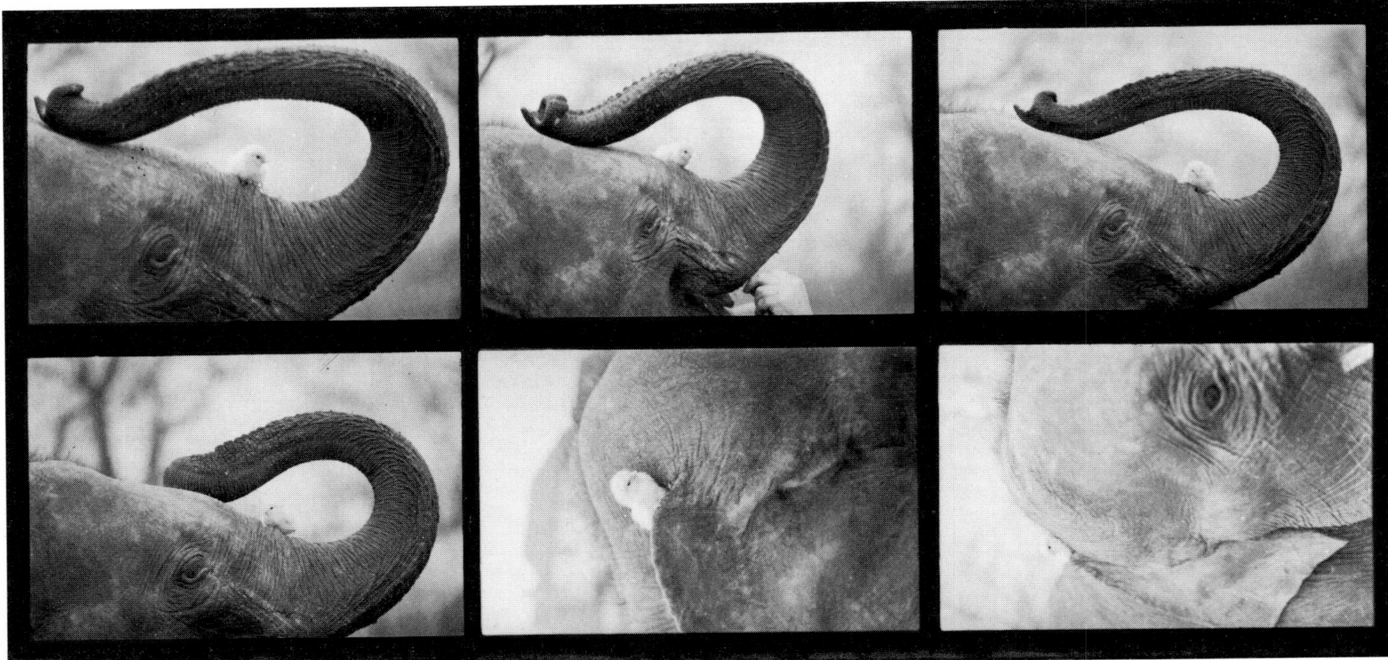

45A Patient photographer, patient chick and elephant; a selection of contact prints which illustrate the endeavour behind the arresting **46A**

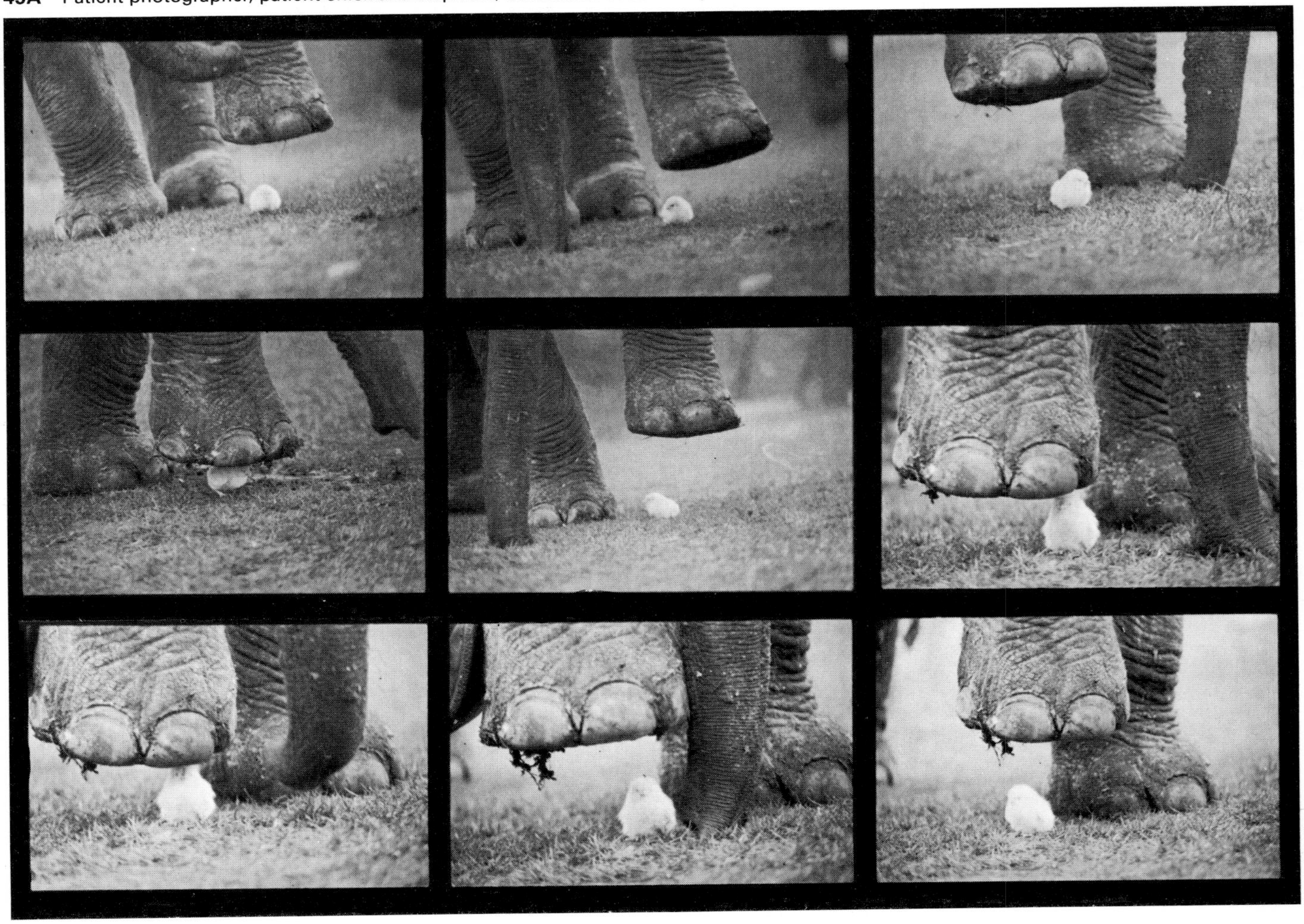

Chapter 3

Three Tests for Selection

No one can do inspired work without genuine interest in his subject and understanding of its characteristics.
Andreas Feininger

47A

Sensational news pictures are their own advocate: they may be meanly sized in many publications but they are not discarded. However, the vast bulk of photographs offered for publication require the editor to have some tools of discrimination—principles or classifications to help his own judgements and to justify them to others. Selections for publication cannot be left to the photographer because he is normally too emotionally involved with his own work; and he cannot, in any event, be expected to judge his pictures against competitors for space and position. It is a pity that much of the selection process falls into the hands of the intuitive school of journalism which degrades the standards because it has none it can explain. There may be a genius among the thousand muddlers but unless he can tell us what he is up to it is no help to the rest of us. My experience of selecting and rejecting pictures at both a local paper and national paper level suggests that publishable photographs have one or more of three values and that pictures which have none of them should be rejected as junk. The three are:

1 Animation
2 Relevant context
3 Depth of meaning

The boy in tears at the end of a village fair race (48A) qualifies in class 1; the chapter opener (47A) is scrap: a posed, featureless picture without meaning. This chapter tests the idea of the three values against the routine run of publication photography.

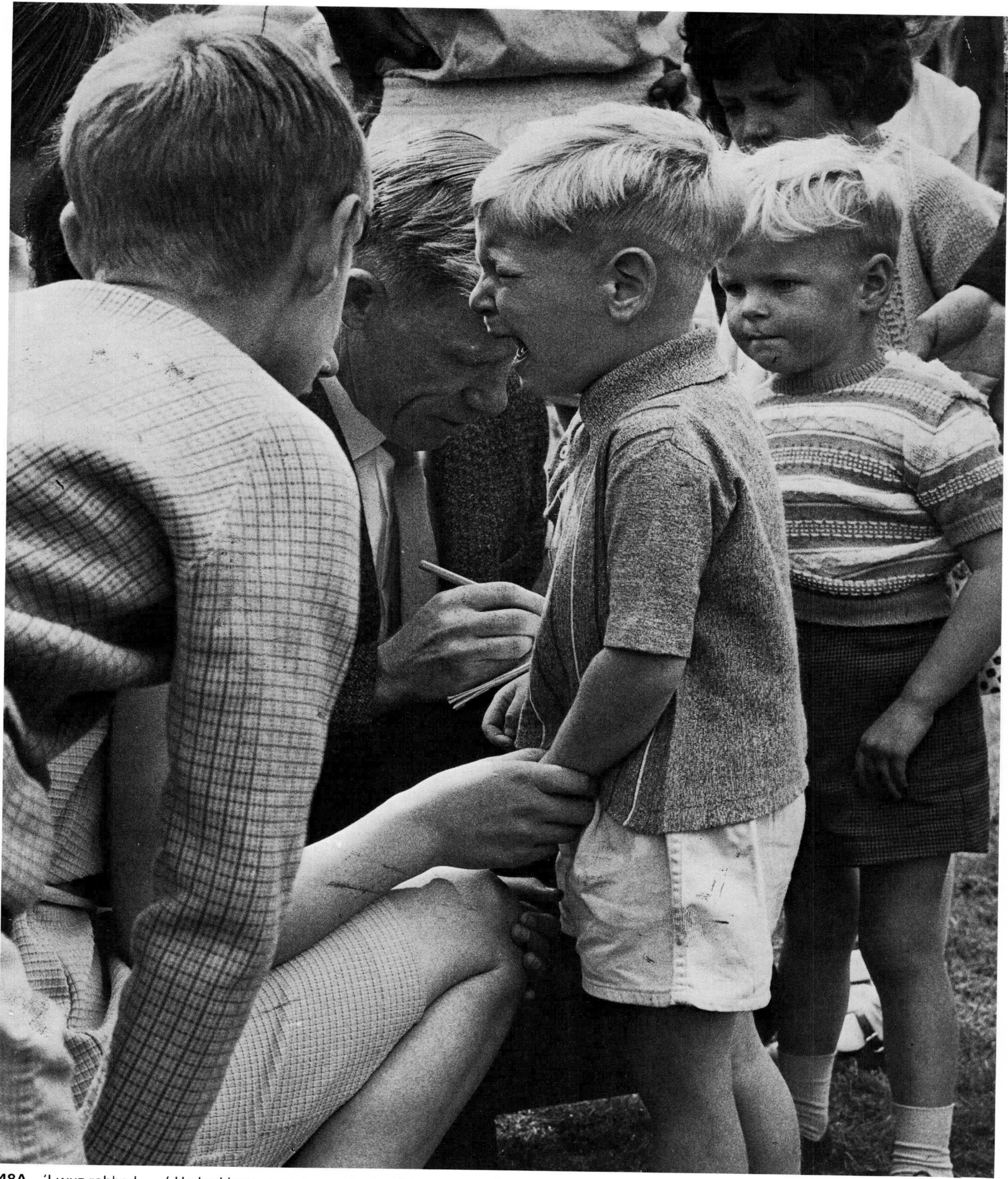

48A 'I wuz robbed. . . .' He had lost a race on sports day. The most routine local event can produce picture stories. From *The Northern Echo*

1: Animation

The chapter opener (47A) is typical of hundreds published every day. The only story they tell is that a number of people have looked at a camera lens: they fail all three of the value tests I have suggested—but most fundamentally they are without any signs of life. Occasionally some wit will write a caption beneath the statuary: 'Enjoying a joke at . . .'

There are two reasons for the prevalence of these dead pictures. First, the circulation manager has persuaded the editorial department that local faces sell newspapers—telephone directory journalism. Second, the editors and photographers have grown bored with what they see as hackneyed subjects.

There is a condescension here which must be resisted. There is nothing wrong with cliché subjects. Life is made up of clichés, of births, birthdays, anniversaries, presentations, prize givings, weddings, christenings, first nights, farewells. All newspapers and house journals must produce a stream of such photographs of average people in predictable circumstances. But the deadness in the pictures is often imported into the event by the photographer and newspaper.

One retirement presentation ceremony is just like another to the newspaper and to the factory manager handing over yet another gold watch for forty years' service. But it is not a routine to the old codger: he gets one gold watch once in his lifetime. It is not a cliché moment to the bride, or to the parents of the schoolboy getting his prize. The good photographer, encouraged to be sensitive to the moment in the old codger's/bride's/boy's life, will try to reflect their feelings and responses. A bad photographer will simply photograph the event, and his laziness will flourish on publications which have never adopted animation as one test in selection.

Here are four examples (49A–50ABC) to support the contention that even the most routine event for the smaller paper can yield good photography if editorial standards determine selection. Weddings, so monotonously recorded, offer rich variety and surprise; the Ilford competition for pressmen had a special wedding section which regularly demonstrated what could be produced by a photographer who is awake.

Tony Spina, writing about (50C) says: 'I never predetermine what kind of picture I am going to get,' and it is a useful injunction for avoiding repetition. Spina had no longer than 20 minutes for the youngsters' golf assignment: 'I swung my 35mm over my shoulder, stuck an extra long lens in my pocket and took off. I had to move fast, shooting good close up expressions on faces and so forth. Then as I started back, I spotted a mother caddying for her son. I settled in a nearby sand trap, and from this low angle I got the shot. Had I gone to the clubhouse to pose pictures, it would not only have been more time consuming, it would have been just another standard "get-by" shot.'

49A How many peas? Animation from fête. By Ossie Stamford of *The Northern Echo*

50A Bored bridesmaid, aged three. Rank Organisation prizewinner for Clive Limpkin

50B There is always something good at some stage in a wedding and reception. The bride and baby is by Alfred Markey

50C Mother as caddy by Tony Spina of the *Detroit Free Press*. The unexpected on a rush assignment

51 A No doubt about it—it's a fire station and a startling view. But compare it with **51 B**

51 B Also a fire station—but no animation, no information, no photograph worth publishing

2: Relevant context

There are occasions when the absence of animation is not decisive, but in all such cases the picture must have information. The lifeless pictures frequently lack a relevant context. They look as if they have been produced in a sterile studio from which every clue to the natural environment has been removed. The neutered subjects, tinker, tailor or tycoon, gaze across the same clean desk or stand against the same grey canteen wall.

For instance, it is anyone's guess what (51B) is all about. It happens to be the opening of a new fire station, but it might have been the opening of a church or warehouse for all the context that the picture presents. And there ought to be any number of possibilities—officials inspecting the fire engine; reflections in a polished bell; firemen opening door with manned vehicle at the alert; firemen sliding down the emergency pole—or fireman on a ladder. Peter McGrath of the *Essex County Standard* was assigned to cover school children visiting Colchester fire station. He began by taking shots of the children squirting hoses and looking at the fire engines and then, hearing that there was to be a demonstration of a turntable ladder, thought of summing up the visit with a picture which included ladder, children and fire station (51A). 'Once I had climbed the top of the hose tower, it took only a little manoeuvring of the ladder to obtain the effect.'

Picture selectors must insist on context. In (52A) Mr. Henry Hartley is properly presented in the story-telling environment by *The Daily Express*. He has been successful in his fight to save the railway line between

A hero steps off the 5.41

THE MAN WHO BEAT BEECHING SAYS 'MAYBE IT WILL ENCOURAGE OTHERS'

52A Not much animation, but the relevant context of the railway station makes the *Daily Express* picture a success

53A Guessing game: Goodbye to cashier or chef, head cashier, or is it a golden wedding? And which one of the handshakers is the hero?

53B Headmistress retires. The children provide animation and a clue to what it is all about. Compare with photograph above

Buxton and Manchester which was threatened with extinction by the Beeching 'axe', he might easily and irrelevantly have been photographed in his solicitors' office.

It is the biggest single weakness of publication photography that recurrent themes are allowed to produce recurrent pictures. If someone retires, then they are automatically shown being shaken by the hand in some featureless room; if someone wins a prize then they are automatically shown with someone else handing them the prize. Editors simply do not consider, or so it seems, asking the photographer to go out earlier and photograph the prizewinner in the activity that won the award—at the piano; at the scene of the rescue; with the winning painting; and so on. Or, in the case of retirements, they could be photographing the person doing his work for the last time, or surrounded by the implements of his craft or profession, or by working colleagues. That is the difference between (53A) and (53B), both local paper pictures of the retirement of a head teacher. The first lacks animation as well as context; the second is lively but it also has teacher-with-children—which is the story. How often are photographs offered which show swimmers without water, champion cyclists on foot, chess champions without chessmen, or scientists in city suits?

Of course, putting the subject into context often requires organisation and some posing but it is better to have a straight-to-camera picture in the right context than a similar picture without any background information. (Groups are a separate subject, of which more shortly.) When a Middlesbrough shipyard won a large order, *The Northern Echo* picture editor had an idea of photographing the two men responsible for designing the proposed ship. That meant a posed shot somewhere, but when the men agreed to be photographed walking through the shipyard (54A) it made all the difference. Editors in doubt about the quality of their own photojournalism should get someone to clip out 50 pictures from back issues, remove captions, and then guess what it was all about.

54A Engineering designer and naval architect. Imagine the men without the background: passable but inferior to this picture with context

3: Meaning

The third test of value is more subtle and requires more description than animation and relevant context. Most people know about animation (smile please), though you would not believe it from glancing at many of the world's great newspapers, but animation is in many ways inferior as a test of selection. Animation may for a moment stop a reader and make him look, but animation can itself become a cliché. Seeking it can rob a picture of significance, as we saw with the London waterfront excavations, page 17; it is significance that sustains our interest and adds to our enjoyment and awareness.

The point can be made, at its extreme, in photographs with no people in them, and several examples follow; but group photography, at its best, also earns its place by the quality of its description. We begin with a picture (55A) which has no animation, no obvious immediate emotional appeal, and whose context has to be explained. But it is a good photograph because it has the third value of meaning. It has also, for a newspaper, the additional attraction of surprise: why, the reader wonders, are they bothering to present a hall table with a clutter of objects?

The answer needs words (as much descriptive photography does). An inquest on a doctor had decided that the doctor killed himself after murdering his wife. Dave Cooksey was given permission to photograph the doctor's flat. The significance of the objects on the hall table, poignantly abandoned next to a framed photograph of the dead couple, was that the doctor had returned from police interrogation and acted at once to conclude the drama. He took off his hat and emptied his pockets of his personal possessions, which included the syringe that had been the instrument of his wife's death and was, in the

55A A portrait of tragedy whose publication value lies in the significance of the objects described. By Dave Cooksey, *Daily Express*

following few seconds, to be the instrument of his own suicide. Dave Cooksey's picture can be characterised as descriptive because its worth lies not in the graphic simplicity of its image but in the richness of its observation. It is a still-life study of violent death that can be read as well as seen. As John Szarkowski has said of such photography, its value is intellectual and literary as well as visceral and visual.

Objects are again invested with significance in (56A), which is a photograph of Ted Simon, an Englishman who decided to ride round the world on a motorcycle. We are given a clear view of the kit he intended to carry—umbrella, axe, chain, torch, frying pan, passport, bandages, oil, tyres, sleeping bag, etc. The background is, of course, deliberately and undistractingly neutral in a photograph like this—a well-lit studio, where the photographer tried different perspectives from a stepladder.

To say that meaning gives value is not to imply there is a single valid meaning to every photograph. People see with their memories and prejudices as much as with their eyes, sometimes drawing contradictory meanings from the same images. Cornell Capa has also reminded us of the limitations of even the supposedly universal language of photography. On page 119 of this book there is Robert Capa's picture of the French woman collaborator being marched through the streets of Chartres, with a baby in her arms and a shaven head, at the end of World War II. When Cornell Capa exhibited his brother's picture in Japan with a laconic caption, Chartres 1944, it meant nothing to the viewers. There was no understanding of the significance of the woman's shaven head, nor was there any cultural equivalent in Japan to that kind of guilt to give the picture sense.

56A A portrait of adventure—man with bits and pieces to sustain a motorcycle trip round the world. By Chris Thornton, *Sunday Times*

57A No human figures, but a picture full of human significance: the missing section of line which led to a rail disaster

TUESDAY NOVEMBER 7 1967 FOURPENCE No. 976

SUN

THE INDEPENDENT DAILY NEWSPAPER

THE FATAL FLAW

Arabian Army 'declare war' on FLOSY

From FRANK DAWES
ADEN, Monday

THE South Arabian Army last night lined up with the National Liberation Front, recognising them as "the only organisation representing the people."

BATTLE

100 KILLED

One week ago inspector warned of track dangers

THE section of railway line missing in the picture was almost certainly responsible for the deaths of 53 people in the train disaster at Hither Green.

In this section there was a crack invisible to the eyes of railwaymen who inspected the line last Monday, Wednesday and Friday—as they do every week.

But on Sunday night, as the 12-coach Hastings-London train roared over the faulty line, the crack widened into a split.

This was probably the fatal flaw that made 11 coaches jump the rails at about 70 mph. Four coaches toppled over. Another coach landed upside down.

Yesterday rail experts removed the 4ft. section of track for laboratory investigations at the railways workshops at Derby.

ANOTHER BREAK

They are trying to find how the faulty section defied detection by every safety-checking device—including an ultrasonic test in June. The line was laid only about a year ago.

Less than 24 hours after the Hither Green disaster another cracked rail was discovered yesterday on the main line near Yeovil, Somerset—25 minutes before an Exeter-Waterloo express was due. The line was closed for two hours while a new section of rail was laid.

A rail spokesman said: "There may have been a hair-line crack there for some time. But fortunately we discovered the break before it became serious enough to cause an accident."

Similar breaks in rail lines are known to have caused at least six accidents in recent years. The number of faulty lines reported last year was 383 compared with 270 in 1965 and 238 in 1964.

The missing section of line which may have killed the 53 people at Hither Green

WIDOW THEFT PLOT CHARGES

TWO BROTHERS were accused last night of conspiring to steal from a wealthy widow who was found murdered last week.

Surgeon dead on raft

They are believed to have been in a cabin cruiser which was in collision with a tanker off Margate on Sunday night.

On trial

Belsky

Cleared—I'm so glad, says driver

By VICTOR CHAPPLE

THE DRIVER of the crashed train,

TODAY'S TRAINS

■ MAIN line trains today will be diverted as they were yesterday. Commuter trains will be "subject to delay and cancellation." It is hoped to resume normal services tomorrow.

57B The simple but powerful presentation of 57A in the broadsheet *Sun*

57C Two symbols of a double-death car crash

Meaning from symbolism

Both the previous photographs, the hall table and the motor cycle kit, were literal descriptions and required a fair amount of newspaper space for their meaning to be clear. Such pictures are rare. This is partly because the newspaper reproduction has so far put a premium on simplicity and force; and partly because, in reaction to dead pictures, we have been over-anxious for pictures whose drama is immediate. Yet there are photographs worth considering for selection which are not descriptive but have meaning through symbolism. They repay attention less richly than the literal descriptive photograph—there is simply less in them—but they have an emotional appeal. Three of the examples are pictures without people, but they none the less have a strong human interest. What they require in the way of supporting text varies according to the intensity of the symbol and our memory and imagination: hardly any words are needed for (58A), black hands on tin plates, a soup kitchen queue in the American depression. The absence of faces is a virtue, not a weakness, for the anonymity of the hands reinforces the idea of individuality eroded by poverty. Nor do we need to be told much to appreciate the meaning of (57C), the victim's shoe in the burned-out wreck. Two other examples, on the other hand (57A and 58B), are almost meaningless without words. The broken railway depends on the associated information that it had been declared the cause of a derailment which had killed 53 people. The simple picture was powerfully presented in the *Sun* (57B). Compare the other creative linkings of words and pictures in Chapter 15. In (58B), again there is not much significance in the visual content—just a man playing patience—and only low-quality description. But the picture becomes highly charged when coupled with the information that the man is Donald Campbell, just before his attempt on the world water speed record. His friend Keith Harrison later recalled that in the nine weeks waiting for the right conditions for the attempt Campbell played Russian patience. On Tuesday he turned up an ace of spaces followed by the queen of spades and told Harrison: 'Mary Queen of Scots turned up the same combination of cards and knew from it she was going to be beheaded. I know that one of my family is going to get the chop. I hope it's not me'. On the Wednesday Campbell was killed in his attempt (see page 177).

58A Meal time, Forrest City, Arkansas, 1937. Documentary symbolism by Walker Evans

58B Waiting for death, Donald Campbell, by Michael Brennan, a Rank prizewinner

59A Stockton High Street, bleary with smog. By itself it is hardly worth publication, but coupled with **60A** opposite. . . .

Meaning by comparison

There are two forms of comparative publication, the suggestive and the documentary. The suggestive employs random coupling to stir ideas. It is more rhetorical than rational—a photograph of a fat man in a Paris restaurant juxtaposed against a starving baby in Nigeria—and we look at it in detail in Chapter 13. Here I am concerned with the documentary comparison which communicates a very clear meaning by precise description—more analysis than allusion. This kind of photography normally features the same subject—High Street 1890 and 1977; the football ground at 10am with men working to clear the snow and at 3pm when the foreground figures are players in action; the face of a man before and after some ordeal; a painting seen in original disrepair and then with the benefit of restoration. One Saturday in a Seventies heatwave *The Sunday Times* received a photograph of a girl of three innocently naked by the Serpentine lake with an avuncular policeman chatting her up. Nice, but by itself a marginal choice. Then we remembered a famous picture at the same spot in 1922 when three boys, similarly naked, were pursued by a policeman intent on preserving public decency. A comparison of the two scenes a permissive age apart made the front page (and that, in turn, gave us another pair the following week when one of the bare boys at the age of 62 came forward to confess all).

Some pictures used in pairs might merit publication on their own. There is a pair by Erich Salomon, better known as the father of candid photography, which shows a Hague conference at 11am during a debate between French and German Ministers, everyone spruce and attentive; and the same scene three hours later, the statesmen smudged by smoke, tiredness and disputation. They are powerful together but interesting on their own. The comparative pictures on these two pages, on the other hand, depend on each other utterly. There had been an argument in the Teesside region of North-East England about air pollution. Some contended that chemical and steel factories were to blame for blotting out the sun on certain days when the wind carried pollution inland. The factories tended to say they were being blamed for changes in the weather. It was not their fault the region was having a dull day. These two pictures (59A, 60A) proved that the critics were right. And together on the page they made a meaningful piece of photojournalism.

60A A few miles further from pollution. Meaningless by itself but proving a point when coupled with **59A** in the page (*see below*)

The midday sun blotted out .... when it's shining ten miles away

ORTHERN ECHO

THAT SMOG ON TEESSIDE

Captured by the camera— smog in Stockton High Street at midday compared with Haughton Village, on the outskirts of Darlington, ten miles away, at the same time.

Exactly a year ago today News Focus looked at the problem of Teesside's polluted air. No one is complacent about it, including industry; but the complaints and the headlines have continued.

What progress are we making?

WHIT Saturday, while the rest of the North- scorched under sun blue sky, Stockton was pped in a blanket of which blotted out

WHAT THE PROBLEMS ARE

that mists have always persisted

Health menace that

WHAT ONE MAN SAYS

Everybody grumbling . . . I wrote a letter

MR. WALTER ROBINSON SMITH (left) security officer at the North Tees Power

61A Line-up: These four are typical of the hundreds in local papers and house journals. You either get the uneasy smiles of 'let's pretend' (*top*) or straight eyeball to lens confrontations which are more honest but are usually deadened by wasteful background. (see especially the middle pair)

61B Bad. This is a phoney, a loosely composed group simulating conversation

61C Better. An advance, posed in less awkward postures and more direct

61D Best. The frame is full of people, and it tells us about the relationships. No doubt who is bos

62A Hell's Angels. A straight to camera grouping but in a revealing context and every face tells a story

Meaning in groups

Nothing in photojournalism has been quite so degraded as photography of groups. They should mean something, at the least tell us something about the people or the occasion, and at their best something about their relationships to the event and each other. Hardly any of those published in newspapers or magazines do. The common fare is at far left—groups like firing squads with marble faces, groups in phoney poses, groups of muddled relationships without context, character or genuine animation. The argument for publication is 'Yes, that may be a dull photograph, but you can recognise people on it. They and their friends will get a kick out of seeing their faces in print and will buy an extra copy or two of the paper.' This is doubtful reasoning and bad photojournalism. Groups are better abandoned than reduced to characterless cannon fodder and this can be done without local rebellion. We proved in an experiment at *The Northern Echo*, when we abandoned groups-for-groups-sake, that newspaper and photo sales were unaffected.

But groups are worth rescuing. Even the humblest publication should be able to organise better group pictures. Three stages of development are presented in a sequence on page 61. At the top we have the traditional embarrassment of a group pretending to talk. People today are so much more sophisticated about the visual world that this kind of thing fools nobody and irritates everyone. Yet photographers have grown so used to the pretence that it is built into their reflexes. 'Mr. Menuhin,' shouts the photographer, 'pretend to play the violin.' We want animation when we can, certainly, but most group participants are dud actors. It is far better generally—as in the second picture—to have a straightforward picture of the group, without pretence. But if that is so then there is no reason why the photographer should not move a stage further and organise the group so that (i) composition is better, leaving no grey holes, (ii) postures are relaxed, and (iii) it is possible that roles and relationships are described.

The arranged group need not be organised so or as rigidly formal as a regimental photocall. There is nearly always a moment for photography when the members are more aware of what is happening in the group than of the camera. Roger Sturrock's Hells Angels (62A) is, for all its naturalness, an arranged group. He persuaded two or three of them to fill the centre and asked them all to look at the camera for three shots. An unposed picture of this group with its

63A A naturalistic grouping which is full of meaning. (It certainly needs the negro men—but does it need the man at extreme left?)

graffiti background would have had its interest, of course, but it would not have given us so many character studies—'the way their eyes meet yours', is Sturrock's phrasing.

To photographers who pull a face at stage management I pass on the attitude of Don McCullin, one of the great photographers of big news, who says of routine group assignments: 'I don't mind bowing and scraping to justify taking their time . . .' For all of us jaded with groups a refreshment is to look again at the group pictures of photographers such as Lewis Hine (for instance, breaker boys coal mine, 1911); Paul Strand (the family); Robert Frank (City Fathers, Hoboken); W. Eugene Smith (Spanish portfolio); and Dorothea Lange whose 'Plantation Overseer and his Field Hands' is (63A). It is not a 'news' picture of course, but it tells a story about the social pattern of the Mississippi Delta in the 1930s, of the relationships of the ruling white man and his coloured workers. As George P. Elliott observed: 'The Coca-Cola ad is for all of them; the machine is his and his foot is on it'. Elliott was commenting, incidentally, on an editing of this photograph for a book about freedom which cropped off the group and left only gritty farmer outside country store as the visual accompaniment to an ode on rugged character. That cropping transformed the meaning of Lange's picture.

Summary groups There is one further class of group photography which is descriptive and meaningful, and this is the summary group. It is the most organised photograph of all, bringing into one frame people and/or objects that are related but not normally seen together. Who keeps a jumbo jet in the air? A summary picture would collect air crew, air controller, engineers and clerk and group them on the tarmac in their kit and with their tools. Whom do we thank for a new musical? We group writer and choreographer, money man and tea lady, cast and commissionaire . . . All the people who work in the Statue of Liberty—surprising idea—is the summary group on page 64. It is an example of the work of Neal Slavin who has made a speciality of documenting groups with props.

The successful summary picture is original in idea, ambitious in organisation, coherent in composition, and detailed in observation; and it needs to be published large with conviction. There are not many on offer.

64A The summary group: Neal Slavin makes a striking picture of the staff who operate the Statue of Liberty

Case History Stanley Devon makes Charles Hill a man of action

65A A reject. The pretence is obvious and meaning and context are unclear

65B A reject. No context and the composition produces lots of grey areas

Winston Churchill, flinging an arrow into a dartboard, once told Stanley Devon: 'You must learn to take your pictures on the wing, my boy'. Devon already had, without Winston's advice. Devon snatched the first picture—and memorable it was—of Hitler's troops marching into the Rhineland in 1936. He was the first great aerial press photographer, flying in one-engined planes with no radios, and the first to fly with the RAF in war action. It was an Air Vice Marshal who dubbed him Glorious Devon. He was in on all the big stories such as Alamein, D-Day, and the crossing of the Rhine. He has been on countless royal tours, notably capable of producing the formal starch or spontaneous human photographs.

The assignment on these pages was therefore very small beer for Devon; but for that reason as much a challenge as any. It was an election in Luton, only thought worth photographing because it featured Dr. Charles Hill, who had made a name for himself as a blunt, warmhearted 'radio doctor'. Nothing was happening or due to happen or likely to happen in Luton when Devon arrived. It was going to have to be a set-up session—but what? Devon persuaded Hill to walk the streets, talk to factory girls, open mail, play trains with his son, and none of the pictures was remotely publishable. The main weakness, Devon realised, was that none of the shots gave a hint of Hill's character or the reason for photographing him. Then he took (66B): Hill the fighter addressing a large open air meeting with gusto, rosette defiantly on his chest. It was, in fact, symbolism for there was nobody listening to Hill when Devon directed him in his role. The readers who saw the picture on the front page were deceived, which is wicked, but the photograph had what the others lacked—animation, context, and meaning. Oddly, Hill, who admired the picture, more and more came to live the role it portrayed.

66A Third reject. The camera angle makes Hill look small and fat

66B Cropped to focus on the fighting Hill, this one was published on the front page of the *Sunday Graphic* and won a prize

Chapter 4

Action

That a horse rushing along at the rate of a mile in one and two thirds of a minute (more than 17 yards in a second) should be seized by photographic art so as to show every limb well and clearly delineated would have seemed wonderful indeed to the early professors of that art.

Editor, *Knowledge*, April 14, 1882

Action photography, for our purposes, divides into three kinds—the analytical which defines fractions of movement too fast for the eye; the emotive which suggests movement vividly but without precision; and the aesthetic. They can overlap. The opening photograph was taken by a stroboscopic lamp which gives a brilliant light for as short a time as one millionth of a second for a single image or a series of images on a single plate, such as those of the ballet dancer (8 flashes each at 1/10,000th of a second). It has all three qualities but less hard analysis than the facing photographs (68A) by Eadweard Muybridge, the father of analytical photography. Muybridge preferred to call his work 'an electro-photographic investigation of consecutive phases of muscular action', and he did more in the 1870s than photograph a horse rushing along. He produced ten or 12 pictures of a single stride, demonstrating that if a horse tried to gallop as the painters had depicted 'he would be obliged to fall down.' (Lecture to the Royal Society of Arts, April 4, 1882.) He went on to photograph men, women and babies, naked and clothed, in stages of walking, crawling, dressing, bathing, leaping, bowling, and much else. He used batteries of cameras, as many as 24, whose shutters were electrically operated by a clockwork device, at exposure times of about 1/1,000th of a second. The horses were photographed when they broke threads which closed a circuit. Today's photographers can tell us what happens with more sophisticated single cameras. The possibilities are immense. But there is more to animation, as we shall see, than simply freezing a moment.

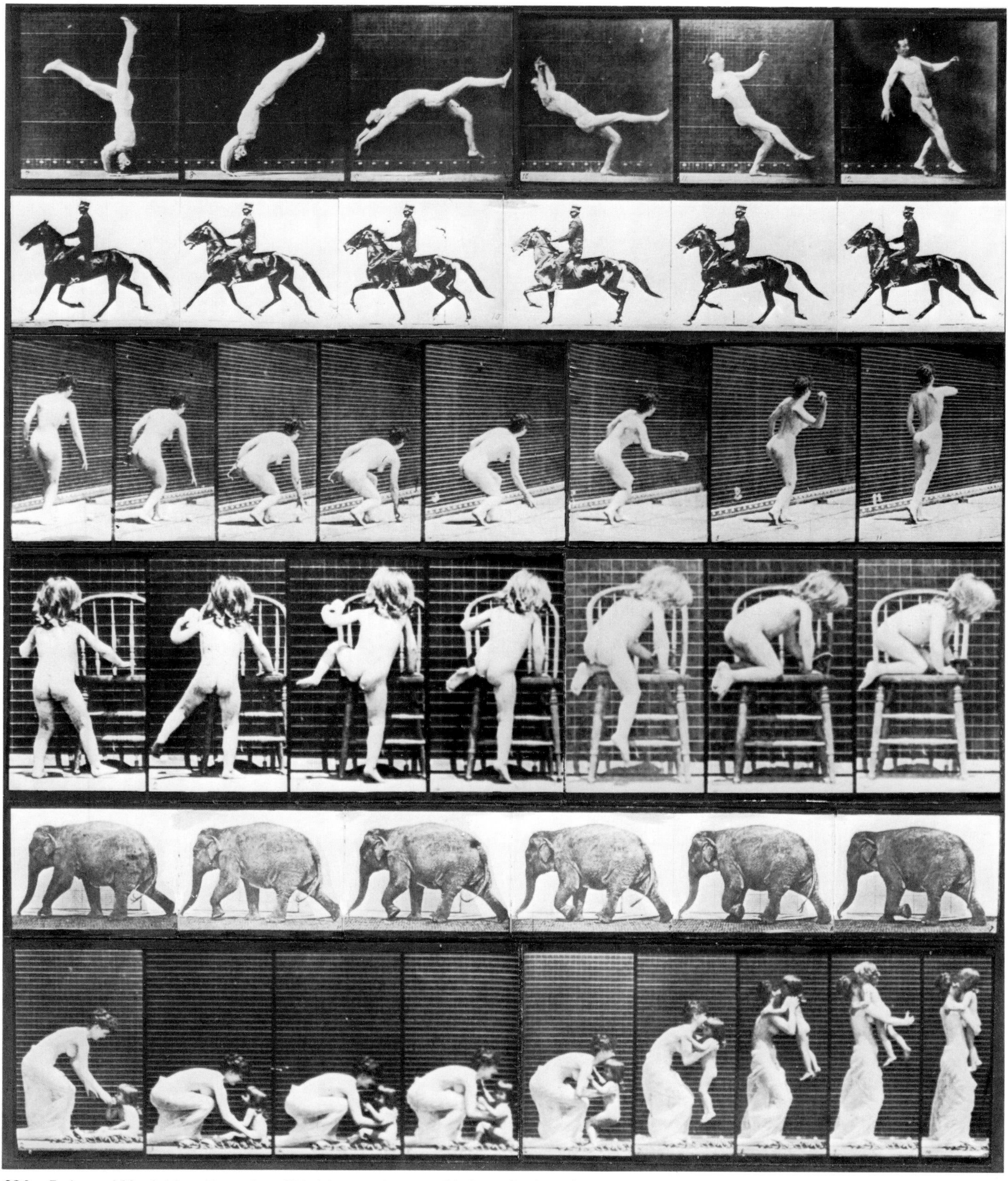

68A Eadweard Muybridge: Examples of his 'electro-photographic investigation of consecutive phases of muscular action'

Action–with four omissions

Animation was one of three value tests suggested for picture selection in chapter three. I have used the word to mean life rather than simply movement: a set scowl or a closed eye may give animation to a picture; and a photograph of a rapidly moving subject may not have much animation. The football picture (70A) is clearly a failure of the kind frequently seen on the sports pages, and the main picture (69A) clearly a success, but why?

The photographer of 70A might protest that it has animation and it is no use responding that the animation is of 'low quality'. It is necessary to analyse the reasons why movement competently frozen has not yielded successful animation; and out of these reasons will emerge an indication of the elements that make an action picture come alive.

1: The animation has no meaning. Information and emotion can both give meaning to a picture. In sport, which will inevitably predominate in this chapter, a photograph may inform us who won or lost the ball or point in a clash between players; who fouled, who scored; it may describe what several players did. Alternatively it may be taken earlier and tell us not the result but the ingredients of a challenge. That is information, essential for armchair critics; even when we know what happened we can ponder how it did. And as well as information there may be emotional excitement in that for both ignoramus and connoisseur. For the man who does not know, it offers an opportunity for the enjoyable or agonising indulgence of speculating 'if only . . .' In 69A we can say 'if only' the full back, Wilson, had got his foot an inch further the extra time in the World Cup would not have been needed. Finally, the action can blend information and emotion if it symbolises the result of the whole match or the performance of a key player. These are characteristics which give meaning to a vast range of photographs. None of these qualities is present in 70A. The moment frozen by the camera is irrelevant.

2: The animation in 70A has no aesthetic quality. An irrelevant action might be satisfying to look at because the photographer has caught an athletically appealing or impressive moment of effort or composed the elements of the photograph to that effect. There is nothing of that quality in 70A; there is in 69A.

3: There is no sensation of movement or energy. A photograph, though still, can represent motion effectively (of which more later), but this still stays still. We know the men have moved because their postures suggest they did, but the composition of the men does not dramatise that or suggest the rough striving of the tackle.

4: The photograph does not concentrate what action there is. Empty spaces here dissipate what energy there was. We only make things worse if, in editing, we crop close in on the players for then we also lose the ball.

The purpose of the photograph should, of course, determine whether the action is 'stopped' for the information or aesthetic appeal of a frozen moment, or whether clarity is sacrificed for emotion and the sense of movement.

69A Alive: The goal that stopped 400m. hearts. Thirty seconds before full-time in the 1966 World

70A Dead: York City centre forward clears the ball in an FA Cup match—or so the caption said

Weber, extreme left, equalises for Germany against England (who won 4–2). Note the expressions

71A Suspense: A save or a goal? A perfect example of tantalising equilibrium in the cycle of movement

71C Going, going . . . By Olle Seijbold, of *Dagens Nyheter*

71B Suspense: The price of a sealskin coat, Kent Gavin, *Daily Mirror*

Key moments

Some actions, therefore, freeze better than others. In this chapter we are concerned with single pictures—sequence photography is considered in chapter 9—and for these singles photographers seeking publication will generally do well to concentrate on one of three moments. First is the moment of suspense of which (71A) is a fine example. What happened to the goalkeeper who dives for the ball as the forward starts to swing for his kick? Everyone will want to read the caption and story to find out—which makes the picture worth page one. (The goalkeeper was knocked unconscious). The same qualities are present in (71B), and in the picture of the assassination of the Japanese Socialist leader (see 108B). The second key moment is the agony or relish of the inevitable in, for example, where nothing can stop the wrestlers bruising the ground. Finally, there is the climax—the truncheon hitting the glasses (72A), the dive (72B). To capture the peak moment in sport when an athlete reaches the apex of performance, the top men shoot before the peak and continue, straddling the target with shots. A motor drive is essential for this, yielding as many as 9 frames a second with automatic priming of the shutter and advancement of the film.

72A Climax: Batoned Linfield supporter by Tommy Collins, *Irish Times*. An Ilford winner

72B Climax: Fulfilment of a dive. Kate Evans from a holiday colour transparency by the author

73A Wide angle race picture. The motion is competently frozen and the focusing sharp, but there is no sense of action. Compare **74A** facing

73B A new world record for the three miles (13 min. 3.2 seconds) between Britain and Germany. But a routine photograph. Compare **74B**

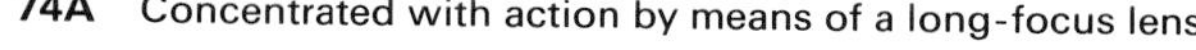

74A Concentrated with action by means of a long-focus lens

74B Angle and timing extract the most from a David Jones finish

Lenses and angles

The photographers who took the pictures on page 73 have tried to photograph key moments by our definition—a moment of climax in athletics and of suspense in racing. But what has gone wrong? Every editor will prefer the pictures above; even at the reduced scale here they are immediately more effective than the larger (73AB). The contrast is essentially one of concentration. In (74A) on this page the action seems right upon us. This is achieved by using a lens of long focal length. 'Normal focal' length equals the diagonal measurement of the negative, so with a 35mm camera where the film is 43 mm diagonally, a lens of 44mm is normal: most 35mm cameras have a 50mm lens. Similarly, the 'normal lens' for the larger negative of a twin-lens reflex is 80mm. A long lens bends light far behind it to produce an image of small area in large scale. Here the long lens gives us a large image of jockeys and without surrounding detail and a powerful sensation of them racing their mounts almost neck and neck. It is an optical illusion since the jockeys are not as close behind each other as they appear to be.

Effects like this are achieved by playing off camera position against focal length. If the photographer moves back and uses a long lens he will both magnify and compress. (Conversely, distances can be stretched out and the view broadened by moving close and using the shorter lens.)

The race picture opposite (73A) is from a wider angle lens of shorter focal length which gives sharp images of both front and following horses. The frustrated punter might possibly be grateful for that extra information, but the photograph gives little feel of a race, and our attention is also pulled by trees and crowds. This is the fault also with (73B) where Christopher Chataway is winning a three-mile in world record time but where our eye is invited to all sorts of different subjects. There is a comic element perhaps in the pedantry of the man with the armband and man in white coat looking down the track, but these indicate further weaknesses in the picture: it is a micro-second later than (74B), reducing the climax, and the angle does not enable us to share the view of the other runners.

The long lens (say 200mm f2.8) is a vital tool for action because much of the time we cannot get close enough without it. But amateur photojournalists might note that newspaper picture editors are averse to lack of focus; long lens photography risks it because of camera shake and because it requires keen accuracy of focusing: there is small depth of field. Of course, as Newman puts it, a 35mm camera on a tripod is a different instrument.

75A All eyes on the jumper—there is nowhere else to look. Karen Karlsen of Norway. By Ed Lacey

Selective seeing

The eye sees subjectively. When we watch the girl high jumper (75A) or the serving table tennis player (76A) we concentrate on them to the exclusion of everything else, discarding a vision of anything which does not interest us. This is where many amateur photojournalists go wrong. They see something with picture potential and assume that the camera will see the same thing. It will not, unless directed and controlled.

The objective lens sees everything presented—the background spectators, the clutter—and presents them faithfully in the print. Here, moreover, their intrusion is always intensified because the edges of the photograph emphasise that all elements within them have a relationship.

No such failure occurred with these two fine photographs. We are absorbed with the action. The golden principle of action photography, more than any other, is that any part of the picture which does not work for it will work against it. Here everything in frame is vitally relevant and suggestive: the jumper's upswept hair, the converging lines in the table tennis service. The low angle helps to exclude inessentials but the key remains that both photographers saw photographically. Both photographs inform—the service in table tennis has only in recent years become so important and so devious as to merit analytical photography—and both photographs have aesthetic value. The timing of the shots is obviously perfect. It is not an accident; it is observation of the movements time and again so that the moment can be anticipated with allowance for reaction time and mechanical inertia. This requires more energy and patience than people realise. Peter Hoare, for instance, won the 1976 Midland Bank sports prize with a photograph of three greyhounds racing round a bend that required five separate visits to the track. He took 30 shots, one shot in each of the six races at five meetings. Having confirmed that the best position was when the dogs were coming out of a bend, the problem was focusing: 'It sounds fairly simple, but it proved to be very difficult. This was due to the speed at which the dogs were travelling and the very shallow depth of focus—about 12 inches—of a 300mm lens at 1/2000 f16'. Hoare says in the end this was as much luck as skill, but nothing would have been accomplished unless Hoare, like the other two photographers here, had begun in Minor White's phrase by thinking photographically—what Minor White calls taking a creatively 'blank' mind to the subject. Or as Edward Weston once put it: 'My own eyes are no more than scouts on a preliminary search, for the camera's eye may entirely change my idea'.

76A All eyes on the ball. Sven Erik Sjoberg of *Dagens Nyheter* reports on a Japanese star's devilish table tennis serve

77ABC In which of these three photographs is the car moving at 30 mph, and in which is it stationary? Answer: only the first car is stationary.

Making the movement flow

So far we have been examining mainly analytical photographs where the movement is frozen. There is a lot of information in the better photographs and they also convey some impression of movement when the subject, though clear, is obviously in motion. With people and animals, and objects in the air, we deduce motion because we know certain postures indicate movement and that what goes up must come down. Since Muybridge in the 1870s there have been enormous advances in our ability to freeze motion. We can now photograph a bullet in flight and the ordinary photographer can employ a motorised camera taking 9 frames in a second at 1/2000th of a second each, or, with the Hulcher, 50 frames a second at 1/10,000th each. (The cine camera is less useful for print since its frames are at the comparatively slow 1/40th of a second needing continuous projection for proper effect.)

Sharp pictures of movement are, therefore, a commonplace, though they require control. Amateur photojournalists of motor racing often, for instance, send in pictures with uncontrolled unprintable blur because they have attempted to freeze the car as it passes directly in front of them. The best position is on a curve for a number of reasons but partly because the cars can be photographed with slower speed when at an oblique angle or when moving towards the camera: The more the motion is at a 90-degree angle to the optical axis the faster the shutter speed required. The subject-distance and shutter speed relationship is simple: when the distance halves, the shutter speed doubles (something often forgotten with a long focus lens which effectively reduces distance).

Very well, which of the photographs of cars have caught the fastest movement? Unlike people, machines and buildings give no posture clues. Car A and B do not appear to be moving at all. This is correct for the first picture but car B was moving and moving faster than C. The difference is that B was taken at 1/1000th of a second which froze the motion but killed the suggestion of speed whereas in slow-moving C the photographer used a technique called panning to suggest speed. And the car which seems to be moving most fast and purposefully—D—is again quite stationary. The celebrated Surrealist painter and photographer Man Ray gave the impression of speed in two ways: blurring the negative and then cropping the photograph on a tilt.

Devices that suggest movement without making it seem inanimate are vital for photojournalists. The most important, in addition to multiple exposure with which the chapter opened, are composition and blur.

There are two basic forms of blur—blur of the subject and blur of the background. Panning is the technique which blurs background while keeping the subject relatively sharp; the streaked background suggests movement and also reduces or eliminates competition for attention. The photographer focuses on the subject and then makes the camera follow its trajectory, at the same speed, relatively, and in the same direction. He shoots in the middle of this pan, beginning to track well before shooting and continuing to swing in the same direction even after the picture has been taken. Blur of the subject is produced more simply—a slower speed.

The second was moving at 30 mph and frozen at 2000th sec f5.6, the third at 20 mph 60th sec f22

78D A Duesenberg at speed by Man Ray. Only the pennant (right), refusing to flutter, gives the game away

79A Mark Spitz churning the water and winning the medals. World Press Photo, Holland, prize for Co Rentmeester of *Life*

79B The spray—as well as the diagonal emphasis—helps the action

79C Tony Jacklin

Composition

Man Ray's lurching car (78D) has a sense of menace, threatening to move in our direction and not harmlessly across the picture frame. This is because of its tilt. The examples on these pages demonstrate how angular lines, notably diagonals, give a sense of motion in a still photograph. Diagonals set up energy tensions. There is a dynamic quality in these photographs which is the outcome of the unresolved tendencies towards vertical and horizontal.

In (80A), for instance, the jockeys seem about to slide off the print and it is interesting to note the extra energy this gives by comparison with the other long lens picture at (74A). All the photographs compare well for concentration with the high jumper and table tennis player at (75A) and (76A). We know that all the frozen postures indicate movement and they are especially effective in capturing expressions of effort.

These observations on composition apply not simply to sports pictures—compare the photographs (99A) of men in a boat and (100A) of a lighthouse.

80A A strong diagonal and a Rank first prize for Chris Smith of *The Sun*

80B Keith Fielding scores a try in England/Wales v Scotland/Ireland

The case for experiment

Three different ways of suggesting motion are represented here—panning, zoom, and debris. In the picture of Reg Harris apparently cycling at speed (82B) Frank Herrmann used a zoom lens which enables the focal length to be changed. Harris was stationary. The effect was produced by taking the shot while zooming.

In (82A) movement is suggested by a special, secondary form of blur—the scatter of sand. Any flying debris has similar effect. But it is panning which is the most viable area for experiment. Frank Herrmann's exciting picture (81A) is an ingenious combination of panning and long focus lens. The foreground jockeys are in focus but he panned to lose background and he had the riders blurred because the long focus lens has little depth of field.

Panning is unpredictable in its results, partly because we cannot be sure constant speed will be maintained by the subject, least of all with athletes. Herrmann says that anything slower than 1/60 gives too blurred an image unless a tripod is used. Mark Kauffman, who has produced

81A Blur gives vivid sensation of motion. For a picture editor to crop off the background, would be a crime

brilliant results with tripod panning, recommends shutter speeds of 1/15 to 1/8, motor drive and the longest lens possible since the further away the lens from the arc being transcribed the slower the pan can be and the greater the control. But that is not all: foregrounds and backgrounds need surveying with care. Intruding obstacles can ruin the effect.

82A The spray effect. Flying debris of any kind usefully suggests motion

82B Illusion. The racer was still and someone was holding the cycle

83A Fleeting anxiety. A. W. Brownscombe shot at 1/15 f11

83B Sudden violence—shot and stage directed by Lyle Wachovsky. He took four rolls

Fear and violence

Blur is more than a vivid symbol of motion. It also indicates turbulence, a disturbance of the status quo. It is therefore very usefully deployed where anxiety has to be suggested—though quite a lot of shots may have to be taken to get the right effect. What we mostly seek, of course, is controlled blur of elements of the picture, or directional unsharpness as it is sometimes called, rather than uncontrolled undifferentiated blur associated with camera shake. The mild panic of the boys running away from the wave (83A) is one example and of course the blur and the debris emphasise motion as well. There is a rougher sense of fear and violence in 83B which was intended to illustrate an article on family fights. It was staged in the confined space of an elevator where the blurred movement of the fist seems more threatening: there is no escape. The camera was hand held, with a half-second exposure, and the movement was shot again and again. Five people were placed in position and the photographer, Lyle Wachovsky, instructed the man to pretend to hit the woman, and the woman to move away at approximately the moment she would have been hit.

Lyle Wachovsky who does a lot of work with blurred photographs believes that they are more convincing because they are more natural. The viewer gets the feeling of being in the centre of the action. 'When something happens very quickly, like someone being struck, observers of the scene do not see the action as sharp and defined. They see it as a blur and so a super sharp photograph of the event would not accurately reproduce what they saw.

Very few people have 20/20 vision and the lens of a camera is always resolving action more finely than we can see it'. For realism Wachovsky often hand-holds his Hasselblad for ten to twenty-second exposures, in natural light.

Case History Robert Capa records the grimness of D-Day

Robert Capa, blown up by a land mine at Thai Binh, Indochina, in 1954, was always edging towards the sound of gunfire. He won renown for his photograph in 1938 of the moment of death of a Spanish Republican soldier and though that picture has been questioned nobody questions Capa's courage and artistry in pretty well every war there was to cover (Spain, North Africa, Sicily, Anzio, D-Day, Israel, Vietnam). When the Allies landed in Normandy on D-Day, June 6, 1944, Capa went with the American troops landing at Easy Red, Omaha Beach. He plunged into the water with the riflemen, bullets ripping around them. He hid waist

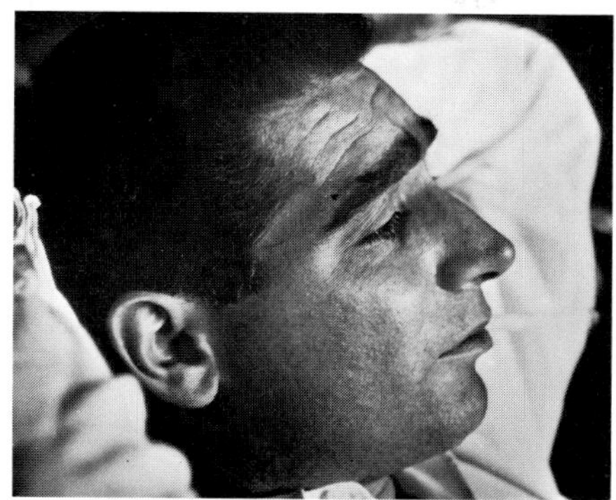

deep in the water behind first a steel obstruction and then a burnt-out amphibious tank taking pictures in a coarse grey light streaked with smoke. He reached the beach exhausted from water and fear, flattened himself on the slanting sand for protection against the bullets and shells and began to shoot with his second Contax without raising his head. In his book *Slightly Out of Focus* (*see bibliography*) he said: 'The foreground of my pictures was filled with wet boots and green faces. Above the boots and faces my picture frames were filled with shrapnel smoke; burnt tanks and sinking barges formed my background'. Capa took 106 pictures but an excited darkroom assistant drying out the negatives turned on too much heat and the emulsions melted. Only eight were salvaged—but how evocative they are, these smudged and grainy remnants of the ordeal at Easy Red.

84A 'If your pictures aren't good enough you aren't close enough. Grain and blur capture the coarse reality of battle action'

Chapter 5

Composition

To consult rules of composition before making a picture is a little like consulting the law of gravitation before going for a walk.
Edward Weston

The airliner above comes in low over the River Thames. In the middle ground are boats and buildings; in the background we see St. Paul's Cathedral, diminished by distance. A photographer might pause to reflect on the lens which has brought the airliner close and still retained St. Paul's in focus. Most of us would 'read' this photograph quickly and simply, our memory and our knowledge of western perspective making unconscious adjustments in interpreting what we see. But the photograph is an illusion (and one which has nothing to do with choice of lens). The reality is on the right at (86C) where the hand of man shatters the linked scale and associated perspective we had assumed. The airliner is a model, and I arranged for two prints, one with and one without the hand, holding the wing tip, for rather more than the negative point of reminding us that we cannot always believe what we can see. I did it to introduce the theme of this chapter: that composition can assist in communicating more effectively. I have already discussed the symbols which enable a photographer to suggest motion in stills of action. We can also, in two-dimensional photography, demonstrate nearness and distance and hugeness and smallness. The photographs (86A) and (86B) build scale into the photograph and the scale element makes the pictures. The graceful black curve in (86B) becomes the bow of a large ship in the moment the eye picks up the dangling painter. And there is more than information here. The size of the man's job is a joke.

86AB Mice and men: Put a finger tip over the mouse or the painter and both pictures perish. Terence McNally, the South African photographer, apprehended the mouse on the stoop of his home, and Esther Bubley, the ship's painter

86C The same airliner as in **85A**, but this time the hand (*left*) gives the game away

Big sugar blockade angers the housewives

FURY OVER MR CUBE'S MOUNTAIN

FURIOUS housewives lashed out yesterday at the big sugar blockade.

Three thousand

By RICHARD STOTT

drive the lorries ourselves."

And Mrs. Regina Dollar, organiser of the National Consumer Protection Council, said:

from the National Housewives' Association will take up the invitation of Tesco boss Sir John Cohen to search his warehouses for sugar stockpiles.

They will inspect his firm's headquarters at Waltham Cross, Herts.

The National Consumer Protection Council an-

A whole heap of trouble

ELEVEN thousand tons of raw sugar lie in a vast heap at a Tate and Lyle plant.

that they too will have to suffer in the new sugar crisis that is sure to hit large areas of the Midlands and Southern

man of the the workers' action committee, was unrepentant about the ban on deliveries.

87A Meaningless photojournalism. The sugar mountain picture is squashed by huge headlines and though intended to show size has no built-in scale indicator. A better photograph below

The potency of scale

Mouse and dog, painter and ship's hull, airliner and man's hand (pp. 85–6) were all devices of composition. The built-in indicators of scale provided corrections and comedy. Yet almost any great photographer who has uttered on the subject of composition rages against the idea that there is any single principle which is valid. Nothing about composition, we are told, can be taught. Paul Strand, for instance, has good practical advice for photographers: 'Photograph a tree, a machine, a table, any old thing: do it over and again under different conditions of light. See what your negative will record'. But when it comes to composition the mists descend. How should a photographer compose? 'Naturally and inevitably by utilising the true qualities of his medium in relation to his experience of life'. It is easy to understand how men like Strand and Weston became hostile to so-called principles of composition. They were caught up in the fatuous debate about art and photography, reacting against people who regarded photography as imitation painting and who discussed photographs in terms of angles, lines, and shapes rather than content. We must preserve the same healthy philistinism today when there is any temptation to sniff at a photograph of a dramatic news event because it is crude in composition or imperfect in focus. Ruskin said the last word on the desiccated analysts: 'It is impossible to give you rules that will enable you to compose. If it were possible to compose pictures by rule Titian and Veronese would be ordinary men'.

Yet, when all this is said, the romantic reaction against analysis has gone too far. It is as if writers were told to ignore the construction of a sentence or warned that no device or structure of prose detected in a Jane Austen novel could ever be used again. In writing, the injunction is to have something to say and to say it well, and in photography, similarly,

88A Desperation. Tiny firefighter against fire bombers of Parliament. By Peter Kempstaff. Compare the effect of **88B**

88B Defiance: Dominating foreground figure of Churchill changes emphasis in picture by Clive Limpkin. See page 90 for discussion

the idea needs to be served by technique. Eric de Mare, in *Photography* (*see bibliography*), has put the relationship succinctly:

'Composition is an essential part of a good photograph; photography as an art has no meaning without it. But craftsmanship is a means and not an end. Expression is the end. If composition is made the end, the result will be self-conscious, artificial and lifeless. Expression and composition are like life and body—a unity. Body by itself is a corpse'.

The romantic nihilism which disdains design is no use to most of us. It encourages ignorance more than it sanctions inspiration. It limits photographic discussion to a series of emotive grunts. And it presides over the production of a lot of bad photographs where even the simplest principles of composition—and it is those I am concerned with—would have transformed the pictorial value. Consider, for example, the photograph (87A) which was published in the *Daily Mirror* at the time of a sugar shortage in the shops. The caption says the picture is a mountain of 11,000 tons of sugar; the photograph, without any scale indicator, might have been of sugar spilled on the tea table. In the bottom picture (87B) we have a man drinking tea and it is an enormous help. But the effect of a human figure varies (consider also (88A) and (88B)), and this aspect of composition requires more discussion.

89A People watch helplessly as the Hindenberg airship blazes with 97 passengers and crew. A powerful composition by Murray Becker

The effect of a figure

The human figure is the simplest effective way of indicating scale and it can, of course, also provide a climax. But if man is the measure of all things the scale effect of the figure varies and so does its influence on what significance we derive from the entire photograph. The three examples at 87–8 give some clue. The introduction of a human figure (87B) confirms that it is a 'mountain' of sugar we see in the background, but we are not induced to marvel at its size. It does not seem so huge that it dwarfs the man drinking tea and that is because he has been photographed in the foreground. The photographer was having a joke that, at a time of sugar shortage, here at least was one person who could have a sweet cup of tea and so it was necessary to make a man with teacup a prominent feature. But a large foreground figure inevitably diminishes a sense of size and vastness in the background. That this scale effect is not the only one is apparent in the comparisons of the two photographs (88A) and (88B) and those on these pages of Germany's Hindenberg airship going up in flames, at the end of its 37th Atlantic crossing. If the human figures are small and distant the frailty of man is suggested. This is what happens in Murray Becker's picture (89A) and in (88A), when the IRA exploded fire bombs at the Houses of Parliament. The size of Big Ben is emphasized in (88A) but the smallness of the fireman against the blaze makes the viewer also feel small in the face of the challenge presented to his institutions and government by terrorism. Completely the opposite significance is suggested in (88B) which offers the defiant statue of Winston Churchill, looming large in the foreground and dominant enough, it seems, to be a shield against any threat. If the first picture is disturbing, this is reassuring.

The Hindenberg photographs all depict what happened in the 47-second explosion that ripped through the dirigible. All give some sense of its size (803ft overall), but (89A) is most successful in scale, significance and symbolism. Because the human figures are small we marvel more at the size of the airship than we do in (90A) and (90B) but we are also made to reflect on how pitiably little individuals could do. The figures create a drama and pathos, a feeling for the trapped passengers and crew, which is lacking in the other photographs. The eye follows the diagonal of the dirigible down to the dots on the ground and back up again to the uncontrollably remote flames. This picture was taken later than the others but caught a decisive moment in the sense we discuss in Chapters 6 and 7.

The exploitation of the human figure can be pushed very far to suggest depth and size. The effect in the Churchill statue can be used to make a big man appear huge by shooting him in close up from below with a receding background. The effect can be controlled and calculated. The further away from the camera is the figure photographed on a structure or landscape, or the wider the angle of view of the lens, the greater is the feeling of depth or dimunition. Scale indicators are essential for publication photography which inevitably compresses. When a ski mountain without skiers is reduced to four-inches square it cannot help but look like an upturned bowl of sugar. Only symbolism can do the trick.

90AB The Hindenberg photographed within seconds of bursting into flames at 7.20 pm, May 6, 1937. But compare **89A**

91A Contrasts in obtaining effect from scale. The outsize nude in Manhattan is by Alfred Gescheidt

Surprise from scale

Electronic brains used to consist of air-conditioned rooms full of equipment. Today the same computing power can be squeezed onto a tiny chip of silicon—the equivalent of 2,000 transistors on a chip perhaps only a quarter of an inch square. How is that minuteness demonstrated? Michael Ward stuck the silicon on a girl's front tooth and asked her to say cheese. The close-up of smiling mouth with a tiny blemish told the story (see introductory pictures). There is never any excuse for failing to provide a symbol of scale where meaning is related to size or distance. Any familiar object will do—postbox against skyscraper, tractor against mountain—but size is more effectively represented by a relationship between the objects. The world's largest pearl should be compared, say, with the head of a match rather than merely held in the hand, a great waterfall, conversely, was all the more impressive when one realised that the shape almost lost in the spray was an aeroplane. Selecting a scale indicator of similar shape helps to concentrate the mind—a pill against a table tennis ball, a wrist watch face against a great clock face, and so on. Alfred Gescheidt did something like that with his comic contrivance (91A) of a giantess accouched, naked, across six shop fronts in Manhattan with people scurrying below. ('Into an empty billboard', explains Gescheidt, 'I double printed a nude'.)

Size is almost always symbolised because we reproduce big objects in a

92A The actual size of fist of Mohammed Ali, a brilliant idea by *Esquire*. It is irresistible to try one's own fist against it

small space. It is a nice moment of theatre when we can break this convention. The bandaged fist (92A) belongs to Mohammed Ali. *Esquire* magazine had the idea just before the world heavyweight fight between Ali and George Foreman, and it published true-size photographs of the fists of Foreman and Ali, both much bigger than the average man's. The *Daily Mirror* reproduced the feature with the headline: 'ACTUAL SIZE. Place your fist over these pictures and see how you shape up!' We can have fun with scale. The mouth of the girl with the silicon smile was reproduced across seven columns, i.e. seven times larger than a normal mouth. That was a trick of scale upon scale. It is very effective in layout, to juxtapose a large reproduction of a small object with a small reproduction of a large object—a big picture, say, of the watchful eyes of a London policeman with a small picture of Scotland Yard. But all of this, plain stuff as it may seem, is wild fantasy. When we look at the daily run of published photographs what is lacking is not a touch of inventiveness, but any idea of scale at all. We are invited, to quote some published examples, to marvel at 'the huge Titan missile silo' (aerial view, flattening sense of size and reproduced at 4 inches square); 'MIT's vast chemical engineering building under construction' (not a human being in sight, it looks like nothing so much as an upturned box of matches), and hundreds of 'giant' this and 'biggest' that whose size remains, for the reader, forever a mystery.

The illusion of depth

A photograph exists on a flat plane. It has no depth. Any idea of depth or distance in anyone's photograph is due to devices of composition, notably diminution, overlapping and aerial perspective. Yet so creative are these that we see space differences simultaneously without having to change the focus of our eyes as we do in daily life. Diminution has already been discussed: our brain tells us that figures which are small must be far away, or that parallel lines converge at a distance. The second device, overlapping, is seen in 93A. The man in the wig overlaps the Queen and is therefore nearer to us; and the spectators, overlapped by the Queen, must be farther away. The technical way to describe this is to say that the man in the wig is on the picture plane—the flat surface through which the picture is seen. Ray Bethers, in *Composition in Pictures* (Pitman, New York, London 1949) describes it as the 'plane which by comparison, establishes all other lines, planes and directions in the space behind it. It is the basis for judging plane directions and for describing two- and three-dimensional space'.

The third device of composition that good photographers practise is aerial perspective. This has nothing to do with pictures taken from aeroplanes. It is the name for the way in which intervening air masses affect our view of distant objects. The further away something is the lighter it will seem, and the greater the contrast with a dark foreground. This progressive lightening of values is evident in nature—the distant mountains 'fade into the background'. In a photograph aerial perspective is a graphic symbol of depth. The photograph of a newly-launched destroyer (94A) on the Tyne is an example of aerial perspective and of scale and mood. The receding foggy background and the dark foreground figures are symbols of size and depth; but the stance of the men is suggestive, too, of north-east phlegm and centuries of ship-building. There has been a gala launching and the flag flies; but have you seen my matches, Fred?

93A Bewigged man, the Queen, the crowd and the building recede from the picture plane, giving us an illusion of depth

94A Colin Theakston of *The Northern Echo* reports the launching of a destroyer and gives a study of retreating visual planes

Examples of framing the subject. **95A** The then Prime Minister Heath framed by the cabin opening—and note the active diagonal **95B** Hungarian rebel **95C** Mother and child, a World Press Photo winner **95D** *Below*: President Kennedy. By George Tames

Framing the subject

Composition can induce concentration. It will not help if the photographer is himself unwilling to concentrate. Many photographers submitting for publication are so obviously undecided about the story the picture is intended to tell. They fail to select. But thinking about principles of composition is one way to develop the habit of selection and organisation. The photographs on these two pages all focus sharply on a single story, and they are all examples of framing—the use of shapes and tones to isolate the subject. Four of the five photographs use dark tones to direct the eye to lighter shades—the exception being 95D where the final frame around President Kennedy is the shape of light coming through the curtains of the White House window. But the effect of the dark tones is different. In 95A and 95B the dark frames are on the picture plane juxtaposed against lighter background and this gives (see page 93) a sense of depth. It is an incidental bonus. In 95C and 96A the black background seems to push baby and infant towards us. Imagine, for a moment, that the mother in 95C had a patterned blouse or the infant stood against flowered wallpaper. A similar technique is to frame the subject with a blurred foreground so that the eye is directed to the sharply focused midfield subject. Everyone groans at the cliché of a photograph with a dark overhanging tree branch but the emphatic photographs here are merely making use of the same idea, demonstrating that a principle of composition is not a prison for the imagination.

The good photographer is composing all the time, whether or not he has a camera. 'I'm always lining things up, measuring angles, noticing the way something or somebody fits into the composition of the space', says Arnold Newman. And Minor White: 'I'm always mentally photographing everything as practice.'

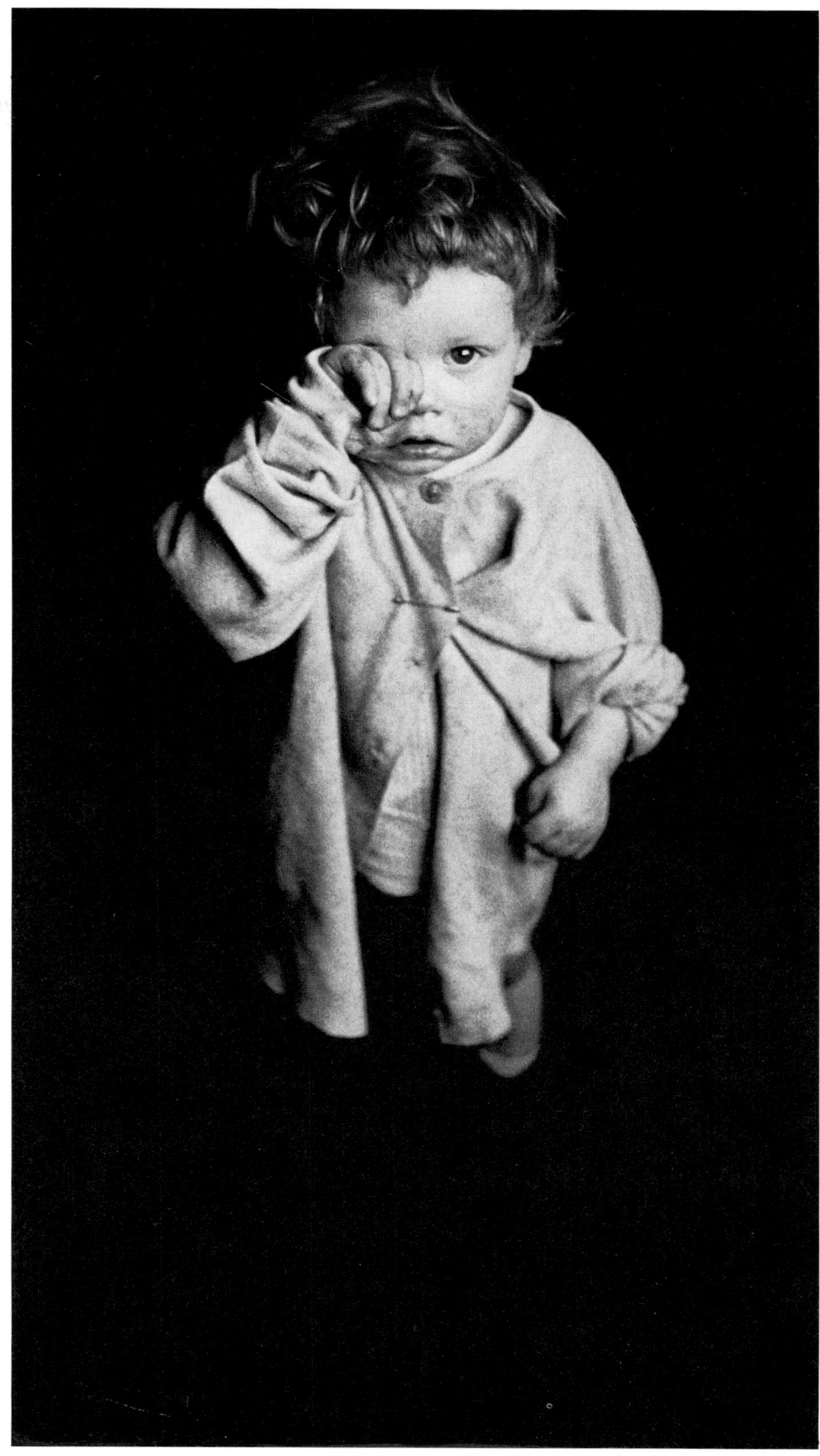

96A Campaigning photography by Snowdon attacking cruelty to children

The corner as climax

We move into trickier territory discussing the emphasis given by lines, tangents, diagonals, curves, balance and the like. It is a ripe area for pretension and the erudite elucidation of patterns that nobody can see but dares not admit. And it has the peril that it encourages photographers to seek patterns to the neglect of the subject. Picture editors, and even photographers, nonetheless, and with due caution, acknowledge that there is such a thing as balance in the distribution of tones and forms, that symmetrical balance is more orderly than asymmetrical (but see *Book V*), and that the dead centre of a photograph is often a debilitating place for the subject. There is to this extent still force in the trite Intersection of Thirds. This suggests that the focus of interest should always be placed off-centre. Imagine the picture divided by three lines horizontally and three vertically. The four intersections of these lines are strong points. (The classical 'golden mean' divides the space in the ratio of 5:8—which is very nearly the same thing.) If the middle is static, and dividing third intersections are strong points, there is no doubt also that a corner can provide a dramatic point to a photograph. Arnold Newman, in his book *One Mind's Eye* (*see bibliography*) reproduces the 18 contact prints of his session with Stravinsky and reveals how he cropped off body, hands, legs, piano legs, and wall, to poise Stravinsky head on hand on the grand piano, at the extreme left corner, a sensational, symbolic portrait. The two pages support the idea of the corner as a point of climax.

97A Dominant corner—Mohammed Ali whooping it up after his seventh round knockout over Sonny Liston, 1974

98A An audacious portrait of Stravinsky by Arnold Newman; it is an edited version of one of a series of prints

98B Illusions of depth and direction. By Stanley Devon

99A Crewman Fred Hansen on the *Vestris*; 'As the last lifeboat was being lowered I jumped into it, taking my last picture on deck'

The energy in a diagonal

Crewman Fred Hansen bought a $8.50 folding Kodak and six rolls of film just before he joined the SS *Vestris* for a Christmas trip carrying 129 passengers and cargo from New Jersey to the Argentine. Off the Virginia Cape the *Vestris*, already listing from overloading, tilted so violently that cargo hurtled through the wooden bulkheads and she began to sink. Passengers and crew inched across the slanting deck, their secure shipboard world now reduced to a handhold on a rail or a rope. This was the picture (99A) Fred Hansen took with his new camera in the seconds before 110 people were lost. He had never heard of the effect of diagonal lines in a photograph. He said later: 'When I got on deck I started taking pictures. Everyone was screaming and yelling'. Fred Hansen had, in short, just pointed his unused camera and recorded a fragment of time in the real world. But in the real world a tilt of this order does make us feel alarmed: there is a raw, physical basis for the idea that a diagonal stress is an important element in composition. Maurice de Sausmarez has explained it: 'We tend to see and interpret by reference to the stable norm of gravitation so that whenever an object or form is placed in contradiction to the horizontal-vertical axis it seems to imply movement'. (*See bibliography.*)

We have already seen the use of the diagonal in action photographs (pp. 79–80) but its influence is not limited to movement. The unresolved tendencies towards vertical and horizontal produce energy tensions which are suggestive of violence, excitement and drama. This dynamic quality is readily apparent in a comparison of two photographs (100A and 100B) of Wolf Rock lighthouse when three men were marooned there by heavy seas and supplies had to be dropped in by helicopter. It is difficult to capture the idea of rough seas when photographing a static object from the air and the drama in 100A really comes from the vertiginous diagonal. There is obviously nothing like this sensation in 100B, but the effect of a diagonal was not appreciated in the darkroom which gamely tried to produce a print with the lighthouse standing straight up as lighthouses do. See also Rembrandt's Storm on the Sea of Galilee.

100B Pretty rather than chilling

100A Stronger sense of drama of relief of Wolf Rock Lighthouse

Repetition and contrast

The difference between a button pusher and a photographer is in the attitude to composition. Romano Cagnoni was very conscious of the picture he was seeking to compose when he took his celebrated photograph of the Ibo recruits for the Biafra army in the Nigeria civil war (101B), a black and white rendition of the original colour slide. He had been attracted first by the shaven heads of 100–150 men running down the road. 'You see one suggestion which is interesting and follow it up'. He stationed himself on the terrace of a house overlooking the drill ground, impressed by the changing shapes of the groups and the beauty of the bodies, and for the next four hours tried to dramatise the scene. He took only 10

101A Blonde Princess Anne in a sea of little black boys in Kenya. By Marion Kaplan

101C Break in the pattern again arrests the eye

shots in that time and knew at once that he had secured with this one a powerful image of war and sacrifice. The shaven, bare-breasted men are vulnerable, anonymous, compressed to a single flesh by the 500mm lens.

Repetition, so subtly exploited here, is a valuable tool. It is another way of suggesting depth (pp. 93–4), so often exploited in architecture where the reduction of similar forms by diminishing perspective—the recession of arches in mediaeval battlements—makes the space comprehensible. Repetition which is then broken is an effective way to point attention (101A and 101C). Princess Anne, framed by the black faces, is also an example of another principle—as so often in a good photograph several positive features may coalesce.

101B Romano Cagnoni waited four hours to make this celebrated study of Ibo recruits in the Biafran civil war in Nigeria

103A

103B

Daines who took **C** *below*

Case History Eyes on the prisoner

Three photographs to emphasise the importance of composition and intention. A gang murder trial is about to begin in a small town and the heavily guarded accused is brought to the court room with a blanket over his head to eliminate problems with evidence of identification. The two smaller photographs adequately show blanketed-prisoner-plus-police-guard. B is better but the third shot goes well beyond these mere mechanics. It exploits the limitations of the human barrier. It uses the policemen, to funnel your eye to the prisoner; it establishes the two corner policemen almost on the picture plane, as unarmed, unshakeable guardians of the law. Michael Daines of Anglia Press who took this excellent photograph says: 'There were dozens of photographers there and a lot of police. They seemed a bit relaxed about following the usual rule of preventing photography within the "precinct" of the court but they did prevent photographers going forward. I made sure I got to the spot where I took the pictures. I had seen that the policemen at the front provided good anchorage points for a picture. I thought of the anchorage first, and then hoped that they would keep their arms folded. I did ask them not to move, but not much more, when I went down to take three shots from the same position with a 21mm wide angle lens. The one that was widely used was the last shot. I always go for strong composition; sometimes it happens, sometimes it doesn't'.

THE GUARDIAN

London Thursday August 2 1973 5p

Nixon stopped ITT case for campaign gift

From SIMON WINCHESTER : Washington, August 1

...vention expenses was revealed last year when a memorandum from a Washington lobbyist, Mrs Dita Beard, was published by a syndicated journalist.

The Administration denied at a Senate hearing set up to inquire into the scandal that there had been any impropriety. But today's document from Mr Colson has confirmed that papers existed in the White House showing that Mr Mitchell had had full foreknowledge of the arrangement with the corporation. Mr Colson expressed concern that "we may not have recovered all the copies" of the paper, which could rightly be expected to be explosive.

The earlier allegations had suggested that the chairman of ITT, Mr Harold Geneen, had been in touch with Mr Agnew, that Agnew had been in touch with Mr Nixon, that Mr Nixon had spoken to both Mr Mitchell and Mr Kleindienst to pressure junior officials in the Justice Department to lay off ITT. The memorandum today would seem to confirm the bulk of the earlier reports, and leave a number of very senior White House officials and Cabinet members open to possible prosecution for perjury and leave perhaps even the President and Mr Agnew open to more serious charges in connection with the pay-off.

STRICT SECURITY was enforced at Braintree yesterday when John Brook and Nicholas D'Clare Johnson were charged with murder and robbery at the Barn Restaurant on November 5 last year. Above: Brook, hidden under a blanket, is led back to the cells. Report page 6

Strike hits car ferries

HUNDREDS of families travelling to the Continent by car ferry face long delays today because of the cancellation of 39 ferry services from Dover and Folkestone. The stoppage results from a 24-hour strike by ships' officers. Newhaven - Dieppe services will not be affected. British Rail said that passengers with bookings would be given priority on all services, including the Seaspeed hovercraft.

Report page 5

Robbers claim letter proves them UK spies

By JAMES MacMANUS

Storm floods homes

South London emergency services were alerted late last night as homes were flooded by a cloudburst. Wandsworth Council summed up the situation as: "Just like the blitz."

Receiving centres were set up at Battersea Town Hall and in private homes to cater for the scores of families forced to evacuate their homes, some of which were seven feet deep in water.

Home loans set to smash 10pc barrier

Loophole shut

Two charged

TV, radio—2

104D *The Guardian* made good use of the picture with a 5-column presentation

Chapter 6

The Decisive Moment

To me photography is the simultaneous recognition, in a fraction of a second, of the significance of an event as well as a precise organisation of forms which give the event proper expression.
Henri Cartier-Bresson

105A Time check: a visual moment of great descriptive interest. President Nixon, hand in one place, mind in another, during a walkabout tour

President Nixon on a glad-handing tour is caught with his sincerity down and we are apt to say the photograph is a decisive moment. It is an arresting phrase but it needs redefinition. It comes to photojournalism by way of 17th Century French theological politics. When Henri Cartier-Bresson produced his 1951 book of photographs with the title *Images à la Sauvette*, his preface recalled the words of Cardinal de Retz that there was a decisive moment for everything in the world (*'il n'y a rien au monde qui n'ait un moment decisif'*). The American publisher Dick Simon fastened on the phrase and published the English language edition under the title *The Decisive Moment*. It has become a commonplace of photojournalism and corrupted. Cartier-Bresson did not, in his prefatory remarks, attach a definition to the phrase, and it has come to be used to describe a dramatic rather than a visual climax, a story rather than a picture. Cartier-Bresson's emphasis was on the visual—on the organic co-ordination of shapes, lines and values. He says disarmingly: 'Few of my photographs qualify'. He is on any definition too modest, but the next two chapters attempt to clarify and refine this creative concept.

Horst Faas was a winner in the World Press photo contest of Amsterdam with his acutely timed photograph

News moments

These are good news pictures, but are they decisive moments? The phrase has come to be pinned on any photograph which happens to have a visual monopoly, as these do, of some unrepeatable news event. But to call them all decisive moments misleads about content and ignores the primacy in Cartier-Bresson's perception of the way content is organised. Used in this loose way, decisive moment is a fiction, a rationalisation of choice, rather than an analytical tool to help us to select photographs for publication and compare qualities.

On content, for instance, consider what is decisive about any of these moments. A different moment, later or earlier, would hardly have made any difference to the value of the exploding plane (108A) or steeple (108C). The photograph of the stabbing of the Japanese Socialist leader (108B) is actually after the mortal sword thrust when officials are trying to stop a second attack. The decisive moment has passed unrecorded. So, too, with the falling mother and child (107A). Stanley Forman had his 135mm camera on motordrive and recalls: 'I remember thinking I don't want to see them hit the ground. I turned away before it happened'.

Secondly, composition. There is certainly no sense of uniqueness in the exploding plane; the pattern of bits and pieces could be quite different without affecting its value as a news picture. There is enough in the falling mother and child and perhaps in the stabbing to meet Cartier-Bresson's criterion that form must give the facts expression and significance—there is a tragic futility about the outstretched hands—but instead of twisting the idea of a decisive moment it is better to reserve that term for moments when decisive content is undisputably synthesised with meaningful form. I propose characterising photographs such as those on this page as News Moments, and others as Visual or Symbolic Moments, so that we can be more discriminating about the decisive moment.

Decisive moments, on my definition, will be fairly rare and there would certainly be disagreement about whether a particular picture qualifies. But that matters less than whether the categories are found to be of assistance in all the phases of publication photography.

107A Caught in a fire the woman fell five storeys to her death, the child lived

108A News moment: De Havilland 110 explodes, with the pilot in it, while giving a display at the Farnborough Air Show

108B (*below right*) A fraction of a second after the stabbing of Japanese socialist leader Inejiro Asanuma in 1960 by a 17-year-old ultra-rightist

108C (*above*) The steeple of Boston's old North church collapses in a hurricane and the moment is caught by amateur Joseph Spallino

109A Frank Hudson (*Daily Mail*) was waiting for Sam King and Dai Rees to come down the fairway when King drove a ball towards the spectators

The visual moment

In news terms there is nothing 'decisive' here. By contrast with News Moments (pp. 107–108) and Symbolic Moments (pp. 111–112) these succeed for visual reasons. Hardly a word is required, though our interest is aroused enough to read any offered. It is the composition which gives enjoyment. For that reason the precise moment of photography is crucial. These are patterns that vanish on hesitation. In 109A there was, and there would be again, simply a crowd of spectators. The visual moment was created by the golfer pulling his shot and the photographer shooting almost simultaneously. In 110C the photographer expected to see the baseball fielder leap for a ball, and caught him receiving, instead, a free cup of spectator's beer. These photographs are different from 110A and B in that they are descriptively full of detailed interest, rather than simply visceral. The baseball picture splits into two stories joined by the column of beer. But they are all Visual Moments. 'Inside movement' said Cartier-Bresson, 'there is one moment in which the elements are in balance. Photography must seize the importance of this moment and hold immobile the equilibrium of it'. Equilibrium will not have been at the front of the minds of the photographers; but it is valuable afterwards

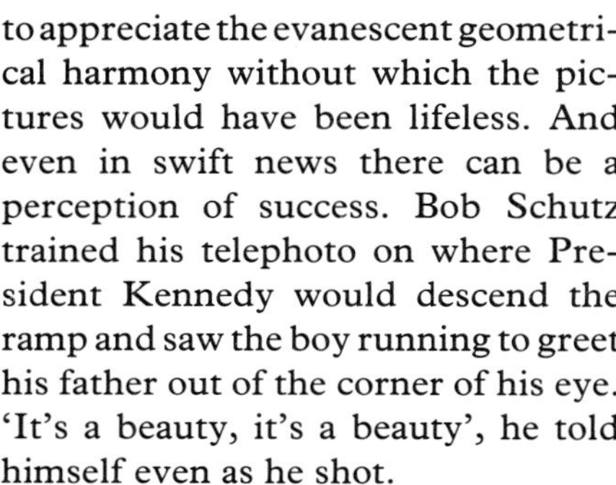

to appreciate the evanescent geometrical harmony without which the pictures would have been lifeless. And even in swift news there can be a perception of success. Bob Schutz trained his telephoto on where President Kennedy would descend the ramp and saw the boy running to greet his father out of the corner of his eye. 'It's a beauty, it's a beauty', he told himself even as he shot.

110A Father and son: John Kennedy, jnr. greets Dad, August 1963

110B A flutter of skirt on the seafront. By Bert Hardy with Box Brownie

110C Al Smith of Chicago White Sox, versus Los Angeles Dodgers and a spectator's beer

111A Black revolt

111B Man flies. The Wrights told a coast-guard how to expose the plate with tripod and black cloth

111C 'I will return', promised MacArthur, and he does, striding ashore on Luzon Island, Philippines, surrendered by America 29 months earlier

112A Oxford, May 1954: Roger Bannister, at 3 mins 59.4, the first man to break the four-minute barrier

The symbolic moment

What we see on this spread is a moment decisive in itself or in its symbolism, but where the pure visual pattern is not significant enough alone to sustain the picture. We have to be told something extra, in words, and believe it. The biplane a few feet off the ground (111B) carries Orville Wright on man's first powered flight, on December 17, 1903 at Kitty Hawk, North Carolina. The 'routine' race picture (112A) is rather more: it is man breaking, for the first time, the barrier of the four-minute mile. The boy looking startled (112B) is Harold Whittles, hearing his voice for the first time by means of a recording and hearing aid which can just be perceived. The men with guns (111A) symbolise the rebellions of the Sixties; they are black students at Cornell University emerging from siege to the shock of a nation. The man getting his feet wet (111C) is General MacArthur keeping a promise to walk ashore in triumph on the beaches of the Philippines which he had left in defeat. Symbolic moments like these can be staged or posed; MacArthur reputedly did it twice for the benefit of photographers. The test is that they should distill the essence of some person, or place, event or era.

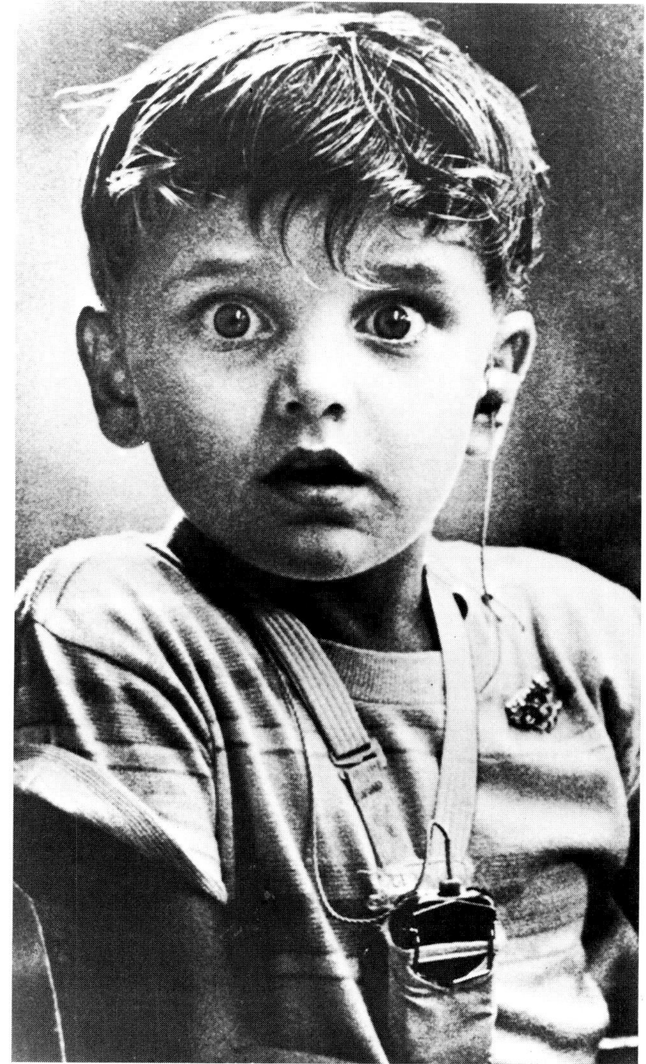

112B Born deaf, a five-year-old hears his own voice

One photograph or several?

John Sadovy has remained disappointed with the sequel to his adventure in Budapest in 1956. Sadovy, a Czech and 15 years a photographer, was sent by *Life* magazine to Hungary when the capital and other townships rebelled against their Communist rulers (and were eventually suppressed by Soviet troops). He tramped the streets for four days as the citizens expressed their resentment in attacks on anything associated with the regime—officials, policemen, Stalin's statue. In the second 48 hours Sadovy was approached from time to time by a man in a leather coat who would direct him to scenes of great ferocity and then disappear. One of these pieces of guidance landed Sadovy outside a building where secret policemen were hiding with armed rebels outside. 'The policemen emerged in groups,' says Sadovy, 'and I saw the jackets of the rebels move. I expected one man might be shot or threatened but they fired on the whole group point blank as the men raised their hands'. Sadovy had his Leica with 35mm lens pre-set for 4 to 15ft and 250th of a second at f11. Within 8 to 10 seconds, photographing on reflex without thinking about composition at all, he had taken the four pictures on this spread. They are terrifying and moving (and some photographers have criticised Sadovy for exposing to public gaze the private moment of death), but it is only 114A which has had considerable publication. Though Sadovy himself has always had 'an obsession, a fanatical belief', in catching 'the moment', he felt then, and feels today, that no single one of these four tells the story of what he recorded that day in Budapest. 'It's a sequence, a story, and it is not told unless all four pictures are used'. It is possible to have sympathy with picture editors who want to give maximum space to the horrifying news moment when the men raise their hands and the bullets strike, but Sadovy surely has a point. There is no need, of course, for all the pictures to have identical sizing, but part of the impact of these photographs undeniably lies in following the anxiety of 113A with the shock of 114A and the sequel pictures add credibility: they really were shot.

The Sadovy story is an example of one of the perverse consequences of too literal an interpretation of the idea of a single decisive moment. Another follows.

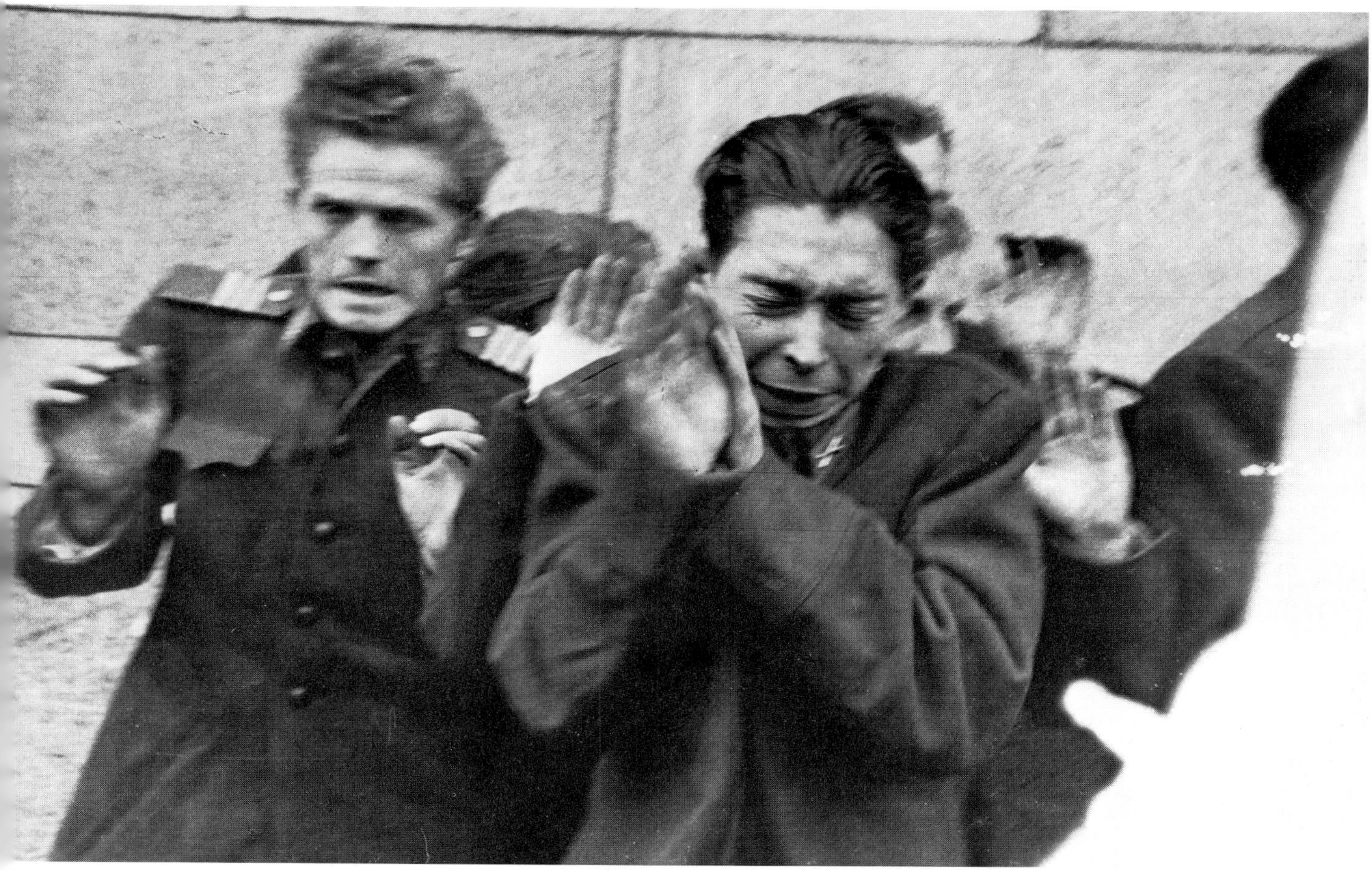

113A–114ABC Killings in Budapest in 1956. John Sadovy (now of Kingston-on-Thames) took these four photographs of the summary execution of Communist policemen by Hungarian rebels. About 80–85 men were shot as they emerged from a building. Six months after he took the picture Sadovy saw a report and a photograph about the blond (*centre* **113A**) who had survived with the loss of a leg.

115 Competitive captions on the day Bannister met Landy. The caption to **A** (*left*) read: 'The moment of triumph is the moment of agony as England's Roger Bannister breaks the tape . . .' **B**'s read: 'This is *the* big moment that decided the dramatic race . . .'

The decisive moment–or the best picture?

The concentration on a single image, encouraged by the idea of a moment which is decisive, is the theme of this chapter and the next, but it is necessary to enter two cautions. There is the risk of suppressing a viable sequence (pp. 113–14) and there is the risk of giving undue weight to a crude idea of 'decisiveness' in choosing between pictures. Cartier-Bresson himself clearly recognised the first possibility: 'The elements which, together, could strike sparks out of a subject are often scattered in time and space'. Reuniting the complementary elements in a picture story is the solution if there is space or interest and if all the photographs are available when they are wanted. But let us discard that possibility in considering the second occasional wayward influence of 'the decisive moment' on picture selection and picture taking. It is well illustrated by the photographs on this spread—taken by different photographers—from the race in 1954 between Roger Bannister of England and Australia's John Landy.

A month after Bannister broke the four minute mile with his 3/59.4 at Oxford, Landy did it as well, and with a new world record of 3.58, just over a second faster than Bannister. Several weeks later the two men met at Vancouver in the then British Empire and Commonwealth Games for the greatest footrace of the century. It was prudent for photographers to ponder athletics. Bannister had a celebrated last-minute sprint so Landy's tactic, it could be reckoned, was to run the first two furlongs at such a pace he would have a commanding lead which Bannister could only challenge at risk of spending himself. Landy did break the field, with only Bannister holding on, five yards behind at half way. At the start of the last lap the gap was 2 yards but half way through it Landy

116A A splendid visual moment. By Mark Kauffman

made a final effort and pulled slowly away. It seemed Bannister was being left just when he had been expected to strike. But he was delaying his sprint until 150 yards out and just as a confident Landy looked back on the field, Bannister passed him at speed. He won by 5 yards at 3/58.8.

Does one of these three photographs represent a decisive moment? The most decisive in the narrow meaning is 115A: nothing could be more decisive than the moment the victor crosses the tape with his challenger behind. It is a competent photograph. It is what I have characterised as a News Moment, since the composition has no particular precision or poignancy. Is this, then, the picture which should be selected above all others?

But wait, there is another moment that was decisive in the race—when Landy looked back (115B). It is not more conclusive but it is more unusual, more intriguing than the routine finish. This leaves us with 116A which preoccupation with a moment of 'decision' would persuade us to discard—and yet what a mistake that would be. It is a superb photograph. The composition is electrifying. Bannister, hair flying, heart pounding, seems to be tearing right into the camera.

The choice between these three pictures is not simple. Something naturally depends on the occasion and purpose of publication. But selection is hindered by the confusion over 'decisive moment'. This is one of the reasons I suggest that in photojournalism we should reserve that term for those few photographs which unmistakably fuse news content and composition and regard the selection here as between News Moments (115A–B) and the Visual Moment (116A). On pages 117–125 I offer a categorisation along these lines of various striking photographs.

117A Cyprus 1964—a Turkish woman mourns for her husband killed in a village battle with Greeks

A truly decisive moment

This is a genuine spontaneous news moment with such a strong composition that it qualifies for inclusion as a decisive moment in the pure restricted sense. Before we learn anything else we can sense the suffering and the companionship of the boy and the woman. It happens also to be a symbolic moment as well as a visual and news moment, for it is a photograph epitomising the tragedy of the Greek-Turkish conflict in Cyprus. The woman, a Turk, has just learned that her husband has been killed during overnight fighting; her son reaches up as much, it seems, to comfort her as seek solace himself. It is this moment which makes the photograph. Our eyes travel back and forth along the line (compare Hindenberg p. 89).

Don McCullin who took the picture had spent the night with the embattled Turks at Ghaziveran. In the morning he could sense that an emotional mood was building up to a revelation. But when it came McCullin did not shoot from the hip. He paused long enough to make an exposure reading and composed almost at the moment of pressing the shutter. 'I always take an exposure reading. Even in battle photography, I go over on my back and read the exposure. What's the point of getting killed if you've got the wrong exposure?' The picture won the World Press Photo award in 1964—but on first publication was curiously and negligently squeezed into a tiny space.

119A Collaborator, 1944. Crowd's glee as Frenchwoman with baby is humiliated for befriending Germans. (Decisive Moment)

119B Celebration. Former US Attorney General John Mitchell with his lawyers after acquittal in post-Watergate conspiracy. (Visual Moment)

120A Fists and faces. One sneak picture was all Bert Hardy dared risk of this dockland fight in the Thirties (News Moment)

120B Estrangement: A couple wait for the hearing of their divorce in Moscow, numb to the presence of photographer Eve Arnold (Visual Moment)

121A The camera as eavesdropper. A visual moment between Mr. Khrushchev and Mr. Gomulka in Moscow. By Dan Weiner

121B A decisive moment combining news and visual moments. It is Benito Mussolini, deposed as a dictator, being rescued from a mountain hideout in Italy by a glider-borne raiding party sent by Hitler in 1943. The photographer has caught a marvellous moment with the eyes, and the graininess adds to the drama

122A (*right*) A horrifying decisive moment. Ron Haeberle photographed the massacre at My Lai, providing damning visual confirmation of the atrocity

Beauty out of Minamata

A mother bathes her daughter, a routine act but a moment of beauty and symbolism in this photograph by W. Eugene Smith, creator of many classic photo essays if not the form itself. He is celebrated for his studies of a Spanish village, Albert Schweitzer in the jungle and a country doctor. When I talked with him in New York, he had only just recovered from head injuries received at the hands of a mob of chemical company toughs in Minamata, Japan. Smith's sense of mission has often made him both observer and participant. In Minamata he and his wife Aileen became friends with families who had been stricken by death and brain damage from eating fish poisoned by mercury effluent. Tokomo Uemura, the girl being bathed, was one of the victims, born alive but unresponsive in 1956. 'I had got to know the family routine well,' said Smith. 'Tokomo was always cared for. I knew there was a picture in the mother bathing her child that would symbolise the family's affection. I asked her eventually if we could make some pictures. There was daylight coming from small high windows, but it was not enough so I used just a kiss of strobe light bounced off the ceiling, and I sank into the background so that the mother forgot about me. I made five or six pictures and then the one I wanted came up. I knew it the moment I took it. It was a picture of love. Then I got sloppy and didn't focus properly. My eyes had filled with tears.'

Smith is fastidious about the use of his work. When I told him I intended to publish the picture as a two page spread he was anxious to know where the fold of this book might intersect it. He does not believe that poor pictures can be made into good ones in the darkroom and he has also had some sharp brushes with picture editors. But he regards as 'nonsense' the idea that a negative is inviolate. He cropped off the top of this picture where the light from the small windows in the full frame would have distracted from the soft light around the mother's face. In making his own layouts (which he prefers to do) he said he often has to crop—'for the benefit of the pictures', and he added: 'The world just does not fit conveniently into the format of a 35mm camera.'

It is fitting, nevertheless, that this chapter concludes overleaf with an enlarged but uncropped 35mm frame

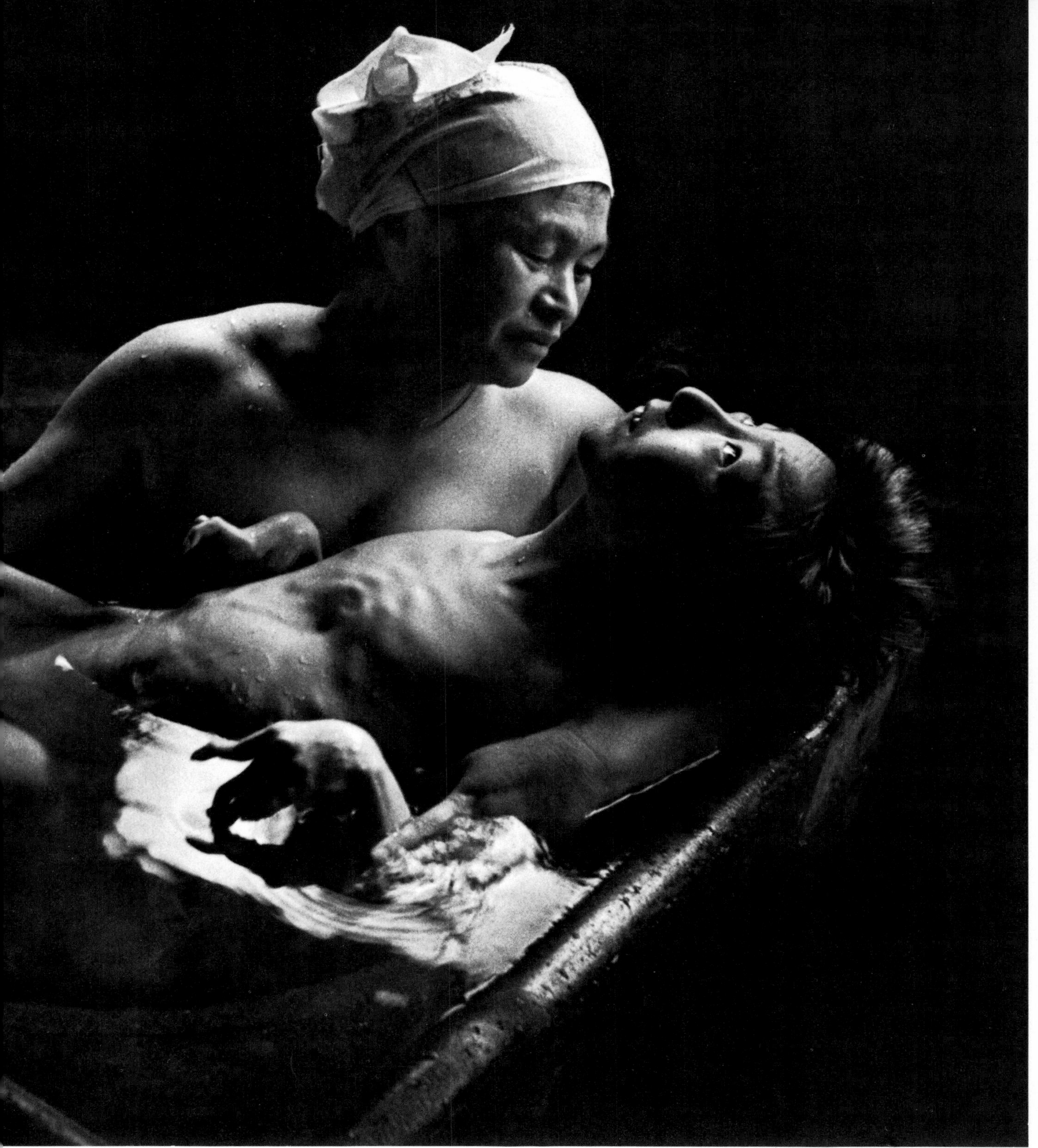

by the inventor of the phrase 'the decisive moment'. It is a moment of news and of visual value, hence a true decisive moment.

125A A decisive moment by the inventor of the phrase, Cartier-Bresson. It is Dessau displaced persons camp, and one of the displace

people is identifying a Belgian as somebody who had been helping the Germans. Cartier-Bresson took two photographs of this scene

Chapter 7

Minutiae of Time and Space

It is a peculiar part of the good photographer's adventure to know where luck is most likely to lie in the stream, to hook it, and to bring it in without unfair play and without too much subduing it. James Agee

Photojournalism's most famous picture, a pure decisive moment, is Robert Capa's of a Republican soldier in the Spanish Civil War at the moment he was mortally struck by a bullet above. The authenticity of the picture has recently been challenged it being suggested it was a staged picture of militia doing battle training for the benefit of the camera. The evidence is discussed in Phillip Knightley's book *The First Casualty (see bibliography)*.

Cornell Capa, who is convinced the picture is genuine, believes his brother was leg-pulling when he gave John Hersey an improbable account of the picture—that while sheltering in a trench he stuck up his camera on the sound of firing and took a blind snap-shot which not only caught a soldier in full frame and in focus as he charged a machine-gun post, but did so at the precise second he fell. Whether that was the way it was taken, we shall never know. To catch a news moment of such poignancy, by any method, and to do it with such powerful composition is indeed extraordinary—and yet Robert Capa did that many times. Luck, as James Agee said, is one of the cardinal creative forces and the photographer has unique equipment for collaborating with it.

Newspapers are often glad, it is true, to get any picture at all from certain events, such as the last hours of President Allende of Chile, and any one of the three opposite (128A–C) would have had universal publication when the pictures surfaced some weeks after Allende was deposed in September 1973. They are news moments. But there were six negatives from Chile and the differences that are possible in apparently similar pictures is demonstrated overleaf (129–30) and is the theme of this chapter.

128AB Negatives No 2 (*left*) and No 3 (*right*) in the strip of six of Allende inside the Moneda Presidential Palace during its siege

128C President Allende (*right in tin helmet*), photographed by an unidentified member of his entourage; on the day he died

129A Picture No 4 from strip of six: a revealing moment, needing space. *The New York Times*, which got the scoop, played it small and downpage

Differences which tell a story

In September 1973 the military in Chile overthrew the elected Government of President Salvador Allende. His fate was unclear. First reports said he had killed himself. Later it was said he had put on a steel helmet and directed the defence of the presidential palace until wounded twice and killed by troops.

All this was verbal and contradictory. Then some weeks after the coup the *New York Times* received six 35mm negatives of the day Allende died, sent anonymously from a member of his staff in hiding. The day of the coup became believable in an extraordinarily more vivid way. The negatives showed him on a telephone, then walking in a courtyard to a door, and finally back inside. It was the fourth contact (129A) which was decisive. It is not a question of better 'art'. It is a question of better news. It is a composition which tells more of the story and tells it better. There is the readiness of the men in the foreground, the President framed in the darkness of the doorway, and the impromptu nature of their defence. All three scan a hostile sky in unison. These are men, it seems, ready to fight and die.

All the negatives had a blemish on the left, an intervening thread. Should it be touched out? Under no circumstances. Where credibility is an issue, there should never be tampering and as little cropping as possible.

This anonymous picture won the World Press Photo Award. Yet numerous newspapers which had given up acres to Chile failed to give it proper space. Even the *New York Times* which got the scoop played it small and downpage. Is it any wonder photographers and picture editors grow cynical about photojournalism?

131A and **131B** Two news moments of the Goodwin lightship disaster. Two hours after daylight a helicopter pilot saw a figure crouched in a corner and hauled him up in a sling. He had spent the night clinging to a rail as seas broke over him. The other seven men were never found; and the visual moment at **132A** is a horrifying idea of what it was like on the night of the disaster

A true picture of disaster

The traditional idea of a decisive moment as a news climax cannot cope with Stuart Heydinger's photograph (132A) of the wreck of the South Goodwin lightship. Photographs 131A and 131B were nearer in time to the decisive news moment of the wreck of the ship and other pictures featured the helicopter and lifeboat rescue teams. But Heydinger's *late* picture is nearer the truth of what happened on the night; it is a visual

moment of stunning ferocity.

This is how it happened. During the early hours of Saturday gales struck the Trinity House lightship with eight men aboard, and dragged it from its moorings, a mystery in itself since it was built to endure even greater assault. The lightship drifted until it struck the Goodwin sands and turned over. Early next morning newspapers sent photographers over by air. Heydinger was always keen to find a pilot who would fly extremely low and was unwilling to go with the first planes on offer. He did not manage to get what he wanted until 3 o'clock in the afternoon. By this time the gale of the night before had started up again and with the wind tearing at the plane and the light fading Heydinger's 'great pilot' flew at 100ft over the wreck. Heydinger leaned out over the side for his shot of the now raging seas, a physical achievement of his own since he was using a heavy Speed Graphic with a 15-inch lens.

That the picture was in focus, Heydinger attributes to his training in zonal focusing on the gentle lawns of Wimbledon. The technique is to use the depth of field scale to determine what aperture will give precision over a predefined area. Heydinger had an added trick: 'At the beginning of the day, I'd stick some tape on the side of the Speed so that I knew the limits for moving the lens backwards and forwards.' Over the South Goodwin lightship there was no time for experiments.

Four scenes from a fire tragedy

The participants and the incident are the same throughout; but there are four quite different possibilities for publication. The photographer was able to record the vain efforts of firemen—one of them Michael Maye, a former Golden Gloves champion—to revive a baby and a boy of 3. They are all news moments and the strongest visual moment comes earliest in the drama (in contrast to the Goodwin lightship, 131–132). It is 134A. The nearest in time to the news moment of failure is 133A but it is confused in composition and shows only one child. In 133B the second fireman distracts. But this picture can be edited (133C) to provide a stronger visual moment, highlighting the fireman in the explicit kiss of life. My own choice would be 134A, where everything concentrates on the children, where there is such tenderness in the outstretched hands, and such a sense of striding urgency.

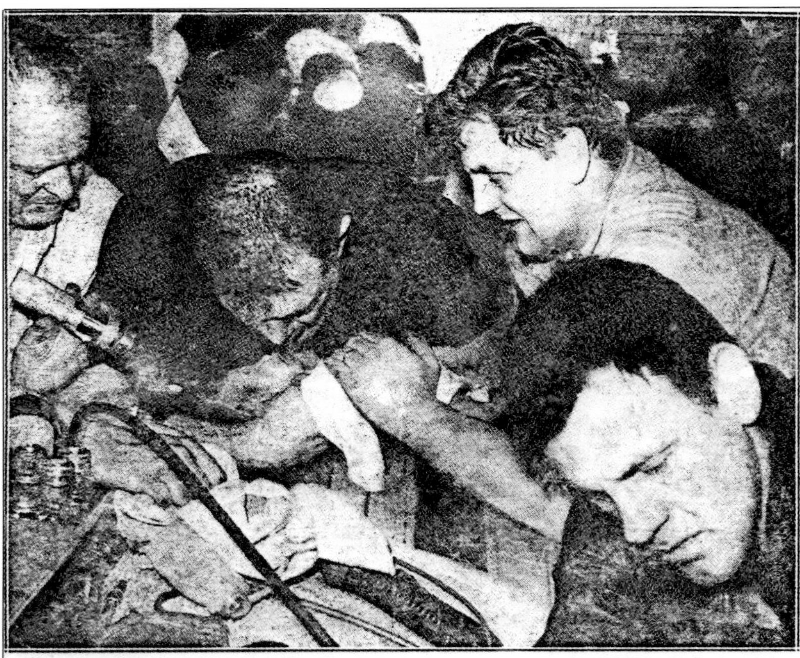

(NEWS fotos by Alan Aaronson)

The Breath Of Life Fails

Fireman Michael Maye attempts to revive Cynthia Alvarado, 2 months, after she and her brother, Carlos, 2, lost consciousness in fire in their home at 490 E. 165th St. Bronx. Both children died despite valiant, prolonged efforts by team of firemen. The two-alarm fire, which erupted in the Alvarados' fourth-floor apartment, routed 100 tenants. See the foto left . . . —*Story p. 3; other pic. P. 1*

133A How the *New York Daily News* published one picture

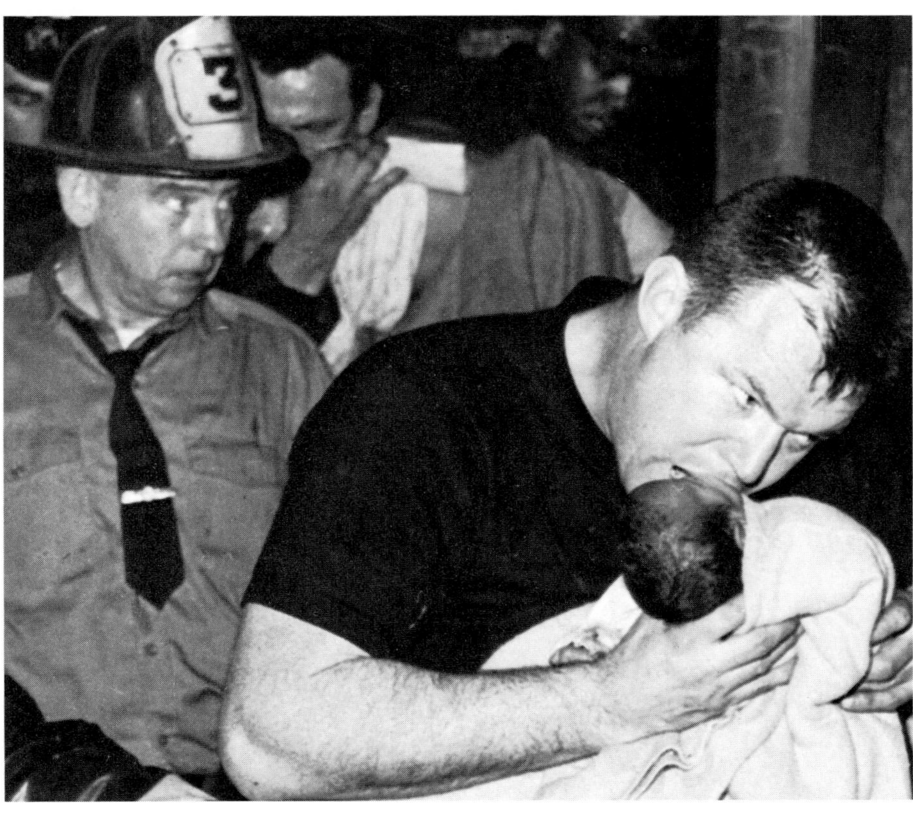

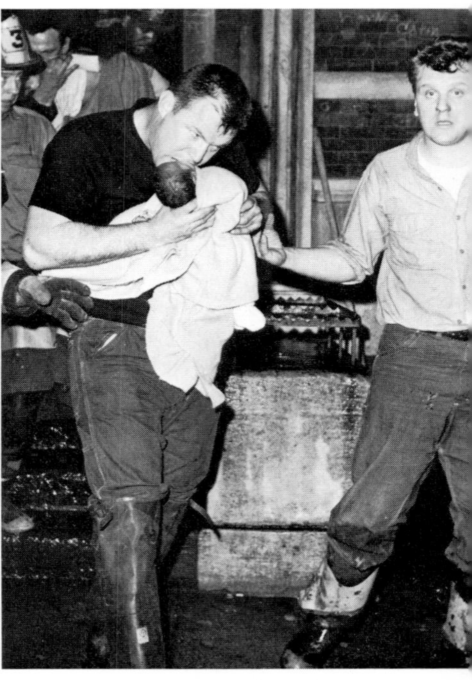

133B (*above*) The gap between the firemen and awareness of the camera distract attention from the central drama. **133C** (*left*) Better than **B**, but the back fireman directs our eyes off the baby

134A A kiss of life on the move for children knocked out by fumes. The strongest visual moment in the set

A split second difference

When a photographer presses the shutter release, in the words of Marvin Krone, a finite fraction of the infinite time of the universe is preserved forever. No other medium can make this possible, but awareness of the profound differences possible in a mega-second is proclaimed rather more than it is practised. I would like a second of infinite time for every occasion in a newsroom I have seen contacts and even prints scanned with a hurried carelessness which cannot fail to miss significant differences. These two demonstrations are of the fractions of time I have in mind.

In 135A we have Adolf Hitler. It is June 21, 1940, in the forest four miles north of Compiègne in France. There is an old railway carriage where Marshal Foch dictated the German surrender in 1918. Shortly after 3.15 pm Hitler enters the car and takes a seat where Foch sat 22 years earlier. Hitler listens as the terms of surrender are read out. Germany has come to Compiègne to wipe out 'its deepest humiliation.' When it is over he cannot restrain himself and photography preserves the fleeting moment of the jig of glee (135B).

The second example records the homecoming of an American prisoner at the end of the war in Vietnam. One became the most honoured news photograph of the year, winning a Pulitzer, the NPPA-Missouri contest and the happy news category in the World Press Photo. Was 136A or 136B the prize winner? It is worth pausing to examine the pictures before you read on.

The picture which won the national and international awards is 136B, and rightly. These are the reasons: **1:** The boy's face is less obscured than in A. **2:** The daughter is caught at a marvellous moment, exuberantly in the air when the gap between her and her father still has its tautness and

135A (*left*) Eight prints of Hitler after the surrender of France, 1940. The visual moment, the fusion of smile and jig with knee at full lift, is caught in the first frame of the second row—and enlarged above: **135B** The photographer was Walter Frentz

drama; A is just past that moment. **3:** The welcoming warmth of the girl's widestretched arms is reduced in A because one of them is obscured. **4:** Perception of the welcoming group is hardly interrupted in B: let your eye run along an imaginary line following the top outlines of the figures. In A the forward flow is broken by an outline shadow between the two girls and the shape of a truck at the right. A is a news moment—but B is a visual moment as well.

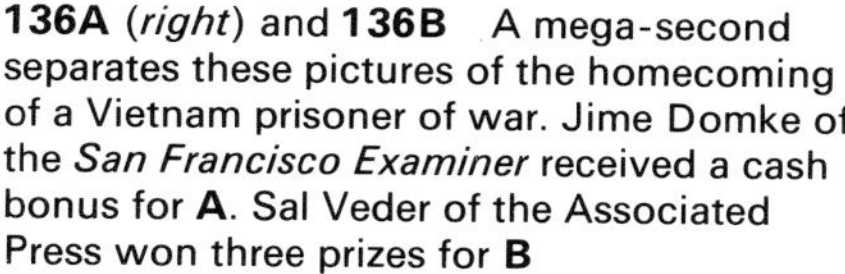

136A (*right*) and **136B** A mega-second separates these pictures of the homecoming of a Vietnam prisoner of war. Jime Domke of the *San Francisco Examiner* received a cash bonus for **A**. Sal Veder of the Associated Press won three prizes for **B**

A

B

A

B

C

137A and **137B** Three beauty queens posed for the traditional moment—then a bee flew at Miss Easington (*left*). Colin Theakstone of *The Northern Echo* was quick enough to capture both the dismay of the girl—and the flight of the bee. It transformed the value of the assignment. The full frame is at **135C**. In publication, the third unnoticing girl—slower than the photographer and distracting—was cropped off. **B** could be used alone or in sequence with **A**

When the props begin to move

Even in photography the ability to preserve and reproduce really thin slices of time is relatively new. In earlier photography, before fast film and split-second lenses, people were more like props in a still life arrangement. So they are here in 137A which is the traditional pose of the three beauty queens, and in 138A, B and C. These are all symbolic moments, and they do not compare in interest with the accompanying visual moments when the props come to life in response to unpredictable accidents. When I asked Cartier-Bresson how he responded to chances like this, he replied: 'When you have a piece of cheese on your plate you put it in your mouth. I am offered a present. I seize it.' It sounds easy and every young photographer knows he does not need practice because he is the fastest gun in the West. In fact, he is often beaten to the draw by an old timer's training and instincts, and he can do with all the practice he can manage. In a recent proficiency test by Britain's National Council for the Training of Journalists, 46 candidates in Sheffield and London were told to photograph an athlete who would appear without warning during a 20-minute period. In the London centre it was then arranged that when he was about five yards from the group of photographers he would raise his arms in the air before running up the steps of the building. The examiners wanted a full-length picture of the runner with arms raised, taken with a 28mm lens. Only about a quarter of the candidates managed this. (Generally candidates also do badly on a studio test with lights, and quite well on features though they often fail to print the best negatives or crop sensibly.)

The next two pages are a different study in the significance of minutiae—the two photographs are taken at exactly the same instant but from a slightly different position. The reader may like to award marks before turning to a discussion on page 141.

A

E

B

D

C

138A–E President Nixon and Mr. Brezhnev toast friendship between the Soviet Union and the United States, on Mr. Nixon's second visit to Moscow. The three **ABC** are symbolic moments, play-acting without much life. But suddenly there is a real visual joke as Mr. Brezhnev spills his champagne **D** and hides his face behind his napkin in mock embarrassment **E**. A visual moment—though the flash reduces tonal interest

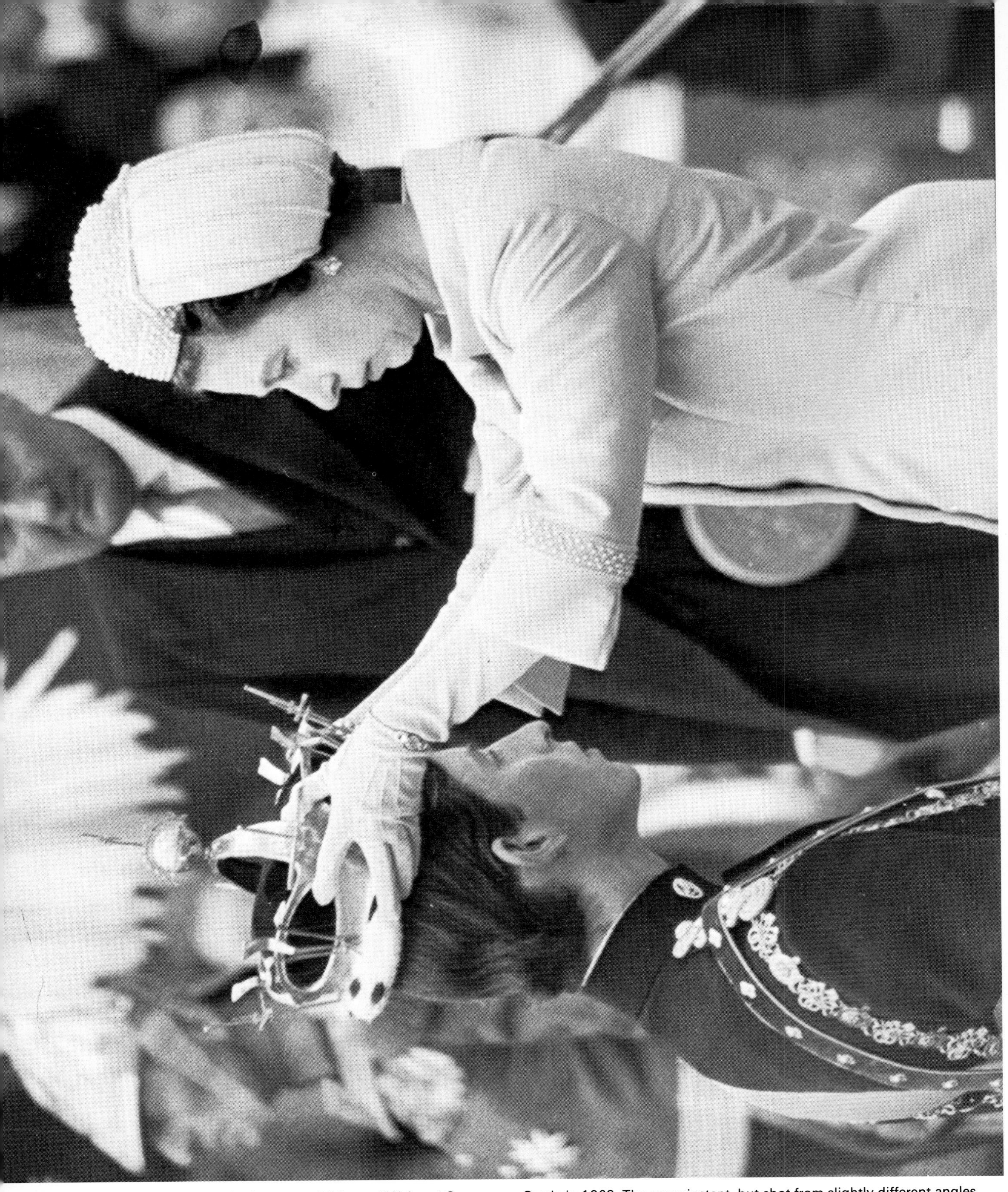

139A–140A Prince Charles is crowned Prince of Wales at Caernarvon Castle in 1969. The same instant, but shot from slightly different angles

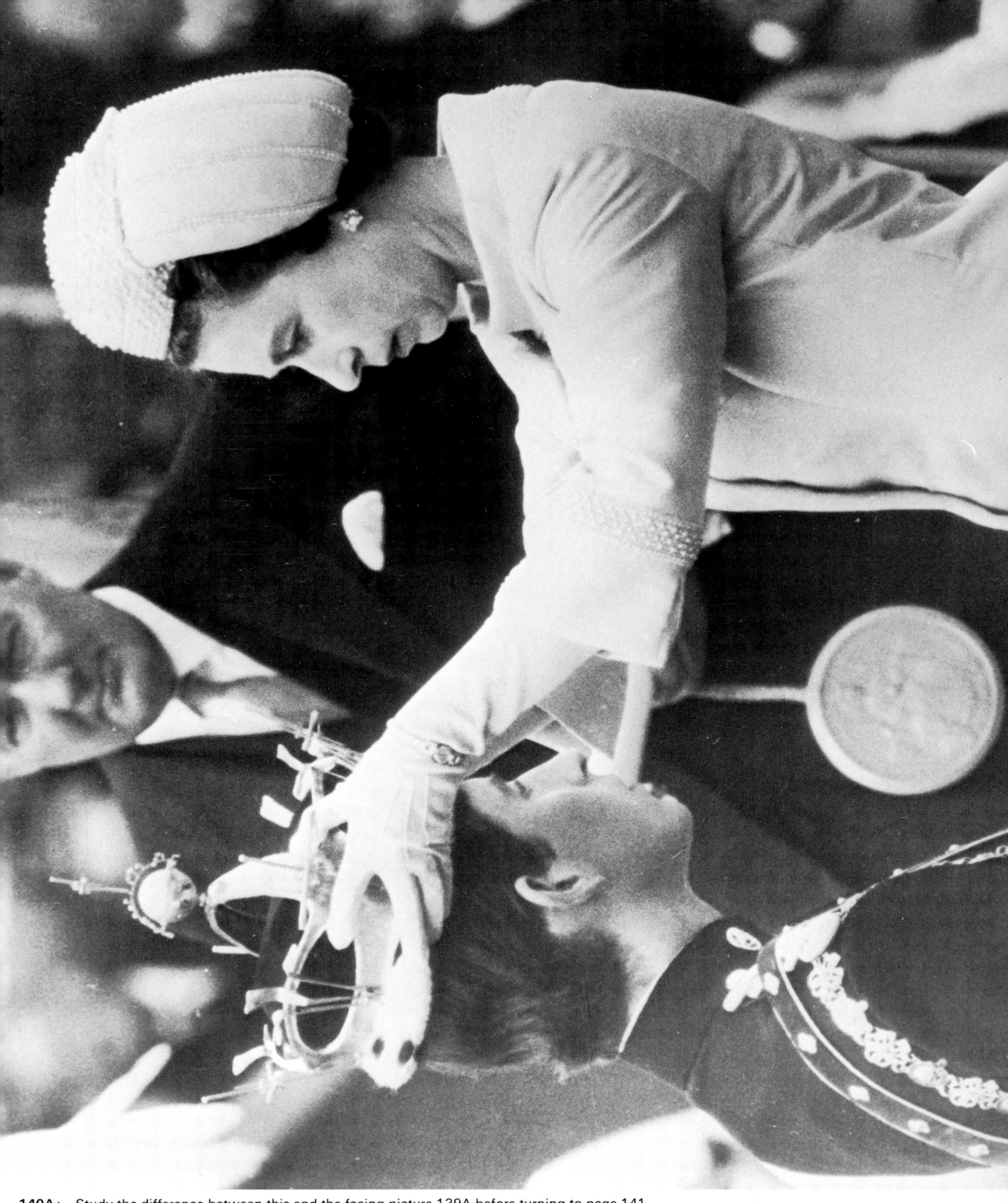

140A: Study the difference between this and the facing picture 139A before turning to page 141

The difference in a position

One of the two pictures of the crowning of the Prince of Wales at Caernarvon Castle (139–140) had considerable publication; the other comparatively little. There are subtle differences in their composition because one photographer, shooting at the same moment, was in a slightly different position. When I asked Cartier-Bresson to judge between the two pictures, he at once turned them upside down: 'That way you can see form better. You are not distracted by the subject.' He ran his finger over the outlines and tones. Unerringly, he chose the more successful of the two pictures. It is 139A–141A below. There is an enlargement in image size in 140A–141B below which temps an initial favourable inclination, but it tells the visual story so much less clearly. There is, first, the medallion blazing away at full circle into the centre of the picture. There is, secondly, the extraneous white blob of the pocket handkerchief of the man behind (Mr. James Callaghan). There is, thirdly, the way the sleeve of the Queen more irritatingly interrupts the profile of the Prince.

All these points were spotted by Cartier-Bresson when the print was upside down; doing that is a valuable tip for forcing attention on visual moments. Reversing the prints of the Vietnamese homecoming (page 136) was similarly revealing.

Small positional changes such as this do not produce significant differences every day. There were two photographers similarly side by side to record the anguish in the Belgian Congo (142A), but it is timing, not angle, which makes 142B more cauterising as a husband's exclamation of grief for his murdered wife. Yet timing has probably had a shade too much emphasis in photojournalism. It has encouraged saturation shooting: bang, bang, bang. Cartier-Bresson, frugal with film, remarks: 'You press the button, you wind the film and maybe the picture was in between.' When a newsman, or an amateur, first arrives on a scene he should certainly get something on to film, but then be invisible and reflective, weighing up the elements, anticipating, and trying different perspectives. The feature photographer's approach is instructive. He looks for 'interesting locations' and timing is secondary. The Belgian Harry Gruyaert explained one picture: 'I saw the strong shapes and planes of this street and waited and waited for someone to walk in'. In India he returned frequently to the same spot at the foot of some steps, always hoping 'something would happen.'

It is a refreshment for a newsman to have assignments where there is room for reflection, for exploiting the permutation of possibilities provided by discrete changes of time and space. This is the endless fascination of photojournalism. The double difference is demonstrated at the bottom of page 142 and again over the page. Badly burned children ran screaming down a road in Vietnam, and the shock of it is tangible reality in Nguyen Kong (Nick) Ut's picture (142D). In timing he caught a visual moment, but he also exploited perspective. He bent his knees so that the viewer can participate on the children's level of fear.

141A and **141B** Crowning the Prince of Wales, spot the difference. These photographs correspond with **139A** and **140A**

142A and **142B** A comparison of timings in the Belgian Congo. 'Why, why, why?' he asks. He is a cement worker driving down a road in Jadotsville in 1963. Congo and Indian troops of the United Nations have just opened fire, killing his wife

D

142C and **142D** A comparison of timings in Vietnam. The shock of napalm burns is direct in **D**, at child's eye level, but muffled in **C**

C

The story of a streaker

A 25-year-old accountant ran naked on to the rugby field in a spontaneous demonstration of something or other when England played France at Twickenham on Saturday, April 20, 1974. Because of the adeptness of two photographers he provided a classic example of the transitory qualities of pattern and moment which transform a picture.

Two photographers were covering the match from one end with long lenses, Ian Bradshaw of the *Sunday Mirror* and Ed Lacey, a sports free-lance. When the streaker ran on the pitch, television was taking a half-time break and the photographers had a duopoly. Bradshaw was in luck. He had been covering the match on a 500mm lens but had gone on to the pitch with a 200mm to photograph a French fan trying to climb a goalpost. It was ideal, giving a better perspective than Lacey's 400mm. Looking at a group of Bradshaw's shots on page 143 (Lacey too had a good sequence) one is struck by the awkwardness of life. There is, building up in the sequence, the single incandescent comedy of (144A): the policeman positions his helmet, he has the satisfied glow of the angler landing a catch, the streaker gazes on him with beatific innocence, his white arms framed on the bobby's serge, and an

Sunday Mirror

Well, it WAS a royal occasion

CLUE TO A SPY'S MURDER

Cigarette holder lead to killers

A POLICEMAN does his duty. It is not, perhaps, the most dignified use of a helmet. But there was simply no time to think of that at Twickenham yesterday. Princess Alexandra was in the royal box and the rest of the crowd of 53,000 were making a right royal uproar. "A darn good try," shouted one fan, no doubt a humorous reference to the rugby

A WOMAN'S cigarette

143–144 Eight contacts from Ian Bradshaw's series on the streaker at Twickenham, beginning top left. The police have their man, and official with coat approaches. The centre picture is the key one: enlarged page 144. The moment passes, but the *Sunday Mirror* seizes its chances with the best picture on the front page (*right*) official, one Mr. Grundy, scurries in with raincoat, the very matador of modesty. Bradshaw's 500mm would have been too narrow in its angle of view to include this crucial figure.

It only comes together momentarily and is gone again sooner than it takes to raise an eyebrow, yet it is transfixed for us by skill and accidents of time and space. 'There is a moment when the luck element ends,' says Bradshaw, 'and the photographer's ability takes over. I am the first to admit that I did not see the official running up with the raincoat . . . My concern was recording the incident and recording it decently as the policeman's helmet was not always completely covering the private parts. However when all has been said about the luck element it comes down to the same situation as any news event. If it happens in front of you and you are a professional photographer you should not miss it. It is what, after all, you are paid for'.

The Editor of the *Sunday Mirror*, Bob Edwards, had no hesitation in giving front-page prominence to Bradshaw's picture; it was immediately reproduced in 35 countries; and, while the French election was in full swing, *Paris Match* presented this view of the British at play in a centre spread open on the bookstands. (France, by the way, won 26–7).

Case History 1/400th of a second on Mount Suribachi, Iwo Jima

The Americans raised the flag twice on Mount Suribachi on the morning of February 23, 1945. It was the fifth day of the invasion of the tiny island of Iwo Jima, five miles long and two miles wide, a crucial staging post in the battle of the Pacific. In 31 days 6,821 Americans died there, including three of the six men photographed raising the flag the second time (148A). This photograph taken by Joe Rosenthal of the Associated Press will live for ever. On this spread there are the other photographs Rosenthal took (145B and 146B) and the picture of the first time the flag was raised (146A), and they serve only to emphasise the uniqueness of Rosenthal's 400th of a second at 12.15 pm on Suribachi. Rosenthal's epic picture has been described as a phoney. It has been said it was posed. Those are lies, based on a misunderstanding and the usual envy of merit. No genius could have posed the picture if he had spent a year in a studio with lights and a wind machine. Rosenthal puts it more modestly: 'Had I posed the shot, I would, of course, have ruined it. I'd have picked fewer men, for the six are

145A Joe Rosenthal: 'It's been a long time. Now I'm shooting auto accidents and football.'

145B Rosenthal's third shot of the flag on Suribachi: 'I got them together to wave and cheer under the flag'

so crowded in the picture that of Sergeant Michael Strank of Gonemaugh, Pennsylvania—who was subsequently killed—only the hands are visible. I would also have made them turn their heads so that they could be identified for AP members throughout the country'. Rosenthal landed on Iwo Jima under gunfire at noon on February 19, three hours after the invasion had begun. In 11 days he took 65 pictures carrying a Speed Graphic and a Rolleiflex, and equipment weighing 25 lbs. Each day he would work his way back to the beach from photographing fighting so that his film could be flown off: one day the trip took 19 hours.

On D-day plus four, at 9.40 am, two patrols fought to the top of Suribachi, an entrenched Japanese observation post, with a 40-man detachment from the 28th Regiment, 5th Division Marine, which had a flag from an attack transport, USS *Missoula*. Rosenthal started climbing with Bill Hipple (*Newsweek*) and two Marine combat photographers, Private Bob Campbell and Sergeant Bill Geneaust. They skirted the minefields and took cover as Marines from time to time threw grenades. About halfway up they met four Marines coming down. Staff Sergeant Louis Lowery (*Leatherneck Magazine*) said the men from the 28th Regiment had raised a flag at the summit and he had photographed it (146A). Rosenthal's group decided to push on, and around noon reached the top. The *Missoula* flag was small, only 54 inches by 28 inches—and it was coming down. The Marines had now brought up a large flag (8ft by 4ft 8 ins) so that it would be visible northward on the island and by ships offshore. Rosenthal says: 'I thought of taking a shot of the two flags, one coming down and the other going up, but although this turned out to be a picture Bob Campbell got I couldn't line it up. Then I decided to get just the one flag going up and I backed off about 35ft. Here the ground sloped down towards the centre of the volcanic crater and I found scrub was in my way. I shoved some stones and

146B Second flag, Rosenthal's second shot

146A Staff Sergeant Lowery's picture of the raising of the first small flag

YANKS SWEEP 5 MILES ACROSS COLOGNE PLAIN

Los Angeles Times

SUNDAY EDITION

FINAL EDITION

SUNDAY MORNING, FEBRUARY 25, 1945

1600 NAVY PLANES ATTACK TOKYO

Yanks Drive Across Plain for Cologne

Massed Guns Smash Villages and Planes Paralyze Rail Lines

All Manila Japs Killed

Fight Ends; Civilians Liberated

TOKYO VOWS DEATH FOR ADM. TURNER

Invasion Fleet Head Must Not Return Home Alive for Killing Our Men on Iwo, Japs Say

Japs Admit Air Armada Rakes City

'Times' Man Tells New Raid to Free Captives

Night Spots Set

Marines Capture Half

147A Front page, but small. How Rosenthal's first shot began its publication life as the most reproduced photograph of all time

147B The full frame of Rosenthal's first shot. **148A** A vertical crop of the same picture

Japanese sandbags on top to try to raise myself about two feet (Rosenthal is only 5ft 5ins). I decided on a lens setting between f8 and f11 and set the speed at 1/400.'

Just as the men, five Marines and a naval medicine corpsman, were preparing to raise the flag a Lieutenant walked between them and Rosenthal. Then Geneaust crossed in front of him with his movie camera and took a position about three feet to his right. 'Geneaust called: "I'm not in your way, am I, Joe?" "No," I shouted "and there it goes." Out of the corner of my eye as I had turned toward Geneaust I had seen the men start the flag up. I swung my camera and shot the scene.'

Rosenthal was not sure he had a picture. 'When you take a picture like that you don't come away saying you got a great shot. You don't know, and within the next few minutes I made another shot of the men putting guy ropes on the pipe (146B) and still another of a group that I got together to cheer under the flag' (145B).

It was this which was to cause confusion later. Rosenthal's film went off and it was nine days later before he got back to Guam press headquarters. 'Congratulations on the flag raising on Iwo', said a correspondent. 'Did you pose it?' Rosenthal replied: 'Sure', thinking of the third, posed, picture which he knew he had secured safely. (He had not even identified the men in the first picture.) It was only later that day that he saw his masterpiece for the first time. 'Gee', I said, 'that's good all right, but I didn't pose that one. I wish I could take credit for posing it, but I can't.'

To this day, Rosenthal—back on the beat for the *San Francisco Chronicle*—calls it luck. It was, he says, lucky that with the sky overcast just enough sunlight fell from almost directly overhead to give the figures a sculptural depth; lucky that the 20ft flag pipe (wreckage from a Japanese radar station) was heavy, which meant the men had to strain to get it up; lucky that an offshore breeze whipped the flag out over the heads of the group; lucky that their feet on the disrupted terrain exemplified the turbulence of war.

These are certainly factors that help to suffuse this still picture with the symbolism of heroic endeavour. Geneaust, who died nine days later on Hill 362, made a fine colour film sequence, but it is the still which is etched in America's memory (see Chapter 1).

Its qualities can be analysed up to a point. There is the energy of the diagonal. Then the acute angle formed by the pole and the outstretched hands leads the eye directly to the flag. Then there is the drama of the unresolved action (compare 136B): the eye goes from the stripes to the space where the flag will (might?) unfurl in the breeze.

'Few artists', said the *Rochester-Times Union* in February 1945, 'would be bold enough to make empty space the centre of their picture. And yet this bit of art from life has done just that. In that space is a vision of what is to be.'

Joe Rosenthal says: 'What does it matter who took the picture? I took it, but the Marines took Iwo Jima.'

Chapter 8

People

Cut off my head and I am 13.
Coco Chanel at 60

Eyes, hands and general body posture usually talk louder than words. But many published portraits seem to have passed through a sterilising chamber. Above is President Sadat of Egypt. He looks at us. We look at him. Nothing passes between us. He might be the secretary of the local golf club or the man who robbed the bank at Monte Carlo. It is the same man in the facing portrait (150A) but this time we learn something about him. Here is a man of some guile and sublety. The hands want to communicate, to convince, to massage. It is not all there is to know about Sadat, but it is one aspect of a man's character, one description of his attitude at one time, and it is valuable for that. Perhaps it is possible for a portrait to do more and sum up a man's 'real' character. Good portraits, we have been told, are visual biographies. But if a gifted photographer can attempt a definitive statement there are limits to how far he should try. News cannot forsake the fugitive moment of facial expression, even if 'out of character', in preference for some synthesis forming in the mind of the photographer. And the pursuit of character and expression, which it is partly the purpose of this chapter to encourage, will be a false trail if it leads to expressive distortion. Art may flourish but photojournalism is not well served when the photograph becomes more important than the subject.

Editors must run from blandness but it is better to have a recognisable record of physiognomy than weak imitations of Richard Avedon.

150A Anwar Sadat pleads his cause. Eddie Adams won third portrait prize with it in the World Press Photo contest in 1975

Sending for the file on Carter

Amateur portraiture is a menagerie of aberration—men with indoor plants sprouting from their ears, noses like 'Schnozzle' Durante, bald heads glistening, and eyes popping; and the photographer himself immortalised in the reflections of the subject's spectacles. These, by and large, are not the failings of the professional supply of portraits—head-shots or mug-shots as the trade says. It is the absence of expression of environment. Features are flattened into pancake mixtures by direct flash or drained in wire transmission. For any well-known person there is sure to be a better choice, but frequently an editorial department asks for a head-shot without examining the range available in the library or on contact prints. *Time* and *Newsweek* set the standards which every publication should observe. Portraits enliven their pages out of all proportion to the space they take; they are chosen with fastidious care for relevance and force, and they draw us into the text. The beginning of making people matter is for editors to reject the glazed-eye portrait monotonously lit from the front by flash so that photographers are encouraged to try harder with available light and bounce flash (and, one might add, the neglected Hill-Adamson device of using a mirror to reflect light on the sitter). The longer lens is essential equipment and the wide angle might be banned. 'No sensible sitter', says Philip Jones-Griffiths, 'should allow himself to be photographed with a distorting wide angle'.

As an example of what may be lost when the choice of head-shot is left to chance, here are some of the photographs produced from the library when I asked for pictures of Jimmy Carter during his successful campaign. Even in this small example—sized for the grid rather than as they might be for publication—there is a rich range of editorial content and reproductive quality. Faces are too important to be published at random.

151A Yes. Well lit, good tonal range. Ideal for a campaign story on the 'unstoppable' Carter

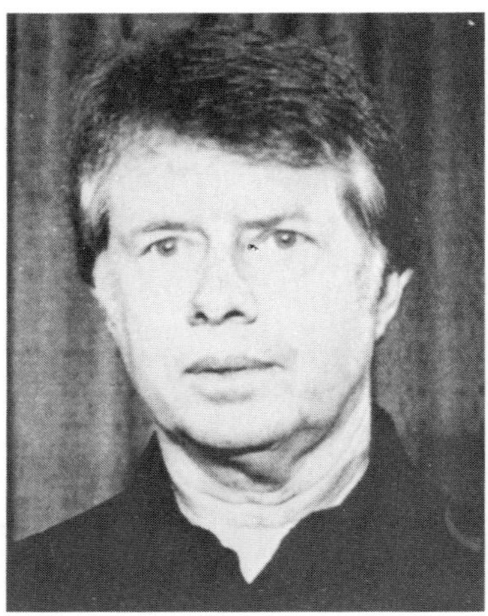

151B Hopeless. All marks of flash—face flattened, eyes a-pop—and tone lost in wire transmission

151C Unlikely. Suitable only with story on diet or campaign eating habits. **151D** Possible since caught in potentially useful pensive mood, but low quality

151F No. Carter with St. Patrick's Day flower but photographed from below and barely recognisable

151E Unlikely. Might illustrate role-playing of candidate at American Legion, but quality too low for general use

152A Yes. Excellent tonal range, relaxed but expressive. Would make a deep single or a double column

152B No—unless seeking hostile shot. Flowered wallpaper background is unhelpful and will have to be faded out in process

152C Yes. Newsy portrait of man seeking Irish vote with St. Patrick's Day flower and badges (one says 'Get Britain out')

152E Yes. Fine concentrated portrait, well lit, superb tonal range, eyes full of interest. Would make a three or four column if desired

152D Hopeless, with or without baby. Caricature of the man produced by wide angle lens used from below

153A Kelvin Brodie changed lenses and positions to produce a varied 'take' of Henry Fonda: this is a small selection from the contacts

Assignment: Henry Fonda and Moshe Dayan

The photographer who can offer a large head-shot which is an honest likeness and has character makes a vivid contribution to modern reporting. It is not easy and the skill should be recognised and encouraged. It is simpler to do while a writer conducts an interview, though this imposes restraints. Tripods and elaborate lighting are out; disturbing the interview by moving the subject or using a flash is imprudent. The longer lens enables a photographer to take a close-up or keep his distance: some people conscious of a camera pointed at their left nostril tend to get a bit twitchy. But that idea cannot be pushed too far—room size sets a limit, and anything over 200mm is hard to hold steady especially when moving around (a 500mm weights nearly a kilo). Kelvin Brodie of *The Sunday Times* swears by a medium telephoto lens at short range. He is a newsman with a kaleidoscopic picture experience but with a happy habit of bringing back powerful close-ups, especially half-profiles that stand out in bas relief and are ideal for newsprint reproduction. 'With a 105mm at three feet', he says, 'you can produce incisive portraits. The focusing characteristics make the subject stand out from background clutter'. Brodie always takes a mixture of telephoto close-ups and standard lens shots, and they are a treasure for the library. Some of the selection from one hour with Henry Fonda, talking to writer Philip Oakes, are shown above (the art editor chose the third from the left, bottom row, reminiscent of Fonda, man of conscience, in *Twelve Angry Men*). Brodie says that when he does not know the subject he finds it useful to arrive ten minutes after the appointed time when the writer has the subject talking. 'Then while I prepare my camera I observe his characteristics—does he smoke, does he tend to cup his hands on his chin, does he play with his glasses? Is there a recognisable mannerism that will make the picture work?'.

A very different assignment was the press conference in Tel Aviv near the end of the Six-Day war in 1967 when Moshe Dayan, Israel's hero of the

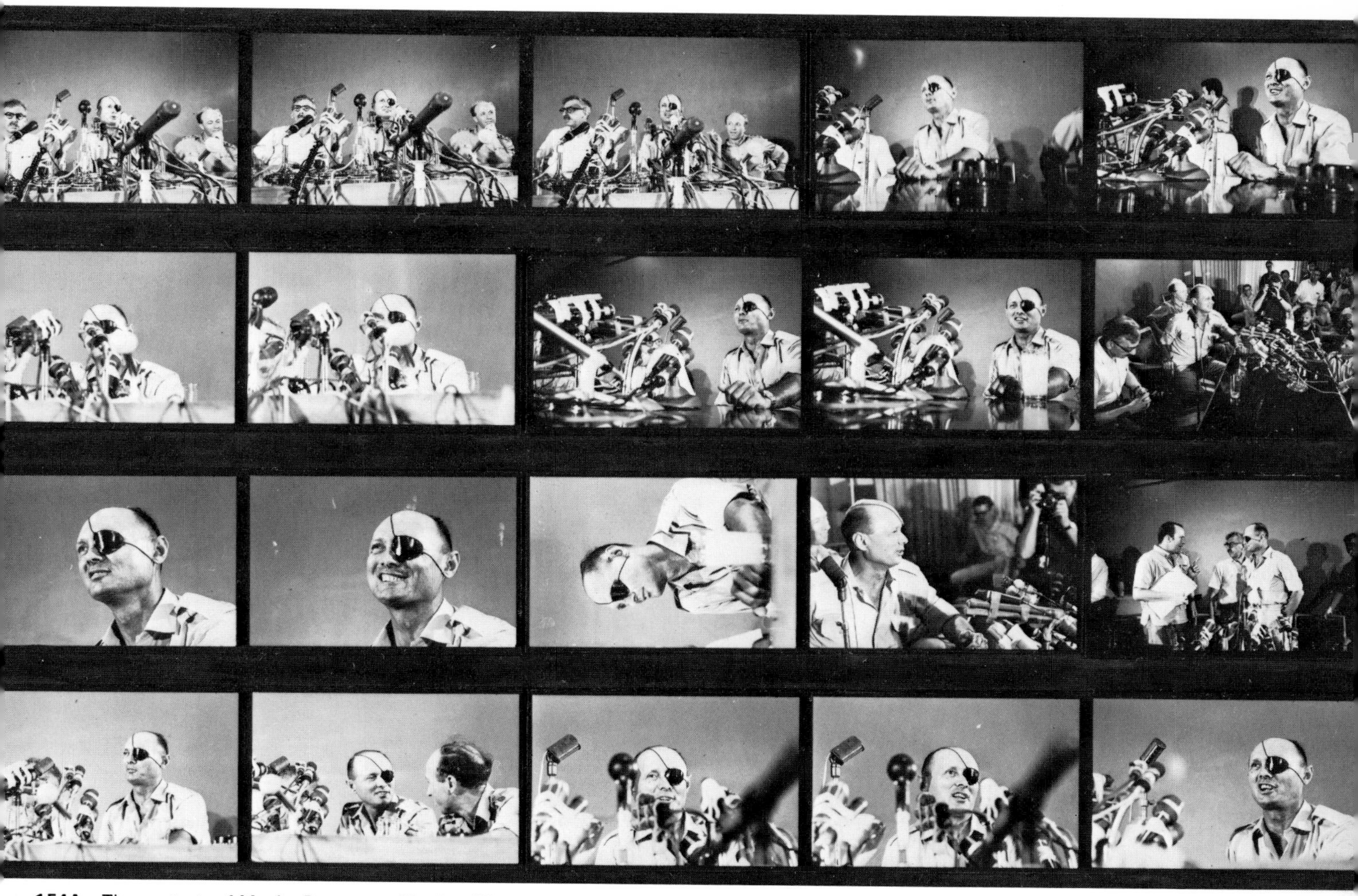

154A The contacts of Moshe Dayan at a Six-Day War press conference suggests the difficulties for the stillmen

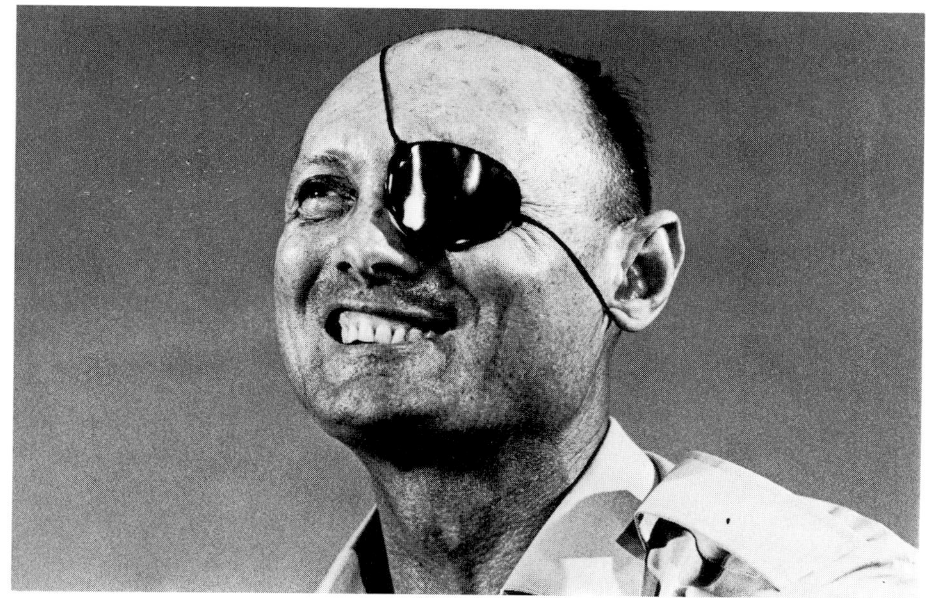

154B A portrait of Moshe Dayan from the contacts above—(Nikon 125th at 5.6)

hour, first showed his face. The room was lit for television and cine-film and Brodie was squashed shoulder to shoulder with other still photographers. A few contacts reflect the difficulties and the success (154B).

Naturally a close-up is restricted in character portrayal by comparison with a portrait which includes the life-style background or the hands which Karsh always tried to include. But the close-up is economical and it is newsy. Or as John Szarkowski has put it: 'As the newspapers prove again each day, there is something fascinating and subtly disturbing about a photograph of a person open-mouthed in speech. The effect can be comic or ludicrous or tragic but the root cause is the same. Life has been arrested'.

A

B

How it felt to both

Edna O'Brien: 'It may have been uneasy because I knew the Godwins socially. Also I am used to being photographed by a man, a stranger, and it's easier for someone like that to tell me what to do'.

Fay Godwin: 'Edna had not been able to stop weeping all morning. This was disconcerting as I felt it might have something to do with my photographing her. I felt we did not connect because she did not want to connect though we had been friendly earlier. Later, developing the film, I heard over the radio about the Turkish airline disaster and wondered whether her grief was a kind of ESP. I have had this feeling about Edna'.

A

B

D

C

Assignment: Edna O'Brien

The solo assignment without a writer is more fragile, though the photographer has more freedom. Almost everybody relaxes more in their familiar environment, home or office. The American photographer Mrs. Rollie McKenna has observed that distractions such as a demanding telephone or a wailing infant help to thaw formality, turning a diffident subject into 'a concerned host putting a guest at ease'. But the atmosphere in a solo session is a subtle affair; and photographers have different ideas about coping. Cartier-Bresson says he can only take pictures of people he knows well and mood is crucial. With Ezra Pound they sat 90 minutes in happy silence and he took ten photographs. At lunch with Coco Chanel, he mentioned somebody who had displeased her and 'it was finished. Everything was spoiled.' Bill Brandt says he hardly talks to the subject or looks at him (page 168). Fay Godwin, the photographer of Edna O'Brien here, 'talks non-stop. I don't want a picture of someone speaking but it helps me find out what kind of person they are.'

Edna O'Brien achieved fame through her novels recalling and cherishing the pains and joys of girlhood in rural Ireland; loneliness is a persistent theme. She was at her home in London for the session, but she is also a sensitive person. 'I'm a tuning fork. Tense and twanging all the time', she once said, and her unease is apparent in 155B and especially outside in the square (156C, D) where the light was hard and glittering. The two at 156A and B are less strained. A, in fact, is quite appealing, but it tells us nothing of Edna O'Brien.

Yet out of a disastrous morning the photographer, Fay Godwin, did secure one successful portrait (155A) which says something about Edna O'Brien's prideful loneliness, and her triumphant (if not happy) emergence from a more primitive background.

A

B

Assignment: A girl in clothes

Barbara Bach, who graces these pages in knitted string tabard and patterned leg-warmers, was photographed in some moments when she wasn't in bed with James Bond (*The Spy Who Loved Me*). As a film star and former model, she was invited to model the clothes by Meriel McCooey, Fashion Editor of *The Sunday Times* colour magazine, and she is here as a simple example of the alluring and absurd, tantalising and highly technical world of people in fashion. We can only peep at it and for a fuller discussion I commend the survey of the top photographers in *The Magic Image* by Cecil Beaton and Gail Buckland (*see bibliography*). Fashion is different from news, which is spontaneous and immediate, because it is mostly a packaged deal. The editor chooses the clothes for a planned feature—garments thought to be news or supplying a seasonal service (it lacks appeal to do swimsuits in January). Once the clothes have been organised, the photographer must be decided on, and that is a whole art in itself, matching their skills and temperaments to the subject: some prefer to work out-of-doors, some are lost if they cannot work in the studios, some can get sex appeal into 15 different dresses a day, and some can manage only one a week. (Eve Sereny, chosen for this assignment, prefers daylight, believing that models respond better.) Then there is the choice of girl. Meriel McCooey comments:

‘ Casting the girl to the garments is of supreme importance: it is absurd to put a sophisticate in ingenues' clothes. In picking the girl it is also important to remember that a newspaper has a mixed readership; obvious, but often forgotten. A mixed readership pays as much attention to the model's face as it does to her clothes. Readers of fashion magazines look at the clothes and don't care if the garments are worn by the Witches of Endor. If a session threatens to be difficult, this sometimes necessitates employing a make-up "artist" (their word—not mine), and a hairdresser. But generally these people are so con-

C

D

cerned with the drama of their own efforts, rather than the overall effect, that usually they prove more trouble than they are worth. All this is placed before the photographer—who then adds his own imagination to improve on the idea (hopefully).

When I first started in fashion, every crease and line would be airbrushed out of the finished product, not just from the clothes, but from the model's face as well, thus giving readers a picture of complete unreality. But art directors such as Peter Knapp of *Elle* broke away from this technique by getting girls photographed in natural situations. Previously, editors chose ludicrous venues where models were drooped over balustrades, walked down curving staircases or, outrageously, Paris fashions costing thousands were photographed against slum backgrounds. Knapp had his photographers set up women in kitchens, in offices, in bathrooms and bedrooms—in real life, in fact.

He advised me once: "Always try to choose a model, that a woman, *any woman*, of a similar type, thinks she could look like, if she had the time and money. And no matter how good a garment is, don't use it if it won't photograph". ❜

There is a varying relationship between the editor, photographer and model. A professional model will know what to do without a great deal of direction, and the editor may have to intervene only occasionally as a control. But here are four photographs from the Sereny–McCooey 'take' and the reader is now invited to make his own choice for publication of a single fashion glamour shot. A clear majority of a small panel of four professionals and a teenager all chose the same print. Check your choice in the paragraph below.

Meriel McCooey, Michael Rand (Magazine Art Director), Edwin Taylor (Newspaper Design Director) and Ruth Evans, selected (158D). But *Vogue*'s fashion girl, Liz Tilberris, preferred (158C), judging the eye-to-eye appeal more fetching. All agreed in the other rejections.

The search for character

There is immediate appeal about the old man in his study (160A). We can borrow the words of one of the early reviewers of the Hill-Adamson portraits: 'The observer cannot help feeling that he is in the presence of the living, acting original'. Nobody feels in the presence of anything much in the comparisons of 159A and 159B. But also 160A works at a second level. The old man is Albert Einstein at Princeton University in 1952. The sense that we are intruding is now compelling: we are looking, with noses squeezed to the window, at a genius in the act of thought . . .

It is, as it happens, a visual rather than a decisive moment, not quite the instant when Einstein realised his theory of relativity. But it is worth celebrating its intriguing nature with the following account which the photographer Ernest Haas prepared for *The Concerned Photographer 2 (see bibliography)*:

‹ Einstein was always posing and looking at my camera and I *never* could get the picture I was looking for—just a second of his being unaware. Also, on top of this, the *Vogue* editor wanted to have a picture of Einstein thinking . . . so we went to the library and we were speaking German, talking about Vienna, and Viennese writers and I said that a certain famous Viennese writer had just come out with a history of culture, a three-volume book, that was very, very fantastic. And he was standing there in front of his library, and I said: 'Do you have the book?' And he said: 'Let me think, where did I put that book' and, finally, I got a picture of Einstein thinking! ›

The picture of Einstein is suggestive of photography's ability to match portrait painting. The painter can produce a synthesis so that we can believe he has captured the 'real' character. The photographer is restricted to giving us one impression at one moment, which affects our willingness to absorb the image as a single verdict. Nevertheless, the unposed, fleeting Einstein has a sense of completeness.

If scepticism remains about the validity of any single print that is no bad thing. The search for character sometimes extends no further than trying to photograph the stereotype already in the photographer's head, a process assisted by the ability of the famous to wear a mask (Churchill would say exactly how he wanted to be taken: 'You do it from there, young man'). The photographer has two basic gambits: to learn about the subject beforehand so that he can, in the idiom of Leonard Freed, play mental chess. Or do nothing at all—a course rarely advised, but followed with some success in formal portraiture by David Montgomery: 'Reading up too much would jade my way of looking and making my own appraisal. I prefer to see them as human beings. With Clint Eastwood I told him I had seen none of his films; but it didn't spoil our relationship. I have no basic idea what I want. It begins when I look through the camera. I don't hide the fact that I'm nervous and not sure what to do.' Montgomery experiments with a Polaroid to test background and light. He prefers straight-to-camera poses: 'I like people to feel they are making some eye-contact with the person looking at them'. August Sander long ago argued that taking people deliberately posed revealed their secret self-image. But let a thousand ideas bloom: only a Citizen Kane would lay down a single prescription in the search for character.

159A and **159B** Albert Einstein with and without gesture but both equally dispiriting by comparison with **160A**

161A The glamour wears thin. Marilyn Monroe at 36, from one of the last photo sessions of her life. By Bert Sterns

Playing roles

Cartier-Bresson says he cannot take portraits of actors because they pose. They do, and it can be tedious. But there may be revelation in a pose. George Barris who took the last picture of Marilyn Monroe, a few weeks before she took an overdose of sleeping pills, had her posing for five hours on the beach and he wrote: 'With the last rays of dying sunset catching her tanned limbs and dishevelled blonde hair, she looked the most beautiful woman in the world. She picked up a glass and bottle of champagne . . . Like an excited teenager having her first sip she held the glass close to her face to let the bubbles bounce off her nose'. Barris, in rent-a-sequin prose, was making Monroe conform to his stereotype of the sex goddess. But the

162A 'One can legitimately accentuate certain things', says Snowdon, 'like a caricaturist'

camera was more perceptive at this time. There are, among 200 shots, glimpses of a different person, and the crack in the mirror really shows at 161A which was taken in a similar glamorous photo-session (by Bert Sterns) not long before the suicide.

Lord Snowdon's Chaplins are different again—a sequence where he may or may not have been playing the little fella, but it is captivating anyway with a man of 86, and a more reflective (more real?) close-up. Snowdon says: 'Photographers should not exploit their subjects. In the old days I did appalling gimmicky pictures but I've tried to become simpler. Now I wouldn't even mind taking a boring picture if it gave truthful information about a human being'.

163A and 163B Which Nixon? Inset B is dismaying, A is warming. Original caption: 'The ultimate accolade—the President gets an enthusiastic welcome from American troops in Vietnam'

163C and **163D** Patty Hearst in contrasting presentations. **C** is Sept 1975, **D** is Feb 1976

People as puppets

Most of us never meet the people in the portraits. Our reality is the caprice of photographers and picture editors. A series of distortions will build a stalagmite of prejudice. A malign photographer does not depend on the off-guard unflattering moment. Camera angle controls the relationship of facial contours to picture frame. A slight sideways tilt can slim a face; it becomes squarer and tougher if jaw and chin lines are run parallel to the frame. Photographing from below can accentuate the tense neck, the bullying chin, the arrogant head angle; doing it under the glare of strobe or bright sun will emphasise anxiety and ageing or a murderous glint in the gaze. The scope for a picture editor is demonstrated on this spread, a manipulation which is the more effective when the words deep-etch the meaning. The girl 'apprehended' on *Time*'s cover is the gun-toting SLA soldier Tania; 'Patty in Court' is Patricia Campbell Hearst, the Berkeley co-ed who was brainwashed and faces trial, innocent until proved guilty. Similarly, the inset Nixon (163B) was wisely used with unfavourable news reports. Imagine it with the ironic caption: 'I am not a crook'. Then imagine the effect of this same caption on 163A. There it would lose its irony; it would support his statement. And it is possible to write a caption to mitigate the damage of 163B: 'Gallant struggle. The President, though exhausted by illness, kept his schedule yesterday for his broadcast to the nation'.

164A and **164B** Vanessa Redgrave may be featured as the beautiful sensitive actress **A** or the embittered revolutionary **B**

164C and **164D** Indira Gandhi, peaceful persuader **C** in the tradition of her father, Nehru, or power-hungry dictator **D**

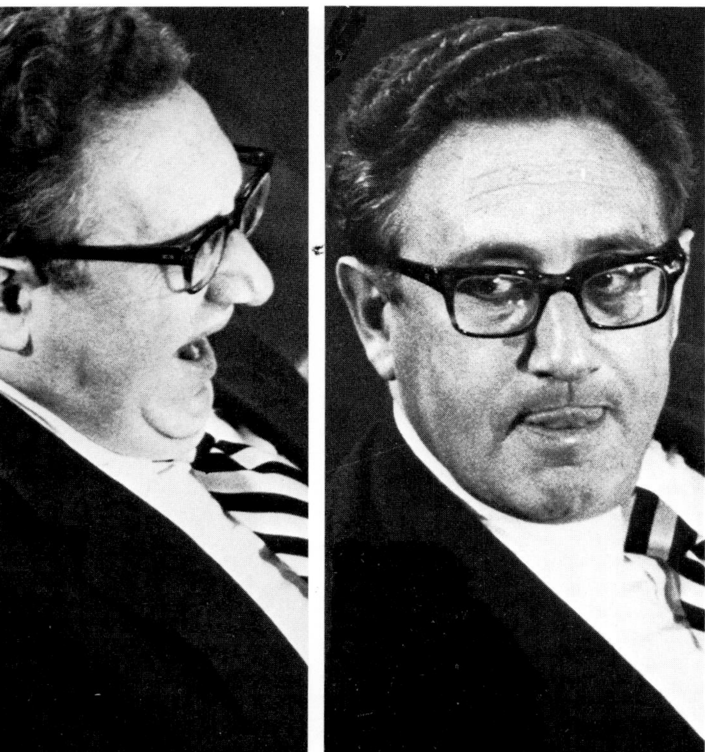

164G and **164H** Henry Kissinger too tired to care **G** or on top of the job, as Secretary of State **H**

164E and **164F** Not much could be done for President Amin but **E** (*top*) helps him and **F** re-confirms the worst

165A Democracy in Action? Harold Wilson, then Prime Minister, meets one of his constituents. The PM—framed (see Chapter 5) by the arms of a pick and shovel labourer—listens impassively to the point being made. The constituent leans forward aggressively. But his fag-end is tucked out of sight in the palm of his hand

165C On the night Sir John Barbirolli will conduct with impulsive ardour; now he doesn't like what he hears

165B Bewilderment equals science. A World Press Photo winner by Vsevolod Tarasewich of the Soviet Union

Men with props

Perhaps Robert Howlett in 1857 began it. He photographed the civil engineer I. K. Brunel not in the conventional studio (where other photographers rigged up Athenian palaces or Canadian forests) but standing plainly in front of the heavy launching chains of his *Great Eastern*, the largest steamship of the 19th century. In this portrait, now in London's National Gallery, Howlett gave us not simply a likeness but the iron symbolism of Brunel's determination to launch his leviathan. It was honest reporting as well as portraiture.

The environmental portrait has

166A Tolkien was stuffed into a smart suit for his picture. Photographer Snowdon and writer Cater persuaded him back into his usual tweeds

been developed and redeveloped since then, pushed furthest by Arnold Newman who often underplays the human form for the sake of expressive design (in his book *One Mind's Eye*, listed in the bibliography, see the portrait of Piet Mondrian which itself looks like a Mondrian abstract, also turn back to Igor Stravinsky on page 98). 'When I make a portrait, I don't take a photograph,' Newman says, 'I build it, seeking all those graphic elements that will express the most common denominator of the subject'.

Four main forms of environmental portraits may be suggested with progressive diminution of the personality of the individual. The simplest is to illuminate an individual by casting him in a context which makes him tick. There are props but he is still the central focus—for instance Sir John Barbirolli in 165C. In 165A the environmental technique is used to bring freshness to a picture of someone so familiar as to be over-exposed. Everyone knows what Prime Minister Harold Wilson looked like and few cared what the workman looked like, but the two together created a new interest. Thirdly, man plus props may be featured to summarise not so much his personality as the characteristics of a group. The blackboard equations (165B) intimidate all laymen into respect for all scientists. Finally, there is the environmental portrait to feature not so much man at work, as man's work (166A). Bill Cater was writing about J. R. R. Tolkien on his 80th birthday. The photographer was Snowdon and Cater answered his preassignment questions with a copy of *The Hobbit* and the information that Tolkien was a great tree lover and had used the tree image in his writings as a symbol of Life. Tolkien's garden backed onto a wooded chine near the sea. 'When we went out in to the chine,' says Cater, 'Snowdon spotted those gnarled tree roots and that was that'.

167A Francis Bacon on Primrose Hill, London, 1963. Brandt uses a Hasselblad. He prints and crops all his own pictures

Atmosphere before vivacity

Bill Brandt, the celebrated London photographer (born 1904), shares a conviction with his close Paris-based contemporary Brassai. 'In my portraits', he told me, 'I try to avoid the fleeting expression and vivacity of a snapshot'. And Brassai emphasised to George Hughes (*Amateur Photographer*, June 18, 1969): 'There are many photographs which are full of life but which are confusing and difficult to remember. It is the force of an image which matters'. Brandt's portraits are very quiet but memorable and it is the environment which makes them. The actual photography takes him little time. 'I am exaggerating but I never compose before I press the shutter'. He hardly talks to the subject or looks at him. 'It often seems,' he says, 'to make people forget what is going on and the self-conscious look fades'. Brandt spends the time looking for background to make the portrait revealing. For his picture of the disturbing painter, Francis Bacon, he had an idea before he went that he would wait until twilight when gaslight would be on and the distant trees would give the mysterious effect he wanted to associate with Bacon (167A).

'The vital elements are often momentary, chance-sent things ... a gleam of light on water, a trail of smoke from a passing train, a cat crossing a threshold. Sometimes they are a matter of luck, sometimes of patience, waiting for an effect to be repeated that you have seen. It is usually some incidental detail that heightens the effect of a picture, stressing a pattern, deepening the sense of atmosphere.'

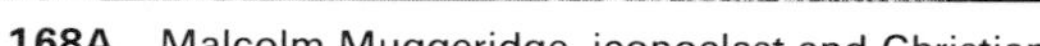

168A Malcolm Muggeridge, iconoclast and Christian

168B Dylan Thomas, London, 1941

168C Pablo Picasso at home

169A A few months from Dallas: determination over Cuba

Private images

The large photograph (170A) is just a man walking in the sand dunes. Only when we know it is John Kennedy, shot dead as President of the United States, at the age of 46, is our interest aroused. We do not need to see more. Memory fills the landscape with mental pictures and emotions: the idea of hope and the aspirations of the New Frontier; the poise and style that enchanted millions; the bravery of the Cuba missile crisis; the defiance in Berlin of the Russian threat to the city: *Ich Bin Ein Berliner!* When Kennedy died most of the single pictures of the President in action, or portraits such as 169A, seemed to give disproportionate stress to one aspect of the man or his career. But the youthful figure walking away from us through the sand dunes enables everyone to turn in on his own thoughts, and sometimes that is the best service photography can render.

170A More than an environmental portrait. There is powerful evocation in the sense of freshness, sand, grass, open sky and a man alone

Chapter 9

Sense in Sequence

The camera should be like the notebook of a trained reporter, to record events as they happen, without trying to stop them to make a picture. Stefan Lorant

171A In minutes this happy crowd in front of the Royal palace in Amsterdam will be broken up by fear and death

The war was over, it seemed. On May 7, 1945, the unconditional surrender of Nazi Germany was signed at Reims, in Eisenhower's headquarters, and announced by the allies. In Amsterdam, the Dutch started celebrating in the historic Dam Square, in front of the Royal palace. Suddenly German *francs-tireurs* soldiers holed up in a building next to the palace began firing on the packed crowd, men, women and children. There was pandemonium. People ran for their lives, fell shot to the ground, helped friends, lay down to escape the bullets, huddled together behind a barrel organ. Forty celebrators in the square died.

No single photograph could tell that story of the shooting. It lay in the disintegration of the crowd. But two pictures can suggest that, and 171A–172A do it. A still sequence may have frames recording such barely perceptible changes that it suggests movement in the cinematographic manner, and there are examples in this chapter. There is nothing of that here. It is a visual fragment, but it is meaningful. The value of a sequence for publication may be less in making movement and more in making sense.

172A Shortly after **171A**: A slightly different angle but a transformed scene. The sequence is from two photographers

Two kinds of sequence

The action sequence suggests movement by recording change in a nearly-similar scene. The narrative sequence concentrates on story to the neglect of movement. The camera records the scene not from the same angle, as the action sequence does, but from whatever angle the story suggests, even though this interrupts physical continuity (see pp. 179–180).

Here are two action sequences—the collapse of a stand at Indianapolis, and a tea party in Thailand where Queen Elizabeth was distracted from watching elephants. All tea party shots are needed at full frame, even though they repeat static elements: the immobility of the other elephant watchers is part of the comedy. (When layout allows it, an action sequence is quicker if laid out vertically so that the eye can jump directly from the focal point of one frame to the focal point directly below).

The collapsing stand (173–174) is a classic action sequence. Amateur photographer J. Parke Randall had been hired for the day by the *Indianapolis News* to help cover the Indianapolis 500-mile race. As he photographed the cars rounding the third bend, Randall heard screams behind him and saw a 30ft. aluminium spectator tower toppling into the crowd. (Two men were killed in the collapse and 50 hurt).

Any single picture would be a winner but the sequence invites constant re-examination of the inevitable.

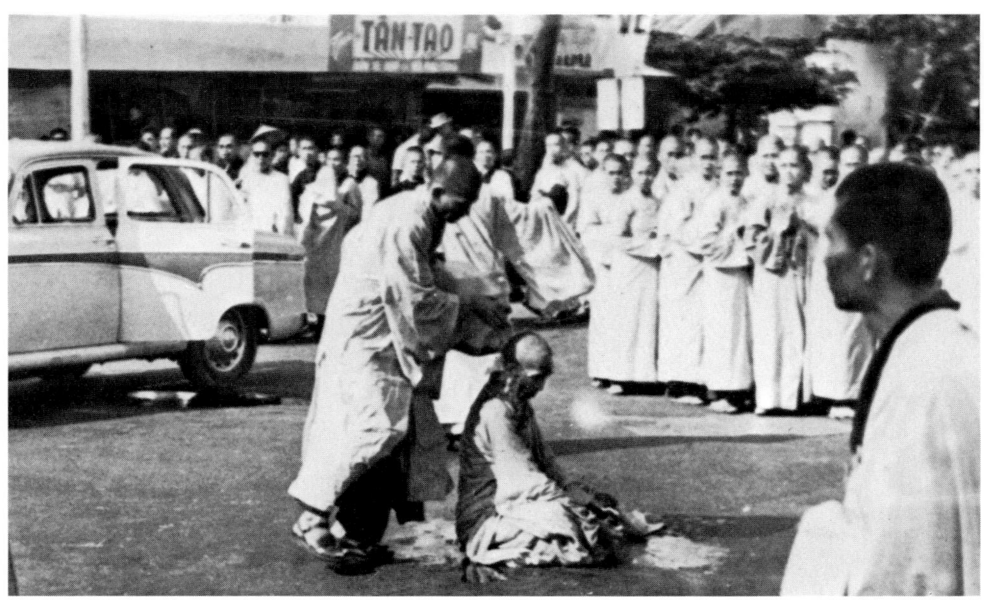

Credibility

The central picture of the burning sequence was seen round the world with the cryptic information that a 73-year-old Buddhist monk had set himself on fire and burned to death, in Saigon, in protest against what he called government persecution of Buddhists. It was a truly incredible event. Many people could not believe that he had died or that the flames were anything more than some piece of magic. Here sequence adds credibility. The three pictures together force home to our minds that the Reverend Quang Duc did have petrol poured over him as he sat in the street (*left*) and that he did burn until he had died (*far right*).

Creativity

We owe the excellent action sequence printed below to a pressman, Robert Coon, who was tired of photograph-

ing death and disaster. Coon was assigned by the *Detroit News* when Richard Ramirez (in check shirt *below*) threatened to throw himself off an 11-storey hotel roof because he had no work and nobody loved him. Coon was appalled by the attitude of the street crowd (deprived, like Ramirez). They were urging him to jump and the photographers were all ready to record his fall. Coon, hoping he could photograph life, went instead to an overlooking building: 'I waited for 45 minutes with much prayer and with only 10 minutes of dusk lighting left was able to photograph the rescue' (a 200mm lens, 1/60 at 3.5). The police persuaded Ramirez to let a priest and a friend talk to him, and then to speak to his mother on the telephone. The wire had been shortened so that he had to come away from the roof edge. A policeman was then able to jump down and save him.

177–178A–F Bluebird races to disaster. The essence of Michael Brennan's action sequence which won a Rank award

THE TIMES

LONDON THURSDAY JANUARY 5 1967

LATE LONDON EDITION

CAMPBELL BOAT TOOK FLIGHT

Risk foreseen: record missed by fraction

Man accused of £1½m. art theft

All eight Dulwich paintings recovered: two damaged

SHOTS FIRED IN POLICE CHASE

JUMPED INTO PARK

ON OTHER PAGES

PAYROLL THEFT AT SADLER'S WELLS

177G *The Times* uneasy compromise between sequence and climax, though the final picture is striking

SHOCK FOR CAR DRIVERS

New insurance blow

SUN

THE INDEPENDENT DAILY NEWSPAPER

AT 320 m.p.h. INEVITABLE TRAGEDY

Campbell—the last picture

Just a second from success

By PETER MOORHEAD

MORE THAN 120,000 motorists insured with the London and Cheshire Insurance Company are to have their policies cancelled.

PROBLEM

By WILLIAM JENKINS

DONALD CAMPBELL plunged to his death on Coniston Water yesterday when he was less than a second away from setting a new world water speed record.

TONIA CAMPBELL Last night's picture

WARNING WAS IN THE CARDS

177H The *Sun* chose a single climax, nearly the full width of a broadsheet page

DAILY MIRROR, Thursday, January 5, 1967

Biggest cut-price company cancels policies

NEW SHOCK ON CAR INSURANCE

By BRIAN McCONNELL

150,000 motorists hit by decision

A NEW shock hit the car insurance world last night when London and Cheshire, the biggest cut-price car insurance company, announced that it has stopped business.

Up to 150,000 drivers were left without insurance

Mast shot off trawler

Court

Claims

Coronation St is blacked out by TV strike

By KEN IRWIN

can't breathe?

Tunes help you breathe more easily

TV row over Campbell widow scene

TWO CHILDREN

Daily Mirror

4d. Thursday, January 5, 1967 No. 19,605

Bluebird begins her take-off to disaster.. over the radio comes Campbell's last anguished cry

I'M GOING!

Like a giant bird in graceful flight . . . spray swirls behind as the nose of Donald Campbell's jet boat Bluebird leaps from the water at 310 m.p.h. Her engines scream in her death throes before she plunges back

POLICE SHOOT AS MEN FLEE IN CAR

By EDWARD VALE

DEATH CHEATS HIM OF FINAL TRIUMPH

A SCENE of terrible beauty — heralding death and destruction— is pictured above.

177I The *Mirror* overcame the limitations of tabloid sizing by opening up back and front pages for a big horizontal with evocative headlining

Over the radio Campbell called 'The water is not good . . . She's going . . . she's going. I am on my back'

Making the most of a sequence

Donald Campbell, the world's fastest man on water, was photographed by still men and television as he streaked along Lake Coniston at more than 300 mph in his jet boat *Bluebird*. Two hundred yards and one second from breaking his own record (276.33 mph) Bluebird leapt 50ft into the air, stood on her tail and crashed back into the lake in a great cloud of spray. When it cleared *Bluebird* had gone and Campbell with her. All this was seen on television and so the morning newspapers had an intriguing challenge in photojournalism. There were blurred pictures from the news reel sequence and still sequences (one of which, 177–178 A–F, won Michael Brennan a Rank award), and there were single photographs.

A sequence should not be discarded simply because of television exposure of moving film. Where the still frames assist understanding they have a value beyond their suggestion of movement. But a sequence with as many frames as *Bluebird* does present space and layout problems. A partial sequence may be the answer if it is possible to eliminate repetition but preserve continuity and meaning, or a partial sequence climaxing in a single photograph which will linger in the memory as a symbol of the disaster. Curiously hardly anybody presented the kind of partial sequence at the top of this page. The *Express* was effective in combining a vertical action sequence for analysis with one big picture for astonishment.

DAILY EXPRESS

No. 20,711 THURSDAY JANUARY 5 1967 Weather: Wintry showers, bright spells later. Price 4d.

● Moment by moment — camera shots to study as Bluebird takes off, somersaults, and finally plunges into Coniston Water

Bluebird's death leap

PICTURE BY EXPRESS CAMERAMAN PETER JACKSON

At 310m.p.h. on the smooth water of Coniston, Campbell's Bluebird, nose almost vertical and engine screaming, somersaults to disaster

THIS IS WHY

The path to disaster: Photonews, Pages 4, 5

300 m.p.h. WAS TOO MUCH FOR A 13-YEAR-OLD BOAT

Express Staff Reporters

DONALD CAMPBELL died on Coniston Water yesterday because he was too brave to admit that he was trying to do the impossible with too little.

He had too little money. In the frustration of waiting, perhaps he showed too little patience. And in his bravery he cared too little for the vital margin of safety.

In the picture above he is pinned in the cockpit of somersaulting Bluebird, a moment from death. But his voice on the radio is calm: *"She's tramping—I'm going—I'm on my back—I'm gone."*

A deep sigh was heard. Then the "G" of this fearsome somersault at over 300 miles an hour would have blacked out the final impact.

The money

As darkness fell over the steel-grey strip of the Lancashire lake last night, and divers and salvage men put off their work until the morning, Donald Campbell's friends asked and answered the question of **WHY**?

TOO LITTLE MONEY: The fact is that Campbell badly needed a new boat. It would have cost £100,000, and he just did not have that kind of money.

As it was he put a new engine into the 13-year-old hull of Bluebird for £10,000—"and he had a difficulty in financing that," said Mr. Eric Norris, one of three brothers who helped design the boat.

TOO LITTLE PATIENCE: Campbell had been waiting at Coniston for nine frustrating weeks for the right conditions for a record run.

When he did look like breaking the record at Christmas his observers were absent. Yesterday, when dawn showed the lake like glass, he could hardly wait.

Mr. Andrew Brown, a Kendal business man who was an official observer, said: "Many times in the past he missed his chance because of the time it took to get the picket boats in position and establish that everything was set to go."

The target

On yesterday's first run Campbell topped the record. He turned straight round for the second run.

If he had waited just a few minutes the turbulence he had set up on the first run would have subsided completely. But he pressed on.

Another observer, Mr. Norman Buckley, said: "He could have come back slower and still beaten the record

He gave me a last wave

EXPRESS MAN BENSON: A GAME OF CARDS

By DAVID BENSON

DONALD CAMPBELL, a desperately superstitious man, felt he was going to die. At his cottage in Coniston on Tuesday night he told me: "I have the most awful premonition that I'm going to get the chop this time. I've had the feeling for days."

To ease his mind we played cards. That started badly, because the pack produced was green-backed. Unlucky green.

We persuaded Campbell to go on. Finally, in his blue sweater—lucky blue—he sat down to a Russian form of patience—and at once he turned up the ace and queen of spades.

"That's it," he said, looking up. "Mary Queen of Scots drew the same two cards the night before she was beheaded."

Switching

There was silence. Then we laughed it off. We got down to a game of pontoon.

It was no ordinary game. Before Donald Campbell would make a call he had to consult his latest lucky mascot, Charlie, a rubber monkey that played the drums when a bulb on its tail was pressed.

"Stick" or "buy" or "twist"? Charlie answered by a roll on the drums.

In fact the little monkey was in good form. Campbell finished £2 up on the night.

But as I left he was depressed, and talked about "the chop." He looked up at the calm night sky. "Tomorrow looks like being the day," he said. "I only hope it is not my last."

Laughing

TONIA FLIES TO LAKE

TONIA CAMPBELL went to Coniston last night by plane and car.

A friend had phoned to her London flat to tell her that her husband was dead.

In fur coat and black silk trouser suit she was met by officials outside Coniston village.

She told them: "I want to go to the cottage. Where is Donald? We've got to get him out tonight."

Mrs. Campbell—she is a cabaret star — was taken to the cottage overlooking the lake.

Later Lady Campbell, mother of Donald Campbell, arrived at Coniston. Her husband, speed king Sir Malcolm Campbell, died in 1948.

LONDON POLICE OPEN FIRE IN CAR CHASE

By GEOFFREY DOWLING

A DETECTIVE fired two shots from a revolver into the air during a gun battle in a London street last night. It is believed to be the first time a Metropolitan police officer has ever opened fire when making an arrest.

It happened in Frithville Gardens, Shepherd's Bush —close to where three policemen were murdered last year and near the B.B.C. Television Centre.

Two men leaped from a car after a chase and blasts from two shotguns were aimed at four officers closing in.

Revolvers had been issued to the police, who were lying in ambush after a tip-off that the two men might be armed.

A violent struggle followed. One man was overpowered but the second broke free.

A B.B.C. employee, 25-year-old Brian Read, of Shinfield Street, Shepherd's Bush, said: "The cars came roaring down the road.

"The police appeared to be shooting as they chased the two men.

"Two policemen pinned one of the men against the car and wrested the gun from his hand."

Later a man was taken to Shepherd's Bush police station.

Art raid charge

Early today, 32-year-old Michael Hall, unemployed, of Knight's Hill, Norwood, was charged at Southwark police station with breaking and entering Dulwich College art gallery and stealing eight pictures.

Emigration boom

The number of emigrants to Canada from Britain and Eire last year is estimated at about 60,000—the largest number for decades.

Wall Street climbs

NEW YORK, Wednesday.—The industrial share prices index rose 4.72 points on Wall Street today, closing at 791.14.

LATEST

JEWELLERY RAID

FAMILY RESCUED

TV, RADIO Page 10

FLEet Street 8000

VERNONS ~~will~~ *did* pay a world record 1st. Dividend Payout of £215,727 in 1966 *and we aim even higher 1967*

IN THE KNOW WITH THE EXPRESS

178A Sequence and climax in the *Express*. Good treatment, though the sequence frames might ideally have been fractionally larger

179A and **179B** (*above*) Soldiers searching through the rubble after an earthquake in Osoppo, Italy, spot hands in the wreckage of a house. **180A** and **180B** (*right*) a father waits for news of his son, trapped in the house **180C** (*right*) His son is dead. But should the picture have been taken?

Narrative sequence

It was dawn in Osoppo, Italy, stricken by earthquake. Soldiers in rescue work (and photographer Bryan Wharton) saw a pair of hands projecting from wreckage. Wharton with a zoom lens on motor drive, operating from 80mm to 200mm, began to record what he saw, not from one position but moving round. In the group waiting there was an old man; his son had been in the wrecked house, he thought, and he had been waiting all night for some sign of him. He held his emotions in check until near the end (180A, B), and then when his son was brought out, dead, he wept on the shoulder of a relative and the soldiers wept with him. This is a narrative sequence with a rhythm and a climax in the large photograph. Wharton had another scene in the sequence, with soldiers and father grouped round the body, and it has been omitted here. But none of the other scenes could be lost without weakening the rhythm of the sequence.

The large photograph exploits the ability of the camera, superior to the eye, to zoom in for a close up. The narrative sequence can make use of this kind of climax more easily than the action sequence, where a change of scale of this kind may interrupt the flow. Of course, the large picture could stand on its own with the headline 'The Moment an Old Man Knew His Son Was Dead', but Wharton rightly argues: 'The justification for the extra space, taken by using the sequence, is that it tells the story more clearly and tells it visually, once. I always take photographs in phrases. Looking always for the one picture which tells the story is a futility.'

On publication in *The Sunday Times*, some people said the main photograph should neither have been taken nor published, because it intruded. That is an understandable reaction, but in Osoppo the people had a different attitude. The photographer was, to them, part of the recognition of tragedy. 'Where are you from? London? You've come all this way to see us . . . make way for the photographer'.

Case History Norman Midgley records the loss of the Thetis

There was enough air for 24 hours of life inside HMS *Thetis* when she sank, 38 miles off Liverpool Bay, on her diving trials in June 1939.

Part of the submarine had been flooded when the inner and outer doors of a torpedo tube were inadvertently opened to the sea, and she lay 150ft down with 103 men on board, 53 of them crew, unable to surface. Their plight was serious but not hopeless. Above them was a tug and the indicator buoy. The alarm was sounded. Then things went needlessly wrong. An RAF navigator made a 7-mile error in the buoy's position, so a night search by the Navy was in vain. Four men escaped by the safety hatch, then it jammed.

Sometime during the night Commander Bolus succeeded in a daring manoeuvre. He jettisoned oil and water so that the lightened stern rose

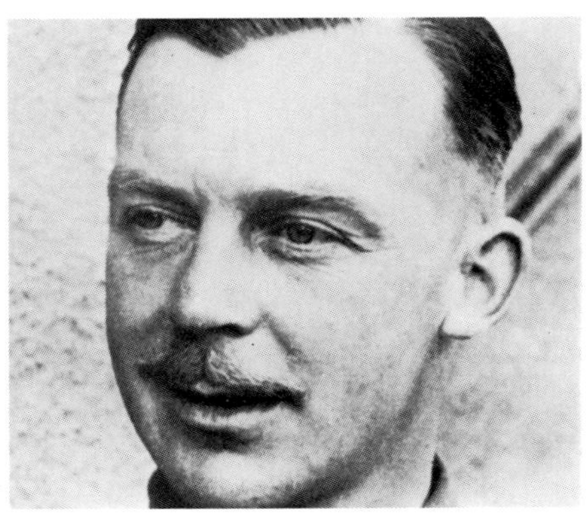

to the surface and was seen at 7 am. There were eight hours of air left. Eight destroyers and the salvage vessel *Vigilant* had arrived. *Vigilant* got a light wire cable round the stern and, with two tugs helping, pulled the tail up a bit more so that a man could attempt to open a manhole showing high out of the water. He could not do it, and a diver failed to find the air connections in the submerged conning tower. At 3 pm when the air in *Thetis* was just about used up the rescuers outside attempted to raise the stern higher still, so that cutting torches which had just arrived could be used to enter the hull. It was then that the final disaster occurred and was photographed by Norman Midgley of *The Daily Express*: 'Photographers from rival newspapers arrived by tug, photographed the tail sticking out of the water and returned to Liverpool. I decided to stay and soon things began to happen'. What Midgley recorded was the *Thetis* twisting on her precarious nose stand and falling, snapping the mooring cable with a sound like a rifle shot. Midgley's pictures were presented in a vertical sequence in the *Daily Express* (182A), horrifyingly compulsive in its drama and finality.

181A Lines to life. Men are trapped inside the *Thetis* whose stern (far left) is held out of the sea by the tug.

182A *right*: Bold numbering and strong black made a graphic presentation of Midgley's action sequence in the *Daily Express*

"HAWSER BROKE ... THE THETIS VANISHED ..." AND DAILY EXPRESS CAMERA MAN TOOK THESE PICTURES

DAILY EXPRESS staff cameraman Norman Midgley watched the sinking of the Thetis through the viewfinder of his camera.

In the Liverpool tug Poolgarth, chartered by the Daily Express, he helped in the rescue work, shared the hope of the crew when they helped to pull the submarine partly out of the water.

The hawser broke. Cameraman Midgley pressed his camera trigger to secure the last picture of the Thetis as she settled below the water.

Here is his story:—

1 p.m—We find the Thetis. The salvage steamer Vigilant grapples her with hawsers.

1.30.—The Vigilant master asks our tug to help. We tie up to his stern.

1.45.—The crews shout "All together." Engines rev. up.

2.0.—"She's coming out," we shout.

2.10.—But the Thetis cants over. We wait.

2.30.—An Admiralty officer climbs from a pinnace on to the tail, inspects it.

3.0.—It means another pull the other way. Tugs strain again. The hawser breaks. Slowly the broken strands curl away. The last one snaps. The Thetis vanishes.

Chapter 10

Picture Editing

It is a rare photographer who can take a detached, cold-blooded view of his work.
Arthur Rothstein

The photograph, once selected, has to be edited for size, shape and story content. This is a world in itself, inhabited by all sorts of hobgoblins. There is one scenario which features coarse picture editors destroying artistic integrity by cropping every print at the sides and top and bottom. There is another scenario where the villain is the layout man who mangles whatever he receives to fit a layout.

These things happen, no doubt, just as on *Life* and *Look* magazines the photographer and editor would pore over 1,000 contact prints, fifty blow-ups and six final enlargements before making the final agonising judgements together in tearful comradeship. The reality in most publication offices is that the photographs receive neither severe cropping nor prolonged examination. They just go in, roughly in scale with the size and shape the photographer's print suggests.

My assertion need not be taken on trust. The published results provide their own damning testimony daily: the example above of Malawi chiefs lined up on arrival at London Airport is from the *Daily Telegraph*. Newspapers—supposed to be the ruthless croppers—abound daily with other examples. The only part of the picture worth publishing is indicated between the lines; if the 20 square inches given to the original had been given to this area instead, then at least their faces could have been studied. There is, in fact, very little editing by anyone. The photograph is sized rather than edited; and sizing is only one of the three final processes of picture editing which is the subject of this and the succeeding two chapters.

184A The casual victor—one of the first photographs of a Khymer Rouge soldier after the collapse of Cambodia. Above is the uncropped print; it is a little too loose

184B This crop enlarges the main image for the expenditure of little extra space in depth—but it is too tight. The loss of the rifle butt is unfortunate. The ideal crop is somewhere between **A** and **B**

Editing for story content

The general run of agency prints is superior to that of the African leaders (page 183), but many of them can be improved with modest cropping. This is not necessarily an agency fault: they rightly leave some margin for the publication, since formats vary. The lines in the four photographs here indicate optimum areas of crop. The deletions are suggested to concentrate attention on the central aspect of the story, and the removal of genuinely extraneous detail means that this key area will occupy more of the allotted space. This enlargement is valuable for impact and in improvin the quality of reproduction, always a worry with newsprint.

It is a pity that the neglect of judicious picture editing is being encouraged by vague ideas that there is something vulgar about cropping. Eric de Maré says approvingly (*Penguin Book of Photography—see bibliography*) that 'most of the famous photographers print from the whole negative'. Cartier-Bresson believes the good photograph becomes meaningless if cropped. He goes further: 'Cropping under the enlarger cannot, to my mind, make up for lack of formal rigour at the time of shooting the picture.' The nature of news photography means that this naturalist philosophy will encourage inertia, rather than preserve purity of form. And this is not a judgement by a mere journalist. Another of our great photographers, Bill Brandt, told me: 'Many of the young pupils who come to me from the Royal College of Art show weak pictures, obviously unedited. They have been led to believe there is something wrong with cropping. I tell them they must do it. I crop all my own pictures in the darkroom'. Arnold Newman reinforced the point: 'Rembrandt and Picasso re-painted and novelists re-write and re-write. Why should the photographer be the only creative artist who is denied the opportunity to improve his work?'

185A The famous debate on capitalism versus communism between Khruschev and Vice-President Nixon. The top is waste, the bottom has a white intrusion, but it's essential to retain the two soap packets, washing machine and sense of a fascinated crowd

185B Bricks against tank cannon in East Berlin, rioters and photographer living to tell the tale. All the right of the picture is waste, diminishing the action. Cropping just above the distant tower building retains perspective

186A An American pilot downed by a rocket in Vietnam is brought out for public humiliation in Hanoi. The bottom part can be discarded to give more space to the key area; but the watching eyes of the crowd have to be retained

186BC A great deal of space is required to publish the full frame of the Apollo 11 rocket on its launch from Cape Kennedy July 1969 with the first men to land on the moon. A vertical crop can retain spectators (foreground) and emphasise the upward thrust of the mission

186D Marines at beleagured Khe Sanh peer through an opening in a bunker. We do not need all the top sandbags: the mind multiplies them. But the corrugated girder at right needs to be kept

Vivid fractions

Shaving the merest sliver from a photograph can make a remarkable difference. Here is a study in the treatment of the full frame (below) of Pope Paul in New York with President Johnson. The *Northern Echo* and the *Daily Mail* rightly decided to concentrate on the heads and crop from both sides. (It is arguable whether the hands should have been retained). But the *Mail* did not go far enough. Leaving the extra margin on the left has two effects. First, it reduces the amount of space available for the main visual story: the faces are noticeably bigger in the *Northern Echo*. Secondly, the remnant of the man with glasses (left) is a distracting irritation.

The Northern Echo

No. 29,740 (Founded 1869) TUESDAY, OCTOBER 5, 1965 THREEPENCE

POPE CALLS FOR 'END WAR' OATH

POPE PAUL VI called on United Nations members last night to swear an oath to change the history of the world: "No more war, never again war, peace: it is peace which must guide the destinies of peoples and of all mankind."

"If you wish to be brothers, let the arms fall from your hands," the Pope told the UN General Assembly in a speech which he had flown 4,000 miles to deliver. "One cannot love while holding offensive arms."

He also took the opportunity to speak out against birth control—"Your task is to ensure that there is enough bread on the tables of mankind, and not encourage an artificial birth control, which would be irrational, in order to diminish the number of guests at the banquet of life."

But it did not suffice to feed the hungry—"It is necessary also to assure to each man a life conformed to his dignity," he said, renewing the appeal he made last December to divert to developing lands at least part of the proceeds saved from reducing armaments.

The world must become accustomed to thinking of man in a new way. "The hour has struck for a halt, a moment of recollection, of reflection, almost of prayer: a moment to think anew of our common origin, our history, our common destiny. Today, as never before, in our era so marked by human progress, there is need for an appeal to the moral conscience of man.

"For the danger comes, not from progress, nor from science. Indeed, if properly utilised, these could rather resolve many of the grave problems which assail mankind.

"No, the real danger comes from man himself, wielding ever more powerful arms, which can be employed equally well for destruction or for the loftiest conquests.

"In a word, then, the edifice of modern civilisation must be built upon spiritual principles which alone can, not only support it, but even illuminate

Mr. Smith meeting Mr. Bottomley at the Commonwealth Relations Office yesterday.

Smith flies in —to tea and biscuits

20 unions snub pay freeze

LEADERS of 20 uni
last night rejected
request by Mr. Geo
Brown, Economics Minis
that pay rises due to 22.
Government skilled en
neers should be "froze
pending an investigation
the National Prices and
comes Board.

Daily Mail

QUEEN AND COMMONWEALTH — News Chronicle and Daily Dispatch — TUESDAY, OCTOBER 5, 196

ou wish to be brothers he arms fall from your s... Swear: No more wa

THE POPE TO THE UN LAST NIG

om STANLEY BURCH
United Nations,
New York, Monday

)PE PAUL
called on UN
bers today to
r an oath to
ge the world's
re history: "No
e war, war
r again."
presented his
onate plea for
as "an appeal
he moral con-
ce of man."
you wish to be
s, let the arms fall
our hands," the
declared in
t. rhetorical
to the General
ly.
cannot love while

Dog pat alertec at trai raid ja

By Daily Mail Reporter

A NEW security patrol was sti
night at Durham Prison after
was to be made to free the three

Senior police officers in the anti-escape plan were alerted at breakfast time on Sunday.

By last night the watch was being eased. But a patrol of dogs was outside the prison wall.

Two vans of the dog squad were stationed outside the back of Durham Jail where the wall is at its lowest, about 15ft.

They were on guard in a lane

NC
sta
n

187A Pope and president (*above*) is full frame
187B (*top right*): is the tightest crop
187C (*right*): an in-between failure

What matters

Another example of millimetre-by-millimetre cropping. Princess Anne was taking tea with school children (full frame below), and both the *Daily Mail* and the *Daily Express* cropped the original. Both cut in from the right where a light area takes the eye away from the Princess and her hostess. The *Express* removed it entirely by cropping from the top as well, but then failed to trim the left side of the picture and so weakened its impact in the page by comparison with its rival. This was expenditure of space on the inessential detail of the school girl's dress and the *Mail* gained by spending the space on a large image of the Princess—within the same total page area.

FIRST OF ALL... BSL South African Sherry

NO. 22,722

Daily Mail

FRIDAY, MAY 23, 1969 — PRICE 5d.

Snoopy does a bucking bronco act in space

That was real wild baby!

From ANGUS MACPHERSON, Houston, Thursday

THE Apollo 10 Moonship hit trouble as it headed back to its command module tonight. It spun wildly for a few moments after jettisoning its 'legs.'

The two astronauts aboard reported a 'wild gyration' which tossed the fragile craft like a bucking bronco.

WHEN THEY COME BACK
. . . the Moonmen will themselves tell the personal stories of their epic journey

Shooting in their excitement at their close-up look at the Moon—they were only a little higher than an airline passenger flies above Earth—the two men tumbled over each other giving a running commentary.

"We're real close, baby . . . This is it, [illegible] . . . we're right on the [illegible]," said Cernan.

Suddenly the names of [illegible]

Comment

Earl Warren steps down

GOOD men are always scarce. We should not miss the chance to praise one such as Earl Warren, Chief Justice of the United States.

For 15 years until his retirement next month Mr Warren has had the job, along with the eight Associate Justices of the Supreme Court, of judging the fairness of his country's laws.

Our own system works differently, for better or worse. But a code of law is only as fair as its judges.

Even the Russian Constitution promises fair trials and free speech. It is men who make justice.

Mr Warren is not a brilliant or witty man. He is no Bertrand Russell or Malcolm Muggeridge. He looks like any American tourist. When he came to London once [illegible]

TEA-PARTY JELLY BABIES FOR PRINCESS ANNE YESTERDAY

Princess plays mother at [illegible]

THREAT TO LONDON TRAINS

Labour man loses deposit

By WALTER TERRY Political Editor

TORY candidate Christopher Chataway won Chichester early today with a record by-election majority.

He was 26,087 votes ahead of Liberal Mr Denys Kinsella, who came second after a recount.

The Labour man, Mr John White, lost his deposit.

The result was:

C. Chataway (Con.) 31,966
D. Kinsella (Lib.) 5,879
J. White (Lab.) 5,257

Majority 26,087

The by-election was caused by the death of Tory Mr Walter Loveys in March. He was 48 and had been the MP since 1958.

Until this morning the safest Tory seat was Warwick and Leamington where, in a by-election last year, the majority was 21,922.

In the 1966 General Election the Conservatives held Chichester by 17,574.

The recount was a surprise. The Liberals and Labour were struggling to avoid third place. The swing from Labour to Conservative was 14.9 p.c., compared with 3.15 p.c. in 1966.

Oddly enough this was better than many other by-elections and was better than many contests over the past two years.

Town hall arrests

Police made ten arrests last night after election more than 30 people demonstrating over housing in the public gallery at Brighton Town Hall.

DAILY MAIL NORTHCLIFFE HOUSE, E.C.4 01-353 6000

LATE NEWS

MOON HITCH

HOUSTON: Cernan Stafford reported that [illegible] still and movie cameras [illegible]

No. 21,449 — FRIDAY MAY 23 1969 — Weather: Very warm; showers — Price 5d.

DAILY EXPRESS

MOON BUZZED—NOW FOR HOME

'We should come here more often'

ROSS MARK, Apollo Control Centre
Houston, Thursday

WITH a triumphant shout—"We's down among them, Charlie—Tom Stafford and Gene Cernan tonight signalled that they had taken their flimsy, spider-like craft down to nine miles and a few yards above the boulders on the moon.

The two men reported: "It is fantastic; its beautiful in blacks and browns. And there's enough boulders to fill the Bay of Galveston back there in Texas."

They reconnoitred the moon's Sea of Tranquility—one of the dark patches situated just right of the centre as we look at the full moon from earth.

That is where the next Apollo mission is expected to make a lunar landing attempt in July.

As arranged they jettisoned the lower half of their craft—which has four landing legs built in. The two men reported that their top half experienced a wild "gyration" and was tossed as though by a bucking bronco.

Then as Stafford and Cernan fired the rocket motors to take their spider-craft, nicknamed Snoopy, up and away to rejoin the command craft piloted by John Young, a flight control official in Huston, Texas, said the way to a moon landing was now wide open.

He commented: "Now we will find that the moon really is American cheese."

Cameras fail

But there may yet be a hitch to the projected landing on July 20. Both cameras aboard Snoopy failed in tonight's low sweep across the boulder-strewn lunar surface. The movie camera jammed and the film packs in the still camera stuck.

Flying 50 miles above the moon John Young, in the command craft nicknamed Charlie Brown, reported to Ground Control that Stafford and Cernan in Snoopy had made a safe descent to nine miles and 252 yards above the surface.

Young said he saw Snoopy skimming the lunar mountains. He added: "They are O.K. down there and mumbling about the boulders. I could see them fine for a while, but I turned to check my radar and lost them."

Ground Control: "Great going, Charlie Brown."

Stafford and Cernan called: "Really, it doesn't look as if we are moving too fast down here. It is very pleasant." Snoopy was then travelling at one mile per second.

Cernan reported: "The only problem is that we don't come here more often. There's so much to do and so little time."

As they ran up the flight path that Apollo 11 will follow to a moon landing, Cernan and Stafford said: "Everything is very easily distinguishable . . . Sidewinder Hill is coming up on the left.

"Now it looks very smooth down there, like very wet clay . . . it reminds me of dry river beds in New Mexico or Arizona . . . we see some rills which look like 200 feet deep."

Snoop starts

The order to go down was given from Ground Control just as Air Force Colonel Stafford, aged [illegible]

The Princess takes tea . . . of 'pretend' black puddings

PICTURE BY EXPRESS CAMERAMAN IAN TORRANCE

Eating jelly babies with her hosts . . . Princess Anne yesterday

Express Staff Reporter

A REAL Princess dropped by for an imaginary cuppa at a make-believe tea party yesterday.

It was laid on at an Edinburgh children's home.

Officials tactfully withdrew while a dozen chattering youngsters, mostly under 10, took charge of Princess Anne.

FIRST came that "pretend" cuppa—followed by black pudding (jelly babies) and lemon curd (dolly mixtures).

"All princesses like a lot of [illegible]

IN THE KNOW with the Express

Vietnam casualties mix-up: Page 2

Emma Soames turned [illegible]

'GET OUT' THREATS TO BRITISH SALESMEN IN US

By PHILIP DITTON

AMERICAN trade union bosses are threatening Britain's fur exports, it was disclosed yesterday.

The Fur Trade Union of the U.S. and Canada wants to ban the import of fur coats [illegible]

YOUR trip to the moon

ADVANCE orders for "Touchdown for the Moon," the colourful spacecraft commander's briefing kit containing diagrams and data sheets for a trip to the moon and back, has passed the million mark.

But ONLY Daily Express readers — and they alone—can buy it NOW to share the thrills and hazards facing the men orbiting the moon, and accompany them on this great venture.

It costs 11s. to personal callers at the Daily Express Books Department, 121, Fleet Street, London, E.C.4. To get it by post send a 12s. 6d. postal order or cheque [illegible]

MIDNIGHT

Labour man loses his deposit

Express Political Correspondent

CHICHESTER has sent Mr. Christopher Chataway back to the Commons with the biggest Tory majority in the country. Result of the by-election, announced early today:—

Christopher Chataway (Tory) 31,966
Denys Kinsella (Lib.) 5,879
John White (Lab.) 5,257
Majority 26,087

General Election figures for Chichester — which covers the cathedral city, the resort of Bognor Regis, and several West Sussex villages—were: Tory, 31,358; Lab. 13,784; Lib. 9,714; majority 17,574.

The blow to the Government is that the Liberal pushed the Labour candidate to the bottom of the poll, and inflicted the humiliation of a lost deposit—involving the unusual situation of having a recount between them to confirm who was last.

Figures

In 1966 Tory Mr. Bill Loveys—whose death has caused the by-election—had a 17,574 majority. In 1959, the Tory high-water mark, it was 21,209. Now Mr. Chataway has raised it in record style.

Mr. Chataway, 38, one-time four-minute miler, Junior Minister and leader of the Inner London Education Authority, said: "The message is clear — Mr. Wilson and his Government must go."

LATEST

TV-Radio programmes Page 12

PHONE (STD CODE 01) 353 8000 TELEX 21841

188A Princess Anne (*above*) is full frame
188B (*top left*): is the tightest, better, crop
188C (*left*): looser crop, smaller image

189A Eyeball to eyeball—the end of a London carnival

A marriage of skills

Hundreds of photographs were taken of the scenes when a cheerful West Indian carnival in Notting Hill, London, in September 1976, ended in rioting and battles with police who had gone in to arrest pickpockets. Only small groups of blacks were involved in fighting and looting, but it was a shock to London because of the bitterness it revealed among younger blacks born in Britain. All the elements were symbolised in the presentation by *The Observer* on its Review Front (**189B**) a visual moment of great intensity. But this was the result of perceptive picture editing as well as of resourceful photography.

BELL'S SCOTCH WHISKY *Afore ye go*

OBSERVER REVIEW

SUNDAY 5 SEPTEMBER 1976

YOUNG BITTER AND BLACK

The Observer invited WILLIAM RASPBERRY, the Washington Post's black columnist, to

black people being robbed by young black hooligans, even if it is to involve an element of risk going in to help them.'

The statement is interesting not merely for its apparent tough-

more than a local neighbourhood affair before last year, when it attracted nearly a quarter of a million revellers.

'That's too many niggers about for their taste,' said a young

that racial problems become more difficult as the size of the rejected minority grows, that the problems are easiest when there are relatively few 'outsiders' to be absorbed. Thus, an American city with a large black population

as another ingre wondrous stew problem

Is it only lack of West Indians that Leicester Square taurants which

The power of close focus
The raw material for the *Observer's* presentation was the full frame on the left, **190A**. It was an excellent news photograph of an edgy moment of confrontation between policemen and young blacks—but the camera also registered trees and houses and background which added nothing to the news and, if left in, would have taken publication space from the main focus of attention. There is plenty of detail as well as drama in what remains (**189A** *above*) and at the size and shape reproduced it took every reader by the eyeball.

Editing for point of emphasis

On March 3, 1974 all 346 passengers and crew were killed when a Turkish Airlines DC10 fell 12,000 feet, out of a clear blue sky, into the Forest of Ermeonville, outside Paris. The jumbo jet cut a path through the trees about 500 yards long and up to 100 yards wide and in this terrible scene of annihilation the remnants of the victims were too tragic to photograph. Captain Jacques Lannier, who led the search, is haunted by one image of two hands clasping each other, a woman's and a man's hand which withstood disintegration. It would have been insensitive to give any other than a general view, and Aubrey Hart achieved this in a moving manner with his picture (above) of the swathe through the forest and a man—a bereaved husband—walking through it.

Should the picture be edited? The answer must lie in what one judges to be the emphasis of the story, and the occasion of publication. The full frame (above) gives equal emphasis to the devastation and the man. Different cropping is suggested if the imagination is to be directed more to individual grief and less to the circumstances of the crash. The crops (right) bring the figure into the foreground with varying effects—he can be made to appear to be walking away—but these describe the scene less well. If the picture is to be accompanied by others showing waiting relatives there is a strong case for the full frame; if, on the other hand, another picture emphasises the devastation, a crop to focus more on the man might supply a missing element.

In later days, when the public has absorbed the idea of the crash, a smaller picture serves as a reminder; versions as limited as those on the far right can be considered. Of course it would be unthinkable to crop like that on first publication.

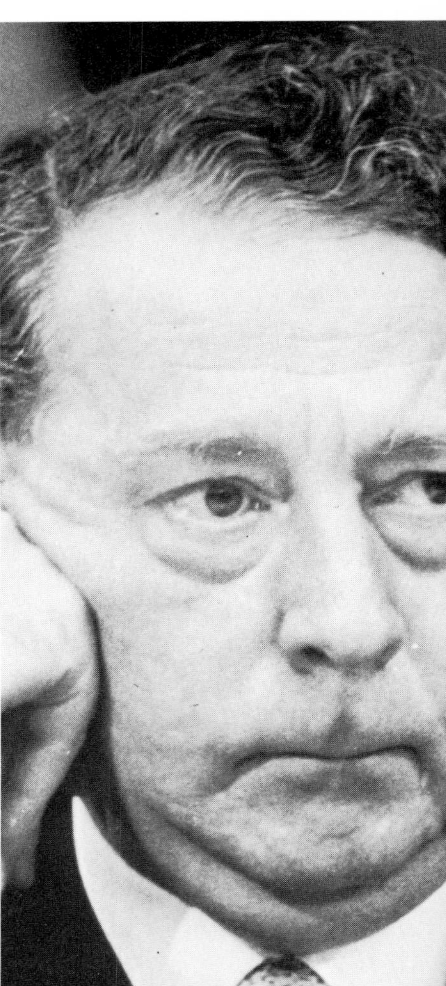

MR. GAITSKELL TO FIGHT "TO SAVE PARTY"

COMMONS DILEMMA AFTER ARMS VOTE DEFEAT

The Times, 1960

The possibilities with a face

Hugh Gaitskell, leader of the Labour party, had an unhappy party conference at Scarborough in 1960. He was attempting to refashion it as a social democratic party, shedding old socialist dogma and remaining firmly in the Western alliance. He promised, on defeat, to fight and fight again; but the photographer caught his dejection on the platform as the debates went against his lead. For first publication (above) it was right to retain the teacup and the glumness suggested by the head resting on the hand. But other crops are possible on later publication. A portrait of a face which is appearing in print almost daily can benefit by exceedingly tight crops, restricting the image to features which express emotion (ears can come off).

The tightest vertical crop is called 'coming in on the eyeballs': a vertical cut is made to the edge of the iris. The limit of such cropping is the point at which the face is not instantly recognisable.

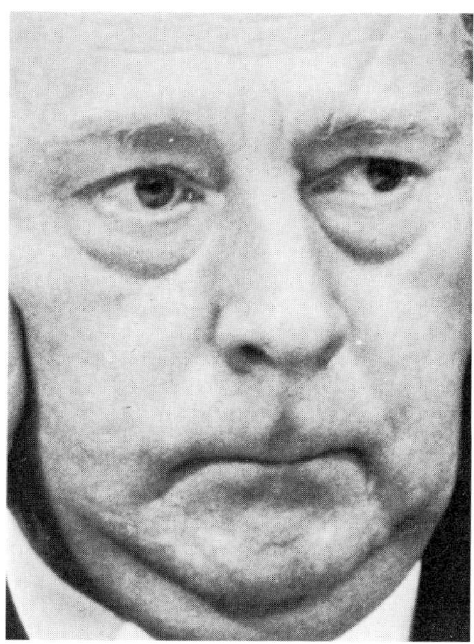

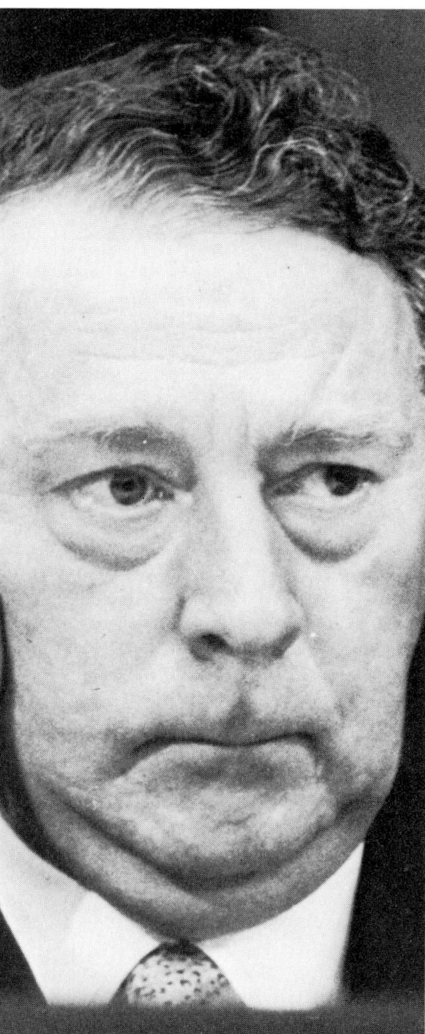

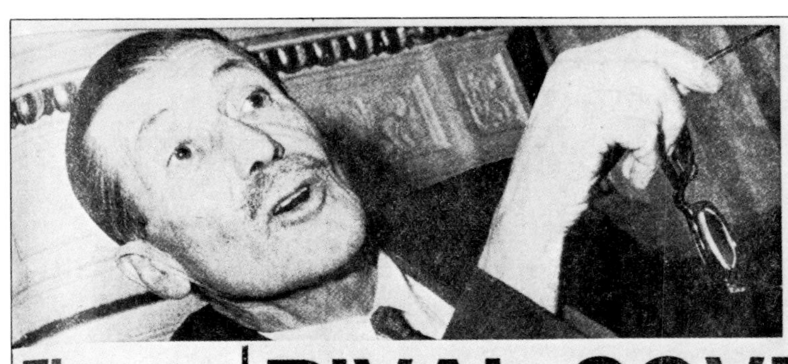

THURSDAY ..

SU

NOVEMBER 18 1965 FOURPENCE

THE INDEPEND

DAILY NEWSPA

The usurper

RIVAL GOVERNO

TAKES OVER

195A (*left*): The original print of Mr. Clifford Dupont, photographed in Rhodesia shortly after he had deposed the British Governor. In **195B** (*above*) the *Sun* cropped it at a tilt to produce a vertiginous horizontal, matching its titlepiece in depth

Cropping for shape

The crop of a picture should normally be dictated by what is in the picture and not by what is on the layout sheet. I have urged elsewhere (*Newspaper Design*, Volume 5) that page design should begin with the main illustration and its size and shape should be regarded as a fixed element to which the other display elements have to adjust. It is less damaging to write a two-column headline instead of a four-column headline than it is to force a deep three-column photograph into a square two-column shape. But there are occasions when these strictures are redundant. There are some photographs which give a surprising range of optional crops; there is more latitude after first prime publication; and if the photograph does suggest or permit an emphasis of shape it can be beneficial to exploit it—either to reinforce the tendencies within the picture or to help the page layout. In a broadsheet, full size newspaper, for instance, there is hardly anything duller than a small square photograph as the main illustration. Its scale is inadequate, of course, but the shape is itself uninteresting and static. Few great artists have painted square pictures. If the right shape for a particular picture is square, when all other points have been considered, then it must be made a big square. A strong vertical or horizontal stress is preferable and here are examples. The *Sun* coped with the awkward spaces in 195A by cropping at an angle and producing a striking—if giddy—effect. The cropping of Mr. Tiny Rowlands of Lonrho (195C) was economical in space yet energetic, forcing the eyes to the beginning of the story.

THE SUNDAY TIMES, MAY 13 1973 — Investment 57

Kelvin Brodie

'Tiny' Rowland

"Accounts show that the net profits before taxation of the company have grown from £158,000 in 1961 to £19.3m in 1972. . . . A large part of this expansion is, I believe, due to my knowledge and understanding of Africa which I have obtained from living there for over 25 years. . . . I have helped to build turnover from about £800,000 to about £230m in the current year. I do not believe that this could have been achieved in the aftermath of the British Empire in the areas concerned without close personal knowledge and understanding. . . . Since I have joined the company, I have been solely responsible with one or two minor exceptions for the negotiations which brought about 400 subsidiary companies into the Lonrho group. In the course of my negotiations I have met the principals concerned. Many of them have become my friends. . . . When I am in London, because of my personal connections, I spend my time by day, in the evening and at weekends, as all who know me will confirm, to the total exclusion of all social life, on the company's affairs."

THE LONRHO CASE

continued from preceding page

Wankel's rotary engine, was a typical Lonrho project. Simple and grandiose in principle, complex and convoluted in detail, it involved among others the mysterious Captain Stefan Klein, a contact of Lonrho director Nicholas Elliott, who was a

details of the Wankel deal are shrouded in a cloak of secrecy and complexity, largely geared to tax considerations. Much of the negotiation, papers and agreements were also originally in German, which only two of the then board, Rowland and Elliott, speak well.

According to Wilkinson, a board

group also had a relationship with the indefatigable Captain Klein, who was still at the centre of negotiations for Lonrho and keen to take a slice of the action as his fee.

Negotiations with this group started on the basis of a 50-50 partnership through a Curacao-based holding company and ended with an 80-20 deal with Lonrho putting up all the money through a Luxembourg company called Loncom SA. (Back in June 1971, Lonrho had bought out 49% of Loncom for £755,000 in Belgian francs.) Lonrho would then create an intermediate holding company called Wankel International of which Loncom would hold 80% and 20% would go free to Bunford, Klein and the

other executives on Lonrho on the one hand and Mr Rowland on the other occurred in 1969-70, when Mr Rowland insisted on pursuing proposals whereby a certain African government should nationalise the assets of two other British companies in the country concerned and then transfer them to a new corporation which would be jointly owned and/or managed by such government and Lonrho. Ultimately, Mr Rowland was prevented from carrying the proposals into effect by circumstances outside Lonrho's control."

The African country was Sierra Leone, in fact, and the companies involved in the suggested na-

Ghana for £15m-plus. An Accra-based middleman, Adolf Pluss, got together with Rowland's old friend Dr Klein and suggested that something could be done in the country next door.

Rowland saw an ideal opportunity to strike another blow at the South African mining establishment and in particular against Harry Oppenheimer of De Beers, the group whose central selling organisation controls an estimated 80% of world diamond sales. If Lonrho could secure management of CASTs, he planned further deals with Tanzania, Russia and Israel to establish a rival world-wide marketing operation.

So a new "shell" company, Diminco, was formed with Andrew Sardanis who had made

realised that this was unacceptable.)

In the end, the whole scheme collapsed when Siaka Stevens staged a *coup détat* and promoted himself from prime minister to president. CASTs was later nationalised but the management contract was granted to the existing management.

Which is the real Rowland?

Ian Hossy

"Lonrho's metalliferous mining division (has built up) from a production rate including associated companies of £1,250,000 per annum 11 years

mutual trust, with heads of state and other influential personalities in these countries.""

Alfred Gerber

"Being Swiss, I was, prior to joining the Lonrho Group, unfamiliar with British company practice and I feel I must express my utter astonishment and dismay at the way in which Mr Rowland runs Lonrho, the complete lack of respect which he pays to the board of directors as a whole, its members individually and its deliberations and decisions . . . In my opinion, his approach (to negotiating with Arab governments and businessmen) lacks sincerity, technical knowledge and methodical approach and, as

reactions of enthusiasm or distaste. For the loyalists, Rowland is the great pan-African adventurer, the man in the Mystère for ever jetting towards new commercial horizons and the high-pocket gambler figuring to bid for Rolls-Royce even with his corporate overdraft escalating towards the £9m mark. He cuts a dashing figure in the rather sedate world of high finance.

To the Lonrho dissidents, however, Rowland presents a different picture. That of a corporate dictator whose flair for dealing has outstripped his capacity to control the £150m group he has created, whose abrasive style and unorthodox tactics have worked against improving management techniques and whose knowledge

195C Economic and dynamic use of limited space. The hand obligingly says 'start reading here'

THE GUARDIAN

London Saturday September 14 1974 6p

LEGGE Locks

HIGH & DRY Really Dry Gin

Embassy gang force France to free killer

BY OUR FOREIGN STAFF

The French Government early today gave in to the demands of the revolutionary Japanese Red Army and released a Japanese terrorist after three gunmen threatened to kill "at intervals" nine hostages they had seized in the French Embassy at The Hague.

A policeman takes cover behind a car outside the French Embassy

Tweedie back on Monday

Hooson alarm over food

Briton freed

Berkeley back

Writer dies

Biker dies

Britain's oil bill may jump by £130M

Going the wrong way: The man with a gun is watching the French embassy in the Hague where a Japanese was holding the French Ambassador and three others as hostages. The full frame is below but the *Guardian* cropped it the wrong way. By cutting off the top it produced a squarish picture and disconcertingly left in the white line of the lamp-post, slicing off a part of the picture. A vertical crop (left) produces a more vigorous picture which would also have benefited the page.

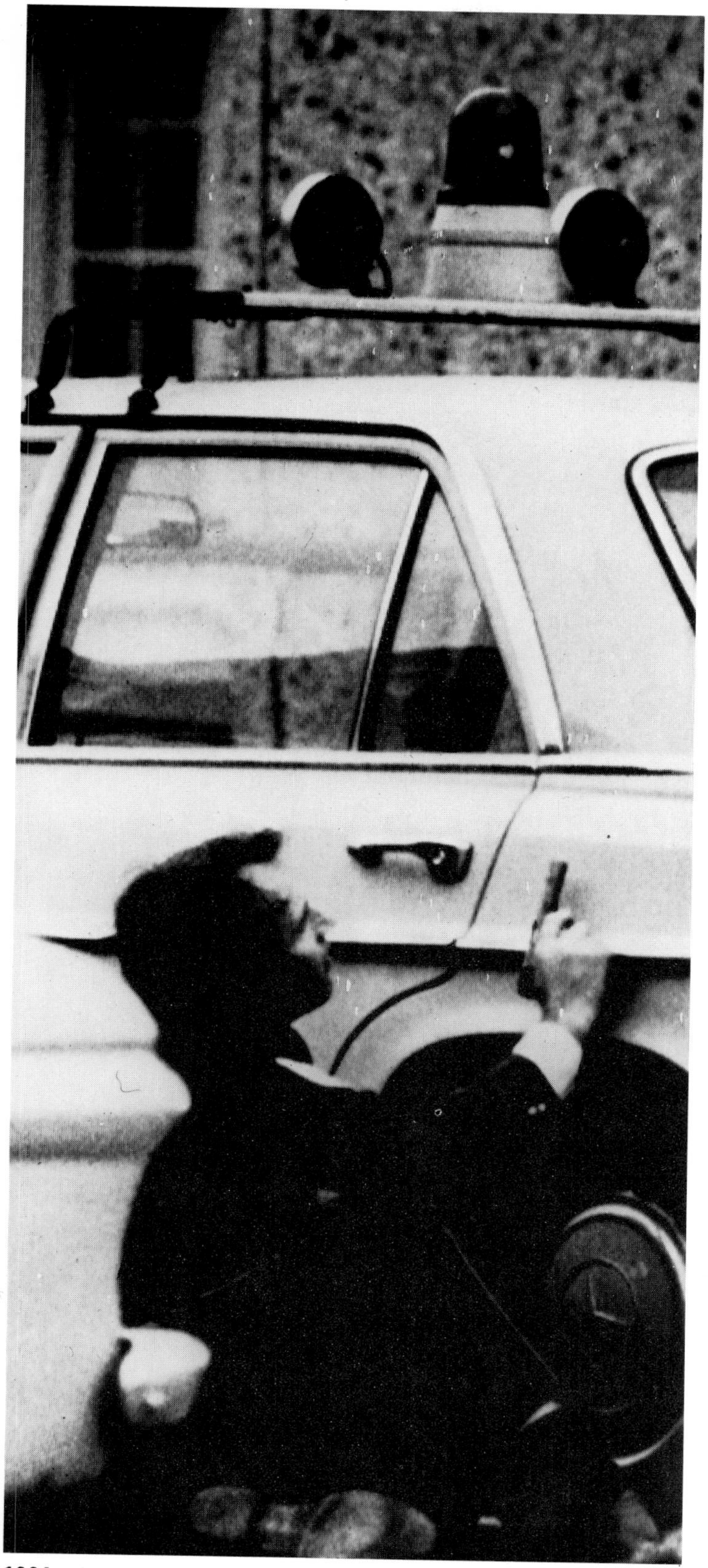

196A A strong vertical crop (*above*) is the best use of the full frame (*right*) of a siege

197ABC Three sizes of a still from a television drama about a vampire villain: even the smallest above gives enough idea of nastiness.

Television

Too Many Flicks Spoil The Ratings

By JACK GOULD

WHAT'S happened? The current television season was supposed to be the big year for movies, with feature-length films supposedly invulnerable to the hazards of erosion in ratings available on the networks every night of the week. So far it doesn't seem to be working out that way.

In the latest audience surveys, none of the network movies finished in the top 20 attractions, and feature films have sagged almost continuously since early September. The apparent droop in movie appeal follows escalation of the cost of films for TV to record six-figure sums.

The reason seems clear enough. Movie saturation of the networks came just at the time when the supply of big hits began to run out, and the home screen found itself caught with an abundance of Grade B presentations. Many of the movies now being scheduled aren't really very much better than the films which TV itself can whip out. The luster of the movie definitely has faded.

It is more than casually significant that the Schaefer Brewing Company, which occasionally has sponsored its "Award Theater" with a pleasant reduction in advertising, has announced the withdrawal of its venture from the New York market because of a shortage of worthwhile features. The same depletion is hitting local stations around the country, and accounts, in large measure, for the Columbia Broadcasting System's acquisition of the Merv Griffin show starting next August. That will spell the final demise of the late movie in most of the country.

The pinch being felt for some time by local stations would seem a clear augury of what lies ahead for the networks. The human race simply does not spawn enough creative geniuses to satisfy the unlimited appetite of the TV screen for material, and a day of reckoning is bound to follow exhaustion of the stockpiles of other media. In relying on movies to fill so many hours of its schedules TV has been living on borrowed time.

*

As is so characteristic of a mass medium, TV added to its troubles by deluging the airwaves with features instead of hoarding its catalogues, and thus inevitably diluted the value of the form as a whole. The National Broadcasting Company not only added a seventh night of movies, but began, in effect, a policy of pitting movie against movie—i.e., "The Name of the Game" against the CBS Friday night movie.

own right. Sales-oriented executives, capable in their chosen field but largely numb in terms of venturous theater, still dominate too many decisions at the TV networks.

It has been a traditional argument of TV that it cannot afford to get too far ahead of its audience, or jam unconventional material into unreceptive homes. But the flaw in this rationale is its assumption that the public knows in advance what it will or will not like. No one conducted a survey establishing a clear-cut yearning for "Laugh-In"; it was the product of professionals with an idea and, once they had a chance to see it, viewers responded with a favorable critical judgment.

In many ways "Laugh-In" is much more than just a passing TV hit. It represents a type of program that cannot be found in theater, recordings or movies, and capitalizes on TV's basic asset of being highly topical and up-to-date. Moreover, it constitutes a breakthrough in the economic notion that a Hollywood show must necessarily be sufficiently bland to survive reruns two to five years hence. The immediacy and pertinency of the one-line sight gags of "Laugh-In" would seem an inherent

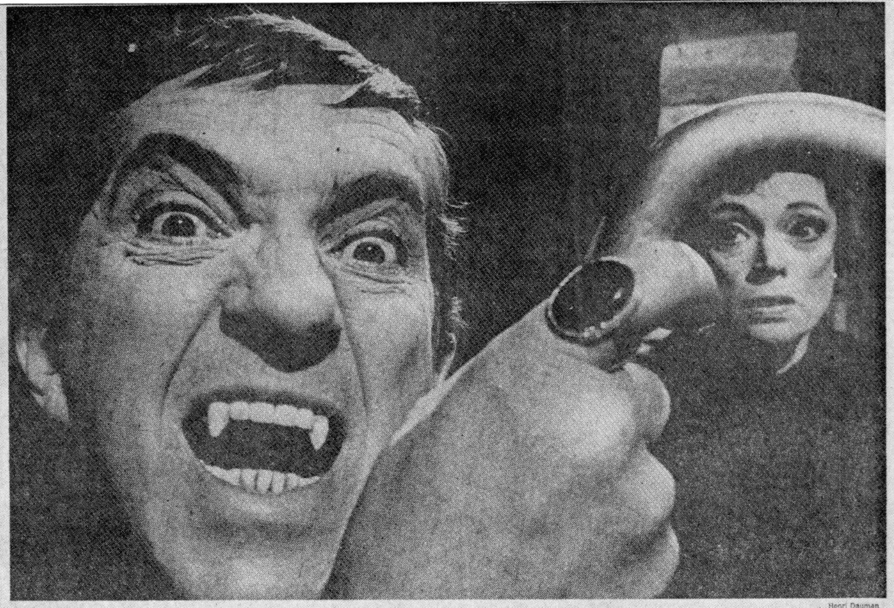

Henri Dauman

Jonathan Frid, playing vampire Barnabas Collins, torments mortals like Grayson Hall every weekday at 4:00 in ABC's "Dark Shadows."
He's got to do his thing—suck human blood

Vampires Are Voluptuous

By ROBERT BERKVIST

WANT to titillate a couple of million housewives and turn on the teenyboppers? Want to see your face on paperback books, sweatshirts, toys? Want your name out of the telephone book and off the bell-plate downstairs? Simple. Bite a few people. On the neck. Leaving two tiny holes. Only in fun. Vampires . . . remember? "Ieeee am Count Drrraaculaahhh . . ." Bela Lugosi then, Jonathan Frid now. Jonathan Frid? Listen:

"I play a guy with a kind of hang-up, like an alcoholic or a sex maniac. He's a loner, an antisocial type—he's got to do his thing, suck his blood. He's hiding his guilt—a lonely man—and the audience saw it, sensed it. They say Lugosi got a tremendous amount of mail, even though *his* version of a vampire didn't appeal emotionally to people, because he struck something in women . . . just the fact that he *bit*. There's a voluptuousness about it, I guess. The other vampires we've had on the show were much more voluptuous biters than

other day, he still seemed a little surprised by it all.

"I don't understand all of this success," he mused. "I mean, I understand it, in a way, and this is why I'm kind of in love with my fans, who saw my potential, saw what I wanted to do. With all due respect and gratitude to Dan's [Dan Curtis, originator and now executive producer of "Dark Shadows"] brilliant idea of having a vampire on the show, it was the fans who made me. The audience, in their letters, were saying, in effect, 'Yes, we know what you're getting at.' I'm a slow study. At first, I was panic-stricken *every day*. I had to wing it like mad. Of course, Barnabas at first was a very vulnerable character, having come back from the dead and all, having to lie about himself, so my own insecurities kind of played into the role."

*

Frid was recalling his debut on "Dark Shadows" back in April, 1967, when everything changed for everybody. The

the handyman at Collinwood—discovered a secret room in the family mausoleum. In the room, a coffin *bound with chains*. Next thing you know, nosy Willie opened the thing and out shot this . . . *hand!* Frid—and Barnabas Collins, the family's 175-year-old vampire—had arrived on the scene. The show's rating took off like a rocket-powered bat out of, well, Collinwood, and soap fans found a weirdo they could love.

Television's first resident vampire proved such a potent drawing card that Barnabas, originally scheduled for a two or three-week stay, became a continuing character on the show. By last summer, fan mail, most of it for Barnabas/Frid, was pouring in at the rate of nearly 6,000 letters a week. Vampire jokes began to, shall we say, circulate (Q: "How does Barnabas get around town?" A: "In his Bloodmobile."), and there were reports that students were cutting classes to watch the groovy new culture hero do his kinky thing.

brought me—if only as a springboard for other things. But I *enjoy* acting on television. There's always a moment every day that's worth playing—a situation to rise to. That's all an actor needs. It doesn't have to be great language."

*

The obvious part of an interview with Frid begins when the interviewer asks, "What's a classically trained actor like you doing in a show like this?" Frid, who grew up in Hamilton, Ontario, played his first role in prep school (Sir Anthony Absolute in Sheridan's "The Rivals"), was president of the Dramatic Society at Hamilton's McMaster University (among other roles, Father Barrett in "The Barretts of Wimpole Street") and, after a wartime hitch in the Canadian Navy, went to England to study at the Royal Academy. "I quit after a couple of terms because I wanted to get out and work. I found that a lot of Canadian actors were making a barrel of money playing Americans—and I'd gone there for classical training! I wound up touring in a London success called 'The Third Visitor,' in which I played an American gangster."

Frid returned to Canada in 1950, got a part in "The Heiress" in Toronto, "sort of hung around the CBC," studied at Toronto's Academy of Radio Arts under Lorne Greene, another Canadian who has since found his own American bonanza, and then enrolled at the Yale Drama School. "I wanted to direct, and I got my masters degree in directing in 1957, but I did more acting up there than anything else. I played a lot of roles, was really spoiled—Caesar in 'Caesar and Cleopatra,' Aufidius in 'Coriolanus'—and I learned a lot about what makes a play tick. I can 'play-doctor' like nobody's business. After Yale, the first job I had in New York was in a production of 'The Golem' down on Second Avenue. I was in 'Henry IV' at the Phoenix, appeared with the American Shakespeare Festival in Stratford, Conn., and acted in 'The White Rose and the Red,' a dramatization of the War of the Roses, and in Wallace Hamilton's 'The Burning.'" Howard Taubman, reviewing "The Burning" for The Times, remarked on Frid's "notable performance as the intense, almost hysterical representative of the archbishop."

In the light of his background and training, it is easy to assume that Frid regards his stint on "Dark Shadows" as nothing more than a lucrative furlough from True Dramatic Art—one of those reluctant sacrifices to Mammon that, when broached, are often acknowledged with a grin and a rather shamefaced shrug. Not so; Frid is not looking for sympathy, nor is he about to look down on his work in "Dark Shadows." "I don't think it's a comedown at all for me. I used to play some Shakespeare — pretty *locky*, barnstorming

Editing for size

Here is one statement in this book which no photographer will contest: pictures are reproduced too small. But there are two points to consider in sizing: legibility and impact. Legibility is the more important. It is pointless to print so small that relevant detail is lost. Legibility indicates the minimum size: beyond that, the question has to be whether it gains in impact to justify the extra space given. Pictures with strong simple detail can be read with surprising ease even when quite small—the Vampire from the *New York Times* (197) is an example. Even at the smallest size it reads well. It certainly springs out more fiendishly at the larger sizes, but space should be used with discrimination so that the photographs which need it get it and because if everything shouts nothing is heard. Two kinds of photographs require size: those which portray a dramatic event or a huge object (especially where scale indicators are weak), and those where there is fine detail. The liner is an example of the first. To reduce it as we do in 198A is to convert gaping into yawning.

198A Fire on an ocean liner—the picture needs size on first-time use. (**B** *below*)

Can it be read?

Some photographs do not have enough content to justify much space. Here is the one that does. At the size below it merits only a glance, and at a glance it is simply two lines of military traffic. The picture cannot be read. When it can, it satisfies intellectually and emotionally. It is a symbolic moment in the six-day war between Israel and Egypt in 1967. Advancing Israeli armour passes a truck of Egyptian prisoners. We need to see the prisoners, in their underwear, hands on heads, and the Israelis taking a cocky look at them.

The picture editor has to cultivate the ability to recognise the descriptive photograph which needs space and to visualise the effect of compression from an 8 × 10 print. For the layout man there is a rough rule: on a broadsheet page the minimum sizes for a solus picture are eight inches single column; six inches double column; five inches three column. And a good face is often worth more than a single column.

200B (*above*): Israeli armour advancing into the Sinai near El Arish passes a convoy of Egyptian prisoners—but we need the scale of 199A (*left*) to see it

RRENDER
HOTEL
RIALTO
BALLROOM
CHOP SUEY
CHAS. P
CAFE
HUTTON · de CORDOVA
PHIL SPITALNY
7TH WAR
WALGREEN CO.
ASTOR BAR

202A (*above*): John Morris, when *New York Times* picture editor, selected this picture for this book as one of their most memorable—so it is, at the proper size, **202B** (*left*)

Legibility plus impact

Times Square, New York, was an astonishing sight the day victory in the war in Europe was announced: so many people.

Perhaps there is no picture editor in the world who would reproduce it as small as it is above, so obvious is the loss of impact and legibility. But there are not many, either, who would give it the space it needed: you have to turn this book on its side to see what can so conveniently be displayed in a newspaper. Most picture editors would size this somewhere between the postage stamp and the poster, and it would be a loss of opportunity. When astronauts first sent back a photograph of the earth as seen from the moon few newspapers responded as *The Times* of London did: a full page 24ins deep × 15ins wide. Newspapers often forget that the viewer who has seen a picture on a 17 inch television, whether of the moon or Brigitte Bardot, is not going to be enraptured by a smudgy four inches of newsprint.

Chapter 11

Creative Cropping

While there is perhaps a province in which the photograph can tell us nothing more than what we see with our own eyes, there is another in which it proves to us how little our eyes often permit us to see.

Dorothea Lange

Rafael Rodriguez, matador, had a great day in the bullring in Mexico City. The crowd stood in admiration. Jubilant fans carried him, bloodstained, on their shoulders as the police tried to clear a path. That is the picture the photographer took and it is reproduced above. It is admittedly small here, but bigger than the contacts you might be editing that day and, with or without a magnifying glass, you are invited to examine the print for the story the photographer did not see. Not until he had developed and printed the picture did he notice it, yet when one sees a print of reasonable size it is fairly obvious. The answer to the challenge is printed at the foot of the page, upside down to discourage cheating and to satisfy the successful.

The point of the exercise is to suggest that the camera's weakness in the hands of an amateur, its total objectivity, may provide some delights in photojournalism. Many a photograph is ruined because the photographer has 'seen' selectively, failing to register the awkward background or confusion of detail which turns up faithfully in the print and spoils his subjective, emotional vision. Contrariwise, in about, say, one contact in 500 there is something in the print which the photographer neither saw nor intended to take, but which provides a point of interest of its own, superior to the original conception. That is so with the photograph used on *The Guardian*'s front page (204A) during the Congo crisis. There is a touching story in it which *The Guardian* failed to recognise—and which the reader is again invited to detect before turning to pages 205–6.

In the excitement what nobody saw was a young pickpocket filleting the inside of the fan's jacket—foreground left

; GUARDIAN

;hester Friday November 27 1964

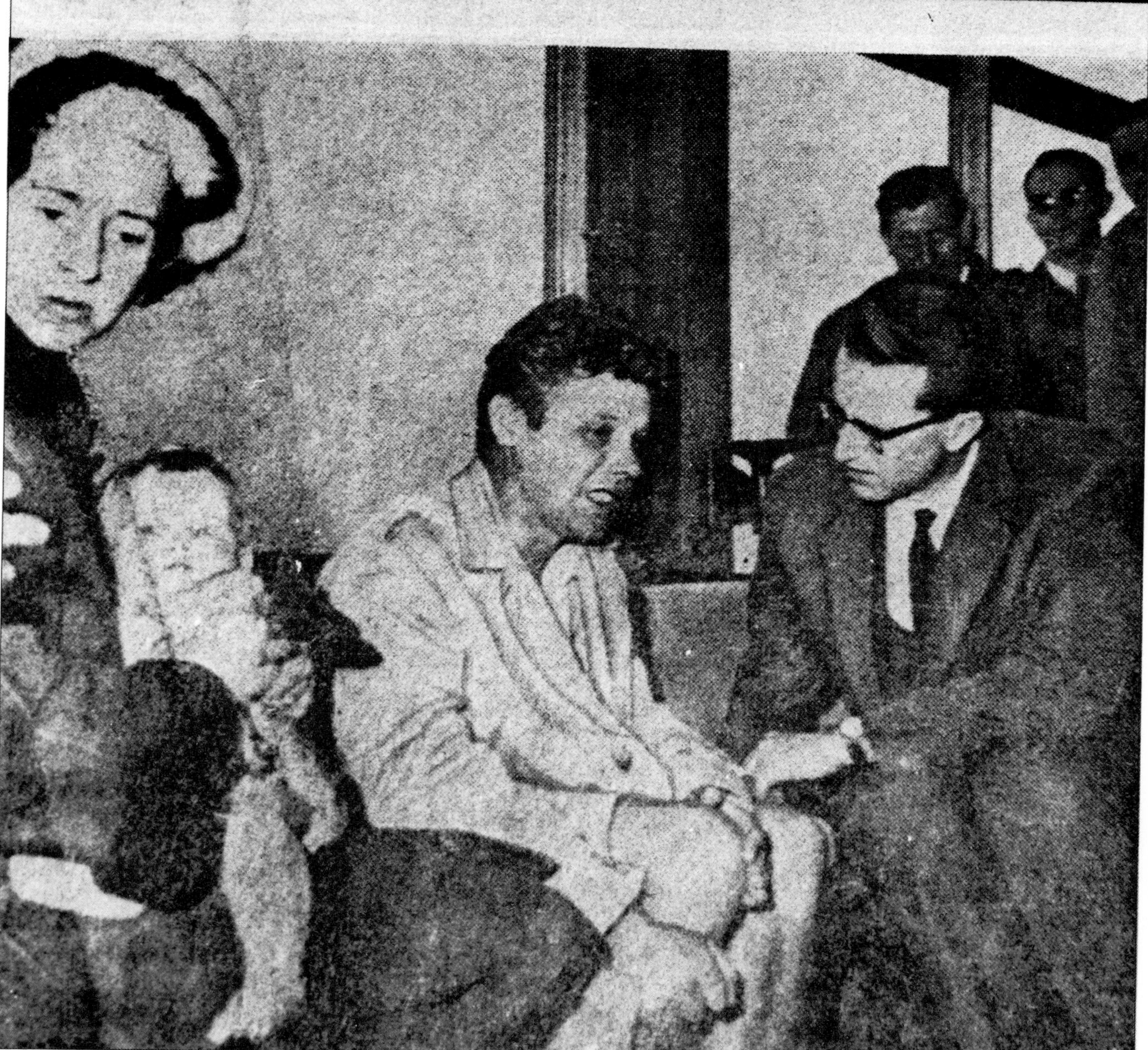

204A *The Guardian* was no exception in using this print exactly as it was received on the wire with the caption: 'King Baudouin and Queen Fabiola of Belgium comforting a refugee from Stanleyville and his 8-month old child at Brussels Airport. The man's wife was killed by Congolese rebels'. But see over

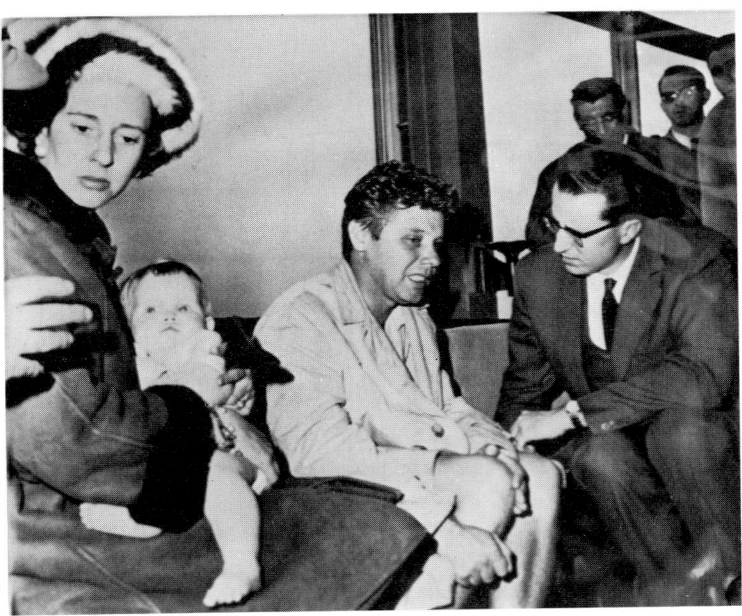

205A The full frame of the King, Queen and refugee; **206A** (*opposite*) is the creative crop obtained from this for *The Northern Echo* (**205B**) (*below*)

The motherless baby

That part of Africa we now call Zaire was in bloody chaos for years after Belgium decided to end 80 years of rule. The new Republic of the Congo descended into a nightmare of army mutinies, killing, looting and rape and a new eruption in 1964 produced yet another stream of European refugees. Pictures of Congo refugees were therefore commonplace, but the one distributed by Associated Press in November 1964 had something special, and it was not simply the presence at the airport of King Baudouin and Queen Fabiola. That part of the news was faithfully recorded by the photographer and almost as faithfully reproduced by newspapers round the world. Yet there was very nearly universal failure to see the real virtue in the photograph.

FLEET (THE FRIENDLY PEOPLE) Rootes Group Agents BUYERS 139/141 NORTH ROAD DARLINGTON for Your New HILLMAN HUMBER SUNBEAM COMMER

The Northern Echo

No. 29,476 (FOUNDED 1869) FRIDAY, NOVEMBER 27, 1964 THREEPENCE

Nediko TEA TIPS DELICIOUS & ECONOMICAL

Stanleyville fighting flares

REBELS IN MASSACRE CITY AGAIN

A husband tells King Baudouin of the Congo horrors.

STANLEYVILLE was a battleground again last night. The Congo rebels driven out of the city by Belgian paratroops, counter-attacked and reoccupied part of the city.

Fierce fighting was going on in the European quarter and one of the African sectors according to reports. Twenty rebels on a golf course near the airport were killed by the paratroops.

And in Paulis, 160 miles north of Stanleyville, a Belgian officer said paratroops were holding the airport and had to stay there to control the situation, which he described as "explosive." The paratroops had freed about 200 rebel hostages in a dawn attack yesterday. One of the freed, Dr. Andre Gotte, Belgian vice-consul, said 16 Europeans and an American missionary had been slowly clubbed to death by the rebels who said they were being killed "because of Stanleyville." Meanwhile the war is being pursued by Major "Mad Mike" Hoare, leader of the white mercenaries in Stanleyville.

A Reuter correspondent said he saw a sniper try to surrender to Congolese military policemen, who told him: "Go away," as the man crossed the road a soldier opened fire, hitting and wounding him three times. Later he saw two Belgian mercenary soldiers searching for rebels fire a burst into a hut and, on entering, find a man wounded in the leg. He spoke to them in Swahili and they then opened fire five times into the man's body.

In one of several anti-West demonstrations yesterday hundreds of screaming students stormed the US embassy in Cairo, set fire to the Kennedy library, smashed cars in the forecourt and broke embassy windows.

In Nairobi and Dar-Es-Salaam yesterday demonstrators protested at the US and Belgian Embassies. In Nairobi, a petrol can thrown at a British diplomatic car parked outside the US Embassy set it on fire. The windows of a

14 die as cruise liner slices tanker

In 1956 the US Atlantic coastline was shrouded in thick fog. A cruise liner was steaming towards New York. A tanker was outward bound. They collided. The liner sank and 51 died — it was the night of the Andrea Dorea disaster.

T least 14 Norwegian sailors from the tanker ... Dagali died yesterday ... collision in fog ... the Israeli liner Shalom 40 miles outside New York harbour.

£ BEGINS TO CLIMB

Caution abroad

THE pound on the foreign exchange market in London yesterday bounced back to its highest level since July 11 following Wednesday night's news of the $3,000m. rescue support by the central banks of 11 nations. Sterling was also marked up slightly on European markets, though full confidence has still to be restored.

In London an early burst of enthusiasm was followed by a lull and slight recession. Then the pound surged to 2.79 and seven thirty-secondths dollars, closing at 2.79 and one-sixteenth, seven-sixteenths above Wednesday night's close.

The upsurge came almost at the time Mr. Callaghan was telling the Commons that Wednesday night's support move would show people's fears about the future of sterling were groundless — and that the Government was going to hold "a strict review" of the whole range of its spending, including overseas defence commitments, to reduce the burden on our balance of payments.

Share prices, too, moved up. Leading shares scored rises of a shilling and more.

The jump in sterling (writes a City correspondent) meant that speculators who have been selling on the assumption that Britain would be forced into devaluation have again burned their fingers.

DEFENCE CUT
Callaghan warns: Page 9.

In New York the pound closed 2.7905 dollars bid, the highest offer for spot sterling since July.

Some European commentators (reports Reuter) said the multi-million support move had given the Government breathing space to work out a cure for the country's underlying economic illness, while others hailed it as a sign of Western solidarity.

A West German Economic Ministry spokesman said: "Any speculator who thinks the pound will ever be left in the lurch will run against a wall of powerful industrial nations."

ROUND-UP

Doctors attack 'miracle' drug

THREE Liverpool doctors today attack the way the new drug Ceporin—developed at Barnard Castle and claimed to be even more effective than penicillin—was launched on the market. It has given rise to false hopes, they say.

Dr. Montague Solomon, Dr. Sylvia Solomon and Dr. Emrys Hopkins say, in a joint protest in the British Medical Journal, that several of their patients have been led to believe that the drug is a miracle cure which will instantly end their illness.

"We have had the unpleasant task of disillusioning these patients, and have found it a time-consuming process involving several patients daily," they say.

"*We resent the difficulties that irresponsible accounts have given, and are angry at the painful disappointments that have resulted.*"

Glaxo replies

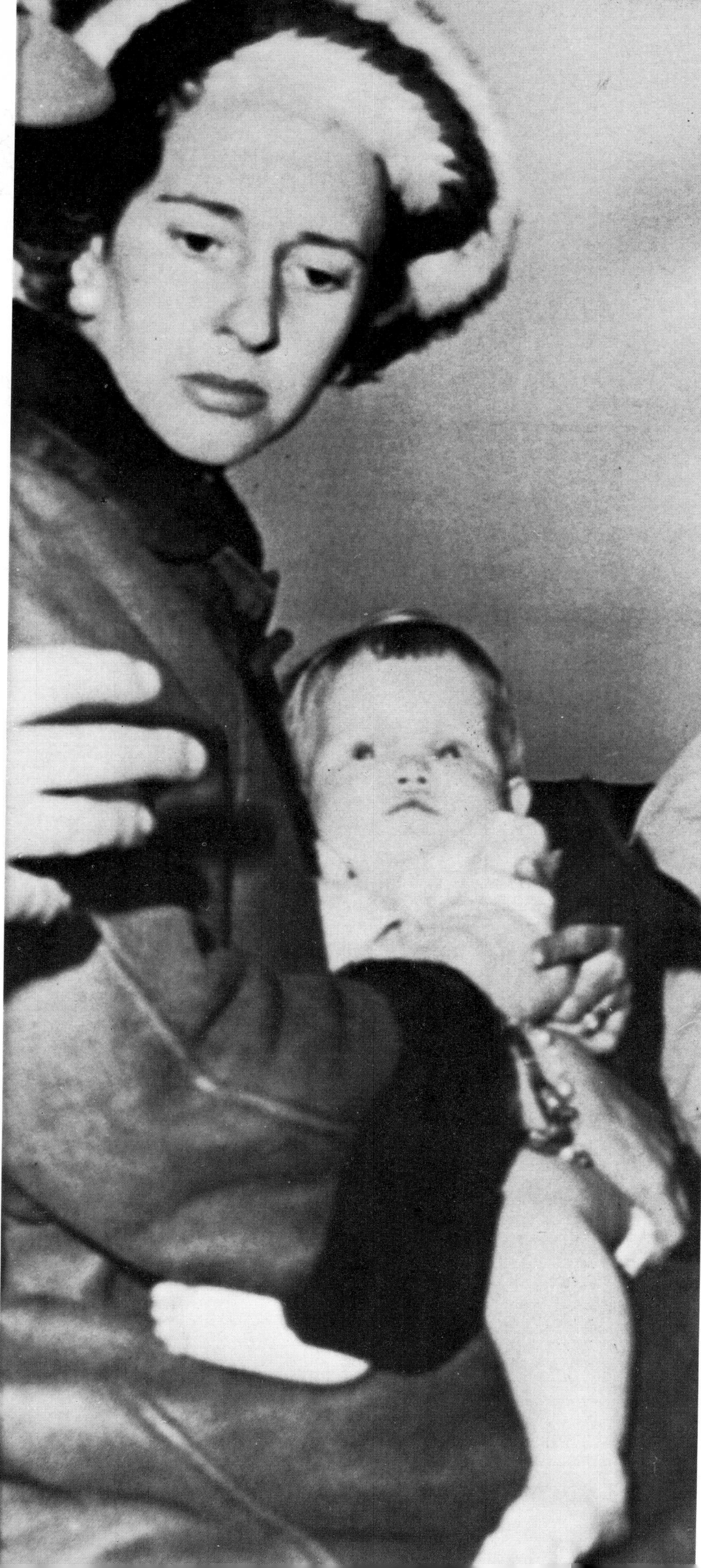

It should, in its original state (205A), have provoked worry since the uninteresting grey area above the refugee's head cannot be cropped off without cutting into the Queen. In 204A *The Guardian*, curiously, made no attempt to cut in from the right where the bystanders are an obvious distraction but cropped in from the left so that it spoiled the shape of the Queen's face. And this is where the real story lay and where the caption in a muffled way pointed us. The man's wife, it said, had been killed by Congolese rebels. It did not go on to make the next statement, which is the key to the cropping the picture requires: that the baby in the Queen's arms is motherless. Once we have received the idea of the Queen nursing a motherless baby our attention moves to the innocence of the child's face and the sadness in the Queen's, epitomising the grief of the Belgian people. Meaning is distilled from confusion.

The cropping (206A) carried out in *The Northern Echo* gives its page (205B) an appeal far superior to that of *The Guardian*. It was possible also to cope with the omission of the King and the father by making a small photograph of these two, which *The Northern Echo* chose to put alongside its main headline, though it might easily have gone elsewhere. The only criticism one might make of *The Northern Echo*'s presentation is that, having decided to present the Queen 'mothering' the baby, it does not point up this poignant feature in a small headline or strong display type above or underneath the photograph (see Chapter 15).

Enlarging the key image

If cropping is neglected in newspapers, creative cropping is virtually unheard of. The distinction I draw is between cropping which accepts the main subject as presented in the print, and cropping which creates a new focus of interest. The first is concerned mainly with excluding extraneous detail; the second is the recognition that a portion within the picture is really its main story. Clearly there are gradations between routine and creative cropping, and this spread is concerned with two photographs which are links between the two related concepts. The editing of Mrs. Eisenhower at former President Eisenhower's funeral (208A) is nearer to routine cropping; and that of Mrs. King at Martin Luther King's funeral (207A) is nearer to creative cropping, though it is a difficult picture. It would be possible, of course, to crop in very closely on Mrs. Eisenhower's face, but aside from a feeling for privacy this would be wrong. The flag on the coffin and the military insignia are both relevant if there is to be a single image from the funeral of the former General. With Mrs. King it is obvious that the background brickwork should go, but how much of the accompanying party should be retained? The suggested crop has the infelicity of cutting through the face of the man at the right; but if he is left in as the sole figure at the right he attracts too much attention. But that is not all. The essence of creative cropping is the tremendous enlargement of the key image. Generally the saving of space on inessentials is such that this can be achieved without giving an inch more space than the original picture would have taken.

There is nothing automatic about such cropping. It requires careful study and trial masking, and there is room for differences of judgment. In difficult cases it is worthwhile, if there is time, having trial stats made to scale.

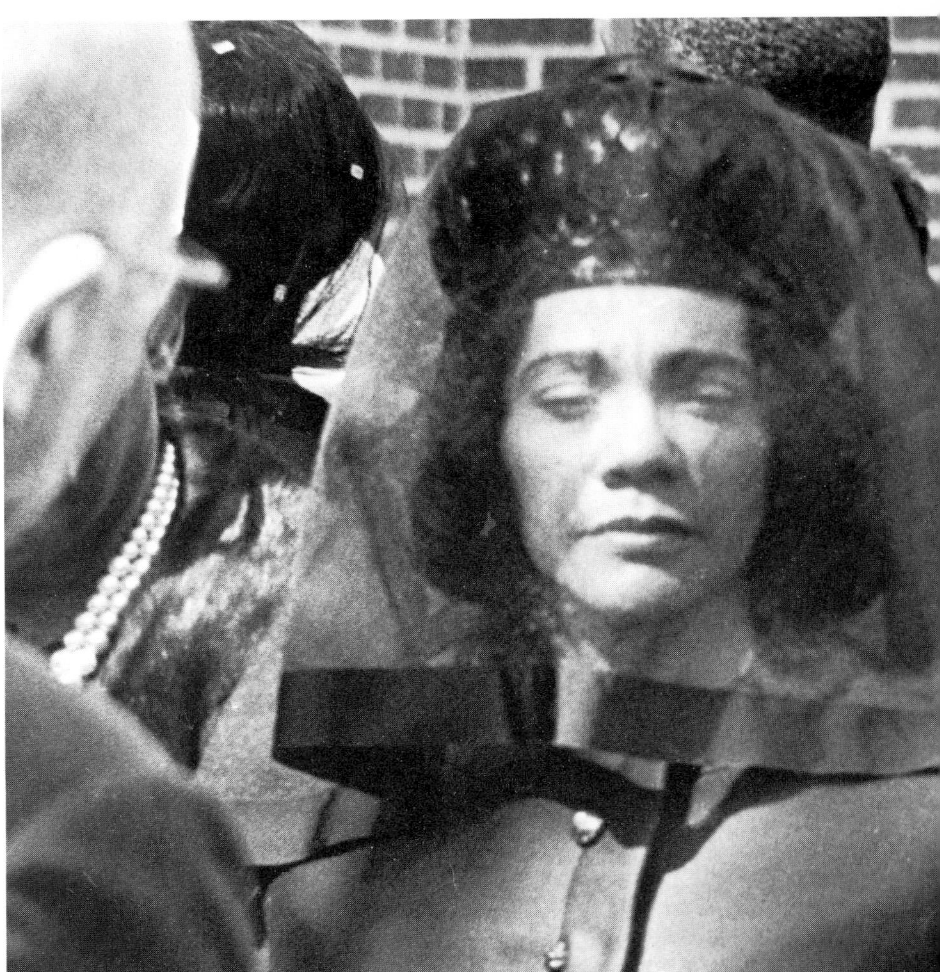

207A and **207B** Mrs Coretta King at the funeral of the assassinated Negro leader Martin Luther King in Atlanta, Georgia, on April 9, 1968. Vast crowds, estimated at anything from 60,000 to 100,000 surrounded the Ebenezer Baptist Church, in the heart of Atlanta's Negro section where Dr. King and his father were co-pastors. At some stage the photographic coverage had to do its best to portray Mrs. King. **A** (*above*) is an enlargement of a detail in **B** (*left*)

208A and **208B** Dwight David Eisenhower, General of the Army and 34th President, was laid to rest on April 2, 1969 in a chapel in the Eisenhower Library grounds in Abilene, Kansas, his boyhood home. **A** (*above*) is a not-too-intrusive editing of **B** (*right*), showing his widow, Mrs. Mamie Eisenhower. She took away with her the foreground flag which draped the casket throughout the military burial service

The two kinds of cropping

These pages compare 'routine' and 'creative' cropping. Here blind Helen Keller, aged 73, runs her sensitive fingers over President Eisenhower's face. Miss Keller, also deaf and virtually mute from infancy, had contact with the world through Miss Polly Thompson who developed a touch alphabet she could spell out on Helen Keller's hand. That is Miss Thompson's hand at the bottom of the full frame (209A *right*.) The story of the hand alphabet, however, was well known. What was new was the meeting with President Eisenhower and the moment when Miss Keller satisfied a desire to 'see' the President's smile. There is such expression in her face, and the hand on the President's face is so extraordinary a sight, that the picture editor made the decision to spend all the space on that. It was a materially small 'routine' crop—though brave—and can be contrasted with (210) opposite.

209A and **209B** Full frame (*top*) and crop (*above*) of the visit to the White House in 1953 by Helen Keller, the blind pioneer in helping the handicapped. By manual sign language afterwards she told her companion the President had a gentle smile

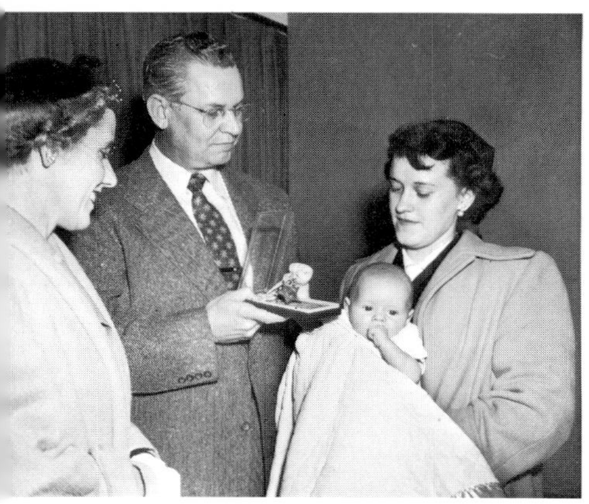

Would anybody have noticed?

Charles Corte's picture of Helen Keller with President Eisenhower (209) was arguably improved by cropping but hardly transformed. It was altogether a memorable photograph. On this page, as with Queen Fabiola (204), creativity lies in a crop which rescues an apparently dull photograph. Francis Colton Hammond, a corpsman in a Naval Hospital, died in the Korean War and was posthumously awarded the Congressional Medal of Honor. The Secretary of Navy and his wife received the widow and her baby son in the Pentagon and the medal was duly presented. This is what the full frame (210A *left*) faithfully records and the picture had little pull. But creative cropping makes a fine news picture out of a passable one (210B *below*). The baby is the story: Francis Colton Hammond, jnr, is having a good suck at his thumb, but he's not letting go of his father's medal.

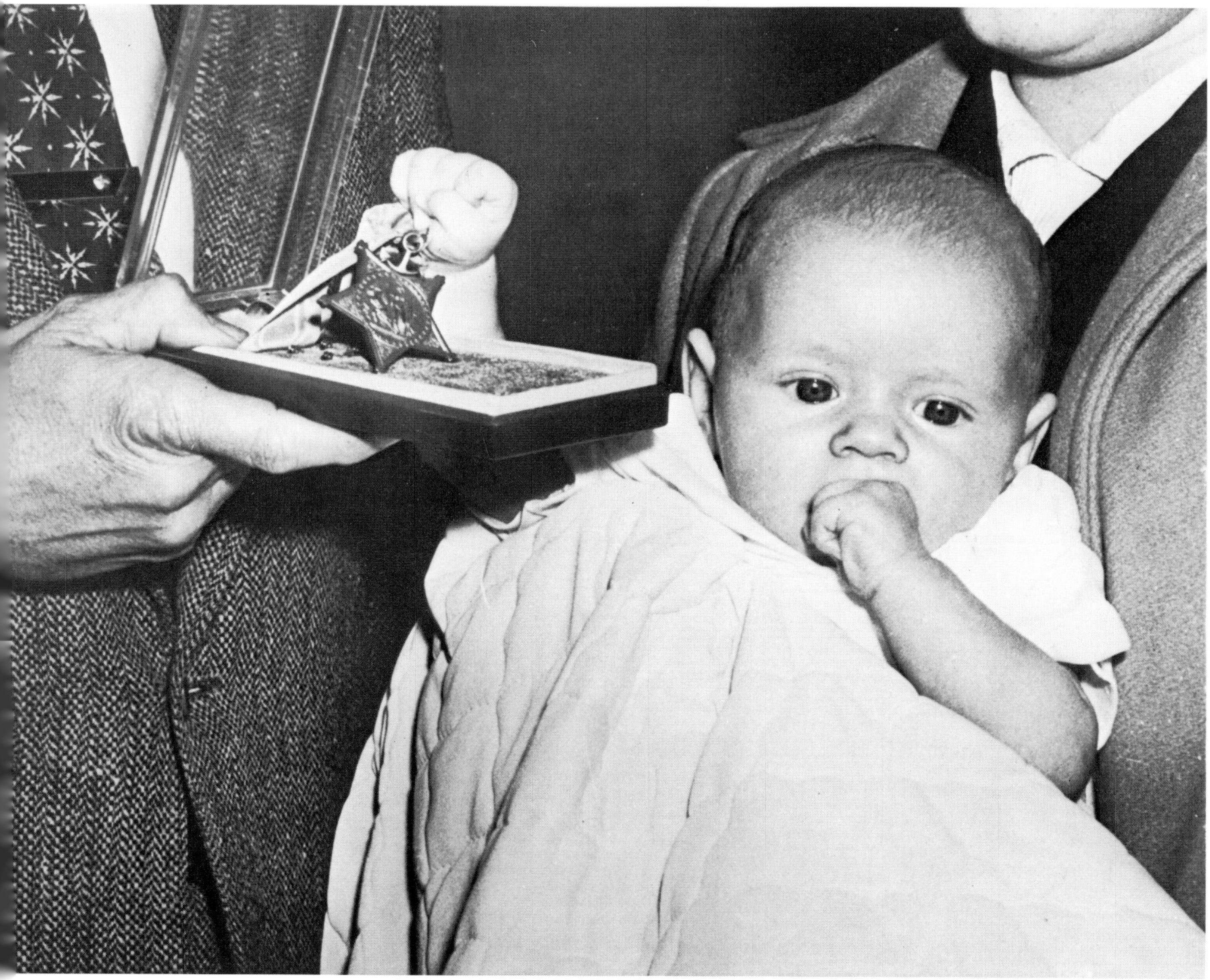

210A and **210B** Full frame (*top*) and crop (*above*) of Francis Colton Hammond jnr at the ceremony in the Pentagon in 1953 to present America's highest medal in the Korean War

211A The Tory Party leadership at conference during opposition days in 1967

211B Creative cropping—Mr Enoch Powell (*left*) and Mr. Edward Heath

Hard choices

It is easy to acknowledge that a significant detail should be emphasised. It is harder to do it in practice. There is a natural temptation to equivocate—to include that little bit extra, such as leaving in Mrs. Kennedy (212C) or the speaker Sir Alec Douglas Home, in 211A. The inclination to do that is strong in 211A since Mr. Powell and Mr. Heath, left and right in 211B are expressing different attitudes to Sir Alec. Mr. Powell had refused to serve in Sir Alec's Cabinet. But though he is back in Mr. Heath's shadow Cabinet, little love was lost between them—the justification for the decisive crop, a striking expression of their alienation.

The top of the Union flag draping the table is retained for context, tonal colour and the directional effect of the lines.

Daily Mirror

FAREWELL

Tuesday, November 26, 1963 • No. 18,642

A little boy's last salute

A BOY stands in the sunlight . . . on his third birthday. But it is a day when his world is in shadow.

It is a day for a brave man's son to be brave. No time for tears.

So John Kennedy salutes as the coffin of his father, the dead President, is borne from St. Matthew's Cathedral in Washington.

It is hard to take in all the deep meaning of the moment.

Honours

He is not thinking—like the great ones who have come to mourn—that it is the President of the United States who is receiving the last honours.

All he knows is that he will never see his father again. . . .

The man who, only a few days ago, romped with him. . . .

The very busy man who was looking forward to his son's very special day . . .

America's saddest day
—See Back Page and Pages 3, 4, 5, 7, 16 and 17

212ABC The family mourning group at the funeral of President Kennedy had to be recorded, but when it was—in many photographs and television pictures—the right treatment of **C** (*below*) was the *Daily Mirror*'s **A** (*left*) and **B** (*above*), John Kennedy, jnr saluting his dead father. It was the boy's third birthday

FLYING ENTERPRISE SINKS IN HEAVY SEAS

MASTER AND TUG'S MATE SAVED AFTER JUMP INTO WATER

The American cargo ship Flying Enterprise sank yesterday afternoon after drifting all day in a strong wind.

Captain Carlsen, the master, and Mr. Dancy, mate of the tug Turmoil, jumped overboard just before she sank and were picked up by the Turmoil, which reached Falmouth last evening. The two men spent the night on board the tug.

SHIP'S LAST MOMENTS

DAY OF DRIFTING IN STRONG WIND

From Our Special Correspondent

FALMOUTH, JAN. 10

The American cargo boat Flying Enterprise sank at 4.10 p.m. to-day, about 41 miles from Falmouth. Just before she sank Captain Kurt Carlsen and Mr. Dancy, the mate of the tug Turmoil, jumped into the water from the funnel of the Flying Enterprise and were picked up

INSURANCE MARKET REACTIONS

GENERAL DISAPPOINTMENT

FROM OUR INSURANCE CORRESPONDENT

When the marine insurance market in London opened yesterday morning it was clear that the prospects of salving the American steamer Flying Enterprise had deteriorated seriously. The change for the worse in the situation was indicated in a first quotation of 50 guineas per cent. to cover the risk of the total loss of the ship, which compared with 25 guineas per cent. quoted at the close of business on Wednesday. By early in the afternoon the rate had risen to 60 guineas per cent.

213A For nearly two weeks the *Flying Enterprise* made front page pictures and headlines (**213B** *above*). Would Captain Carlsen go down with his ship, or see it to port? The picture story required skill and courage. On one mission, the plane took off in sunshine but ran into thick cloud near the ship. Pilot and photographer went down to fifty feet: 'We'll find the ship', said the pilot, 'when we hit it'

213D After eight days, a scoop picture—Kurt Carlsen, with a cheery wave from the side of his ship

213C Almost gone . . . but by this time the drunken *Enterprise* was too familiar a sight for such a picture to be noteworthy

Uplift for a running story

The captain stayed on his sinking ship in the Atlantic and the world watched. For nearly two weeks the ship kept afloat, tilting more to the ocean every day, sometimes in tow, sometimes adrift in storm. The drama of the ship, the *Flying Enterprise*, and its captain, Kurt Carlsen, began on December 30, 1952, when the fifty passengers and crew were taken off by the American vessel *Southland* in the worst Atlantic gale in thirty years. The 6,711-ton *Enterprise* had a 60° list to port, but Carlsen refused to leave. Every newspaper was soon clamouring for a photograph, and in a day or two, there were hundreds of publications of the aerial views of the ship (such as 213A). It was a week later before a great scoop picture was taken (213D): a photo plane took off in bad weather, saw a hole in the cloud and went through to find Captain Carlsen waiting for them, clinging to the deck rail. By this time, in desperate endeavours, the tug *Turmoil*, from Falmouth, had secured a tow line to *Enterprise* and another act of great daring had taken place when the tug's mate, Kenneth Dancy, had leapt aboard the ship to help Carlsen. There were more photographs of the *Enterprise*, its list increasing, as the *Turmoil* towed it nearer safety. The one at (214A) would have been unexceptional at full frame, after so many pictures of the listing ship. However, creative cropping and enlargement showed us for the first time Carlsen and Dancy together in their ordeal, lolling against the deck rail like two men leaning on a garden fence during a Sunday morning chat. There is none the less a marvellous sense of danger and queasy disequilibrium in contemplating this crop with the conflict of diagonals from the funnel and the guard-rail. Less than 24 hours later, the tow line broke, the ship lay at 90° on the roll in bad weather. Both men plunged into the sea and 'swam like hell', just before the *Enterprise* went down.

214A (*top*) appears to take the story no further. But cropped as in **214B** (*above*) it is a different picture altogether

DAILY HERALD

No. 13079 (C) Tuesday, February 14, 1961 Price 2½d.

Fair and Free

THE FLIRTING HUSBANDS
See Page 10

ESCAPE OR MURDER?

SATURDAY'S HERALD POSED THE QUESTION

Now Lumumba's death threatens civil war

CONGO REVENGE FEAR

U.N. alerts troops

THOUSANDS of Europeans in the Congo last night feared a wave of vicious reprisals against the murder of ex-Premier Patrice Lumumba.

The brink

The certificates

One of the last pictures of Lumumba. With him, Joseph Okito.

Crash train blazes—3 die

A PASSENGER train burst into flames after smashing into a goods train at 40 m p h last night. Three railmen were killed and 10 other people were injured.

The fire was in the first coach of the four-coach passenger train. Fifty firemen fought the blaze at Baschurch, Shropshire, and it was under control after an hour and a half.

The dead were the driver and fireman of the passenger train and a railman travelling on the train.

Jumping

Way out in front!

TEMPLEGATE, top of the racing tipsters, raced further ahead yesterday.

His nap won at 11 to 2, and these selections now show a profit on a £1 stake of £12 3s. 6d.

And his double succeeded, too, at 16 to 1. On the season his doubles show a profit of £55 8s. 6d.

You CAN'T AFFORD to miss the Herald!

See Page 11.

Now Touche may resign

POLITICAL CORRESPONDENT

SIR GORDON TOUCHE, the Deputy Speaker, will decide today whether to resign after the unprecedented Opposition attack on him which alleged collusion with the Government.

CONFIDENCE

Debate: Page Nine.

Michelmore trapped in lift to studio

By PHILIP PHILLIPS

GET HART

'SURPRISE' IN RHODESIA PLANS

By HAROLD HUTCHINSON

THE Cabinet is ready to impose the Northern Rhodesia Plan on the Africans and the white settlers despite the protests of both sides.

Belsky's Cartoon

George Formby ('I'm lucky') to wed teacher

HERALD REPORTER

GEORGE FORMBY is to marry again — just 50 days after the death of his first wife Beryl.

SAID 'YES'

Venus probe is going well

Thousands of the once-deaf are asking...

The arrest of Patrice Lumumba, former Congo Premier, was documented in news photographs in December 1960. He and two of his ministers were shown in Leopoldville as prisoners, roped together in an open truck. The pictures were worth reviving on his controversial death in February **215A** (*above*), leaving the Sunday newspapers with nothing. *The Sunday Times* had a dreary picture of a London protest march (**215C** *below*). *The Observer* scored (**215B** *right*) by creative use of the same library pictures

THE SUNDAY TIMES FEBRUARY 19, 1961

The Economic Factor

TWO Ks WATCH THEIR STEP

U.S.-Russian Tightrope

By HENRY BRANDON

WASHINGTON, Saturday.

THE Kennedy Administration, despite the provocative Russian threat of unilateral intervention in the Congo and a "declaration of war on the United Nations," remains for the time being undeterred in its intention to seek what the President has called "harmonious" relations with the Soviet Union.

Cool and Confident

Looking Over Shoulder

"Border" Industries

Police push back pro-Lumumba demonstrators in London last week.

This map shows the provincial boundaries of the Congo, with the distribution of some of the main tribes.

Was Lumumba Murdered a Month Ago?

BY A SPECIAL CORRESPONDENT

ELISABETHVILLE, Saturday.

HARDLY anyone in Elisabethville thinks Lumumba died in the manner described by the Katanga Government—escape followed by death at the hands of loyal Katanga villagers.

THE QUEEN GOES TO CALCUTTA'S RACES

By GAVIN LYALL

CALCUTTA, Saturday.

INDONESIA IS ARMED FOR NEW GUINEA BLOW

By RICHARD HUGHES

HONGKONG, Saturday.

INDONESIA'S Defence Minister, General Nasution, I learn, has informed President Soekarno that Indonesia has now achieved "decisive air, naval and army superiority in the New Guinea area," and can seize Dutch West New Guinea "in a three-week campaign, with or without United Nations intervention."

Australian Firmness

Police Step Up Patrols to Find Algiers Bomb Rebels

By STEPHEN COULTER

PARIS, Saturday.

Maquis Group

Laos Peace Plan

Vatican Paper's New Look

By HENRY THODY

ROME, Saturday.

A NEW look is planned for one of the world's most widely quoted newspapers, the Vatican's

From the library

The murder of Patrice Lumumba, deposed pro-Soviet Premier of the Congo, was news early in the week. He was said to have been killed by hostile villagers after escaping from

imprisonment. The daily newspapers (215A) were able to fall back on photographs of the occasion two months before when Lumumba, accused of inciting an army mutiny, had been exposed to public humiliation in Leopoldville. The story developed all week but only *The Observer* made a virtue of the absence of live news photographs. Its picture editor, Denis Hackett, noted a detail in the picture library file on Lumumba—the searing change between the face of Premier and prisoner. Hackett cropped and enlarged the faces to produce a feature (*below*) which made other Sunday coverage seem lacklustre (215C).

From triumph to humiliation:

THE SHORT LIFE OF LUMUMBA

THE political career of Mr. Patrice Lumumba was shortlived but startling; it symbolises the sudden and unprepared emergence of African nationalism and its involvement in world politics. Less than a year ago, on July 1, 1960, Mr. Lumumba, aged thirty-five, became the first Prime Minister of a newly independent country the size of Western Europe. It was after his career in the Civil Service had been ended by a short gaol sentence for embezzlement that he turned to politics and in 1958 founded the Congo's first real nationalist party, the *Mouvement National Congolais*. In November, 1959, he was in prison again, for provoking riots against the Belgians in Stanleyville, but two months later he was flown from prison to Brussels for the round-table conference which gave the Congo its independence. After the return of the Belgians he went for help first to the United States, then to the United Nations and finally to Russia. In September President Kasavubu deposed him, and he remained in his house under United Nations protection until his dramatic escape and recapture last December.

Memorable faces

The portrait of Franklin Delano Roosevelt (217A) celebrates the man at full flower, in mid-passage of an unprecedented twelve years of Presidency. It is a famous picture—but also an example of creative cropping, since it is only a section from the full frame (218C) of a 1939 news shot. It is, when cropped, an excellent symbolic moment (see pages 11–12 and 110–111), but the full frame barely allowed us to focus on the tilt of Roosevelt's cigarette holder, a shorthand cypher for confidence.

The powerful head of President Sukarno, suspicious and menacing (218A), was taken by *The Straits Times* from an apparently ordinary picture of him addressing a mass rally (218B). Graininess here increases, if anything, the sense of rough power.

218A What a hundred thousand people at a rally missed—a close up of the face of President Sukarno which the picture editor provided from **218B** (*below*)

18C It's FDR, but at first glance there is so much going on that this icture would not merit the attention it deserves. In the detail (**217A** *left*) nere is a magical moment when features and mood and props coalesce to roject a generic image, one that FDR will live by, one by which he will be neasured and worshipped. It's a political icon, made up in part of patrician ince-nez, jaunty cigarette holder, and that fighting jaw

Case History Highlighting of a visual moment

A mountain of waste from coal mining slid down a Welsh valley and struck the village of Aberfan in 1966. Children in the village school were entombed just after morning prayers. Altogether 116 children died in the wrecked building, many more were injured and 28 adults were killed also. Early news photographs and television showed rescuers digging all night, and aerial views depicted the path of the mountain that moved. They gave only the vaguest idea of what had happened. Photography is limited in its power of analysis. It required graphics to give Aberfan scale, explanation and meaning (see Graphics page 317).

But one first-day news photograph did suggest the emotional catastrophe: Melville Parry's, showing a child being carried from the school wreckage (220A). We can relate to it more easily than the aerial views (front pages at 219A and 219B). The picture won prizes for Parry and his paper, the *Merthyr Express*—but is the full frame the best exposition? It takes time for one's eye to fasten on the child in the policeman's arms, and the posture and expression of the woman just to the right is unclear. Perhaps this is a case for severe cropping, confining oneself to the central image of rescuer, child and woman? This loses much of the crowd and wreckage, but since it is only one of many pictures being published about Aberfan, it could be argued that it is right to concentrate all the space on the single visual moment. This is a crop which is demonstrated on page 221. It is as if we had used a zoom lens; suddenly we are right at the emotional axis of the scene. Yet we have lost something. Other pictures may show the wreckage, but this picture, denuded of its background, has lost the relevant context I advocated in Chapter 3. It could be a policeman comforting a child anywhere; there is not enough which is distinctive about this detail to justify its visual monopoly. The right answer is to match this concentrated view with the background wreckage, and especially to retain the striding figure high on the heap of rubble, which gives context, urgency and scale. This crop, and the original full frame, can be compared by folding back page 220 to face the similar sizing on page 222. It is a cropping decision that requires experiment and justification and it leads us directly into a discussion of cropping problems.

LIVERPOOL DAILY POST

Whole generation of children buried as Aberfan slag tip hits village school

200 LOST BENEATH THE MAN-MADE MOUNTAIN

Premier flies to disaster area

Councillor gave a warning in 1964

Freedom honour for St. Helens alderman

THE TIMES

200 LOST AS COLLIERY TIP ENGULFS SCHOOL

Mothers join in night search for their buried children

85 BODIES RECOVERED, 36 INJURED

Prime Minister promises all help

ABNORMAL RAIN BLAMED BY COAL BOARD

Paint flung at President's car

LAUNDRY CHARGES PEGGED

C.B.I. furious over order

Strike ties down 51 ships in London

'Estate Duty Planning'

Send for free copy

BOY WATCHED TWO OF HIS FRIENDS BEING SUCKED AWAY

219A and **219B** Front pages on the day after the mountain moved tended to concentrate on aerial views

220A The human scale of the disaster—the prize winning picture of a child being carried from the wreckage of the school

221A An extremely tight crop of the full frame at **220A**. *Right*, **222A**, the preferred crop. The figures in the foreground and sides of **220A** have been excluded. The directional value that one or two of them have is destroyed by other postures which divert attention from the central scene

Chapter 12

Cropping Problems

A photograph is usually looked at—*seldom looked* into.
Ansel Adams

Cropping can often improve and occasionally transform. It can also create an untruth and ransack a photographer's perception. Much of the art of picture editing lies between these two sentences. The stress of the previous two chapters has been on the rewards for vigorous cropping, but it would be a calamity if the present lethargies were replaced with zombie cropping. Cropping is more complex in photojournalism than in personal or exhibition photography. There is not only the composition of the photograph to consider; the occasion and place of publication must also influence judgement. A good photograph may have to be cropped because it has been overtaken by other visual news (the *Flying Enterprise*, page 214, for example), and a bad photograph cluttered with 'extraneous' detail may have to be published full frame if news makes the clutter relevant. And over-riding any consideration of art is photojournalism's obligation to the truth. The photograph opening this chapter is of Mrs. Margaret Trudeau with her husband Mr. Pierre Trudeau, the Canadian Prime Minister, shortly after her controversial absence with the Rolling Stones in 1977 (and before their formal separation). They are in the dressing-room of a ballet dancer who is demonstrating a movement from Romeo and Juliet and Mrs. Trudeau is miming it. At full frame the picture represents normal, engaging behaviour. But some newspapers cropped the ballet dancer where the black line appears, defensible perhaps to lose the dull area but indefensible without caption explanation of what was going on. They made Mrs. Trudeau seem to be some loony doing a gig.

DAY TIMES

reports every n
London's not-so
IN COLOUR

MPs

p
d

nt

ttending the Parlia-
arty meetings until
nentary Party had
pportunity of deal-
allegations against
y had had an
of explaining
ion; and until the
s wisdom or other-
decided to with-
hip."
id Winnick, who
the Government in
was also critical:
y opposed to the
from party meet-
e colleagues who
ast Thursday."
ditionalists, with
, seem to agree
ilkin should have
the liaison com-
ne link between
ary Party, the
t and the Whips.
Douglas Houghton,
of the parliamen-
has summoned the
to meet tomorrow
Wednesday.
in, however, is
to defend himself
His case will be
Chief Whip must
val every time he
s M Ps individually
be placed in an
situation.
hough, most of Mr
tics breaking sur-
night appeared to
e of the fact that
n committee has
a new code of con-
uide M Ps. This
issued in a week's

Philip Jones-Griffiths

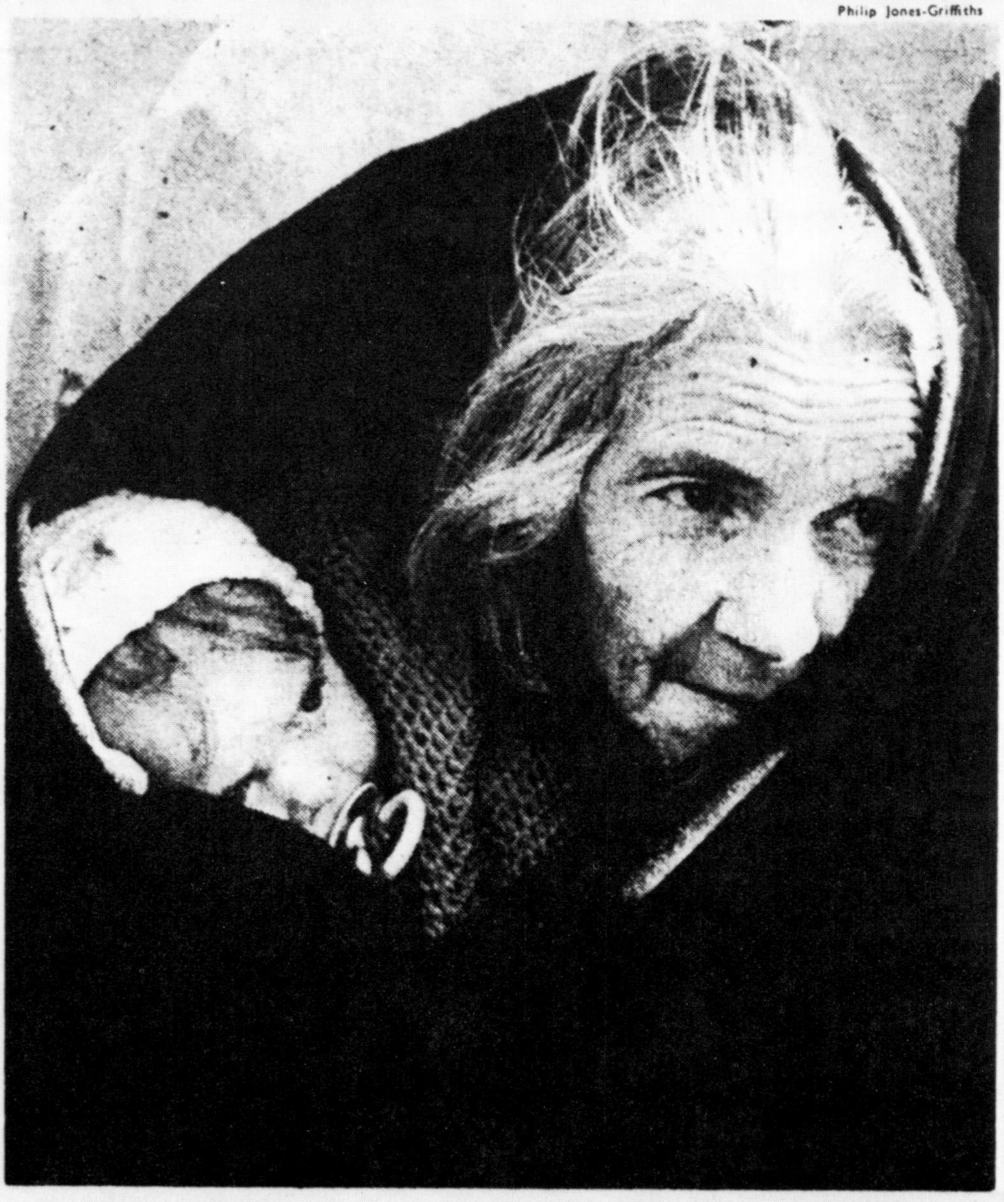

One picture sums up the terror of Sicily . . . old and young, homeless and terrified

Disease hits quake victims

YET ANOTHER strong earth tremor rumbled through Western Sicily yesterday as sickness and disease spread among the 60,000 made homeless by the week's earthquakes, which have

Doctors report that pneumonia, bronchitis, influenza, scarlet fever and whooping cough are rampant, particularly among the homeless children.

tered tents between them. About 80,000 people have either left or been evacuated from their wrecked homes in the quake-hit provinces of Palermo, Trapani and Agrigento. Officials

Tories t
Vorster:
We'll se
you arm

By Peter Schirmer
Johannesburg, Saturday

A NUMBER of leading
Conservatives are indica
the Vorster Government
if they return to powe
total ban on arms export
be relaxed, according to
sources in Pretoria.

For this reason, they ar
ing South Africa not to be
hasty in placing long-term
and other contracts with
European countries, as a
of Mr Wilson's arms ban
Christmas.

Several Tory M Ps and
trialists are making
individual efforts to pe
South Africa to postpon
trading switch. Reports
indicate that Britain's po
Confederation of British
try is indirectly backin
campaign, which includes
writing to South African
papers, visits by British
Missions—this year there
be a record 10 missions
exporter groups and cha
of commerce—and visits by
M Ps and supporters.

Among other M Ps, Sir
Douglas-Home is due to
three weeks here as gu
the South African Found
and will have talks wi
Vorster, the South A
Prime Minister. These
likely to cover the Simon
Agreement, which Sir
negotiated in 1955.

Official Tory policy do
favour a complete lifting
ban and would bar weapo
"internal repression."
Britain would again se
South Africa aircraft, fr
and other naval vessels.

Lord Watkinson, a
Tory Minister and leadin
porter, has written in a
paper that he is "glad th
Opposition has now
pledged itself to revers

224A A forceful front page news photograph—but is it the right crop? See page **225A** for full frame

The influence of format

Philip Jones Griffiths went into Gibellina in Western Sicily, devastated by earthquake, and sent back this expressive study in stoicism. *The Sunday Times* (224A) cropped it to feature old woman and baby, with the implication that the baby's mother had been a victim. The concentration was total; all background was painted out. Was this sensible editing or desecration? It is not possible to say without being aware of the circumstances. News photographs are part of a flow of visual information, not abstract pieces of timeless art. The earthquake occurred on Monday and the picture was circulated at the weekend when it was secondary news. The crop turns on questions which have to be considered together.

1: Content: Was anything lost by exclusion? Yes, in the grouping of men. Jones Griffiths rightly says: 'I

225A More than 20,000 were made homeless and 300 died in Sicily's 1968 earthquake. This is the full frame, of which **224A** is a detail

thought their size and strength increased the feeling of the vulnerability of woman and child'.

2: Competition: How much was the picture pre-empted by earlier ones depicting the demeanour of victims? There had been views of people, though less well composed.

3: Story: Was old woman and baby a story on its own? It was suggestive but inconclusive; there was not text detail to support it.

4: Space: Was there room to publish full frame at meaningful size? The earthquake could only exceptionally claim space on the front page. With *The Sunday Times*, the space was given because of the photograph and more could not have been spared.

On balance, therefore, the crop was the right one for that newspaper on that day—but for magazine or exhibition or book the full frame is best. This is a judgement which Jones Griffiths accepts. He believes that with cameras producing a $2\frac{1}{2}''$ square negative cropping is inevitable, but with the rectangle of a 35mm it is possible to crop 'in the camera'. He does not, however, complain here. 'For a magazine I would want to see it all used, but in a news page I expect concentrated blocks of information and images like this'.

There is no doubt about the bad cropping of 226A and 226B. But see page 227.

226A (*top*) and **226B** A soldier comes home from Vietnam and prisoners from jail help out with flood defences. But the essential element of both stories has been cropped off. See page 227

Infelicities and occasional idiocies

Zealous cropping killed the story points in both the photographs on page 226. In 227A we see the discarded crutch first and then the soldier on one leg, home from Vietnam. In the cropped version it is possible to see that he has only one leg—if you look. But a newspaper picture has to catch a glancing eye in fractions of a second, and without the crutch or a pointing headline the reader may not linger enough to appreciate that this is not just another welcome-home picture. Even if we do read the cropped version quickly, we are deprived of the emotional sense of the photograph in the joyously impetuous nature of the reunion. The temptation to crop springs here from a natural initial desire to lose the large grey area to the right, but even that has a role in diverting attention to the crutch.

The second cropping (226B) is even less defensible. The Mississippi was in such flood that $1\frac{1}{2}$m people had been made homeless, and everyone capable of helping was called in to strengthen the levees. Such was the crisis that even convicts were let out to join the co-operative effort (and later had their sentences commuted). That point can be made in the cropped 226B but the pathos lies in the deleted chains at their ankles (227B).

After every cropping there should be a pause to ask: what has been lost? Is the cropped photograph more or less distinctive than the original? That question would protect 228A. There have been thousands of photographs of the Queen Mother with hand raised in greeting, so that to come in close on the lower part with a horizontal crop (white dotted line) is to emphasise a banality. It is the pyramid of waiters and waitresses and chambermaids and clerks which makes this photograph distinctive. A vertical crop (black line) is feasible but full frame is best.

Is it possible that essential details such as this can be cropped off? The answer must be yes. Agencies producing many prints for distribution often generate howlers. They fail to check that each print is identical; ears, and arms and legs are lopped off in the darkrooms without anyone, it seems, noticing. Clock and layout conjugate most of the newspaper horrors, but photographers' 'paranoia' should begin in the darkroom abattoir.

Every photographer has a private asylum of idiocies. Eugene Smith recalls a Puerto Rico paper reproducing his Minamata picture (123A) without the mother. But infelicities rather than brutalities are the commoner currency. A failure to appreciate the significance of space is probably the commonest error, and it is the subject of the next spread.

227A Ruined by the cropped crutch in **226A**

227B Convicts at work—notice the essential detail cropped in **226B**

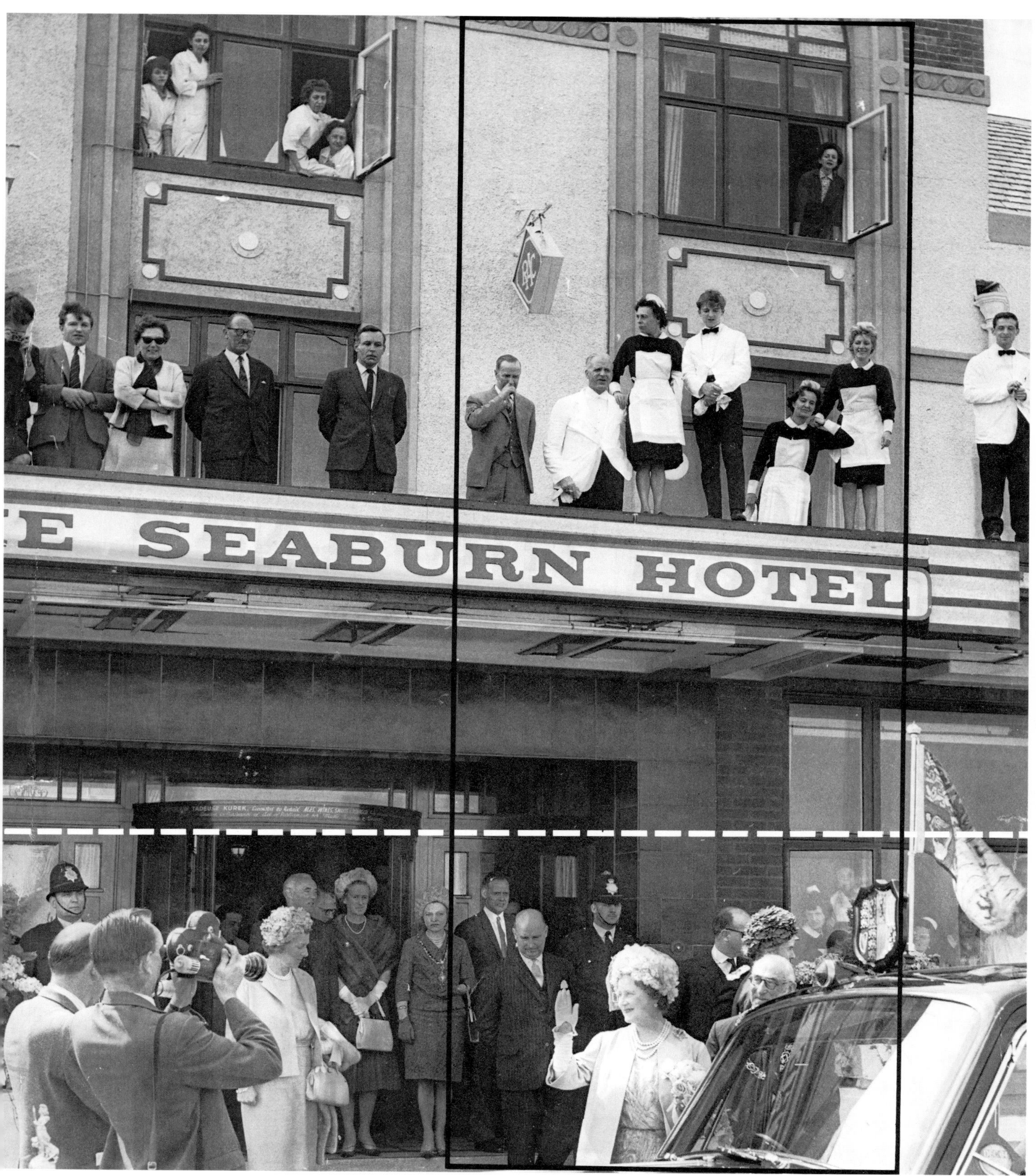

228A The Queen Mother's farewell is a visual story in two levels and both must be retained (compare with **110C**)

229A The South Korean villager had been shot and left to die by the invaders; his last warm breath created the other opening in the falling snow

Active space

There are no short cuts in deliberations about cropping. Patient and gradual experiment with before and after maskings is the only way. It is certainly unwise to assume that an area is expendable because, considered in isolation, it contains no detail of significance or nothing at all. The total effect of each trial crop must be judged: the whole is more than the sum of the parts. The photographs on this spread are at first glance prime candidates for the blue crayon, yet none of them can tolerate any more cropping because in each the apparently wasted space has a positive function. The zealous cropper might easily crop from the right in 229B, to

229B A news shot of a Turkish gunman in Cyprus. The photographer, Don McCullin, worried that it looked like a feature film frame the shadow or even the gunman, but it would ruin the flow of the photograph. The man must have space to run into, space which gives direction and creates expectancy. With all photographs of people running, walking, leaping, riding we have to consider whether there should be more or less space for them to run, walk, leap and ride into.

'Empty' space can also frame an image. In 229A it is the snow which fell and buried the body of the South Korean villager. Not a flake more can be taken off. In 230A every wave is necessary and in 230B the bleak emptiness of the stage and the hostile blackness of the forum point up the forlornness of the girl.

230A The scoop picture confirming that Sir Francis Chicester was alive and well, rounding Cape Horn in a force 7 gale on his single-handed circumnavigation

230B What it's like to be up there for the first time. A debut at a children's dancing matinee. By Beverley Goodway

Document or dramatisation

Jeffrey Miller, a student at Kent State University, Ohio, lies in a pool of his blood (231A). President Nixon had ordered American troops to invade Cambodia, and the extension of the war to defend Vietnam produced protest demonstrations. What happened at Kent State where the National Guard opened fire on students and killed four remained a subject of contention. A reader wrote to AP to challenge this picture: 'There seems to be a very unusual conjuncture: photographer, victim, distressed young lady, and yet no distressed and interested bystanders and no evidence of bleeding. The distressed young lady seems to be more interested in the camera than in the victim . . . and the victim has fallen in an uncommonly orderly fashion'.

But photography was helpful in the later reconstruction of events and this picture was authentic enough, testifying to the location and number of witnesses, some unaware of the tragedy: many said they thought the Guardsmen were firing blanks. As evidence, 231A needs full frame but as news it is primarily an emotive picture which focuses on the girl's outstretched arms as a symbol of anguished protest. That is the point of emphasis if the picture is to be treated as drama rather than documentation. *The Times* cropping (232A) was the worst: too heavy for documentation and too small for drama. The *Express* (232B) was better but the *Mirror* (232C) was best, picking up in the headline Nixon's characterisation of students who protested.

The remnants of bystanders are untidy, but there is not much that could be done, short of retouching; the figure on the right might arguably have been excluded but at some cost to the central figures. There is a compensation. The horizontal shape reinforces the line of the student's body and the girl's arm. John Filo, a photography student, took the picture: 'I didn't react visually. This girl came up and knelt over the body and let out a God-awful scream. That made me click the camera.'

231A John Filo, a student, borrowed a camera and a zoom lens to take this Pulitzer prize winning picture from 30ft

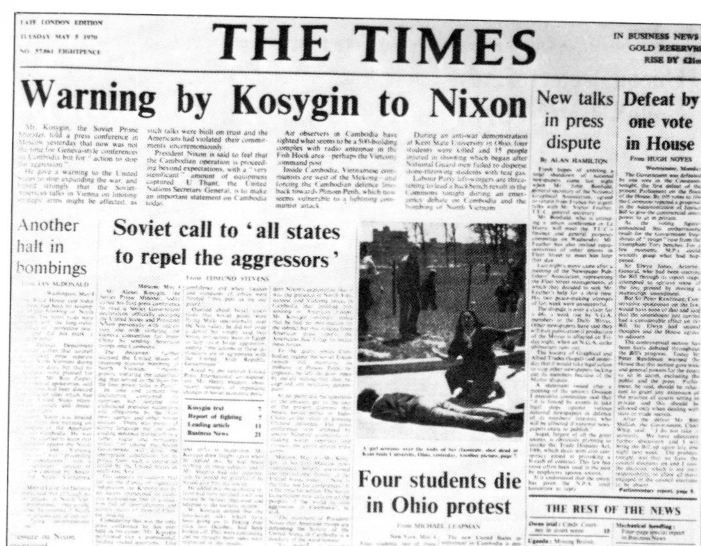

LATE LONDON EDITION
TUESDAY MAY 5 1970
No. 57,861 EIGHTPENCE

THE TIMES

IN BUSINESS NEWS: GOLD RESERVES RISE BY £31m

Warning by Kosygin to Nixon

New talks in press dispute

By ALAN HAMILTON

Defeat by one vote in House

From HUGH NOYES

Another halt in bombings

From IAN McDONALD

Soviet call to 'all states to repel the aggressors'

From EDMUND STEVENS

Four students die in Ohio protest

From MICHAEL LEAPMAN

THE REST OF THE NEWS

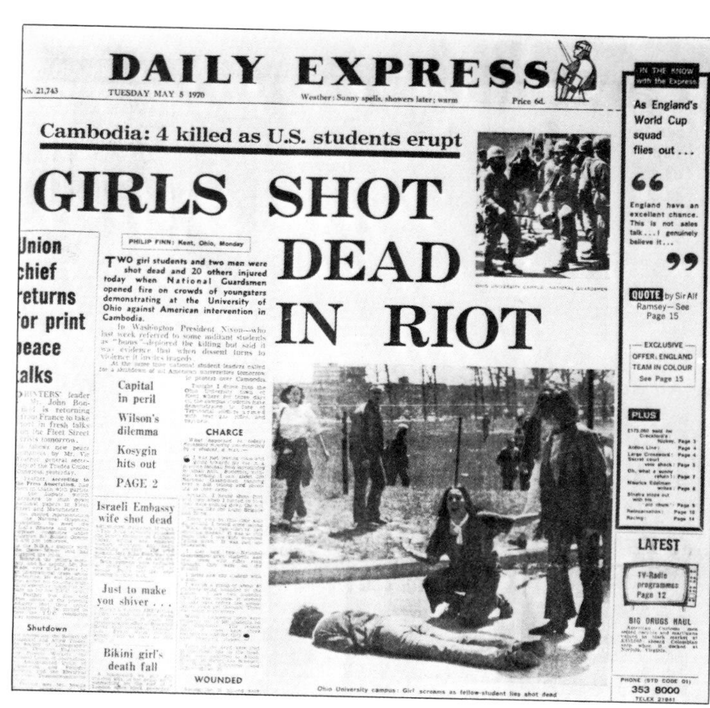

Kosygin text
Report of fighting
Leading article
Business News

No. 21,743

DAILY EXPRESS

TUESDAY MAY 5 1970

Weather: Sunny spells, showers later; warm

Price 6d.

Cambodia: 4 killed as U.S. students erupt

GIRLS SHOT DEAD IN RIOT

PHILIP FINN: Kent, Ohio, Monday

TWO girl students and two men were shot dead and 20 others injured today when National Guardsmen opened fire on crowds of youngsters demonstrating at the University of Ohio against American intervention in Cambodia.

Union chief returns for print peace talks

Capital in peril

Wilson's dilemma

Kosygin hits out

PAGE 2

CHARGE

Israeli Embassy wife shot dead

Just to make you shiver . . .

Shutdown

Bikini girl's death fall

WOUNDED

Ohio University campus: Girl screams as fellow-student lies shot dead

IN THE KNOW with the Express

As England's World Cup squad flies out . . .

England have an excellent chance. This is not sales talk . . . I genuinely believe it . . .

QUOTE by Sir Alf Ramsey—See Page 15

EXCLUSIVE

OFFER: ENGLAND TEAM IN COLOUR

See Page 15

PLUS

LATEST

TV-Radio programmes Page 12

BIG DRUGS HAUL

PHONE (STD CODE 01) 353 8000

232A *The Times* cropped too much for documentation and under-sized for drama. **232B** *The Express* scored on sizing but failed in headline words to create a single picture-headline unit. **232C** The *Mirror* cropped for the central image and effectively linked words and picture.

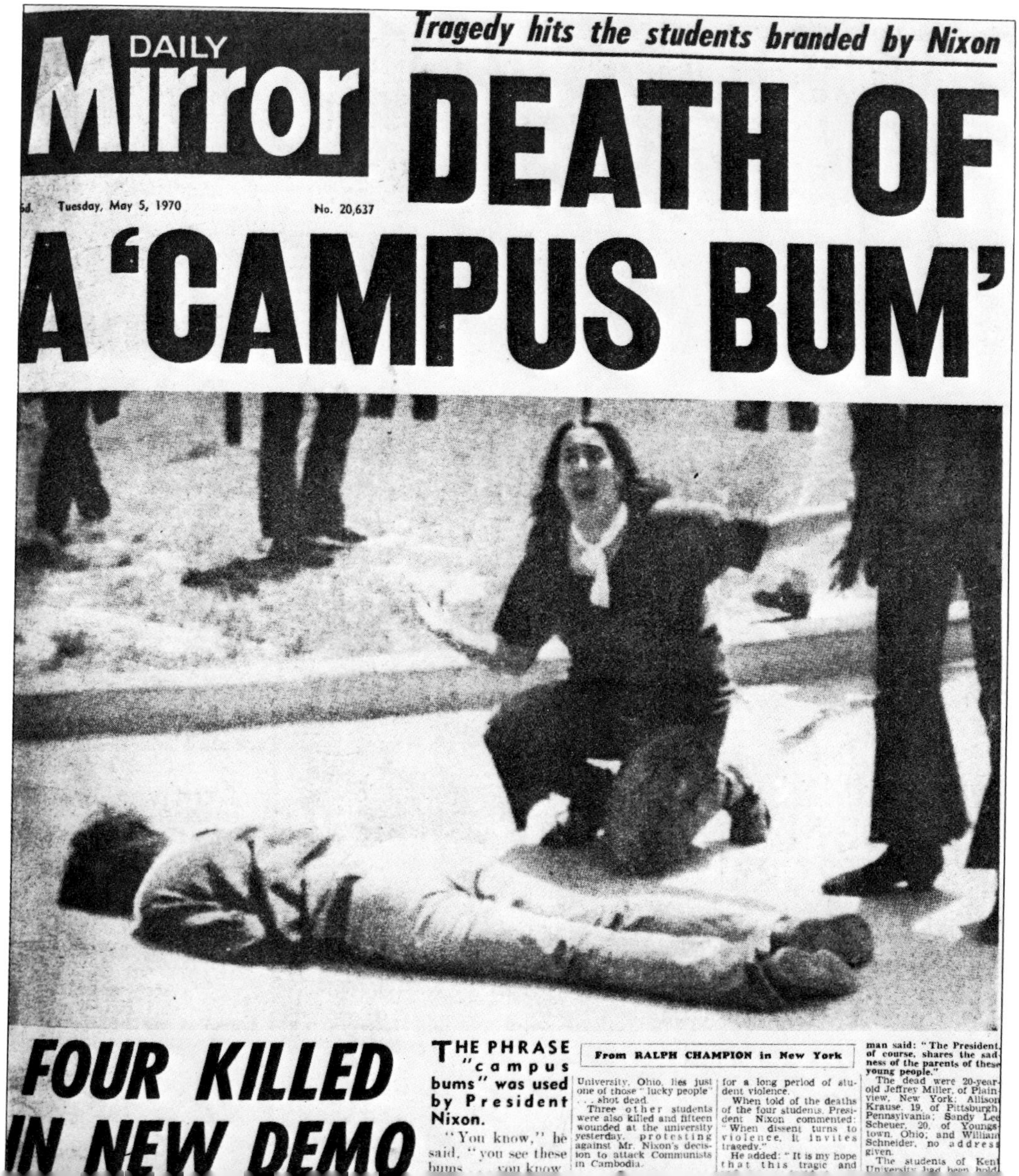

Tragedy hits the students branded by Nixon

DAILY Mirror

6d. Tuesday, May 5, 1970 No. 20,637

DEATH OF A 'CAMPUS BUM'

FOUR KILLED IN NEW DEMO

THE PHRASE "campus bums" was used by President Nixon.

"You know," he said, "you see these bums . . . you know

From RALPH CHAMPION in New York

University, Ohio, lies just one of those "lucky people" . . . shot dead.

Three other students were also killed and fifteen wounded at the university yesterday, protesting against Mr. Nixon's decision to attack Communists in Cambodia.

for a long period of student violence.

When told of the deaths of the four students, President Nixon commented: "When dissent turns to violence, it invites tragedy."

He added: "It is my hope that this tragic and

man said: "The President, of course, shares the sadness of the parents of these young people."

The dead were 20-year-old Jeffrey Miller, of Plainview, New York; Allison Krause, 19, of Pittsburgh, Pennsylvania; Sandy Lee Scheuer, 20, of Youngstown, Ohio; and William Schneider, no address given.

The students of Kent University had been hold

233A Shortly after 4.30 pm on February 7, 1952, at London Airport, the new Queen Elizabeth II is met by her Prime Minister, Winston Churchill. Detail from **233C**

233B Three Prime Ministers, past, present and future, and the Lord President of the Council await their new Queen; another possible crop of **233C**

The Queen's return to London

A small figure in black comes down the steps of the aircraft at London airport: Elizabeth Alexandra Mary, who had gone to Kenya as a Princess, is setting foot on English soil for the first time as Sovereign. King George VI had died the previous morning. The full frame, (233C *below*) presents an intriguing cropping problem. For reasons of protocol (or the want of a longer lens) only creative cropping can give us a picture the photographer might have visualised, but could not take: the close-up of the new Queen descending and her Prime Minister, Winston Churchill, waiting with bowed head. This crop (233A) enlarges the Queen's face and posture and there is an active expectancy in the gap between Sovereign and the First Minister.

Given three or four columns this was a powerful photograph, but does it lose too much? The figures to the left of Churchill represent homage from the Government of England, the leading Privy Councillors in the Cabinet. There are three Prime Ministers, past, present and future—Churchill, Clement Attlee and Anthony Eden. Retaining these suggests the square of 233B, but this is surely an ineffectual compromise. The full line of Ministers has a real news point and the horizontal shape emphasises a moment of respectful obeisance. This is such a historic moment that, even for a newspaper, the line of Ministers should be retained, with the crop indicated by the straight black line so that the BOAC headline lettering would not create a problem by clashing with a news headline). A magazine might well print full frame.

233C Queen Elizabeth II setting foot on English soil for the first time as Sovereign with her Privy Councillors waiting to greet her. The black line is a suggested newspaper crop

EL SALVADOR
EGYPT
UNITED STATES
UNITED KINGDOM

Propaganda

Cropping is not merely an aid to art or journalism; it may be a tool for the unscrupulous. The most notorious modern example was exposed during Senator Joe McCarthy's witch-hunt of alleged Communist sympathisers in the United States during the fifties: his excision of other figures from a snapshot to make it appear that the Secretary of the Army had been solicitously friendly with McCarthy's aide, Private David Schine. Many photographs lend themselves to such manipulation of the truth. As an example, 235A left is the full frame of a debate in the UN General Assembly in which the Soviet delegate Andrei Vishinsky was denouncing the US delegate, Cabot Lodge, with Britain's Sir Gladwyn Jebb downcast in the middle. It is susceptible to different crops to support different meanings. It could be cropped as in 236B *below*—curiously, the print supplied to *The Sunday Times* had more of the scene but did leave off Cabot Lodge. It could then support the idea that Britain was the object of Russia's scorn—a false impression since on this occasion Britain and the Soviet Union were on the same side in trying to gain representation for India to peace talks after the Korean armistice. The US was opposed to Indian admission and Britain and the US untypically parted in the vote. Another crop (236A) could support opposing captions suggesting either (correctly) that Britain was fed up at finding itself on the same side as the shrill Mr. Vishinsky or (wrongly) that Britain was failing to take a proper part in a grave debate.

235A (*left*) The sense of crisis in Mr. Vishinsky's harangue is reduced by the tranquillity of the other delegates. But the picture is capable of several crops (**236A** *top* and *236B above,* for example) to produce a variety of meanings

Chapter 13

The Third Effect

To see life; to see the world; to eye witness great events; to watch the faces of the poor and the gestures of the proud; to see strange things—machines, multitudes, shadows in the jungle and on the moon . . . to see and take pleasure in seeing; to see and be amazed; to see and be instructed.
The Manifesto of *Life* Magazine, 1936

Stefan Lorant, that brilliant editor, who is one of the fathers of photojournalism, recalls seeing a man who looked like a bulldog. He looked round for a picture of a bulldog that looked like a man and published the two side by side in *Lilliput*, the small-sized English picture magazine he edited in the thirties (he was also of course the first editor of *Picture Post*).

That was one of the first juxtapositions or couplings, producing what Wilson Hicks later dubbed the principle of the third effect: 'When two pictures are brought together their individual effects are combined and enhanced by the reader's interpretative and evaluative reaction'. This may sound high flown for bulldog-man, but the coupling of two pictures offers much more than the possibility of a mild joke from similarity of design within each frame or the simple comparisons of then and now, here and there. Lorant, pioneer of the form, developed it for political attack, coupling a flinty portrait of Rockefeller with a beatific peasant and labelling it poverty and riches. He created uproar with a spread comparing Prime Minister Neville Chamberlain and a particularly dozy llama.

Coupling can play off any two images and do it with a minimum of words since they comment and sustain each other. None is needed for the presentation on these pages of the control room and the astronaut (though there are further words about them on page 242). It is not hard to dream up couplings and the reader is invited to think of six or seven before turning the page for a selection put together for this chapter to demonstrate some of the range—from facial resemblances to social comment.

238 Cameraman on the moon, and co-astronaut from Apollo 12 in 1969 caught in the reflection, both dependent on ground control

239AB The Greta Garbo look (*right*) and (*behind*) the real Greta Garbo

239CD Mr. Khrushchev: wolf in wolf's clothin

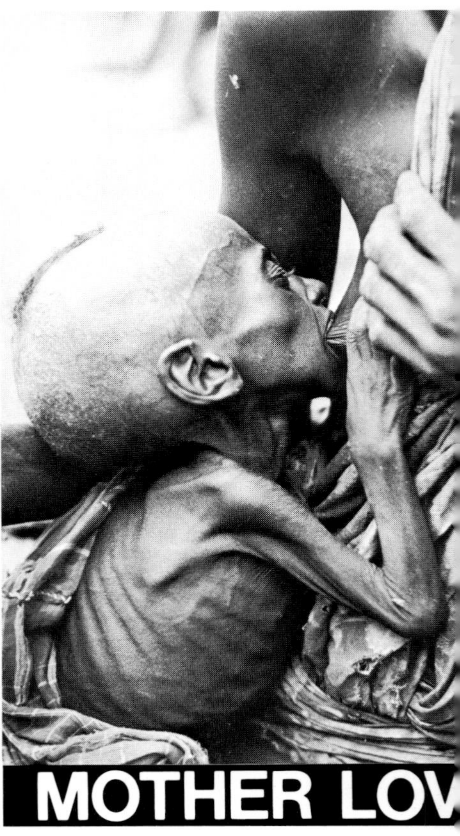

WHATEVER NEXT!

SMALL BOY MAKES GOOD

242B One of Hitler's SS officers took the photograph in Warsaw in the spring of 1943, with the caption 'Pulled out of dug outs and led to death', when the Jewish ghetto was destroyed. Used with a picture of Hitler it makes a forceful combination

Conviction and design

Ideas in two pictures may collide or coalesce to produce a chain reaction of other ideas, the infinite regression of images reflected in facing mirrors. The two or more pictures in a sequence are limited to portraying incremental changes in the same scene. But almost anything that can be imagined can be coupled (Lorant says he keeps ten to twenty thousand pictures in his head) and this gives a range of opportunity as rich as the imagination of the creator and the associative ideas of the viewer. The form is capable of communicating a blinding truth and, much more than the single picture, an inflammatory lie (and of course it can stretch the borders of the banal). Where creative flexibility ends and manipulation begins is a matter for judgement. The pictures of the men in the control room looking at their man on the moon (237–8) are suggestive of teamwork and isolation, the dependence of the astronaut on the control room and their eagerness in turn for his success. Yet if the generalisation is valid the particulars on which it is based are a misrepresentation. The astronauts in 238A had been to the moon and back three years before the men in the control room were photographed and even then they were not looking at an astronaut. They were listening to Vice President Agnew following the launching of Apollo 17, in 1972.

Coupling has design facility. In the moon coupling the eye is directed from one picture to another. Friends and enemies can be made to look at each other, grimacing or grinning. Scale can be compared and dramatised. And juxtapositional design can be exploited to reinforce the central thrust of an idea. The silhouette of Hitler (*left*) is overpoweringly dominant against the Jews being herded to the concentration camps from the Warsaw Ghetto.

There is nothing particularly clever about the design or the underlying idea; that is the source of this example's success. It is forceful because it is simple. It is a huge mistake to assume that more means better. Two pictures can provide a third effect, but there is no automatic progression. Three pictures may add up to nothing, cancelling rather than reinforcing each other's point. It is particularly tricky to collect more images and fuse them in a montage in a single frame. The design of any montage is troublesome for a start. Different units have to be fitted in at different scales which requires sensitive judgement if weird effects are to be avoided; and the shapes have to interlock smoothly as if they belonged together. Multiply the units and you multiply the problems. Even the best publications make a mess of things: ambition outruns art. For even more fundamental than design is the basic concept of a montage. What is it trying to say? There is all too often a collection of images but no conviction. It is the prevalent weakness of picture pages to which we now turn.

A cautionary note

Coupling has its snares. Two mediocre pictures may couple to produce a third effect equal to the power of the first-rate photograph, but it is no reason for stinting the search for the most fitting images. Secondly, coupling represents such an obvious effort it runs the risk of being ponderous: nudge, nudge, wink, wink. And thirdly it is not an end in itself. The principal virtue—or vice—is the ability to relate what it might never be possible to present within a single photograph. It is pointless to do it where a single picture makes the point as well, which is the superiority of the marine with the head tucked underneath his arm.

243ABC The replacement of the portrait of ex-President Nixon (*top left*) with the portrait of President Ford is laboured as a coupling. The single picture works better also because of the indignity of the arm across the portrait. The idea of discarding is stronger

Mirror picture power puts a Soccer thug behind bars

CAUGHT IN THE ACT

1975: Photographer Peter Cook first catches Scott in action.

1977: Monte Fresco snaps Scott at Spurs' match on Saturday.

SOCCER thug Mark Scott was behind bars last night . . . thanks to the Mirror.

A picture taken by photographer Monte Fresco during the Spurs v. Manchester United game on Saturday showed Scott in the thick of terrace terror.

And it meant that TWICE in the past two years, Mirror cameramen have captured his savagery at White

Within hours of Scott's picture being published in yesterday's Daily Mirror, fans phoned us to link him with a picture published by the Mirror in 1975.

And yesterday, police admitted: "Without the Mirror pictures, we would have had trouble getting the thug into custody.

PICTURE ONE was snapped by Sunday Mirror cameraman Peter Cook two years ago when fighting broke out during the Tottenham-Chelsea relegation derby match.

Scott, then 18, was seen lashing out

By JOHN JACKSON

grimacing in pain, reeled under blows thrown by angry fans.

The 43-year-old constable was savagely beaten. Yesterday it was revealed that he will never walk the beat again because of his injuries.

PICTURE TWO was the fast work of the Daily Mirror's Monte Fresco as Spurs and Manchester United fans clashed last Saturday.

Wisbey, who saw Scott throw a stone and then a rock at opposing fans. Scott disappeared into the crowd.

Two hours later, P C Wisbey spotted Scott in Tottenham High Road and arrested him. He was bailed to appear at Tottenham Magistrates' Court yesterday accused of possessing an offensive weapon.

On arrival at court with his father, Scott, a wood machinist, of Carters Mead, Harlow, Essex, said he would be pleading not guilty.

P C Wisbey produced the Daily

Scott changed his plea to guilty.

Magistrate Samuel Kershen w… told he had two previous convictio… for Soccer violence and had serve… three months in detention la… summer.

Mr. Kershen told Scott: "The la… stretch of detention obviously had … effect, so you will go back for anoth… three months."

While Scott was awaiting senten… his father was shown the first pi… ture.

"Hell," he said. "I know nothi… about that. That's it then."

News twice over

Coupling is normally a device for suggesting ideas, but this example from the *Daily Mirror* makes news—and it is a testimony also to the assertion in the first chapter on our readiness to remember still images (pp. 1–10). Monte Fresco took the picture on the right in 1977 when there was violence on the terrace at the Tottenham Hotspur and Manchester United match. Within hours of the picture being published, soccer fans telephoned the *Mirror* to link the attacker of 1977 with a picture they remembered being published in the *Mirror* in 1975. The *Mirror* made a search and found a remarkably similar picture by Peter Cook of the *Sunday Mirror* showing the same youth pounding a trapped policeman with his fist, during a Tottenham-Chelsea match. (The policeman was so badly hurt he had to leave the beat.) As it happened police as well as photographer had observed the 1977 incident and the youth appeared in court. He said he was not guilty. Then he changed his plea: he was confronted with the *Daily Mirror* picture.

Beyond coupling: The picture page and the picture story

The picture story is the ultimate expression in photojournalism. It documents as well as dramatises. It can be looked at again and again and when its message impresses it is passed on to the other people. It is immediate in effect, conveniently permanent in record. But the more pictures one uses on a page the harder, not easier, it is to succeed. There must be a strong motivating idea and it is the absence of any idea at all which dooms the variety picture page, long beloved of British local papers and every other American newspaper. This throws together, say, one smiling politician at a fête, one car crash, one girl being crowned Miss Dakota or Miss Birmingham or one pony/dog/lion which has similar appeal. There is an attempt to give this pizza-pie of a page a unity with headings such as Today's News in Pictures, which it isn't, or It's a Strange World, but there is in such efforts as little conviction as there is meaning in the dissonant contents headline which typically runs Big New Factory—She's Crowned—Too Hot for Him—Champion Bull. The newspaper must produce order from chaos, it must integrate words, pictures, and drawings to create understanding. The variety picture page creates a half-tone ghetto, divorcing pictures from news and depriving the other pages of the relief they gave. It sufficed perhaps when it was an achievement to engrave a half tone at all, but not for today's visually more sophisticated world.

A single subject presentation is preferable, but it has to be emphasised that when it has no theme or thought it is not a picture story or a picture essay. It is, in the phrase of Eugene Smith, a parking lot of pictures. The two terms, essay and story, are used interchangeably in newspapers and magazines, essay being preferred by photographers who want to give themselves artistic airs or who happen to have missed a sequence. A distinction might be suggested. The picture story is essentially narrative, the record of a single event or aspect of it, or a simple chronology such as the account of the first year in the life of a baby (245A). It may imply a comment, but it is descriptive rather than declarative. The essay is not confined by time or event. It may attempt to photograph a generality, an abstraction or a trend—marriage, permissiveness, friendship, women's liberation, competition—and the photographer is restricted only by his imagination. The essay will argue and analyse rather than narrate; it will make points. But it is not for that reason superior. High School (245B) is an essay, a study of the emotions aroused by school sports matches, which is one of seven produced by Jim Richardson from devoting 18 months documenting the everyday events of Rossville High School, Topeka, Kansas. The party's over (246B) is a story, an account of the final stages of the Republican convention in 1976. The common feature is development. Both 'read': we can *see* what is being said. In both the words work with the pictures: the pictures are not simply illustrations of the words.

There are four processes to the successful picture story/essay: preparation; photography; selection; and combination. Luck will make a great single picture sometimes a picture story; it will never produce the development and depth for a picture essay, requiring several pages of a magazine or a whole page of a newspaper. Time must be spent on research, not merely locational but intellectual as well.

The photographer will naturally ponder how the story can be interpreted visually, but he cannot do that unless he first understands what it is all about. The ultimate in dedication must be Eugene and Aileen Smith's visit to the Japanese town of Minamata. They expected to stay there for a few days as part of a three-month picture tour, but they became first

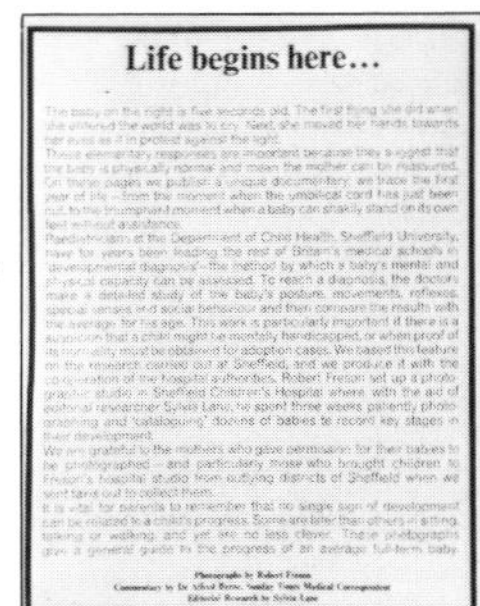

Life begins here...

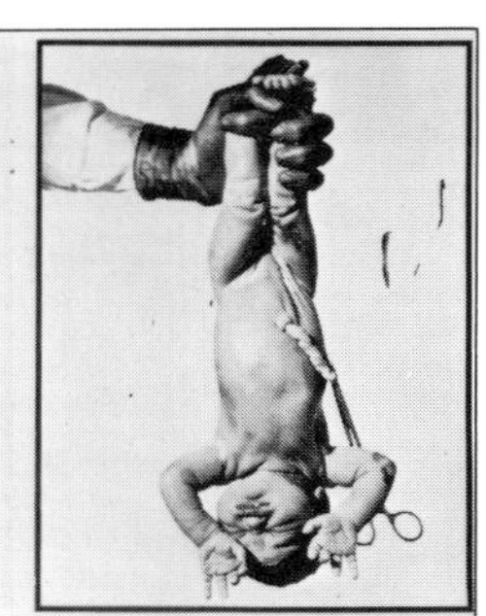

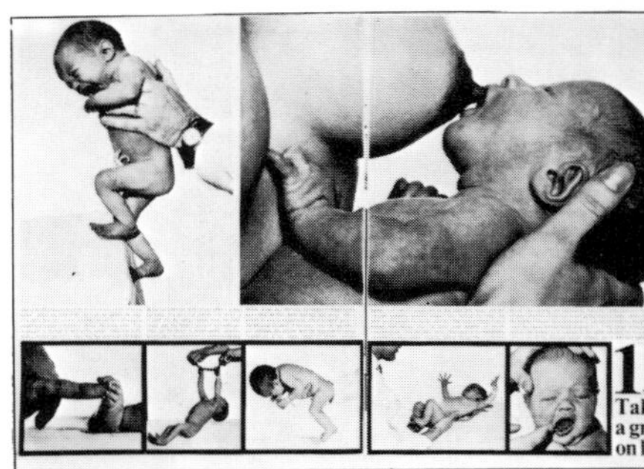

245–6 A BABY'S YEAR: Chronological picture story with the theme on each page elaborated bel

HIGH SCHOOL 3

'When you win they really crowd around'

245B Picture essay

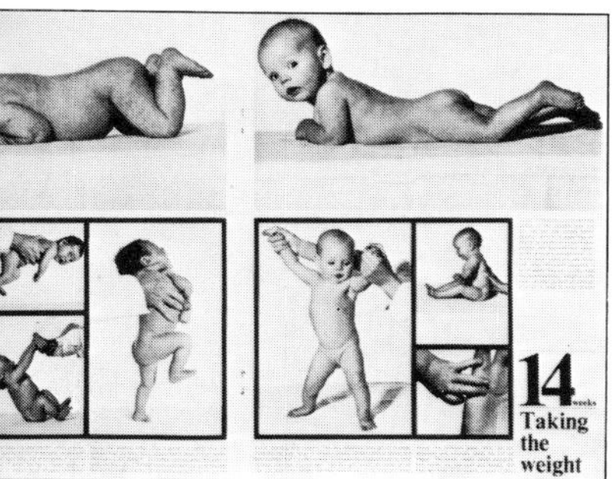
14 weeks Taking the weight

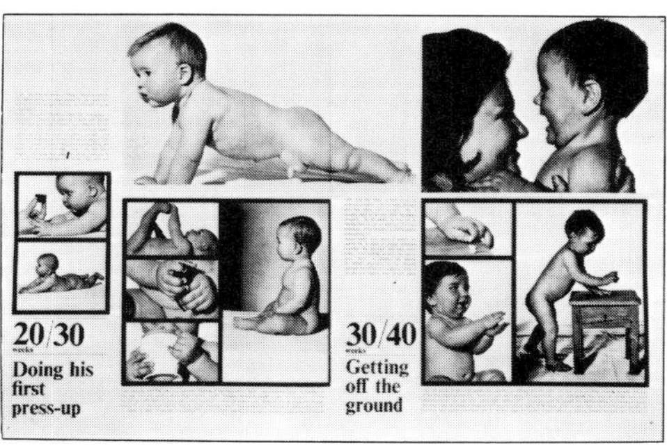
20/30 weeks Doing his first press-up

30/40 weeks Getting off the ground

52 weeks Standing on his own feet

The ultimate moment of the first year when the baby succeeds in standing entirely on his own makes a vertical counterpoint to the opening picture

fascinated and then passionately involved in the way 10,000 of the people had been poisoned by a chemical company discharging mercury waste into the sea. They spent three years documenting the story, Eugene being beaten up once by the company's goons and nearly blinded (see 123A).

Behind Brian Brake's success with his Indian monsoon lay two years of reading, off and on, and preliminary showings of slides to ordinary people in Calcutta. He realised that there had to be a flow not merely in the chronological content but also in a cycle of colour. These are heady exemplars. The baby story (245A) is a demonstration of more routine forethought. It was not acceptable to wait 12 months and photograph the same baby—good ideas have a way of occurring to more than one person at the same time—so different babies at different stages were photographed. The photographer would have spoiled the flow if he had allowed changes in the background to obtrude. Robert Freson, brought in early, appreciated the point and his technical skill preserved continuity.

The party's over but the battle's ahead

246B Picture story

Where flow is lacking the fault may lie with the photographer who shot from the hip, or it may lie with the designer—the layout man or picture editor on a newspaper and art director on a magazine. A sensible photographer relishes rather than resents the sharpening of focus that an art director can provide in selection, combination and projection. Selection has to be ruthless. The notable temptation in newspaper picture pages is to squeeze in an extra picture. It is almost always a mistake since it impinges on the space for the others. It is better to make a single decisive statement and reduce the subsidiary pictures in scale, or discard one, than to start sizing down what was intended to be a big opening picture on the basic idea. A newspaper text page may well contain as few as three or four photographs. The selection is not a job for the photographer. Mike Rand, art director of *The Sunday Times Magazine* and a campaigner for photography, believes photographers do not know their best pictures. 'They get too involved in them. They try to explain the picture to you, to tell you what the picture is saying. I regard myself as standing there for the reader and if I can't see it I don't want it explained. I have, on occasion, gone through a final set of 50 with Don McCullin to select the last 10 and then I take them away and lay them out. I would never let a photographer change them at that stage unless he made out a very strong case.'

The selection and combination carried out by the art director is a parallel task. Ten pictures selected in isolation may unquestionably be the best ten but they may not work together. Links may be missing. Some of the 'second best' will have to be preferred. Eugene Smith even says he has from time to time removed the strongest picture from an essay 'because it would be like putting a strong speech in the first act and throwing the whole play off balance'. There must be trial and error, matching this picture with that, turning everything back to front and starting again. The physical organisation of this matters since the combinations have to be reshuffled time and again. Black and white prints, if there are a lot, may be laid out on a floor; at the *New York Times*, John Morris introduced a magnetised wall so that he could literally throw the prints at the wall and arrange them in quick conference. On a magazine, scaled photostats are the easiest method.

WEEKLY ILLUSTRATED—August 4, 1934

MUSSOLINI

WHAT IS HE PLANNING?

These pictures were taken by special permission in the Dictator's study by a "Weekly Illustrated" photographer

EVENTS of the past few days have focused the eyes of all Europe on Mussolini, the Italian dictator.

The shooting of Dr. Dollfuss, Chancellor of Austria, by Nazis set the whole world thinking of those events in Europe, twenty years ago, which embroiled Europe in four years of war.

• • •

To-day Mussolini holds the scales of European peace in the balance. For Dollfuss was not only a political sympathiser with Mussolini. He was his friend.

The German confederates of the Nazis who murdered Dollfuss know that Hitler, their leader, and Mussolini are at loggerheads over the question of Austria's independence. Does the Italian dictator intend to strike? And if he does, what of the rest of Europe—can the other countries keep out of this quarrel?

Some say Mussolini will not strike in vengeance alone.

But Hitler covets Austria, and Dollfuss was murdered in cold blood because he would not tolerate dominance by Hitler.

So what if Hitler now decides to go ahead with his ambitious plans?

The moment a German Nazi steps across the Austrian frontier in aggression—will Mussolini strike?

The answer can only be "yes." The war won for him a part of Austrian territory, and he will not stand by and let it be taken from him.

• • •

Thus the democratic countries of the world have before their eyes the amazing spectacle of three different brands of Fascism up in arms against each other, with the dread prospect of a bloody clash.

Europe is watching Mussolini with anxious eyes.

IN THE TEMPLE OF FA

Signor Mussolini in his great study he Palazzo Venezia, in Rome. Of such size is the room that a visitor corner. The fascist emblem can be seen ove

Fascism has risen to power in Germany, Italy, and Austria, along paths strewn with brutality, murder, and oppression.

Are neighbouring countries going to be dragged into another age of horror because the greed for power remains unsatisfied?

• • •

Now the nations of Europe are reiterating their pledges—"We stand by Austria"—"We shall see no bloodshed"—"There must be no victimisation of Austria"—and so on.

Troops are on the move. Secret planning, accusations, denials and counter-accusations—where is it all leading? Again we look at Mussolini—the man who cursed Europe with the first Fascist régime and who now sees his rivals close behind him.

• • •

The pictures here show Mussolini at work in his magnificent suite at the Palazza Venezia, in Rome. The haughty mask, the pose of the Mighty Leader, is forgotten, for the Italian people cannot see him in his study.

That is why these pictures are of particular interest, for Mussolini's face is seen as it really is—and not as the Italian people believe it to be.

247A The classic combination—of pictures and of photographer (Felix Man) and editor (Stefan Lorant). Lorant produced it in *Munchener Illustrierte*, then Britain's *Weekly Illustrated*, in 1934: the world was intensely curious about the dictator known in England as the sawdust Caesar. Lorant says: 'I had a hundred pictures to choose from. The big picture is Mussolini far away, so you get the feeling of the visitor who comes into the room as I did and I saw this huge room with the small table. So that was obviously the large picture. Then I wanted to show how he worked, like an animal poring over his papers, so that was a large picture to illustrate his kind of showmanship. I finished with the four different pictures at the bottom so that the eye is taken from the right corner—just like it is in a painting—down to the left corner and then to the bottom right'

248A Wimbledon—notable as a contrast with Mussolini and an innovation in candid photography. Lorant took the pictures himself for his weekly *Illustrated*, with a Leica that had a mirror arrangement attachment that enabled him to point the camera in one direction while actually photographing spectators next to him. He was able to obtain natural pictures of people who had no idea what he was up to. On the

August 4, 1934—WEEKLY ILLUSTRATED

…inute to reach the Dictator's desk, which stands in the

(*Continued from page 246*)

The art director, in all this, is not a mere maker of patterns. He has to consider how a story fits into an issue. He is familiar with traps such as the photograph that is excellent as a print but is disrupted at the fold when used as a double spread. But most of all he must choose in combinations calculated to enhance the special quality of the picture, and to arouse and sustain interest. There are many techniques. Grouped picture pages whose content is of the same scale and viewpoint are monotonous. Contrasts of content, scale, colour, texture and timing are required. The reader's attention can be directed—a figure on the left can move our attention into the page.

There is no place for competing with the content of the photographs by clever layout. This is one of the fundamental understandings that developed in the various German magazines in the thirties, then *Life* and *Picture Post* (but for the origins see Tim Gidal's book in the bibliography) and is one of the reasons why Stefan Lorant's double spread on Mussolini (247A) is justly famous. He simplified, as he puts it, 'the prevailing hodge podge'. Wimbledon (248A) also by Lorant, is an enchanting comparison from the period.

Layout shapes should basically be determined by the shapes of the photographs—but it is absurd, especially when there are a few pictures to choose from, to make a fetish of not cropping at all. This inevitably produces great chasms of white on the page; it is a major failing of even the best American newspapers and some later *Life* essays. Photojournalism is assisted by the bold simplicities and sense of the value of space exhibited in *Stern* magazine, *Paris Match* and, at their best, the British Sunday colour magazines.

In summary, the picture story or essay should be distinguished by these features:

1. The basic idea should be clear. In layout this almost always means opening with a key statement.
2. There should be a flow. It should be orderly so that it makes sense but it should not fall away. A good magazine picture story ends with a statement almost as powerful as the opening.
3. Design techniques, notably of coupling, sequence and contrast should be used.
4. The layout should be simple.

layout Lorant says: 'I had taken perhaps 100 pictures and I knew I wanted a montage, so I made a circle in the centre to show all the players and around the circle I wanted to show all the people who watched the game. People on the left had to face right and people on the right to face left. It's really a very simple layout'

The take

This is not the layout for a picture page. It is a glimpse of the range the photographer should produce when engaged on a picture story or essay. He has to shoot for content, for elaboration of the basic idea. But that is only the beginning. A picture story will require changes of scale, sequence, proportion, perspective and tonal values. This often means shooting the same scene with different lenses from different viewpoints and with different shapes in mind. Photographers tend to return with lots of horizontals all requiring a double spread in a magazine or four columns in a newspaper. This often foils an exciting combination.

We are looking at only part of the take of marines in training by Eddie Adams, but it is a superb demonstration of professionalism. The full take would make either a long or short picture story on marine training or a picture essay on the theme of, say, discipline. It deserves to be pinned to the lid of every photographers' gadget box; and rescaled and laid out by every art director.

No. 2563 26 May 1968 Price 1/-

THE SUNDAY TIMES

THE FRENCH REVOLT: EIGHT-PAGE SPECIAL — The full story on pages 7 to 14

'As for the future, it depends not on us, it depends on God'

De Gaulle speaking to the new US Ambassador yesterday

Mary McCarthy in North Vietnam 49

IN COLOUR: The British king who sold out: his villa and his life uncovered

Hoyle on Lovell 57

J W Lambert on Ustinov and Osborne 53

Lanning Roper on the big show at Chelsea 42

Spitting flame, a tear gas gun hurls its missile at Paris demonstrators behind the barricades near the Sorbonne

Paris police ordered: get even tougher

CASUALTIES

Machine guns awaited Cohn-Bendit

EIGHT-PAGE SPECIAL — THE FRENCH REVOLT — 1 — HOW IT BEGAN

Bedroom sit-in was the spark

The making of a hero

Secret police on the campus

THE SUNDAY TIMES, 26 MAY 1968

THE FRENCH REVOLT — 4 — HOW IT EXPLODED

The turmoil of the streets at night is lit by fires: it is like the Liberation twenty-four years ago, and like Detroit and Washington last year and this

Workers cook Renault's goose—Peking-style

A Chinese kind of revolution

'Le Chien-lit, c'est loi'

THE SUNDAY TIMES, 26 MAY 1968

THE FRENCH REVOLT — 5 — HOW THE REVOLUTION SPLIT UP

Hussein backs hotel strikers

Unions do a power deal with Fortes

In the vast Renault shed at Billancourt, where strikers meet each morning, solidarity suddenly becomes something tangible and very moving

What the unions want for themselves

By Stephen Fay, Labour Correspondent

Exploring the possibilities

Newspapermen tend to envy magazines for photojournalism. The magazine certainly has some advantages. Apart from generally superior printing, there is the congenial concentration of the double-spread, the basic design unit, which is not interrupted by awkwardly shaped advertising or any other distraction. There need not even be a margin between the pages or, with full bleed, any margin on the page at all. The nightmare of the newspaper picture story is a page or spread that looks fine on editorial page proof but is ruined as soon as the display advertising is included; it may include a dominant half-tone or strident type. In the best-regulated houses, of course, no picture page is designed without a proof of the associated advertising, and sometimes white space or a thicker dividing rule will help.

But despite these problems, the broadsheet newspaper has the virtue of scale—the Mussolini magazine spread (247A) would work very well as a half-page broadsheet—and the possibility of page sequence is always there for a major event. As an experiment, we have taken the *Sunday Times* section of the 1968 French Revolution (251–2) and with the same material but with more time produced the top section of three spreads to exploit the picture possibilities (253–4). The 1968 troubles began with a minor clash. The Paris Latin Quarter became a battleground between students and French riot police and then eight million workers struck and occupied the factories. Students and workers marched together shouting 'De Gaulle adieu' but De Gaulle

THE SUNDAY TIMES, 26 MAY 1968

The magazine that will ever be on the bookstalls

THE FRENCH REVOLT 2 HOW IT BEGAN

Symbol of the broken pen

Danny, the inflexible

Students occupy the Odeon: the first of the citadels has fallen

The doctrines of Lenin, Mao, Marx...

Too many for too few places

THE FRENCH REVOLT 3 HOW IT ESCALATED

The fatal order of Rector Roche

The elegance of Paris disappears under mountains of rubbish—the unlooked-for "barricades" of the dustmen's strike

Minister's daughter sides with students

Violence after Sorbonne closes

From education to death duty

Plan your family's finances with Towry Law

TOWRY LAW & CO. LTD.

YOUR WINDOW ON THE WORLD

THE ILLUSTRATED LONDON NEWS

Increased Interest Rate

CO-OPERATIVE PERMANENT

THE SUNDAY TIMES

Price to be paid

THE FRENCH REVOLT 6 COMMENT

AN END TO HIS VANITY

BY SIRIUS

Le Monde

MORE THAN DE GAULLE AT RISK

BY FRANK GILES

WESTMINSTER CHIEN-LIT

BY RONALD BUTT

NO PLAY TODAY

BY JACK FINGLETON

THE FRENCH REVOLT 7 THE PATTERN OF VIOLENCE

Brutality across the barricades

Last night France seemed set for still grimmer turmoil in its streets. The battles have become organised set pieces. No longer do the professional strongmen of the CRS—Special Riot Police—face only amateurs across the improvised barricades. This report describes the action and analyses France's embryonic civil war

Cheers for attack on a young woman

How the students learned to fight

ABBEY EVENT

rallied the nation and the revolution effectively ended with a million-or-so De Gaullists parading up the Champs-Elysées. *The Sunday Times* written narrative was excellent, and there was a splendid set of photographs, but we failed to make them into a picture story. The pages displayed are the front page (*top left*) and then the right-hand opening of a section inside the paper. Coupling was used effectively on page one of the section pointing Daniel Cohn Bendit, the student leader, at the riot police and again between De Gaulle (facing the wrong way) and a rioter (pages 6–7). But otherwise there was little attempt to relate the pictures in their spreads. After this strong opening the second spread (2–3), has students on the left and mountains of uncollected rubbish on the right—fine as single picture but inconsequential as a spread and making no narrative contribution.

The revision on the next two pages suggests six pages in three spreads. It has the benefit of scale, but apart from that its superiority is that it reads and it makes its points visually. The pictures are no longer merely appendages to the words.

The opening is a spread. The riot police are scaled for a dramatic street-wide shape, but we also zoom in for a close up of an argument between a marcher and a gendarme. The next spread (3–4) has a change of scale in the riot policeman sandwiched between the running figures and the new protestors occupying the factories and marching the streets with banners. The top section of the final spread personifies the conflict and concludes the story. There has been a beginning, a middle and an end.

The top sections of three experimental spreads *linked 1–2; 3–4; and 5–6 across these pages.*

1

THE FRENCH REVOLT

1 Opening statement of conflict. This is the top half of the spread facing the top half (**2**) on page 254 —

3

3 Development. The crowd scenes on **1** and **2** dissolve explosively in an action sequence—facing new trouble on **4** →

5

which they overcome the snags is impressive. Six or seven years for a power station is slow by their standards but good building by most criteria. They are not helped by the remoteness of their sites, at Almaraz in the lonely plains of Extremadura, or Asco in the beautiful valley of the Ebro (near where Jack Jones was wounded in the Civil War, I was incessantly reminded). Carrying 300-ton components there over twisty mountain roads has been a major engineering feat in itself.

But while the Spaniards could make a go of everything else, even a decade ago their mechanical engineering was nowhere near nuclear standards. "We looked all over Spain to see what we could buy," Quent remembers, "we found a lot of rough shops; they hadn't the plant and quality analysis was unknown. But the word was out that there would be a lot of work."

So the incentive was there, but government help was crucial. Firms that wanted nuclear orders were invited to sign detailed undertakings to do a significant proportion of the work locally from the start, and then to develop their technology and reduce the import content. In return they would have the benefit of a decree, known unknown. But the word was out that there would be a lot of work."

So the incentive was there, but government help was crucial. Firms that wanted nuclear orders were invited to sign detailed undertakings to do a significant proportion of the work locally from the start, and then to develop their technology and reduce the import content. In return they would have

Now he is in production in one end of his handsome new factory while the other end is still being finished off. "But we have orders to meet, we are in a terrific hurry, we couldn't wait."

The equipment at Santander is superb, with the extra advantage that it is on a deepwater port so that its cranes can lift an 800-ton pressure vessel straight from the factory door on to a ship. In three years time Equipos Nucleares is contracted to be supplying three sets of components a year—pressure vessels, steam generators, main piping, and perhaps even the finely-machined reactor internals. By then it will be using mainly Spanish raw materials too, as the steelworks and forges race to catch up with the new technologies.

It is all a new world for the Spaniards, struggling against a desperate shortage of skilled workers and good managers. But the opportunities are bringing experienced men home at last. machine operators from Germany and petrochemical engineers from the Far East. The technocratic style, driven hard by the government, has a strong French flavour. Palacios claims: "We are only five years behind the Italians and we will overtake them because we are more decisive." The excitement is infecdesperate shortage of skilled workers and good managers. But the opportunities are bringing experienced men home at last. machine operators from Germany and petrochemical engineers from the Far East. The technocratic style, driven hard by the government, has a strong French flavour. Palacios claims: "We are only five years behind the Italians and we will overtake them because we are more deci-

which they overcome the snags is impressive. Six or seven years for a power station is slow by their standards but good building by most criteria. They are not helped by the remoteness of their sites, at Almaraz in the lonely plains of Extremadura, or Asco in the beautiful valley of the Ebro (near where Jack Jones was wounded in the Civil War, I was incessantly reminded). Carrying 300-ton components there over twisty mountain roads has been a major engineering feat in itself.

But while the Spaniards could make a go of everything else, even a decade ago their mechanical engineering was nowhere near nuclear standards. "We looked all over Spain to see what we could buy," Quent remembers, "we found a lot of rough shops; they hadn't the plant and quality analysis was unknown. But the word was out that there would be a lot of work."

So the incentive was there, but government help was crucial. Firms that wanted nuclear orders were invited to sign detailed undertakings to do a significant proportion of the work locally from the start, and then to develop their technology and reduce the import content. In return they would have the benefit of a decree, known which they overcome the snags is impressive. Six or seven years for a power station is slow by their standards but good building by most criteria. They are not helped by the remoteness of their sites, at Almaraz in the lonely plains of Extremadura, or Asco in the beautiful valley of the Ebro (near where Jack Jones was wounded in the Civil War, I was incessantly reminded). Carrying 300-ton

5 Denouement. First the challenge to Gaullism is made explicit—and then it is answered. . . . →

2

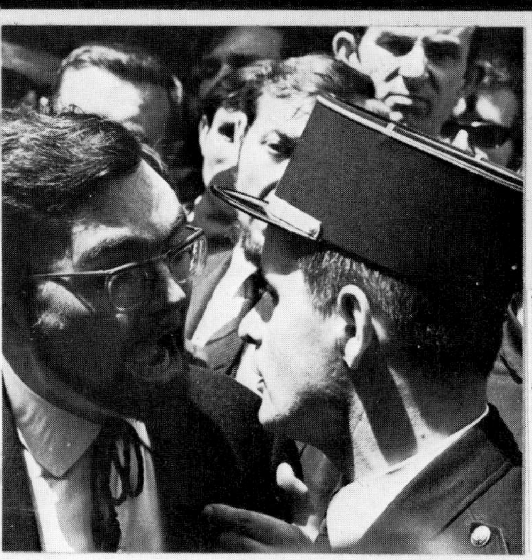

Jack Jones was wounded in the Civil War, I was incessantly reminded). Carrying 300-ton components there over twisty mountain roads has been a major engineering feat in itself.

But while the Spaniards could make a go of everything else, even a decade ago their mechanical engineering was nowhere near nuclear standards. "We looked all over Spain to see what we could buy," Ouent remembers, "we found a lot of rough shops; they hadn't the plant and quality analysis was unknown. But the word was out that there would be a lot of work."

So the incentive was there, but government help was crucial. Firms that wanted nuclear orders were invited to sign detailed undertakings to do a significant proportion of the work locally from the start, and pressure vessel straight from the factory door on to a ship. In three years time Equipos Nucleares is contracted to be supplying three sets of components a year—pressure vessels, steam generators, main piping, and perhaps even the finely-machined reactor internals. By then it will be using mainly Spanish raw materials too, as the steelworks and forges race to catch up with the new technologies.

It is all a new world for the Spaniards, struggling against a desperate shortage of skilled workers and good managers. But the opportunities are bringing experienced men home at last, machine operators from Germany and petrochemical engineers from the Far East. The technocratic style, driven hard by the government, has a strong French flavour. Palacios claims: which they overcome the snags is impressive. Six or seven years for a power station is slow by their standards but good building by most criteria. They are not helped by the remoteness of their sites, at Almaraz in the lonely plains of Extremadura, or Asco in the beautiful valley of the Ebro (near where Jack Jones was wounded in the Civil War, I was incessantly reminded). Carrying 300-ton components there over twisty mountain roads has been a major engineering feat in itself.

But while the Spaniards could make a go of everything else, even a decade ago their mechanical engineering was nowhere near nuclear standards. "We looked all over Spain to see what we could buy," Ouent remembers, "we found a lot of rough shops; they hadn't the plant and quality analysis was Now he is in production in one end of his handsome new factory while the other end is still being finished off. "But we have orders to meet, we are in a terrific hurry, we couldn't wait."

The equipment at Santander is superb, with the extra advantage that it is on a deepwater port so that its cranes can lift an 800-ton pressure vessel straight from the factory door on to a ship. In three years time Equipos Nucleares is contracted to be supplying three sets of components a year—pressure vessels, steam generators, main piping, and perhaps even the finely-machined reactor internals. By then it will be using mainly Spanish raw materials too, as the steelworks and forges race to catch up with the new technologies.

It is all a new world for the Spaniards, struggling against a

which they overcome the snags is impressive. Six or seven years for a power station is slow by their standards but good building by most criteria. They are not helped by the remoteness of their sites, at Almaraz in the lonely plains of Extremadura, or Asco in the beautiful valley of the Ebro (near where Jack Jones was wounded in the Civil War, I was incessantly reminded). Carrying 300-ton components there over twisty mountain roads has been a major engineering feat in itself.

But while the Spaniards could make a go of everything else, even a decade ago their mechanical engineering was nowhere near nuclear standards. "We looked all over Spain to see what we could buy," Ouent remembers, "we found a lot of rough shops; they hadn't the plant and quality analysis was

2 The students who faced the police on the streets face them across the newspaper page

4

4 Target: A close up of Authority which is the target of the growing protests

6

6 The assault of youth (**5**) is met with a vigorous response in the Gaullist march down the Champs-Elysées

Chapter 14

Words with Pictures

The basic unit of photojournalism is one picture with words. Wilson Hicks

Photographers and art editors tend to be snooty about headlines and captions (sometimes called cutlines in American newspapers). Cartier-Bresson says that if a photograph is really evocative it carries its own message and the only caption it needs is a label of when and where. 'The who or what and the why are incorporated in the subject—or should be—and the how is unimportant.'

In fifteen years of discussion of photojournalism at the international conferences at the University of Miami there seems to have been hardly a photographer concerned about the words that might go with their pictures, and art editors often produce 'exciting' layouts which relegate captions to obscurity or condemn them to unreadable settings. The excellent digest of the exhaustive Miami proceedings edited by Professor R. Smith Schuneman (*Photographic Communication, see bibliography*) contains some wisdom from a copy editor who was with *Life*, but the photographers are busy burning incense: their obsession with images is evident in the titles of the discussions ('Signals, Channels, Icons . . . The Photographer's Changing Vision . . . Images and Impact'). This is understandable. But photography is not photojournalism and significantly Professor Schuneman has had to redress the balance by including an extract from *Words and Pictures* (*see bibliography*), the book published in 1952 by the late and celebrated Wilson Hicks, an executive editor of *Life*.

Wilson Hicks, knowing what he had to contend with in the fifties, said words were not a subordinate but an equal partner of the photographer. He was stretching the point, but it was then—and is today—a necessary antidote to the idea that words pollute photographs. This is a piece of intellectual debris from the early idea that photography was art or it was nothing. There are certainly photographs we see as unequivocally and completely as a painting and which do not need even a title. They crop up in journalism less frequently than in photography, perhaps a few times a year. They may be a visual illustration of a verity which words render into a commonplace—that wars or famine cause human misery—or confirmation of a known event (The Conquest of Everest, page 2), or they may make a point merely by composition as in the photograph of the policeman on point duty (256B). But rarely, with the overwhelming mass of newspaper photographs, are we satisfied by such simple statements. Our curiosity requires more information which can be supplied only by words. Emphatically this does not mean we are dealing with an inferior photograph. To demonstrate faith in photography, it is not necessary to forsake rationality. The wordless picture story may have an aesthetic rigour but words can enhance both emotional and cognitive values. They are not competitive; they are complementary. They identify people and places, the first essential. They explain relationships. They fix the time. They may elaborate on what is happening. They can point to an elusive detail. They can attempt to counter our irritating perversity in each drawing different, even contradictory, meanings from the same image. They can confirm mood. And with a single photograph only words can explain how the event occurred or what its effect might be.

It has to be admitted that all too often words do none of these things or do them very lamely. Headlines and captions are written and published which give the reader in possession of eye or brain the feeling of being overdressed. The typical *Daily Mirror* headline of 1915 (256A) which tells the reader unashamedly what to think, at least identifies the Kaiser and the Serb (and has a saving jingoistic piquancy today), but the words with most photographs in most newspapers are numbingly irrelevant and especially in captions.

The Daily Mirror

CERTIFIED CIRCULATION LARGER THAN ANY OTHER PICTURE PAPER IN THE WORLD

No. 3,550. Registered at the G.P.O. as a Newspaper. THURSDAY, MARCH 11, 1915 **16 PAGES.** One Halfpenny.

THE KAISER STARES AT THE UNDAUNTED SERBIAN AND SEES ONLY CONTEMPT WRITTEN ON THE PRISONER'S FACE.

256A *Daily Mirror*, 1915: What to see, what to think

256B Which way? But words are superfluous

Captions

Lord Northcliffe, surveying a dull page, told them to put a pretty girl picture in it, according to his biographer Tom Clarke. They brought him a selection, but the first he picked up had no name on it. 'Who is it?' asked The Chief. Nobody knew. 'Put it in', said Northcliffe, 'under the caption, "Who is it?"'.

Too many captions are hardly more informative. Many might be classified as 'You don't say!' captions. Beneath a photograph of President Carter speaking the caption says:

> President Carter speaking

Beneath a picture of the Prime Minister entering a car it says:

> The Prime Minister enters his car

There was a publicity picture of a man wearing an Apollo spacesuit standing in the street talking to a London policeman. The man in the suit had all the gear—visor, space helmet, dials, white suit, heavy boots, gloves. The caption commented:

> The space suit poses a sharp contrast with the policeman's uniform above

This tendency of caption writers to treat the reader as a moron is easily corrected by the editor striking his employee a hard blow on the head, twice, with a blunt instrument. When he comes to he should be reminded of the what? where? when? why? questions the picture raises. What was President Carter speaking about? Why was he apparently happy? Where was the Prime Minister going? What was the man in the space suit up to?

The war on vacuity does not require a writer to answer every one of the who-what-why-where questions—certainly not when a story accompanies a picture and the hope is that the picture will draw the reader into the text. One extra tit-bit of fact will do: it may have to do on those awkward occasions for text editors when there is very little in the story. An actor's car broke down at his wedding and there was a comic story about his rescue with a photograph of a powerful car being pushed to make it start. In several papers it attracted this mind-softener:

> Friends push the groom's car after it broke down

I will not punish the reader by recording the common headline. What can be done with the caption? The point of the picture is that a glamorous car has gone embarrassingly on the blink. It is hard to write that in the caption without visual-verbal duplication or irrelevancies (such as the names of the pushers). But, with one factual snippet, it can be done:

> The groom and 150 sleeping horses

Identification, which is vital, is always helped by a factual nudge:

> Horizon's Leonard Koven:
> Chasing 80,000 tourists

Simple name captions are almost always too bald. A name plus a quote is one of the most useful nudges and often takes only the same space:

> Mr. Lee: 'It's fantastic'

Time and *Newsweek* appreciate the baiting power of a caption with their famous teaser lines:

> Dayan: How to crash a party

Instead of saying on a ballet photograph

> Baryshnikov and Haydee dancing in 'Hamlet Connotation'

Time tantalises:

> Baryshnikov and Haydee: Oedipal fantasy in a sleepless night

Captions to scenes from plays are too often simple name-and-play; a line of the dialogue, or a summary of the theme enlivens.

And if *Time*, especially 'Burton in Equus: Portrait of a divided self', sometimes seems a cryptic parody of itself, it is a risk any newspaper should prefer to the daily banalities. There is a story with a picture of a man digging and the caption says:

> Mr. Gus Oliver busy with spade

In the same space a teaser caption would have attracted the reader to the story if it had flirted with the why? of caption writing:

> Mr. Gus Oliver digging for a fortune

Nothing I have said about the what-why-where-when should obscure the fact that identification, the who?, is the key requirement. When I say this I am conscious of the capacity of caption writers for mischief:

> Mr. X with chimpanzee (the chimpanzee is on the left)

This is an international ailment. In *Photographic Communication* Mr. Kastner has told us about the early days at *Life*: 'We were all saying things like "Smile on face is forced". "Hat on head is awry". We identified everything. The clincher in one story was "Corpse in foreground is real".'

Still, the risks of literalism have to be faced, such is the sloppiness of simple identification in newspapers. In the ordinary picture of a small group, everyone should be identified, and normally by full name. Identification means saying who is who and not simply listing names.

Obvious, you would think. But every day the reader is expected to know that the man in the middle is the public health officer for Barnsley or Syria's chief of staff.

Identification should be from left to right except when the picture is concentrated on one person as more important than the rest. It is then legitimate to begin with his name and this gets round the small awkwardness of identifying an over-familiar face.

One further qualification:

When the news figure is surrounded by many people, perhaps even a crowd, it is not possible to identify everybody. Names are here often an irrelevancy: but what must be identified is the role of the crowd, as onlookers, petitioners, wives of candidates, demonstrators, veterans, licensed victuallers . . .

Captions must be in the present tense and be brief and vivid (delete 'the picture shows' and 'in the picture'). There is no excuse for waffle such as that produced by the caption writer confronted by a sleeping tiger:

> Practising the gentle art of peaceful relaxation before getting to the more serious business of playing to the gallery of hordes of human visitors, this placid polesquatting jungle puss indulges in the luxury of 40 winks atop a plinth in the tigers' enclosure in London's Zoological Gardens, Regent's Park

It is information that we want, not elaboration of the obvious. Often this means adding facts that cannot be drawn from the photograph but which put the image in a context:

> Peasants at Camporeale beg for bread from the relief columns after the Sicilian earthquake that killed 300 in their beds and led at least another 80,000 to flee the area in search of safety

This caption gives a sense of meaningful proportion to the photograph; the begging of the peasants the reader can see is symbolic of a wider disaster which he cannot see. But words can help a photograph to perform its function even when they concentrate on the content of the photograph:

> Newly vested with the Pope's gold, silver and jewelled triregnum—three crowns set in tiers—John XXIII makes the sign of the cross, blessing urbi et orbi (the city and the world) as the attendants bless themselves

We can see the Pope is wearing *something*, we learn what it is; we can see he is doing *something*, we learn what it is; we can see he is speaking; we hear the words.

A photograph is enhanced in value when a significant detail is explained. Pictures of demonstrators carrying banners with slogans in a foreign language are often muffed. There should be a translation. When British readers see a picture of the Queen's state visit to Germany which includes placards proclaiming '*Wir Grüssen die Queen*' he is entitled to know whether, behind the umlaut, the natives are friendly. They were.

> 'We welcome the Queen,' said the banners outside Hamburg Rathaus

It is hard to advise on light captions. Good writing helps and it often helps to try to imagine a spoken comment on the picture. An apt word or phrase is all that is needed. A weekly paper's picture of students trying to break the world record for the number who cram into a telephone kiosk began:

> Breathe in, everybody . . .

Caption and headline writers should, of course, see what they are writing about, and that means seeing the edited picture.

> Citizens of Rhotak made heroic efforts to prevent flood water entering the town. In the picture they are seen throwing sandbags in a bid to save the town

Not so. The heroic citizens had downed sandbags to pose for a smiling picture for the photographer.

Typography

Once upon a time a journalistic genius had the idea of putting words underneath a picture. We all got used to looking there for them. Too often today the layout man, especially if he ranks as an art editor, feels square if he does something as simple as this. Captions in magazines suffer most, all too frequently separated from the photograph. They should always be immediately adjacent. The commonest newspaper vice is to run portmanteau captions so that the reader has to wend his way through this kind of thing (a real example from *The Times*):

> Above, an Indian forward picket in the Himalayas; top right, a patrol sets out and (bottom) heaving a gun when the towing truck gets into difficulties; top far right: looking across to Chinese positions in Sikkim, and (bottom), the Indian Air Force drops supplies to a forward post

Only Chinese Intelligence Officers with 6–6 vision can be expected to complete this scrutiny.

Readers should at least be assisted by having the identifying words in a different typeface, and preferably by having each caption on a separate line. It is sometimes impossible, even with the best intentions, to do justice to a photograph and have every caption directly underneath every picture—the ideal—but it should always be easy to find and read the caption.

Legibility is a second failing. Captions are set too wide and too small. The type should be distinct from the text type: 9pt bold captions are best in a newspaper set in 8pt. Big pictures require big captions: 10pt or 12pt. Ideal setting measures are discussed in Book II (*Handling Newspaper Text*).

Captions should be indented a little at each side, say an em or an en, and then set centred, but a caption should never begin with a paragraph indent. Captions should never be all in caps, but a few words in caps at the beginning, as a kind of mini-headline, may usefully set the tone for the picture, or signal a theme.

> THE LISTENERS: Senator Edward Kennedy, middle row, left, did not comment on the speech but others did—largely along party lines
>
> THE CRITICS: The House Minority leader, right, and other GOP leaders said at a news conference they would try to trim 10 billion dollars from the proposed budget

The intro phrase in caps is a useful device in all kinds of caption, but to repeat the same words in the body of the caption is ponderous:

> FATHERLY ADVICE: Prince Charles playing polo at Windsor Great Park yesterday receives a bit of fatherly advice from the Duke of Edinburgh during the interval

Thematic captions can be lower case:

> Vance (left), willing
>
> Acheson, suspicious
>
> Kissinger, wily

Credits

A picture credit to the photographer and/or agency is indispensable. It is absurd that writers get by-lines but photographers often go unmentioned. The simplest method is to run it tight up against the block in any neat position. Alternatively the end of the caption can be tagged. But the style should be consistent.

Picture headlines

The most effective way to present a photograph is to headline it with a few fitting words so that the words and pictures have a unity of effect. An instant perception of the event, as disaster or joke, achievement or near-miss, is what we seek: headline-picture captures attention and then the caption elaborates. It sounds simple enough, but success is elusive. When I came to select examples for this book from what I thought I remembered as striking presentations in *The Sunday Times* I was dismayed by the frequency of two failings: the layout relationship between headline type and picture was not close enough, and the words failed to match the meaning or mood of the picture. What happens, I think, is that when a striking set of pictures arrives, we concentrate our excitement and judgement on selecting, cropping and sizing, and forget that the average reader comes to the photograph in the page without our knowledge of the event. The mental context of viewing is different; there is a gap of understanding which we have to bridge with the headline before we can expect the reader to be drawn to the caption.

Everything, of course, must pull together. The moving picture of St. Paul's Cathedral (259A) during a bombing raid in World War II was not inaptly headlined 'War's greatest picture: St. Paul's Stands Unharmed in the Midst of the Burning City' (259B)—but the effect and the conviction about the worth of the picture were marred by biting a corner off the picture for a display ad.

The *Daily Express* treatment of its picture of the funeral of King George VI succeeds by force. It mildly offends one rule but emphasises the point of the picture so simply and directly. Instantly, without having to recognise individuals or think at all, we absorb the idea: *three* Queens. The scale of headline matches the scale of the picture. The offence is that it is a picture of three Queens mourning (Three Queens Mourn); but not quite a picture of three Queens *praying*. If we are told to expect a picture of someone at prayer we expect to see them kneeling; perhaps the three

Daily Mail

FOR KING AND EMPIRE

LATE WAR NEWS SPECIAL

SHERLEY'S

WAR'S GREATEST PICTURE: St. Paul's Stands Unharmed in the Midst of the Burning City

Hitler Planned Monday Swoop

London was to Blaze First

America Moves

LATEST

100 to 1 Backing for Roosevelt

HAVOC COULD HAVE BEEN SAVED

Fire Spotter Off: Firm Fined £20

China Seeks U.S. Planes

Churchill Sees London's Ruins

Morrison on Radio To-night

500 Were Killed in Manchester

259A St. Paul's Cathedral rises inspiringly from the smoke and tumult of the London blitz, but if the German bombers failed the advertising block on the front page of the *Mail* did damage to an otherwise excellent presentation (**259B** above)

DAILY EXPRESS

No. 16,113 Price 1½d. TUESDAY FEBRUARY 12 1952 CONTROLLING SHAREHOLDER LORD BEAVERBROOK Weather: Cold

The week of tribute ... PICTURE EDITION

TO THE QUEEN ... Our loyal devotion and our complete conviction that she will, with the Blessing of God, uphold the liberties of all her peoples.

TO THE QUEEN MOTHER ... With her aid, the King was able to surmount his trials ... an ordeal he could not have endured without her aid.

TO QUEEN MARY ... May she find comfort in the affection which flows to her from all who have watched and admired her through these long years.

MR. WINSTON CHURCHILL TO THE COMMONS ASSEMBLED IN MOURNING YESTERDAY

THE THREE QUEENS PRAY

AT THE LYING IN STATE

Express Staff Reporter

THREE Queens of England—Queen Elizabeth II, the Queen Mother, and majestic Queen Mary—tried to fight back their tears yesterday as they stood beside the bier of King George VI, lying in state in Westminster Hall.

Queen Elizabeth mourning a father, stood a little in front at the head of the coffin. On her right, two paces behind, was her mother mourning a husband. On the other side was Queen Mary mourning a son.

THE EMOTION

[illegible]

THE SILENCE

[illegible]

THE SALUTE

[illegible]

THE CROWN

[illegible]

260A THREE QUEENS of England. Queen Elizabeth II, Queen Mary and the Queen Mother, at the funeral of King George VI, February 1952

SUNDAY TIMES EXCLUSIVE . . . THIS WAS BLOODY SUNDAY AS THE BULLETS FLEW . . .

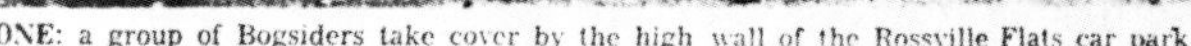

ONE: a group of Bogsiders take cover by the high wall of the Rossville Flats car park

TWO three men start to crawl towards the Rossville Flats. Among them is Patrick Doherty (left)

Photographer Gilles Peress

Death in Derry

These photographs and the map (right) show where a man called Patrick Doherty died in Londonderry last Sunday. It is for the Widgery inquiry to decide how and why he died. The Sunday Times is passing these pictures to Lord Widgery.

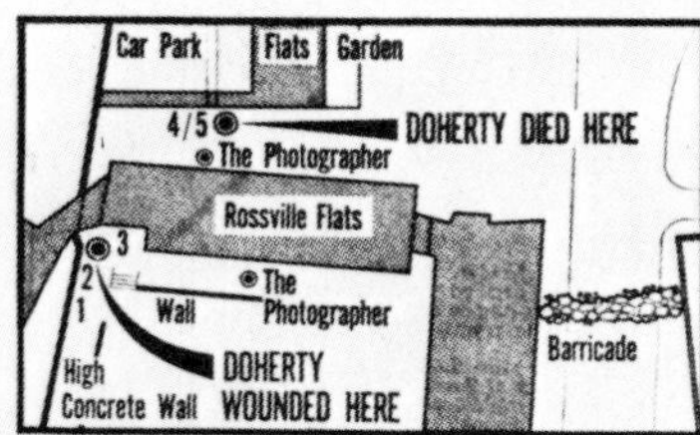

Numbers refer to the pictures on this and the opposite page.

GILLES PERESS is a 25-year-old French photographer who has been working in Northern Ireland for the Magnum International News Picture Agency since 1970. Last Sunday he walked at the head of the ill-fated Civil Rights march in Londonderry, photographing the youths at the Williams Street barrier. Later he ran up Chamberlain Street towards Rossville Flats.

He continued up Chamberlain Street and went through the passage under Rossville Flats and on the far side saw a dead or dying man and another crawling towards him to help him. "I photographed that scene and also a young man trying to find shelter by lying flat on the ground behind a small tree," says Peress. "Going along the wall of the flats, I saw and photographed a man shot in the eye and a young man shot in the stomach."

261–2 DEATH IN DERRY.
Eye and word go together in this presentation from *The Sunday Times* showing one of a number of men who died controversially when troops opened fire on a Londonderry riot in 1972. The sequence of photographs across two pages is held together by a long strapline. It is white on black, but it is restrained in sizing and does not get in the way of the pictures. There is a map to locate the photographic drama and captions lead 1–5 across the spread to the final emphasis of the death picture

(continued from page 259)

Queens were at private prayer—they were standing in the street as the coffin was taken off the gun carriage—but perfect picture headlines satisfy without suspicion every expectation they arouse. In later editions the headline was changed to The Three Stand Alone. This is where caption and picture headline differ. The headline must affirm what we can see. The caption must avoid that; it must supplement. If the headline says Factory Fire, the customers are entitled to ask for their money back if we simply show a gutted factory without flames or fireman with hose. An American daily had the dramatic overline Millworker Fights Fire 60ft Up. That is fine as the headline on a news story, but when it is presenting a picture we expect to see the gallant man actually suspended vertiginously above the smoke. All we got, in fact, was the man posing for a picture, on the ground, without a whiff of smoke or vertigo.

The occasions are rare when the overline properly strays beyond the visible, and then it should do so deliberately:

FIVE MINUTES AFTER THIS PICTURE THE PRESIDENT WAS DEAD

This requirement to deliver the goods is the only limitation on the picture headline. It shares with news headlines (see Book III) the desirability of short words, but the style is freer for three reasons:

1 Comment is permissible. The photograph of a Vietcong prisoner being executed in the street (page 5) was headlined acceptably 'Savage Saigon'. And another horror picture: 'Even for Uganda a picture unsurpassed in brutality.'

2 The phrase that would not make sense by itself often makes good sense with a picture. Even a single word can forge a link with a picture: Triplets, Hero, Victim, Rescuer . . . and there are more striking single-word presentations (p. 269).

3 Label headlines, frowned on for news stories, are acceptable and often preferable.

. AND A MAN CRAWLED TO THE END OF HIS LIFE

E: Doherty is hit—the handkerchief worn for CS gas is no protection against bullets. He crawls on

round the corner, Doherty collapses and a man moves out from cover to help. But he is too late . . .

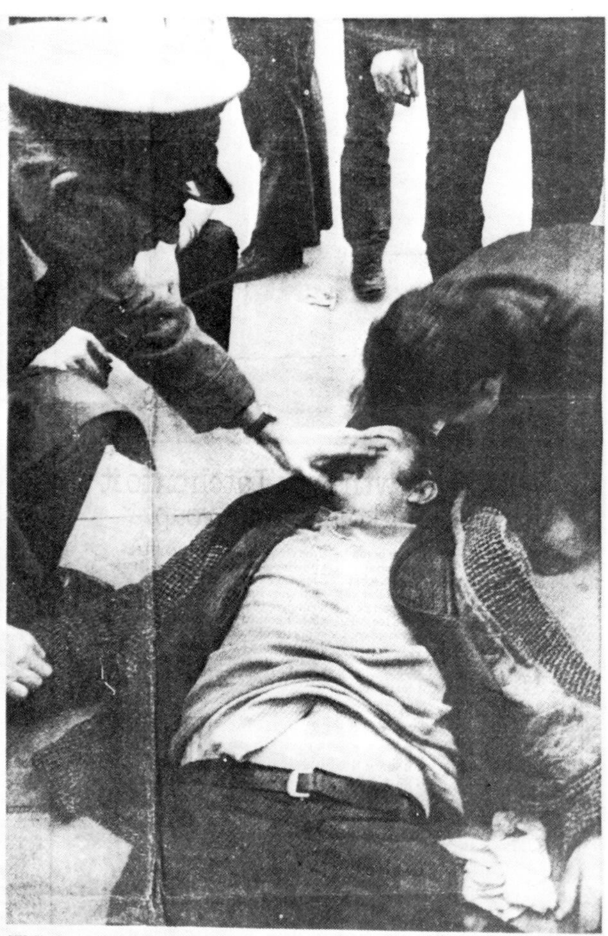

FIVE: an ambulanceman delivers the verdict. Patrick Doherty is dead

262 TRAIN CRASH (*right*). The remarkable fact when the train came off the line at 60 miles an hour was that so many people were saved. The photograph by itself would have been unfocused in meaning: are we meant to exclaim in horror or relief? The headline leaves no doubt, creating from word and image a strong single effect

DAILY EXPRESS

No. 19,015 MONDAY JULY 17 1961 3.30 a.m. forecast: Drizzle, improving later Price 3d

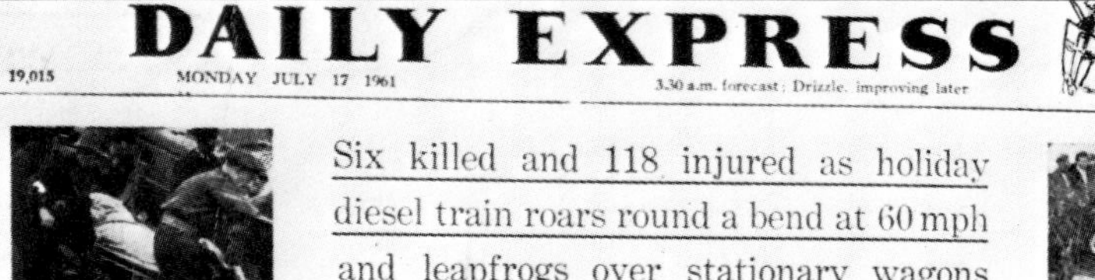

Six killed and 118 injured as holiday diesel train roars round a bend at 60 mph and leapfrogs over stationary wagons

ALIVE! OUT OF THIS

Seconds after the crash they stream to safety. A woman weeps. Behind: The second and third coaches, with hardly a window broken, rear into a crazy leap-frog over the trucks

Men on the track

Ted Hill warns

The major

RIVIERA THIEVES GRAB £715,000 ART

From RICHARD KILIAN: Paris, Sunday

4.30 a.m. LATEST

HUNT FOR MAN ON MOUNTAIN

263A The original photograph of jubilant guerrillas on wreck of VC10

Five attempts

The word-and-picture successes on the previous pages look easy enough: but we professionals muff it somewhere every edition. Here are five attempts by British Sunday newspapers to make effective use of a striking Saturday picture. Arab hijackers had forced a British airliner to land in the desert. The passengers became hostages for an Arab guerrilla girl arrested in London called Leila Khaled. On Saturday night Khaled was freed and the guerrillas, who had been threatening to blow up all the people in the plane, allowed them off—and then blew up the plane. The newspapers received this photograph of guerrillas doing a jig of joy on top of the ruins of the VC10 with rather more wreckage to the right than shown here (263A). Nobody got it right.

The Sunday Times (264A) sized the picture well, but weakened its effect

WORLD EXCLUSIVE

Sunday Mirror

LADY BIRD JOHNSON TELLS HER SECRETS

9d. September 13, 1970 No. 387

Jeers—at Britain's expense

Moment of triumph for Arab terrorists atop the crumpled remains of Britain's hijacked VC-10.

By JOHN GRAHAM, Political Correspondent

BRITAIN is prepared to release Arab hijack girl Leila Khaled to protect the lives of 250 British citizens in Jordan.

The concession was announced by Premier Edward Heath last night after armed anti-British mobs rampaged through Amman's hotel district.

The statement came shortly after the hijackers blew up the three airliners stranded on the desert "Revolution Airport." It said:

"To avoid any misunderstanding or possible loss of life, the Government wish to let it be known that they are prepared to return Miss Leila Khaled to an Arab country as part of the satisfactory settlement of the problem of the detained passengers and crews of the three aircraft."

Mr. Heath made the concession public first with the approval of seven of his Ministers and then of his full Cabinet.

Earlier, the new British Ambassador in Amman, Mr. John Phillips radioed that but heads of the Popular Front for the Liberation of Palestine were inciting crowds in the streets with the story that Britain was not prepared to free Leila under any circumstances.

Broadcast

They said they had heard this in a radio broadcast. But by late last night the British authorities had still not traced the alleged broadcast.

Earlier yesterday Government sources in London said that so far they had "conceded nothing" to the guerillas who might have "expectations but not assurances."

On orders from the Prime Minister, the new statement was immediately and repeatedly broadcast in Arabic on the BBC's external service.

It was also flashed to the Ambassador and to the International Red Cross in Amman in an effort to reassure the mobs that Britain is willing to hand the girl over.

But this would only be as part of a deal for the return of all the hijacked prisoners.

They had, in fact, previously been conveyed to the Red

Continued on Back Page

Leila Khaled . . . now she waits to be set free.

LEILA TO BE FREED

by THE EDITOR

THE DAY John Kennedy was assassinated Lady Bird Johnson, wife of the new President, began keeping a diary.

Almost every day for five years she dictated her account of events, great or personal, as she experienced them.

I have just finished reading an advance copy of the diary, soon to be published.

It is warm and womanly, revealing and frank, a history of our time told through the words of a wife and mother.

LADY Bird Johnson's White House Diary is the publishing event of 1970—which every man and woman will want to read.

That is why the Sunday Mirror—in the face of vigorous competition—is soon to begin serialisation from the diary.

This major coup has been negotiated by the Sunday Mirror and the eminent publishers Weidenfeld and Nicolson, who will be publishing the British book version.

NEVER before has there been such a candid account of the life and times of one of America's great Presidents.

Mrs. Johnson tells of her intimate family problems . . . the tragedies of the Kennedys . . . 4 a.m. phone calls . . . anecdotes of the famous.

She also discusses frankly her role in shaping her husband's decisions—and his personal future.

You can read this compelling document first in the Sunday Mirror. Watch for further announcements.

LADY BIRD JOHNSON

C

The blast that shook the world

The People

No. 4630 Sunday, September 13, 1970 9d.

'MY SIX LOST YEARS'

The amazing case of the wife who cannot remember her husband

LIFE was like most mothers' for this pretty young wife.

Then . . . suddenly . . . she forgot EVERYTHING about the past six years of her life.

She forgot her husband.

She forgot her baby.

Even her body was a stranger to her. The one she remembered had changed over the six totally forgotten years.

Her story is incredible, tragic. And she still can't remember.

The story of her unique human drama—by the young wife herself—begins next week in The People.

IT IS ONE OF THE MOST REMARKABLE AMNESIA CASES IN HISTORY.

THIS WEEK don't miss the great story of how the present Chancellor of the Exchequer once tried to burrow his way out of a prison camp like a human mole—FILLING UP THE TUNNEL BEHIND HIM AS HE BURROWED. See pages 7 and 8.

'WE WILL GIVE UP LEILA IF...'

● Dynamite blasts the desert air . . . and the VC-10 British airliner is shattered.

Pieces of wreckage fly through the air. And, alongside, stand the two other hijacked planes . . . they are next on the guerillas' demolition list.

Soon after the dust and the debris settled, the jubilant guerillas stood proudly (inset) on the engine cowlings of the VC-10, all that remained of a once-proud gleaming airliner.

HOWLING anti-British mobs armed with rifles and grenades rampaged through the streets of Jordan's capital, Amman, yesterday, after hearing rumours that Britain was refusing to free girl guerilla Leila Khaled.

Britain makes it official

by TERENCE LANCASTER in London and KEN GARDNER in Amman

KIDS, YOU WERE GREAT!

THE TEENAGE brothers who kept their turtle alive . . . the girls who kept their heads despite taunts by their guards . . . the little boy called Richard who walked up and down cheering everybody up . . . these were some of the marvellous British children from the B.O.A.C. hijack plane.

WRIT BY BEATLES

'Prisoners'

Warning

FRONT PAGE SPORT

And now the latest, the greatest—the new No-Hope Cup

Alan SMITH EVERY SUNDAY

IT GIVES ME great pride and pleasure, as the actress once said, to announce the arrival of a new football competition—the No-Hopers' Cup. This will be sponsored by Annie's fish and chip shop of Billericay High Street. The final will be played on a wet Wednesday afternoon in Workington.

Dream

ADVERTISEMENT

Would you like to speak a foreign language?

by failing to display some words about it. They could have run across the top of the picture or in place of the headline on the left about Israel.

The Sunday Mirror (263C) is the best of this bunch because of the simple relationship of that headline 'Jeers—at Britain's expense'.

The People (263B): Unlike the others, it received, in time, a photograph of the explosion itself. It decided to run both, by insetting the joyful guerrillas, and arguably weakens both pictures. *The People* appreciated the need to sell the picture in words, but the positioning of them in the top left of the page is obscure and the wording a little exaggerated.

Sunday Telegraph (264C): Like *The Sunday Times* it fails by lack of a headline, and two pictures here are less impressive than one big one.

News of the World (264B): Sandwiched by two sans headlines, the picture hardly has a chance.

THE SUNDAY TIMES

13 SEPTEMBER 1970 • No. 7685 • Price 1/3

THE TROUBLED HEART — the first of a three-week series on the CARDIAC CRISIS — COLOUR MAGAZINE

40 hostages still held: Leila can go

PALESTINIAN guerrillas blew up three hijacked airliners yesterday, and said they were holding 40 hostages indefinitely as "prisoners of war" but that all others could go free. In all, about 60 hostages were unaccounted for: five Britons are still held by the guerrillas in addition to BOAC crew members.

A split in the guerrilla movement came into the open when the central committee of guerrilla organisations announced it was suspending from membership the Popular Front for hijacking and destroying the planes. The Committee said it would take a firm stand against the Popular Front.

In Geneva, the International Red Cross said it was suspending negotiations with the guerrillas.

In London, the British Cabinet, breaking silence on the future of Leila Khaled, the guerrilla girl held at Ealing police station, announced that it was prepared to release her, though not at once. This move was made to avert a riot of Palestinians threatening in Amman as crowds surged through the streets inflamed by news of the hostages' release.

BOAC has offered free flights to London to parents of children freed by the guerrillas. Airline staff will care for the children until parents arrive.

London brokers estimate that the destruction of the hijacked aircraft—including the 747 Jumbo at Cairo airport—will cost insurers nearly £20 million.

Hijacker Leila Khaled's own story, page 13
Four-page special begins page 11

JERUSALEM

Israel fears for the missing victims

By Eric Marsden

Victory jig from Arab guerrillas on the VC10 that bit the dust. Cost to the Popular Front, a few pounds of gelignite; cost to BOAC around £4m.

ROBERT MORLEY with Vanessa Redgrave in LOS ANGELES 25

BEFORE AND AFTER THE FIRST OF A NEW LOOK! SERIES

THE BOOT TO GO WITH THE LOOK designed by Edward Rayne

A

SUNDAY TELEGRAPH

No. 500 September 13, 1970 Price 9d.

HOW TO END AIR PIRACY P.16
Secrets of Soviet Security Police P.6

ARAB MOB MENACES HOSTAGES

British pledge to free Leila: planes blown up

AN accusation by Palestinian guerrillas of "British treachery" led last night to a mob of Arabs howling outside the Intercontinental Hotel in Amman for the blood of nearly 200 airline passengers and crews released from the three hijacked planes in the Jordanian desert, and to emergency action by the British Cabinet.

The mob of Jordanians, led by armed guerrillas, also demonstrated outside the British Embassy, shouting abuse at the staff. The sudden street violence came after the Popular Front for the Liberation of Palestine had told its members that Britain would not release Leila Khaled, the girl hijacker, under any circumstances.

A radio broadcast apparently incited the crowds. After an emergency Cabinet at 10 Downing Street, a statement was broadcast by the B.B.C. to Jordan, "to avoid any misunderstanding" that the Government would free Miss Khaled as part of a satisfactory settlement.

Hostages freed, 40 still held

By JOHN MOSSMAN in Amman

WOMEN and children passengers from the three aircraft hijacked by Palestinian commandos were freed from their desert "prison" at Revolution Airfield yesterday and driven in convoy into Amman.

Ballerina to write for SUNDAY TELEGRAPH

By DAVID FLOYD

No. 10 statement is broadcast to Arabs

By IAN WALLER, Political Correspondent

RED CROSS BREAK OFF TALKS

ISRAELIS MAY ACT IN JORDAN

Venice mourns tornado dead

ARMED GUARDS IN U.S. AIRLINERS

By DAVID ADAMSON in Washington

FREE record reveals your hidden ability to speak a foreign language

OTHER PAGES

LATE NEWS

C

NEWS OF THE WORLD

SUNDAY, SEPTEMBER 13, 1970 No. 6,616 PRICE NINEPENCE

WEATHER Sunny, some showers. OUTLOOK: Rainy

The Paper with the MOST

Cabinet move on Leila

THE CABINET held an emergency meeting last night and then issued the following statement:

Triumphant terrorists stand on the wrecked VC10. Total cost to airlines—£8,500,000

I SEE REBEL PUNCH UP OVER HOSTAGES' FATE

FROM INSIDE THE ARAB GUERRILLAS' SECRET HEADQUARTERS REPORTER SIMON REGAN SENDS AN EXCLUSIVE WORLD SCOOP ON THE LIFE-OR-DEATH ROW OVER 300 HIJACK VICTIMS.

● News of the World reporter SIMON REGAN was in the Palestine guerrillas' secret headquarters when the live-or-die fate of the 300 hijack hostages hung in the balance.

Vicar forgot the bride

Doctor Miriam works on a pill for men

ALL THE LONELY PEOPLE

£200,000 Soccer star rarin' to go

More for MEN
More for WOMEN
More for the YOUNG

Haven't you sometimes thought… I wish I could speak another language

B

Daily Mirror

EUROPE'S BIGGEST DAILY SALE

5p Friday, May 16, 1975 No. 22,177

The moment they knew that the marines had won

VICTORY is ours! This was the moment of triumph for President Ford and his gleeful men.

America's display of strength had crushed an enemy who later said they were too weak to resist.

Laughs, smiles and shouts burst around the President's desk as the hours of waiting ended.

President Ford, Secretary of State Henry Kissinger and the other top White House advisers had just learned that the Communist Cambodians had freed the 39 American seamen captured with their cargo ship, the Mayaguez, two days before.

The seamen were taken to a US destroyer by a small fishing-boat flying a white flag after a massive display of American strength.

Stormed

Two hours before, a US destroyer, her guns blazing warning shots, had closed at speed on the Mayaguez off the Cambodian coast.

US Marines stormed aboard. They found it abandoned. The Cambodians manning the Mayaguez had jumped over the side.

Ford's First Stand had ended in a partial victory. But there was still danger for 160 US Marines defending a beachhead on the Cambodian island of Koh Tang.

Most of the Marines — who are nick-named the "Leathernecks" — had landed there from helicopters on President Ford's orders to search for the American seamen.

But almost immediately they came under heavy fire from perhaps 1,000 Cambodian troops.

The Leathernecks ran up the Stars and Stripes—and fought back.

More Marines were sent in to help them, and the fierce battle raged for fourteen hours.

Cambodian fire brought down three helicopters, but then the Communists were shelled by US destroyers and strafed by jets.

The Marines gathered their wounded together and waited for dark. Then more helicopters went in and lifted them off.

Many were wounded and one was confirmed dead. But sixteen men—nine Marines and seven helicopter crewmen—are missing.

After the helicopters left, two destroyers sailed slowly offshore calling through loud-hailers: "If any Americans can hear this, give some sign. Fire your weapons. Wave."

Engines

Powerful binoculars swept the foreshore. Every so often the destroyers stopped their engines to listen. There was no response.

It is almost certain that the missing men are dead. But if they are alive President Ford may decide to

Continued on Page Two

From ANTHONY DELANO in Washington

WHOOPEE IN THE WHITE HOUSE

Sinatra's £1,000 shopping spree

Centre Pages

DAILY EXPRESS

No. 23,293 Friday May 16 1975 Weather: Showers; bright spells Price 6p

WHO'S GOT THE LAST LAUGH NOW

The moment Ford tasted victory and America regained its pride

Victory at last . . . President Ford shares his moment of triumph with his right-hand man Henry Kissinger and three aides in the White House as the news came through from Cambodia

OH BOY, we did it! The Mayaguez crew had been freed and

that America was now regarded by the world as "The Chicken of the Sea"—

Air hunt

Sinatra in at

Labels and idiom

There is a virtue in a label headline because it thrusts attention on to the picture; capturing the idiom of the real or imagined dialogue goes one better but it is tricky. The label can point the significance of a picture that is apparently dull: THE ROOM WHERE PEACE WAS SIGNED.

It can also give a lift to routine: THE FACE THAT LAUNCHED A THOUSANDTH SHIP (on a Greek royal at the launching of tanker 1,000). The commonest labels derive from who, where, when: The man who . . . The street where . . . The moment when . . . The last capitalises on the photograph's capacity for freezing a second. The front pages of the *Daily Mirror* (265A) and *Daily Express* (265B) enable us to compare the force of label and idiomatic headline.

President Ford is photographed with his aides when they first had the news that U.S. marines had retaken the American ship *Mayaguez*, captured at the end of the Cambodian war. The *Express* WHO'S GOT THE LAST LAUGH NOW is strong stuff—implied comment as well as idiom.

At a Miss World contest in London, watched by 150m TV viewers, the *Daily Express* had a picture taken backstage fractionally after an official had whispered the result to Miss Peru and her eyes were closing in a faint.

To have headed that MISS PERU BECOMES MISS WORLD would have emphasised to readers that they already knew it from television and MISS PERU FAINTS would have missed the piquancy of timing. The *Express* rightly had a label THE MOMENT THEY MADE MISS PERU MISS WORLD; but it scored again with another label: The scene you did not see on television last night.

'The moment' is, however, a phrase to ration. Where there is a strong news photograph (not seen on television) it is often better to employ something

265A and 265B THE MAYAGUEZ INCIDENT. Which is the better headline treatment of the same photograph?

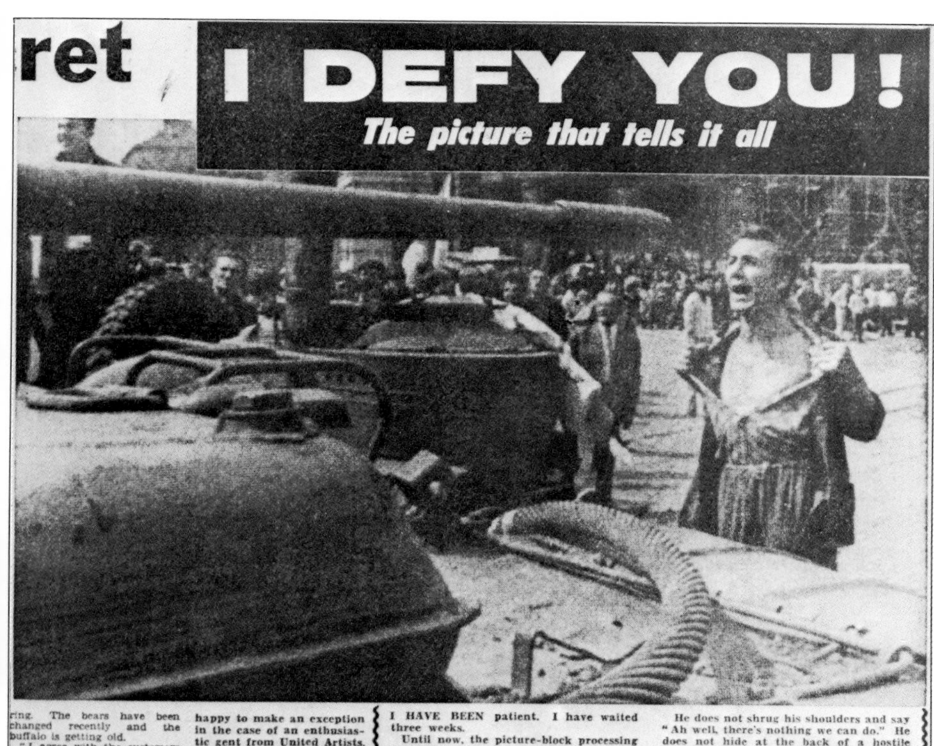

ret

I DEFY YOU!

The picture that tells it all

ring. The bears have been changed recently and the buffalo is getting old.

"I agree with the customers—they should not be advertised if they are not appearing, but the posters were printed some time ago."

If this is the only way the travelling circus can hope to survive, I can only wish them bon voyage to obscurity.

Nameless

IT IS NOT my habit to use the material sent to me in heaping measure by the film publicity boys. But I'm happy to make an exception in the case of an enthusiastic gent from United Artists.

He has come up with a photo of a scene from an Italian-made Western. It shows six men on a gallows about to be hanged, and it panders to the perverted instincts which once caused crowds to flock to public executions.

It is a pleasure to mention the item in the hope, and I mean this sincerely, that the film enjoys no success whatever.

It is also a pleasure not to mention the film's title.

I HAVE BEEN patient. I have waited three weeks.

Until now, the picture-block processing dispute in the newspaper industry has prevented me from publishing what is, in my opinion, the most powerful, significant picture of the Czech tragedy.

It is August 21, 1968. A Czech—in his thirties or forties, I would guess, and probably a married man with children—faces the long, menacing gun barrel of a Russian tank.

He is still in pyjamas and dressing-gown—awakened by the shattering realisation that the Russians are not only coming. They have come.

He does not shrug his shoulders and say "Ah well, there's nothing we can do." He does not hide at the back of a hostile crowd. He walks up to a tank, bares his breast and shouts defiantly: "So you would make our land your concentration camp? Rather you shoot me dead!"

Having watched the new TV series about the Home Guard, "Dad's Army," I have been thinking: What WOULD we have done if the Jerries had taken over?

Would I—would you—have had the guts to stand in front of a Tiger tank like this and shout "Shoot and be damned"?

A thought to ponder on with your bacon, eggs and toast today.

266A THE LONE CZECH. Because of an industrial dispute, the picture editor of the *People* had to wait three weeks to use this photograph. He used his delayed opportunity to effect

266B HIS LAST PICTURE. Taken by Leonardo Henrickson as he was shot by his subject. Published in the *Daily Express*

NEWS

The moment I died

By the man who took this picture

Leonardo Henricksen, his pictures are the evidence

PEOPLE once believed that a murderer's image was imprinted on the eyes of his victim. Today this old myth has a tragic parallel.

The picture on the left was taken by cameraman Leonardo Henricksen during the abortive Chile uprising at the end of June.

It was his last.

The soldier standing on the truck fired the rifle he is pointing directly at the camera and killed the Swedish - Argentinian cameraman who was working for Swedish TV.

Now the soldier may pay.

For now Chilian court martial prosecutors have exactly the evidence that once British police looked for in vain when they photographed the retinas behind the eyes of Jack the Ripper's victims. . . .

A picture that says: "This is the moment I died — this is my killer."

CLOSE-UP ON DEATH, the soldier on the truck pointing his rifle straight at the camera fired, the cameraman fell

approaching a news headline: Joe Bloggs crashing at 100 mph. But there is no escaping 'The moment' treatment in 266B THE MOMENT I DIED was a remarkable headline on a remarkable photograph. It was taken by the cameraman featured in the display during street troubles in Chile. It was his last picture. He died from a bullet fired by the soldier standing on the back of the truck.

I DEFY YOU (266A) is a successful use of both idiom and label—rightly leading with meaning of the picture and using the label as reinforcement. This was taken during the 1968 Soviet invasion of Czechoslovakia.

Armchair picture editors might like to try alternative headlines: MAN AGAINST TANK (too obvious), THE BRAVE SPIRIT OF THE CZECHS (too wordy), PRIDE AND POWER (abstruse)

Idiomatic headlines are fine when they are sensitive, but riskier. When an elephant upset a tea table at feeding time, the temptation should have been resisted to write: OOPS, SORRY,—SCUSE ME. Far better: THE ELEPHANT WHO CAME TO TEA. But there are successes. A civil servant beauty queen named Miss Whitehall (the home of British government offices) is neatly headed: I REMAIN, SIR, YOUR GLAMOROUS SERVANT . . .

When soldiers in the Royal Army Service Corps exchanged their hats for those of the Royal Army Ordnance Corps, The *Northern Echo* headline writer did well to pick up Army supply idiom: NEW HAT: REBADGED: NEW REGIMENT FOR THE USE OF.

There are two keys to writing idiomatic headlines: to be in tune with the mood of the picture and to realise that the reader, too, is seeing it. Thus: POPE BLESSES AMERICA AT SERVICE is tolerable as a text headline but flat for a picture heading, whereas 'GOD BLESS AMERICA! GOD BLESS YOU ALL!' adds the impression of sound to the still photograph. It uses the reader's recognition of the Pope to take him into the story. It rejoices in the occasion.

267A LINK-UP: American soldiers, fighting from the West, meet their Russian allies, fighting from the East, at Torgau on the Elbe, April 1945

DAILY EXPRESS

SATURDAY APRIL 28 1945

HITLER'S EMPIRE, SPLIT IN TWO, MAKES ITS LAST STRUGGLE

Allies from East and West unite, then turn to deliver the final blows

THIRD REICH IS DEAD

'THE YANKS ARE HERE'—'THE RUSSIANS ARE HERE'

At 4p.m., April 25, in its 13th year

HANDSHAKE ON TWISTED GIRDER LINKS ARMIES

From SELKIRK PANTON: Torgau on the Elbe, Friday

THE Third Reich of Adolf Hitler is dead. It died in its 13th year at four o'clock on Wednesday afternoon, when General Courtney Hodges' First U.S. Army linked up with Marshal Koniev's First Ukrainian Army and cut Germany into two parts, north and south.

WINE, SONG AND MUSIC

Panton was a prisoner

TWO ARMIES MOVE TO PINCER MUNICH

GENOA IS CAPTURED, NEARING VENICE

Himmler men shoot Goering

SAYS GERMAN

4.30 a.m. LATEST

HITLER PLANS WITH GREIM

ROME CALLS FOR MUSSOLINI

Petain sleeps by death post

Nuns at his door

REDOUBT A MYTH SAYS DIETMAR

'When Berlin goes, all is over: Hitler is there'

From JAMES WELLARD: U.S. 9th Army, Friday

DIETMAR: WE ARE CUT TO THE QUICK

AND THIS IS DIETMAR SAYING IT . . .

Victory prizes for young composers

Mussolini is 'caught at

Simplicity

This, said the *News Chronicle*, was a picture the world will never forget. It is the day American and Russian troops met after battling across different sides of Europe.

The *Daily Express* (267A) muffed the presentation. The main headline wording—premature by several months—did not talk directly to the picture; the headline that did was tortuous ('THE YANKS ARE HERE'—'THE RUSSIANS ARE HERE'). Far too many headlines were competing for attention; and the picture was under-sized.

The whole point of the story was the link-up and the *News Chronicle* (268B) did it simply and brilliantly. It is hard to think that this could be bettered by anybody today.

News Chronicle

4 a.m. EDITION

SATURDAY, APRIL 28, 1945

ONE PENNY

LINK-UP

Secret is out: Americans and Russians met at Torgau on Elbe at 4.20 p.m. Wednesday

THEY have linked up. These words, flashed round the world last night, announced the conclusion of two of the greatest military marches in modern history.

From the banks of the Volga the Red Army has battled 1,400 miles to the west; from the beaches of Normandy the Americans have fought 700 miles to the east, and at Torgau on the Elbe, in the heart of the Reich, they have at last met.

From London, from Moscow, from Washington the news was announced simultaneously.

At 4.20 p.m. on Wednesday patrols met; on the following afternoon the link was firmly forged.

Actually there were two points of contact—the first at Torgau; the second 25 miles to the south-east at Groba, a suburb of Riesa.

The three leaders issued messages. "This," said President Truman, "is not the hour of final victory in Europe, but the hour draws near."

"Our task and our duty are to complete the destruction of the enemy," said Marshal Stalin.

"We meet in true and victorious comradeship," declared Mr. Churchill. "Let us all march forward upon the foe."

OFFICER IN JEEP MADE CONTACT

Home-made banner waved from castle

From STANLEY BARON

News Chronicle War Correspondent

A picture the world will never forget

Mussolini caught: Goering said to be dead and Hitler dying

The Big 3 tell the world

PETAIN ASKS FOR PORTRAIT OF DE GAULLE

DECORATION FOR TIMOSHENKO

BELL'S SCOTCH WHISKY *Afore ye go*

Daily Mail

NO. 23,235 — SATURDAY, JANUARY 23, 1971 — PRICE

CAUGHT!

A burglar at work

NEXT WEEK FROM PARIS

SANDY FAWKES

with the lush new clothes for spring and summer

TODAY

By RODNEY TYLER

THIS is the picture which caught John Trott attempting to break-in — and put him in jail for two years.

For, as he approached the window of a £20,000 house in St. John's Wood, London, the owner stepped from behind the curtains and took a flashlight snap.

And the picture won him a judge's commendation at Inner London Sessions for his 'coolness and skill' in a dangerous situation.

On the day the picture was circulated to the police 41-year-old Trott was recognised and arrested at his home, where silver from another robbery was found.

The story behind the picture started the night marketing executive Anthony Coombs, 29, went to bed early at his home in Woronzow Road, N.W.

At 9.35 p.m. he heard a noise by the front door, crept downstairs and saw a shadowy figure through the frosted glass pressing at the door.

After one or two attempts the man gave up and moved off.

But Mr Coombs thought he might try again, so he fetched his 35mm. camera and flash apparatus and edged into the dining room.

He was just in time to see the figure drop over the seven-foot wall into his back

Slasher Nixon shakes

More Post Office

BURGLAR TROTT CAUGHT BY THE CAMERA

269A BURGLAR. All five headline words are needed, but CAUGHT! was rightly bigger. One of the few occasions justifying an exclamation mark

Pages with punch

Words help pictures; but passenger words have an especially debilitating effect on picture headlines. The *Daily Mirror* had a strong picture page of Mrs. Jacqueline Kennedy at the President's funeral, but spoiled it with the heading: TRAGIC JACKIE, SO COURAGEOUS IN HER SILENT GRIEF. The last six words add nothing. We can pare and pare again with a picture headline (always provided it meets the generally preferable layout requirement of running the full width of the picture). Whereas a one-word news headline would be a cryptic absurdity, a one-word picture headline can make sense. RENDEZVOUS was effective over the first photograph of a boat meeting Chichester after his voyage round the world. PROOF was the word over the first pictures demonstrating the existence of Soviet rocket sites in Cuba. Here are other examples of economy.

Sunday, 1,357,556
Daily, 1,193,297

DAILY NEWS

NEW YORK'S PICTURE NEWSPAPER

EXTRA EDITION

Vol. 9. No. 173 56 Pages — New York, Friday, January 13, 1928 — 2 Cents

DEAD!

Story on page 3

269C ELECTROCUTION. The *New York Daily News* photographer took this first, illicit photograph of an execution by strapping a camera to his ankle

Daily Mail

MONDAY, AUGUST 4, 1975

NIGEL DEMPSTER MAIL DIARY PAGE 13

MAIL WORLD EXCLUSIVE Philby and Blake, both now with Russian wives, meet near Moscow to talk over the legacy of their betrayal

THE TRAITORS

KIM PHILBY and George Blake—two men whose names have become synonymous with the word 'traitor'—meet over a bottle of wine in a garden near Moscow. Theirs is a strange friendship. The only thing they have in common is their treachery.

Now, the Mail can reveal exclusively, both have Russian wives to ease the loneliness of their self-... woman 20 years his junior. Her name is Nina and she is Philby's fifth wife. He was divorced some years ago from Melinda Maclean, former wife of Donald Maclean, of the spies Burgess and Maclean.

George Blake, now 52, and his wife, Ida, an interpreter at Moscow's Scientific Institute, have a four-year-old son named Mischa. Blake fled to Russia after making a spectacular escape in 1966 from Wormwood Scrubs, where he was serving a 42-year sentence.

269B Scoop picture with punchline (it would be weakened if smaller type explanation intervened between headline and picture

Daily  Mail

WEDNESDAY, APRIL 30, 1975 6p (CHANNEL ISLANDS 7p)

Frightened, abandoned and waiting for its fate . . . that is Saigon as 30 years of war reach a climax with a Dunkirk in the Sky

THE END

JOHN EDWARDS
Mailman who is remaining in Saigon

THE Americans went out the way only they can. They staged an aerial spectacular, a Dunkirk in the sky that went on all day and deep into the flare-ridden night.

It was the biggest one-way trip in their history.

They went in their king-sized 'choppers' . . . Green Giants . . . Hueys . . . Chinooks. And they went fast. Scrabbling and pushing their way into the big birds, with the curses of the Vietnamese ringing in their ears.

Their farewell from the broken, abandoned army of the Republic of Vietnam were fusillades of automatic fire, triggered as much in contempt as in anger.

So now there's nobody left in town any more. Except the Vietnamese for whom there's no way out.

And they crouch in a Saigon like it had never been—still and frightened, abandoned and waiting for its fate.

Pleading

What that fate will be we will know in a few days or hours when the new masters arrive. Big Minh's government of national surrender are desperately pleading for the the only thing left to beg for . . . mercy.

Is mercy a Vietcong virtue? This is the city to find out.

Stairway to safety . . . Americans and refugees clamber to an airlift helicopter

Desperate fight to leave

270A LAST DAY. It is the end of the long war in Vietnam and the last refugees queue all day for a rooftop airlift rescue by American helicopters. The picture is thin but intriguing; and *Daily Mail* picture and headline synthesise memorably well

Chapter 15

From Print to Page Ethics

A seven-bath developer is no substitute for thought.
Terence Donovan

19 MARCH 1972 No 7762

THE SUNDAY TIMES

NEWS DIGEST
19 March 1972

China explodes new A-bomb

Howard Hughes 'may end silence'

Maoists threaten Soviet planes

Bhutto woos Russia

Two new Heath plans for Ulster

1: Resident British Minister
2: Proportional Representation

Big Craig rally sounds warning to Westminster

COLOUR MAGAZINE

BARBER'S BUDGET AUCTION

THE WIFE BELOW STAIRS

HAVE FUN PLAYING TENNIS THE HELDMAN WAY

PLEASURES & PERILS OF OLD AGE

The perils of putting with ARNOLD PALMER

The treasure lies in the contact sheet which offers a positive print, at actual negative size, of every negative the photographer exposed. Contacts are always disappointing to the inexperienced eye. The images are tiny, the prints too often are not the quality needed for judgment. It is a fatal error, whether of ignorance or indolence, merely to scan them with the naked eye. Every contact needs to be examined with a contact magnifier in a bright light, and it takes practice. When a contact is blurred there is a simple way to tell whether the flaw is in the original negative or is due to faulty proofing: have a look at the numbers which run with the contacts. If they are also unsharp the error is in the proofing, not the photography.

The contact sheet at 272, a meeting between Heath and Pompidou, had the conventional two-shots, but the picture editor was intrigued by the juxtaposition on part of one contact of two famous noses in silhouette and that made a deep double column on the front page. But between contact and page there are several steps which this chapter will, in part, describe.

There are two other systems for black and white selection. One is for the picture editor to examine negatives in the darkroom. This has the disadvantage of limiting the number of people who can discuss the work; and the more people who handle negatives the greater the risk of damage from fingerprints, dust and scratches. The other system relies on the photographer to present a handful of finished prints. It saves time but photographers are not the best judges of their own work and rarely do they have eye or eagerness for creative cropping.

A contact sheet of 35mm film recording President Pompidou meeting Prime Minister Heath. 'Herr' (*bottom right*) identifies the photographer Frank Herrmann

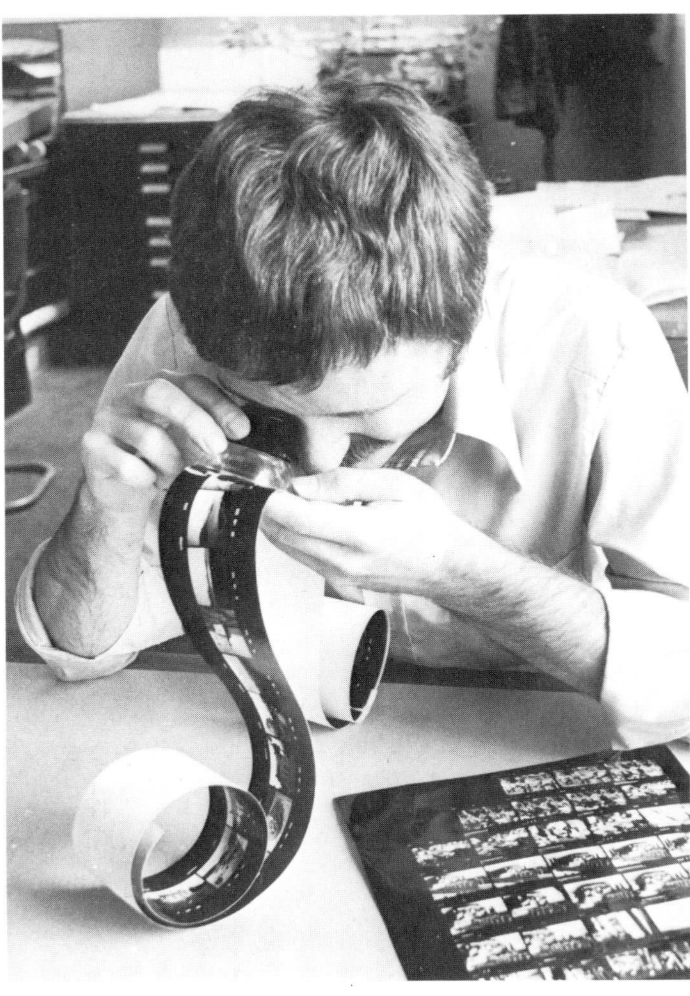

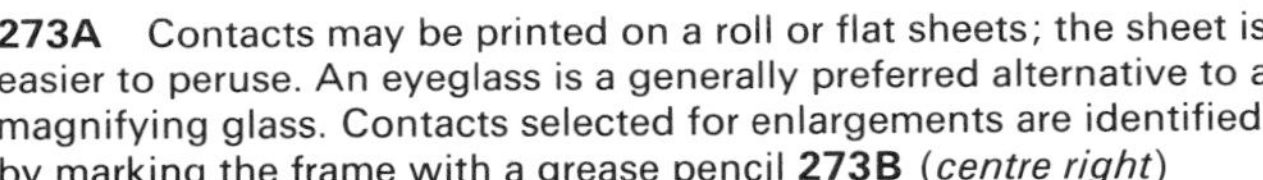
273A Contacts may be printed on a roll or flat sheets; the sheet is easier to peruse. An eyeglass is a generally preferred alternative to a magnifying glass. Contacts selected for enlargements are identified by marking the frame with a grease pencil **273B** (*centre right*)

Steps to high quality reproduction

Robert Benchley once remarked of the first issue of *Time* that it looked as if the pictures had been engraved on slices of bread. It was a defamation not only of *Time*—one need not even hasten to say their standards are first class—but also of engravers. Many of the smudges that pass for half-tones in newspapers owe their murk to other sources; and good reproduction may require detective work at stages from print to page. In letterpress newspapers the engraver's proof should be compared with the photograph and with a proof from the foundry casting. The height of the block in the forme (which needs to be accurate to a ten-thousandth of an inch) should be checked, and the control of inking and pressure on the presses, always bearing in mind that in rotary letterpress some pages print better than others. (One quick clue is to examine the other half-tones on the same page; if they are reproducing well, the fault lies before the casting.)

None of the later stages can do much if editorial departments persist in trying to reproduce photographs whose quality must turn M. Daguerre in his grave—flat and grey prints with little tone range. What is required is sharp detail, broad pattern, and a full gradation of tone. The sharp detail is often called 'contrast', which is misleading. True contrast—solid blacks and whites—would reveal little detail. We should look for tone scale, for highlights and shadows with details crystal clear. Of course some news pictures have to be accepted despite being technically imperfect, but nothing can justify the frequency with which newspapers present inky blobs described as 'fire damage', or 'flower show' or 'the distant border', to name

A

B

C

three subject areas where there is inadequate tone differentiation.

The darkroom can help a lot. It should be asked for prints larger by about a third than the intended reproduction. Some idea of the tonal scale possible from the same negative is shown at 274A–C, part of the frame 274D selected from the contacts. Which would you choose? There is only one and the eyes alone suggest the answer. A at left is too light, and in C the face will print as a dark smudge. When we have the tonal scale like 274B (*centre*) we are ready for the next stage.

274D Enlarged print from marked contact **273B**. All the faces **ABC** *above* are a section of **274D** but printed lighter and darker

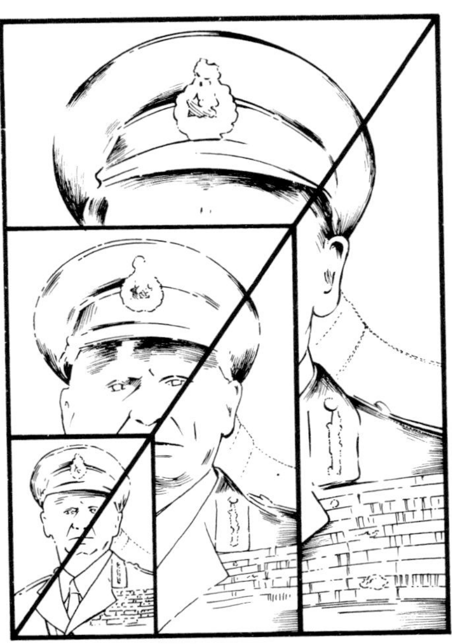

275A (*left*)

Scaling a print for a layout

The diagonal is the key to geometric scaling. The rectangle chosen for reproduction—all or part of the print—will reduce or enlarge in fixed proportion along the projection of a line from corner to corner. A new rectangle can be produced at whatever point the diagonal lines intersect a line from the edge of the print (as indicated at 275A). In a newspaper a rough decision is normally made on column width when the print is being reduced. The width of two-columns, say, is marked off along the top or bottom line of the desired rectangle. The depth of reproduction this will produce is then indicated by the length of a 90-degree line from this two-column point to its intersection with the diagonal.

Scaling and cropping instructions are given in one of three ways: Marking the front with grease pencil (not recommended); marking the back with a soft pencil either by placing face down on a light box or holding to a window; or by using tracing paper. This is the best method and we carry it out below with a full frame of 274D and the intention of scaling for the reproduction at 276B.

1 Materials: Drawing board (preferably tilted); T-square; 45 deg. set-square; Perspex ruler; felt pen; tracing paper; masking tape. Tape print down at two corners, keeping image square to T-square

2 Tape tracing paper over print with masking tape—pressure sensitive tape, not clear Sellotape which rips off emulsion. Judge likely crop mark and draw right angle in top left corner

3 Measure width of final reproduction from top left corner. Drop a line to the required depth and complete reproduction rectangle

4 Run a diagonal line from top left corner to opposite corner—and then, continue it so that a new rectangle can be formed which will encompass the preferred area of reproduction

5 Complete the new rectangle. First draw a vertical line from conclusion of the diagonal and then complete the horizontals

6 You now have two rectangles; the smaller one is the reproduction size and the large one is the area which will be scaled down

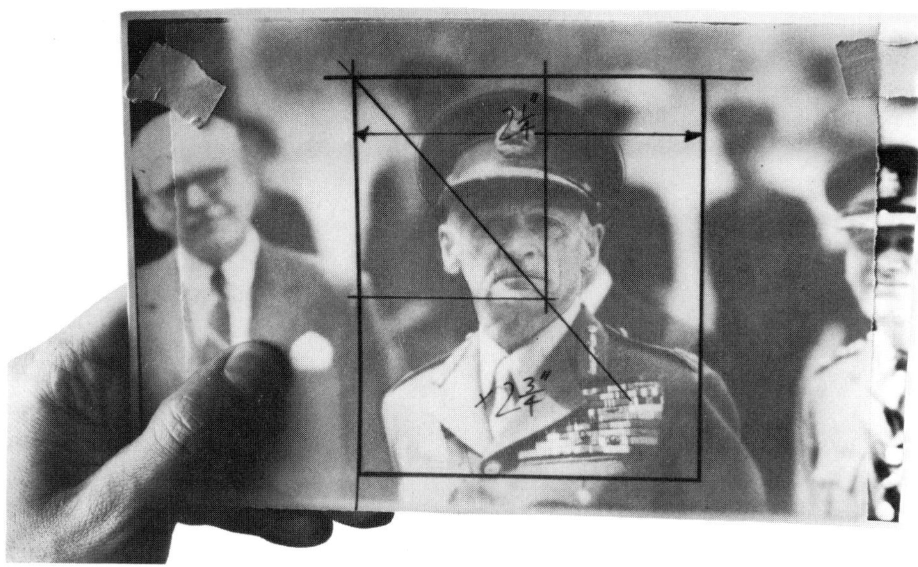

276A (*left*): Scaling a portrait. **276B** (above) the result, at actual size

Two ways to scale Monty

Our completed tracing overlay can now been seen over the full print of Field Marshal Montgomery (276A *above*). Any rectangle which intersects along the diagonal (see 275A) can be reproduced at $2\frac{1}{4}''$ by $2\frac{3}{4}''$ (the smaller rectangle). The area we choose is reproduced right at actual size (276B). It represents a big reduction on the real size of the image—don't be misled by its apparent size similarly with the scaled down photograph above. A precise determination of the final crop area is made by removing the masking tape and moving the tracing paper on the surface of the photograph, examining variations through the rectangular window we drew.

When the ideal area has been fixed the tracing is struck down again and print and tracing with instructions sent to process.

Another way is the proportional calculator. You find the original print width $4\frac{1}{8}''$ on the inner scale and align it with the desired width on the outer scale. The new depth will be the figure on the outer scale opposite the actual depth on the inner scale. A window gives the percentage reduction and the engineer will accept a single instruction 'reduce 53 per cent'.

This magic wheel is a vital tool for magazines publishing from small positive transparencies. The page designer works by pasting photostats of artwork on a full scale layout sheet. He looks at the transparency, estimates the size of the preferred area and uses the calculator to determine what percentage of enlargement this means. The darkroom will then produce the enlarged stat from the full transparency and the designer can use any part of it he wishes for his layout.

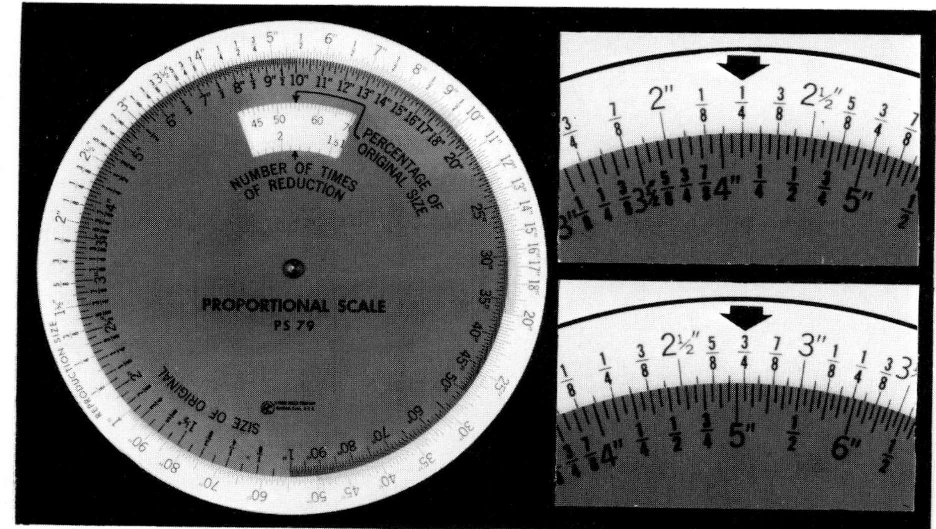

276C The proportional calculator. Monty's original print width of $4\frac{1}{8}''$ is aligned with the design width of $2\frac{1}{4}''$ (*top left*) and the new depth ($2\frac{3}{4}''$) is indicated opposite the original 5" (*bottom left*). A window (*above*) shows what percentage reduction this is

Handling

Conserve the image. Photographs should never be cut, nor crop marks indicated on the front (277A *right*). Even writing on the back is risky. Ball point or hard pencil comes through as embossment on the surface and can appear in print. Masking tape should be used for attachments, not paper clips (as at top centre); and if clips have to be used the print should be protected by a buffer of cardboard. A print should never be folded or rolled since it cracks the emulsion (as through the boy's sunglasses; right lens as we see it). These are rules for current reproduction and also for preservation: today's images are tomorrow's history.

Reversing

Layout is sometimes stymied because a figure looks the wrong way, especially in couplings (Chapter 13) and combinations. Process can solve this by reversing or 'flopping' the image as in 277B. But floppers must watch tell tale-points such as hair-partings and lettering. Which is Moshe Dayan's blind eye? Some flops invite giggles: an informed *Observer* magazine feature on Oxford's rowing was caught with its shorts down with a photograph in which all the Worcester College oars went into the water on the wrong sides of the eight.

Retouching

Strong detail which mars composition can be painted out in process (277C). Less obtrusive detail can be faded out in the etching.

In areas where skilled retouchers are not available even an amateur can improve a print by removing wire streaks and painting in 'dividers', outlines where whites melting into off whites are lost in reproduction. It requires a few fine sable brushes, a range of five grey watercolours which can be mixed judiciously (or a bottle of Indian ink and a pot of process white), and a resolution never to touch a face.

A

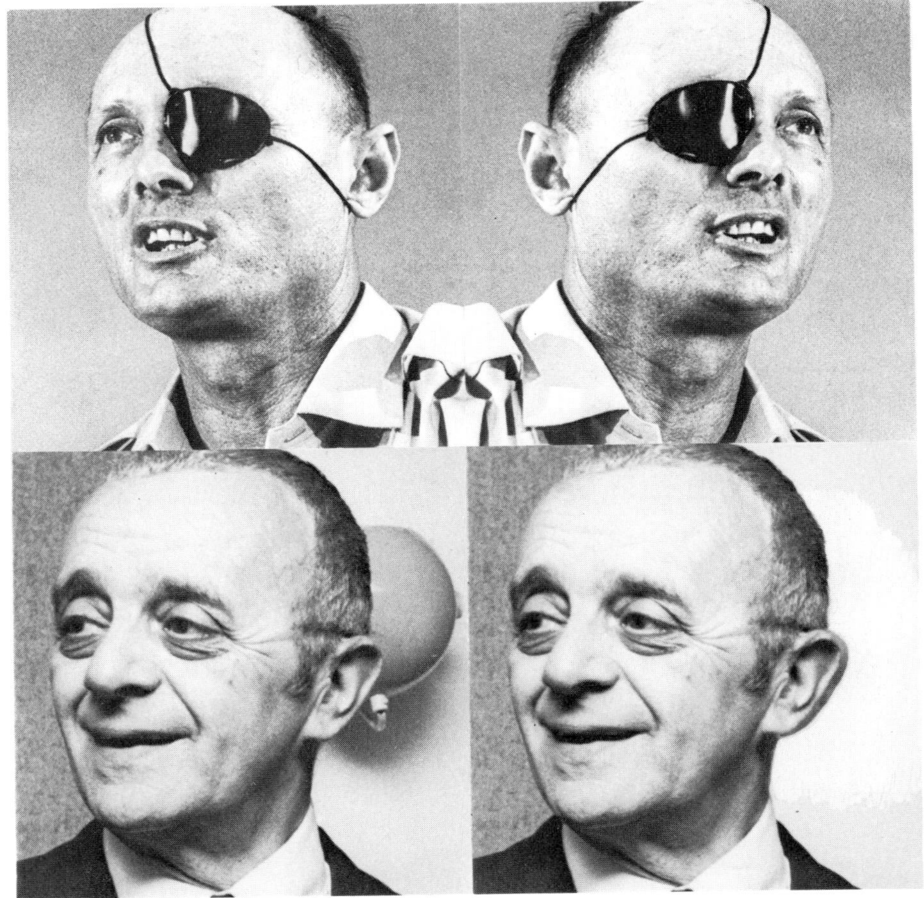

B

C

A

B

C

Angle cropping

Sometimes the content of a picture is not conveniently—or economically—caught by a straight crop. The tilted crop, demonstrated here, may be the answer. This story was about Jean-Bedel Bokassa, 55-year-old dictator of the Central African Republic. Not content with being president, prime minister and minister of defence, justice, information, agriculture and stock breeding, health, aviation, transport and mines, he had declared himself emperor of his 1,600,000 people and ordered a jewelled crown. A routine single column crop (278A) could not be tight and properly show the emperor's current finery, but a slight tilt in the original (278B) produced both a tight crop and a full display (278C).

A necessary caution about angled cropping is that watch has to be kept for background details, particularly horizontal and vertical lines (windows, fireplaces, picture frames, etc). If these become too angled, the viewer is disturbed by disorientation. This is another area where process paint may be usefully employed, fading or obliterating the intrusions.

A Squared-Up Half-Tone
Made with a relatively coarse screen of 55–65 lines to an inch for most newspapers, up to 85 for offset and 150 for glossy magazines. The screen must match paper, ink and print methods.

B Cut-Out Half-tone
The silhouette may be complete, as here, or a partial projection from a squared up half tone. Ideal for losing ugly background, popular for fashion shots. Obtained by marking required outline on tracing overlay.

C Bleach-Out
The continuous tone of the photograph is converted to single black and whites of line reproduction. The big advantage is that it retains high legibility at very small sizes, e.g. in logos.

Variations on a theme

Line conversions of photographs yield possibilities for editorial or technical improvement. Process departments can offer a few variations normally but hundreds can be produced by specialised firms, such as Headliners (UK) Ltd. who have provided the specimens of different treatments of Barbara Bach, viewed earlier on page 157 through the normal halftone screen. The technical facility is to make good reproduction possible in all processes—and at smaller sizes. The editorial bonus is to add texture, drama or fun. In the circle screen example we have targeted in on the mouth as if preparing an illustration for a beauty feature. The commonest use of a line conversion is to add life to an over-familiar photograph which is required for feature display.

65 Halftone dot screen high contrast
Useful for poor printing

Mezzo 75 line
Ideal texture for fashion photograph

D Tone overprint line

Type added to Example A. If reproduced half-tone, the blackness of 'OK' would become grey, so strength is retained by making 'OK' separately as a line engraving and stripping the negative into the halftone negative.

E Tone Cut-Out Overprint Line

Half-tone cut-out overprinted on line engraving of type. The lettering is drawn or pasted on Kodatrace (Permatrace) overlay and attached to the photograph with masking tape. Good tracing paper may also be used.

F Tone Reverse Line Overprint

The same as E but with process instructed to reverse type into white. The commonest error in this kind of work is to make the type too small forgetting that it scales down with the half tone. The background makes **E** (*left*) the most successful overprint

Circle screen 30 line
Any 'target' area can be specified

12 Halftone dot screen
Coarse dots for drama or disguise

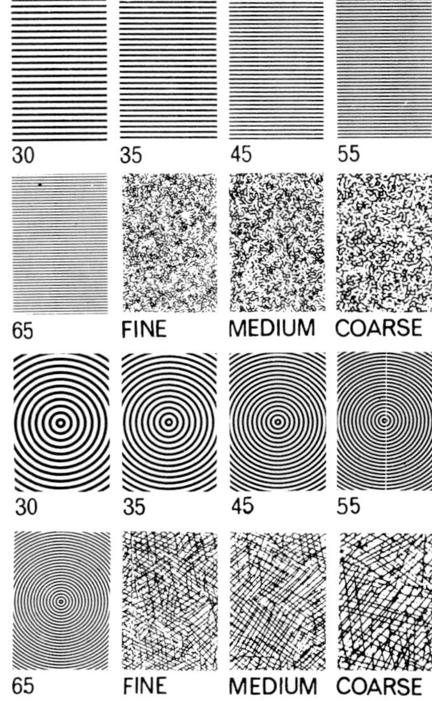

A few of the other examples of line conversion screens by Headliners (UK).

Six shots, a 500mm, and a set of staples

Trooping the Colour before the Queen is an annual ceremony in London, photographed to the point of tedium. But Peter Dunne and *The Sunday Times* picture desk converted it into a front page spectacular. Some days before the ceremony Dunne went to the top of New Zealand House overlooking Horse Guard's Parade. A 105mm lens gave the whole scene from parade ground to Big Ben but it did not produce a big enough image on the negative. A 500mm lens gave the right size of sharp image—but only for parts of the view. Dunne therefore decided to photograph the Trooping in several sections. On the morning of the ceremony he made a dry run, using a 500mm Nikon mirror lens mounted on a motorised F2 body, locked on a heavy tripod. When later the Guardsmen marched Dunne took six over-lapping horizontal shots in a vertical pan (right 282A), quick enough to keep the right time on Big Ben. Six big prints were too much for scaling machines and six sets of tracing was daunting so the picture desk stapled the prints together and asked process to do what it could to make the joins invisible. They did, fusing sections at architectural joints of ledges and roof-tops (281B). Joining lines such as that in a montage gives the preparing eye a guide and the viewing eye a perception of natural flow. There is a trap in every montage, a false detail which, without care, can spoil the effect.

THE SUNDAY TIMES

Grassroots Liberals will pick the leader

Callan tells war trial: I am responsible

COLOUR MAGAZINE

Ascot favourite

Exclusive: the oldest face in the world

281A In page the big view was coupled with a close-up of the Queen taking the salute

B

282A The six sections which made one picture: a little overlap is always required to help in the later join-up

The Join-up

A line of secret servicemen, police, officials, and American Ambassador Richardson confronts the world on the arrival of Henry Kissinger at London airport for a meeting with Prime Minister Callaghan (far right 284). The picture is striking. But it was never taken. It is a combination of three separate photographs taken on the same occasion (*right*) and in that way similar to the Paris composite on page 33. But this is the work of the picture editor, rather than the product of a photographer's intention to shoot separate sections; and the demonstrations here show the capacity of the join-up or composite for creating images. How it is done is explained below.

Trace it: A Jordanian policeman conciliates Israeli border guards over the right of an Arab and his family to cross the bridge. One print (*top right*) showed the Arab and family; the other omitted the family and the Arab's head is down, but in this one the Israeli's accusing arm and the policeman's placatory hand make a visual moment. The appealing elements from the prints were therefore combined in a single picture for publication by tracing the parts required from each print and giving process the 'intention tracing' with the prints.

The same tracing technique is used in the common task of moving two people closer. But in complex composites where prints of different scale are to be combined each print is viewed on a scaling machine—vital for any elaborate work—which projects an image to any scale. The relevant sections are then traced.

D

E

F

G

284D–G Going too far? Composites can be misused. At the simplest they can suggest that two people are friendlier than they are. At the most devilish they can combine incidents from different occasions to create a lampoon of incongruity or a lie. The determining question should be whether the composite misleads. This is a questionable case—the signing of a memorial book at the American Embassy in London in tribute to the late President Eisenhower. The composition was strongest in the top picture (**D**) but this is a composite achieved by fusing the best elements of three pictures (**E, F, G**) below it. The Marine, it will be noted, is present on only one of these three prints. It was effective but it meant portraying people as being present at the same time when they were not. That might or might not be harmless, but you cannot tell. It would certainly puzzle the people in the pictures—and if they realised what had happened, erode a little of their faith in the newspaper. And how the woman in the headscarf (*right*) seems to have grown . . .

'Publishing a photograph of Queen's Park Rangers' footballer Stan Bowles embracing a topless 19-year-old model was a matter of editorial discretion said the Press Council when it rejected a complaint against the Daily Mirror' NEWS ITEM.

There are four areas of sensitivity: violence; intrusions into privacy; sex and public decency; and faking. The passage of time has transformed public tolerance in areas of taste—female belly buttons need no longer be painted out—but it has hardly affected the awkwardness of judgements on gruesome photographs, and privacy will increasingly bother photographers and editors.

A California court ruling on a magazine photograph of a husband and wife caught the emphasis of public anxiety: 'Members of the opposite sexes engaging in amorous demonstrations should be protected from the broadcast of that most intimate reaction'. It was the privacy of Australian tennis star Miss Evonne Goolagong, rather than public susceptibility, which provoked the Press Council's censor on the *Sun* for publishing drawings purporting to show her in the nude. Nobody in Britain frets about seeing bare breasts any more, as a reader, unless it is the *Sun* worrying whether the day's nipple count is higher in the *Mirror* (even *The Times* has had a lusciously naked lady in an advertisement—for fertiliser). The unthinkable of yesterday is commonplace, though the vulgarity borders run a different course between Catholic and non-Catholic countries, as British dailies circulating in Ireland appreciate. The climate is such as to lend a fairly preposterous air to some of the objectors and defenders. The complaint about the *Mirror*'s photographs of the embracing Bowles said it brought football into disrepute. The editor said the *Mirror* thought the Football Association had erred in attempting to ban footballers embracing on the pitch 'and this could best be highlighted by showing a well-known footballer embracing an attractive model'. As the *Mirror* would say: who's kidding?

The Press Council has produced some suggested rulings. It will not tolerate faking. It has rebuked the *Daily Mail* for a montage which made a cemetery seem more macabrely visible from an old folks' home than it was. But easily the most severe of the Council's adjudications has been for intrusions into private life and grief; there is no doubt these are widely resented and we ignore them at our peril. The Council has censured photographs of relatives in distress, people in prison, and surveillance of public figures in private places. It deprecates photographs of funerals unless they are public occasions. The public nature of the event and the person is the crux of it. When Lord George-Brown tripped and fell after resigning from the Labour party he was cruelly splashed over five columns on the front page of the *Daily Mail*, but the Press Council rejected a complaint of sensationalism. A picture of a public official who fainted during a church service was similarly justified as 'an incident which occurred during an important public event'. The *Daily Mirror* was upheld after it had presented a three-column picture, headlined 'The Brute', of a man who beat a child to death.

The lines are harder to draw on violence. I wonder if anyone turning through this book felt a moment of unease at the inclusion, in a discussion of presentation, of the picture on page 269. The front page of Ruth Snyder in the electric chair earned the *New York Daily News* national condemnation. If our sensibilities seem more leathery today, what would we feel if on tomorrow's front page we saw a photograph of a woman's execution by guillotine or hanging? As many people might be offended as they were in 1928. This would not make publication wrong, but it would

285A Generation gap: The publicity stills for *A is Born*, reflecting the change in attitudes to sexu display between 1954 and 1977

285B Too distressing to print? Readers of *The Northern Echo* thought it was and complained

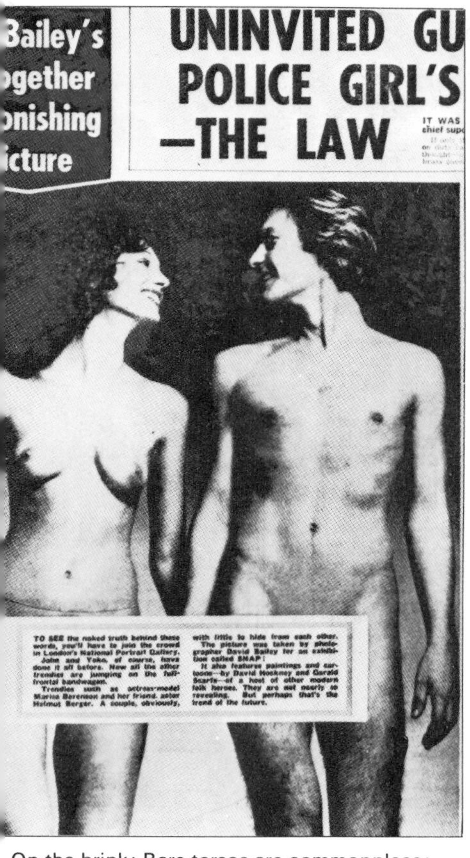

Bailey's
ogether
onishing
icture

UNINVITED GU
POLICE GIRL'S
—THE LAW

IT WAS
chief sup

TO SEE the naked truth behind these words, you'll have to join the crowd in London's National Portrait Gallery.

John and Yoko, of course, have done it all before. Now all the other trendies are jumping on the full-frontal bandwagon.

Trendies such as actress-model Marisa Berenson and her friend, actor Helmut Berger. A couple, obviously, with little to hide from each other.

The picture was taken by photographer David Bailey for an exhibition called SNAP!

It also features paintings and cartoons—by David Hockney and Gerald Scarfe—of a host of other modern folk heroes. They are not nearly so revealing. But perhaps that's the trend of the future.

On the brink: Bare torsos are commonplace; *Sun*'s incision in David Bailey's full frontal ore joke than censorship

onditional Surrender

Page 4

Only Answer to Japan

Justifiable shock? News that the victim was ian took the steam out of protests in America

make it require more justification today than the simple assertion of Mr. Frank Howard, managing editor of the *Daily News*, that they did not want to disappoint the readers who liked to be taken to big events. Violent photographs do cause distress to many people and that has sometimes to be accepted; but to inflict distress at random is to weaken the case for doing it at all. Circumstances must determine cases, and certainty is elusive. In fifteen years of editing first a provincial daily and then a national, neither immune to controversy, it is the response to a single photograph which still most perplexes me: the coffin in the foreground of a burned out car (285B). By telephone, letter and personal visits scores of readers of *The Northern Echo* let me know their outrage at this photograph. It was news, we said, it was common practice to publish accident pictures, it was a reminder of the toll of the roads. The argument did not convince. Perhaps in a national newspaper the picture would have escaped rebuke. A smaller community may expect its paper to bind wounds, not expose them. Or perhaps the starkness of the coffin does transgress some taboo?

The general defences to publication of this picture seem to me as sound today as they did then, but there is a limit to their validity. I would not have published a picture of the burned remains of the driver, yet that, too, would have been a warning of the dangers of the roads. Many newspapers, rightly I think, chose not to publish the car crash pictures of the actress Jayne Mansfield showing her head impaled on a shard of windshield glass and her body lying several feet away on the roadside. There has to be some fitness of purpose; and a constant awareness of the capacity of a photograph to excite deep emotion. With the offensive photograph, two questions help: is the event it portrays of such social or historic significance that the shock is justified? Is the objectionable detail necessary for a proper understanding of the event?

It was supremely right, on this test, to publish a whole series of sensational photographs. Ronald Haeberle's pictures of dead and terrified villagers at My Lai were not the gratuitous violence alleged against the publishers. They were evidence of a massacre. They were the reality of war. The beheading of an Australian soldier (286B) by a Japanese officer was horrifying but a testimony to the nature of the war in the Far East. It would have been better if decades of American editors had not suppressed gruesome photographs of Southern lynchings; this was more a protection of the lynchers than public morals. It was necessary, again, to show the charred bodies of the Jews murdered by the Nazis—but it was, on the tests suggested, merely pandering to morbid curiosity to portray the heap of burned bodies of people trapped in a Chicago street car. It did not explain anything and there was no need for a salutary shock or for confirmation.

Neither was there any justification for the pictures of Lee Harvey Oswald lying on a pathologist's table with the post-mortem stitches crudely visible. We knew he was dead. But a picture of the dead Hitler, however gruesome, would be published everywhere today just as Che Guevara had to be seen (see preface).

There is one new worry today: the presence of the camera may invite or encourage violence for the sake of the publicity. The classic example is that invitation to a bayoneting on a polo field in Bangladesh where some photographers walked away without taking a picture and others stayed to record 'the event'. Perhaps the murders would have happened without the camera, and certainly the conflict of duties is understandable. But if to take and publish those pictures was correct, and on our tests publication was permissible, it was surely demeaning to photojournalism for the Pulitzer Committee to award the picture a prize.

Chapter 16

Graphics and Illustration

The main function of graphic design in contemporary communication is the translation and condensation of ideas or problems into visual forms in such a way that they establish a short cut to understanding. Will Burtin

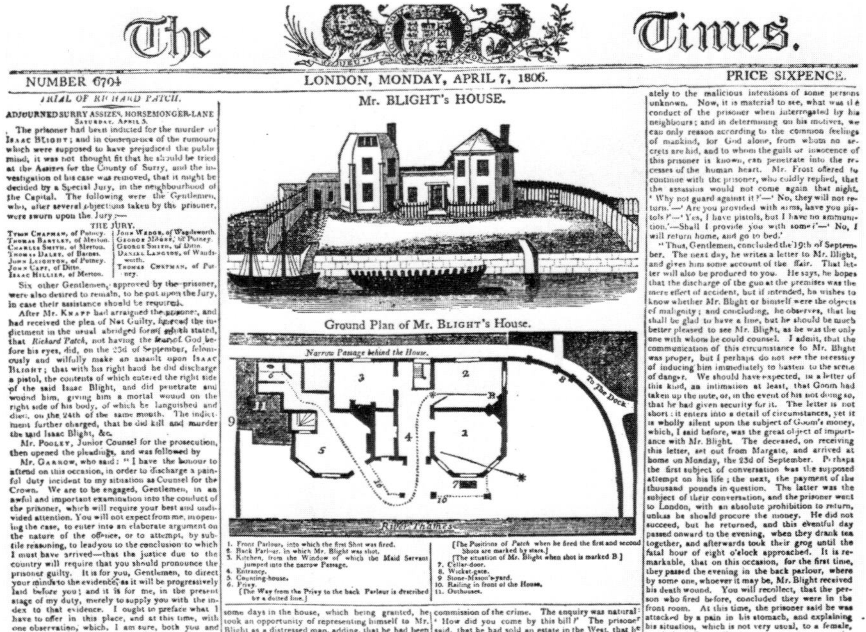

The Times.

NUMBER 6704 | LONDON, MONDAY, APRIL 7, 1806. | PRICE SIXPENCE.

TRIAL OF RICHARD PATCH.

ADJOURNED SURRY ASSIZES, HORSEMONGER-LANE
SATURDAY, APRIL 5.

The prisoner had been indicted for the murder of ISAAC BLIGHT; and in consequence of the rumours which were supposed to have prejudiced the public mind, it was not thought fit that he should be tried at the Assizes for the County of Surry, and the investigation of his case was removed, that it might be decided by a Special Jury, in the neighbourhood of the Capital. The following were the Gentlemen, who, after several objections taken by the prisoner, were sworn upon the Jury:—

THE JURY.

TYSON CHAPMAN, of Putney.
THOMAS BARTLEY, of Merton.
CHARLES SMITH, of Merton.
THOMAS DALEY, of Barnes.
JOHN LEIGHTON, of Putney.
JOHN CAPP, of Ditto.
ISAAC HILLIER, of Merton.
JOHN WADOR, of Wandsworth.
GEORGE MOORE, of Putney.
GEORGE SMITH, of Ditto.
DANIEL LANGTON, of Wandsworth.
THOMAS CHAPMAN, of Putney.

Six other Gentlemen, approved by the prisoner, were also desired to remain, to be put upon the Jury, in case their assistance should be required.

After Mr. KNAPP had arraigned the prisoner, and had received the plea of Not Guilty, he read the indictment in the usual abridged form, which stated, that *Richard Patch*, not having the fear of God before his eyes, did, on the 23d of September, feloniously and wilfully make an assault upon ISAAC BLIGHT; that with his right hand he did discharge a pistol, the contents of which entered the right side of the said Isaac Blight, and did penetrate and wound him, giving him a mortal wound on the right side of his body, of which he languished and died, on the 24th of the same month. The indictment further charged, that he did kill and murder the said Isaac Blight, &c.

Mr. POOLEY, Junior Counsel for the prosecution, then opened the pleadings, and was followed by

Mr. GARROW, who said: "I have the honour to attend on this occasion, in order to discharge a painful duty incident to my situation as Counsel for the Crown. We are to be engaged, Gentlemen, in an awful and important examination into the conduct of the prisoner, which will require your best and undivided attention. You will not expect from me, in opening the case, to enter into an elaborate argument on the nature of the offence, or to attempt, by subtile reasoning, to lead you to the conclusion to which I must have arrived—that the justice due to the country will require that you should pronounce the prisoner guilty. It is for you, Gentlemen, to direct your minds to the evidence, as it will be progressively laid before you; and it is for me, in the present stage of my duty, merely to supply you with the index to that evidence. I ought to preface what I have to offer in this place, and at this time, with one observation, which, I am sure, both you and

Mr. BLIGHT's HOUSE.

Ground Plan of Mr. BLIGHT's House.

1. Front Parlour, into which the first Shot was fired.
2. Back Parlour, in which Mr. Blight was shot.
3. Kitchen, from the Window of which the Maid Servant jumped into the narrow Passage.
4. Entrancy.
5. Counting-house.
6. Privy.
[The Way from the Privy to the back Parlour is described by a dotted line.]
[The Positions of *Patch* when he fired the first and second Shots are marked by stars.]
[The situation of Mr. Blight when shot is marked B.]
7. Cellar-door.
8. Wicket-gate.
9. Stone-Mason's-yard.
10. Railing in front of the House.
11. Outhouses.

some days in the house, which being granted, he took an opportunity of representing himself to Mr. Blight as a distressed man, adding, that he had been

commission of the crime. The enquiry was natural: 'How did you come by this bill?' The prisoner said, that he had sold an estate in the West, that he

ately to the malicious intentions of some persons unknown. Now, it is material to see, what was the conduct of the prisoner when interrogated by his neighbours; and in determining on his motives, we can only reason according to the common feelings of mankind, for God alone, from whom no secrets are hid, and to whom the guilt or innocence of this prisoner is known, can penetrate into the recesses of the human heart. Mr. Frost offered to continue with the prisoner, who coldly replied, that the assassins would not come again that night. 'Why not guard against it?'—'No, they will not return.'—'Are you provided with arms, have you pistols?'—'Yes, I have pistols, but I have no ammunition.'—Shall I provide you with some?'—'No, I will return home, and go to bed.'

"Thus, Gentlemen, concluded the 19th of September. The next day, he writes a letter to Mr. Blight, and gives him some account of the affair. That letter will also be produced to you. He says, he hopes that the discharge of the gun at the premises was the mere effect of accident, but if intended, he wishes to know whether Mr. Blight or himself were the objects of malignity; and concluding, he observes, that he shall be glad to have a line, but he should be much better pleased to see Mr. Blight, as he was the only one with whom he could counsel. I admit, that the communication of this circumstance to Mr. Blight was proper, but I perhaps do not see the necessity of inducing him immediately to hasten to the scene of danger. We should have expected, in a letter of this kind, an intimation at least, that Goom had taken up the note, or, in the event of his not doing so, that he had given security for it. The letter is not short: it enters into a detail of circumstances, yet it is wholly silent upon the subject of Goom's money, which, I said before, was the great object of importance with Mr. Blight. The deceased, on receiving this letter, set out from Margate, and arrived at home on Monday, the 23d of September. Perhaps the first subject of conversation was the supposed attempt on his life; the next, the payment of the thousand pounds in question. The latter was the subject of their conversation, and the prisoner went to London, with an absolute prohibition to return, unless he should procure the money. He did not succeed, but he returned, and this eventful day passed onward to the evening, when they drank tea together, and afterwards took their grog until the fatal hour of eight o'clock approached. It is remarkable, that on this occasion, for the first time, they passed the evening in the back parlour, where by some one, whoever it may be, Mr. Blight received his death wound. You will recollect, that the person who fired before, concluded they were in the front room. At this time, the prisoner said he was attacked by a pain in his stomach, and explaining his situation, which is not very usual, to a female,

When Richard Patch shot Isaac Blight, *The Times* of London carried on its front page two diagrams to make the mystery clearer. One was an elevation of the house where the deed was done and the other a ground plan with explanatory symbols of where the body had been found and so on. These were excellent newspaper graphics, both short cuts to understanding. But *The Times* which had the inspiration to commission the sketch plans was *The Times* of 1806 (287A *above*).

In the following 150 years few newspapers have done anything. Every day there is plenty of news that cannot properly be told by words, notably news whose essence lies in visual and spatial relationships, calling out for illustration by graphics. If that sounds a mouthful, consider the headline:

RESCUERS DIG FOR MINERS
TRAPPED BY RISING WATER

Spatial relationships are the heart of that drama, and the outsider cannot understand it without graphics—a diagram of the underground workings, locating men, flood water and rescuers, an indication of the scale of distances between them and the rate of progress. A straight photograph cannot do this.

The same is true of drawing. That it may be more than decorative, or that graphic art can create an entirely new dimension of communication, is appreciated by only a handful of publications in the world.

I do not want to provoke an esoteric discussion about that term 'graphics'. Let me elaborate the

288A The wedding of Princess Anne—an identifying drawing for the benefit of television viewers

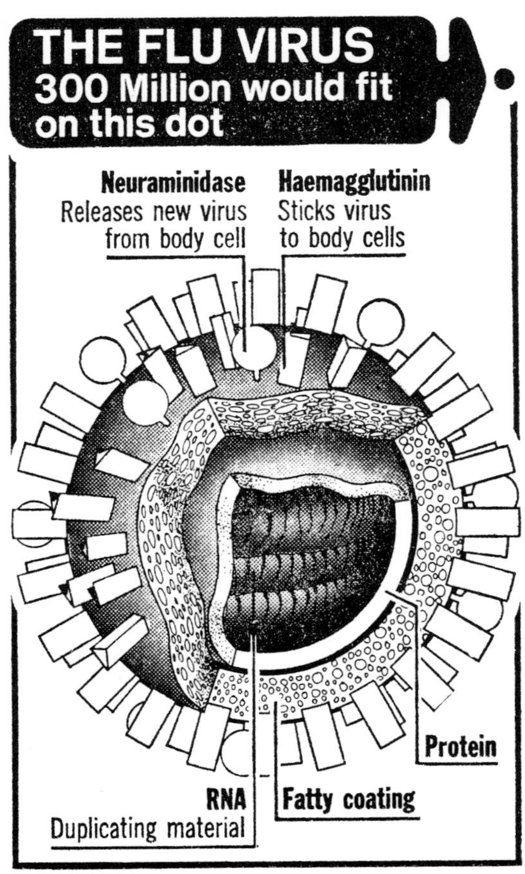

289A Fact graphic

distinction in the way I think most useful for print people. A single drawing illustrating a feature is not graphics. It is an illustration. So is a single photograph in a news story. But both become graphics if sign systems or words or symbols are made an integral part of the drawing or photograph.

Graphics at the simplest level is the X which marks the spot on the simple map; or the directional arrow to indicate that an article is continuing on another page, or the photograph with identifying labels.

But there are much more sophisticated possibilities for information graphics where symbols and art together diagnose a complicated issue more succinctly than is possible in words alone. And there is a second area of graphics which is also worth attention—where display type and drawing provide a more economical but more evocative display unit. This divides graphics into two arbitrary divisions which I call fact or information graphics and flavour graphics. Flavour graphics are essentially decorative. Fact graphics are concerned not with images but with information. The distinction between the two categories is suggested by examples 289A and 290A: The Pleasures of Life is a flavour graphic and The Flu Virus is a fact graphic, which demonstrates the exceptional value of the form. Here we have compactly a drawing of the wretched virus which was making millions wilt, and a startling example of its infinitesimal scale.

Of course the distinctions between fact and flavour are not exclusive. A good flavour graphic arouses attention and that assists perception; and a well-executed fact graphic can be a decoration.

Of the two forgotten forms of journalism the fact graphic is most within the reach of the average small town newspaper. Journalist and printer together can manage 'X marks the spot' without the skill of graphic designer. Photographs and maps can be labelled, and firms such as Letraset, Normatype, Zip-a-tone and Chart-Pak supply tone and texture sheets which are easy to apply to artwork. Letraset's sheet of symbols is especially useful (catalogue: Letraset Ltd., Webber Street, London S.E.1., or A. I. Friedman, 25 West 45th Street, New York).

But headier things are also possible. The bankruptcy of the entire newspaper will no doubt be predicted at the recruitment of a youngster from the local college of art, but that is what I suggest as an enrichment to the barrenness of the average enterprise. He will need knocking into shape. The colleges tend to be long on aesthetic self-expression and short on practical draughtsmanship.

The shortage of reportorial drawing in the press is not all the fault of philistines in the media. Art schools have indulged themselves in courses on the poetry of painting instead of teaching the real skill of drawing. David Hockney has attacked the progressive abandonment of the teaching of drawing and he is right: 'I don't see how you can make pictures with reference to the real world without drawing, yet in some art schools they have life classes only once a week, if at all. It is total madness'.

On graphics, Edwin Taylor, as Design Director of *The Sunday Times*, has observed: 'Students emerge from art schools with too many specimens of full-colour double spreads aping popular magazines . . . and too few specimens analysing the break-up of the

290A Flavour graphic

Torrey Canyon or the pattern of traffic in the English Channel, or a lucid statement on the evolution of reptiles.'

But, if an editor knows what he wants, the weaknesses of the art school graduate can be overcome and his strengths exploited.

If the editor insists on accuracy and clarity he can allow the designer to experiment with a variety of style and graphic techniques. Creativity can be released without damage to communication. This has been our experience at *The Sunday Times*. The British re-awakening of interest in the possibilities of graphics came in the early Sixties at the *Daily Express* when the then Editor Edward Pickering and Assistant Editor Harold Keeble appointed Ray Hawkey as design director. The *Express* did not manage to maintain its pioneering, but the *Observer* (which recruited Hawkey), *The Sunday Times*, and *The Daily Mail* all took up graphics. The advance at *The Sunday Times* has been pushed by several designers, notably Michael Rand, Peter Sullivan (who doubled as *Sunday Times* top graphic man and head of graphics at the Canterbury School of Art), and by Edwin Taylor who made several imaginative innovations and began training art college graduates as designer-journalists. The names deserve mentioning for what they did, but to emphasise also what a few individuals can do in a verbal-visual partnership.

The partnership can be particularly fruitful because of what both have to offer. The journalist should supply clear information and insist on clear expression; the designer should supply graphic distinction and insist on limiting the information to what can be graphically expressed. Clearly, there is going to be a lot of arguing and there should be certain understandings. The journalist must really recognise that his beloved words are indeed only one way of communicating, that if he wants to tell somebody the way from A to B it is better to draw a map than to talk. He must not press the designer to overweigh the graphics with words. He must not expect a six-day sequence of the Middle East war to be dramatised in six inches and ten minutes. Emphatically, he must recognise that the design department is not just a service department. Good graphics emerge from a partnership or they do not emerge at all.

Sheer design skill could not have produced the drawing (288A) of the scene inside Westminster Abbey for the wedding of Princess Anne—several days before it took place. The artist needed information on who would be where and what they might be doing and wearing. The distinctive feature of this co-operative effort was that it enabled the paper to give its readers one view of the royal wedding the world would not see because television cameras were banned from positions in front of the bridal couple.

Graphics offer a unique facility for this kind of advance portrayal. The commonest example, of course, is Surveyors' Surrealism, impressions of proposed building schemes complete with happy people and improbably mature trees (forget cars, lorries and a sense of scale), which the alert newspaper will check by commissioning its own visualisation. But there is scope for being so much more than a development detective. Graphics can let us see the unseeable—the intricacies of surgery, the supposed functions of an anti-ballistic missile system, the big event before it has happened.

None of these things is possible without a library. The artist designer cannot draw out of his head the inside of a racing car, the blood flow of the human heart or the flight panel of a moon rocket. Few newspapers or magazines have anything approaching the proper kind of information storage and retrieval systems required: swift, certain, clean and comprehensive. Computer technology could help enormously.

For his part, the graphic artist has to try to absorb the spirit of journalism. He must have a mind as well as an eye. He must learn to respond to the rough imperatives of time and directness.

If he finds all this a chore or if the examples in the following pages distend his fine art nostrils it will be better all round if he absconds to an advertising agency or dedicates himself to murals in the Aegean.

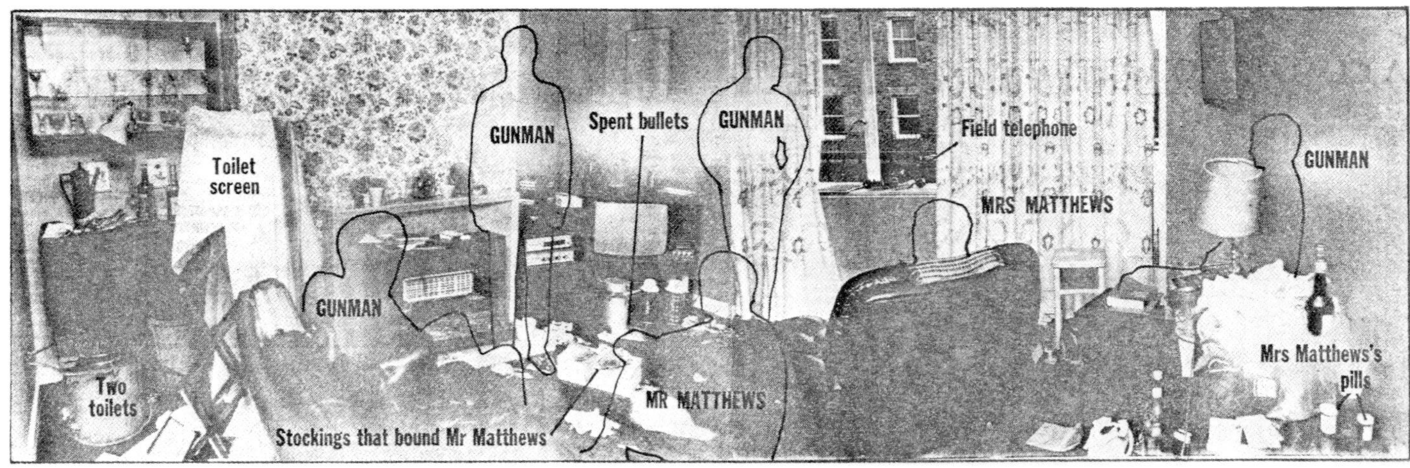

Supplementing the photograph

The simplest fact graphics are additions or adjuncts to photographs so that the photograph tells more. The examples of labelling a photograph here are simple enough—the top one is graphically primitive—but both add immensely to understanding. The arrow line traced on the terraced houses by the photographer Ford Jenkins shows the path of a 12-inch shell through 13 houses in Lowestoft, Britain, during the First World War bombardment; nobody was hurt. No photograph could show that, nor was any photograph taken of the sitting room at Balcombe Street, London, where four Irish gunmen held Mr. and Mrs. Matthews hostage for six days while the police kept siege outside. When the Matthews were freed police allowed photographers into the empty room and, though that was interesting, the pictures published told us little compared with this superimposition of shapes and words.

Labelling photographs is also effective for marking key features that can be seen but are not readily identified. The most massive unenlightenment is provided by the usual run of pictures of architectural planning models. They are usually taken from above, as if the reader inhabited cloud 7, and surprisingly few newspapers label the landmarks.

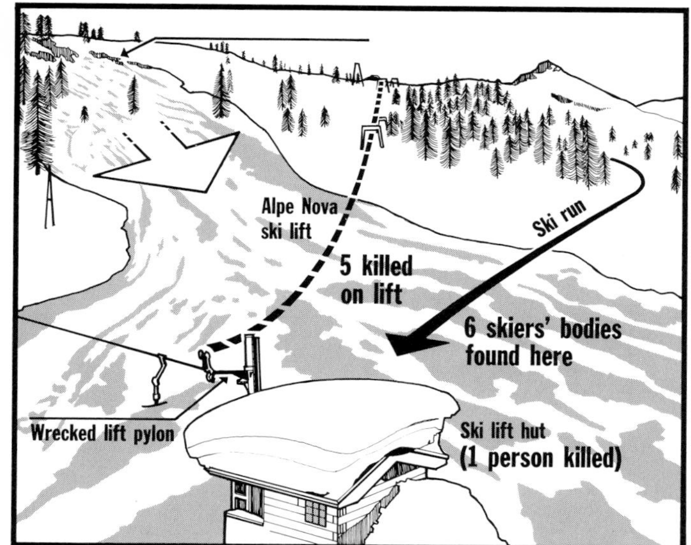

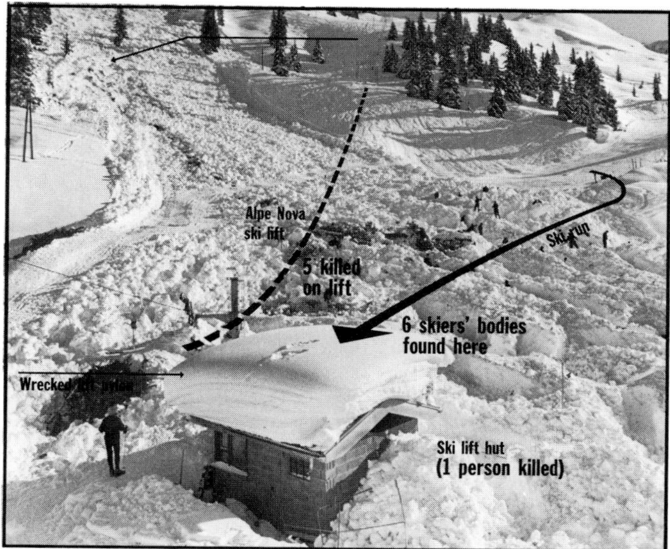

	Birmingham	Newcastle	Belfast	Cardiff	Glasgow	Manchester	Doncaster	London	Luton
SEPT	●●●● ○○○○	●● ○○○○○	●●●●●● ○	● ○○○○	●●	●●●● ○○○○	●●●	● ○○○○	●● ○○○
OCT 14	●●●●● ○○○○○	● ○○	●●●●● ○	○○	●●	● ○○	●●●●	○○	
OCT 20	●●●● ○○○	● ○○	●●●●● ○	○○	●●	● ○○	●●●●	○○	
NOV 22	●● ○○○○○	● ○○	●●●● ○	○○		○○	●		

● Skilled
○ Unskilled

There are many news photographs where labelling helps, but sometimes the information is more crisply imparted by abandoning the photograph, except as a reference, and producing a diagram. Compare the relative clarity of the labelled photograph and the diagram of an avalanche disaster. The diagram works at small scale. In newspaper reproduction, the labelled photograph required excessive space.

An alternative to the fact graphic is the small sketch to accompany a photograph. Where we have an erratically grouped crowd of people who need to be identified, the solution is a small sketch of the silhouettes, each numbered, and the numbers given names in a caption.

Simple fact graphics can replace news stories of continuous prose, especially where alternative sequences have to be described (for which the 'logical tree' method is ideal) or where the prose throws up considerable repetition. The bottom chart is the visual way of tracing how many of 50 men in different regions had got work in four months after becoming unemployed. It was simple and took less space than the repetitious verbal recital of the same facts. (As a chart it would have been improved in colour and comprehension if the men had been represented by different Isotype symbols of workers.)

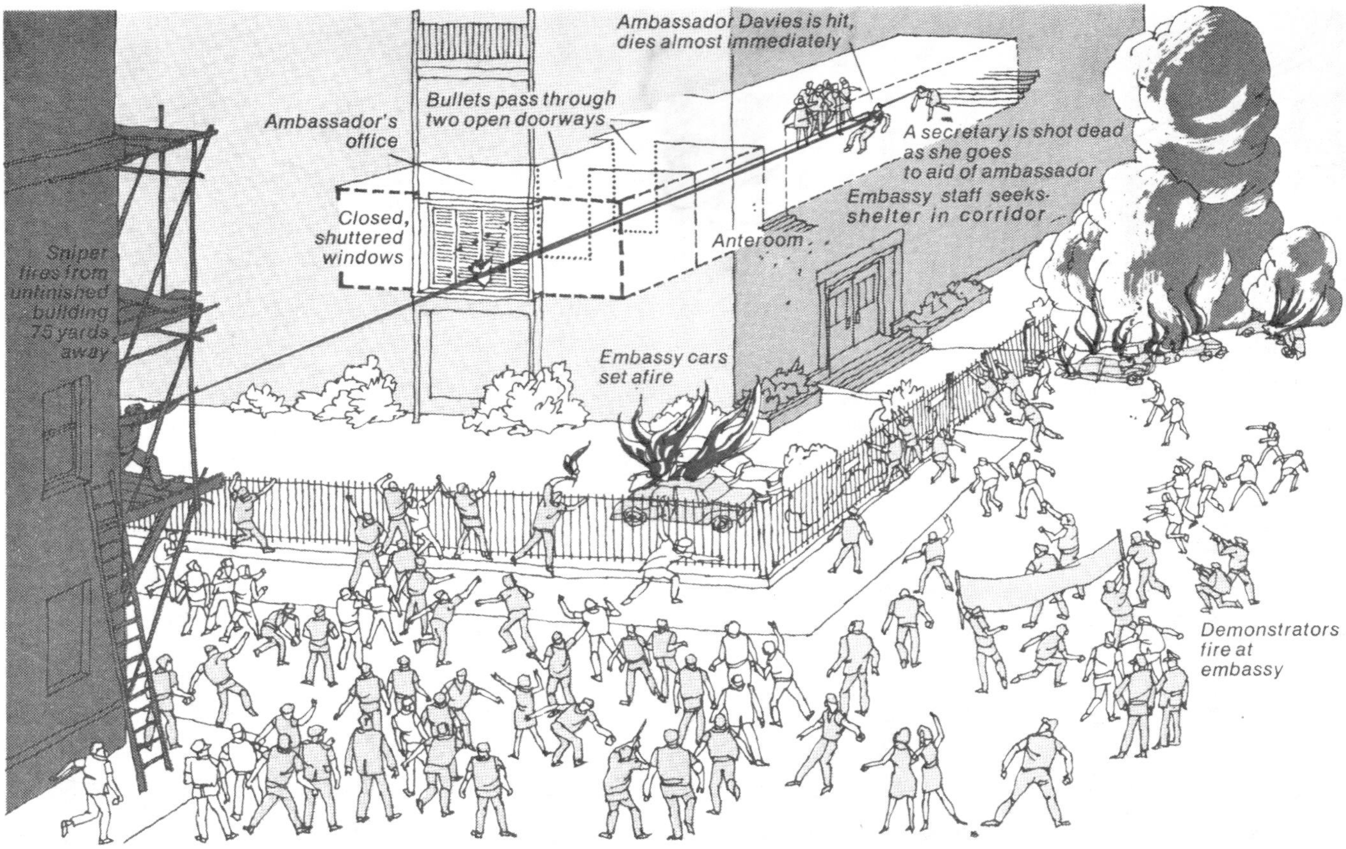

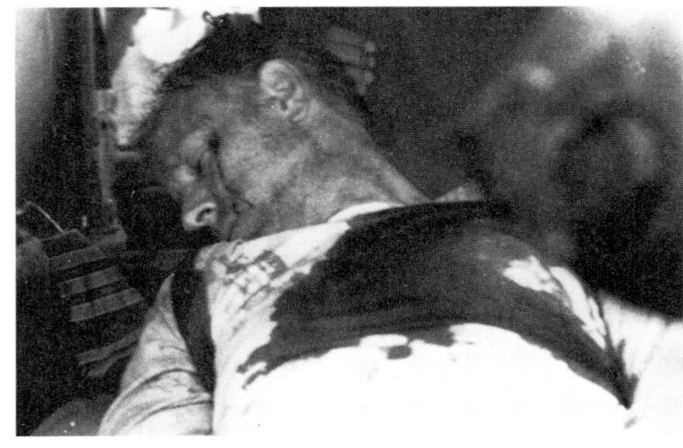

Replacing the news photograph

Scores of photographs may be taken and fail to tell the story. It may lie, invisibly, behind walls or security. It may lie in a sequence and one frame is missing. The storming of the American Embassy in Nicosia is an example. Archbishop Makarios had been deposed in Cyprus and Turkey had invaded the island. Anti-American rioters burned Embassy cars, threw rocks, took down the American flag and some of them with rifles fired at the building. One of the bullets somehow killed the Ambassador and another killed a secretary. The agencies supplied many pictures of various events, four of them reproduced here, but no accumulation of the photographs told the story as well as Don Mackay's fact graphic in *Newsweek*, one of the few magazines—*Stern* is another—which realises what graphics can do.

It plots the incidents. It explains how the bullets struck the victims after penetrating closed shutters: note the use of white to delineate the open route to the inner room. It is also marvellously economical. There is no reason, of course, why a drawing like this should not be accompanied by a photograph and the obvious one would be of the murdered Ambassador.

The second example (*top right*) is

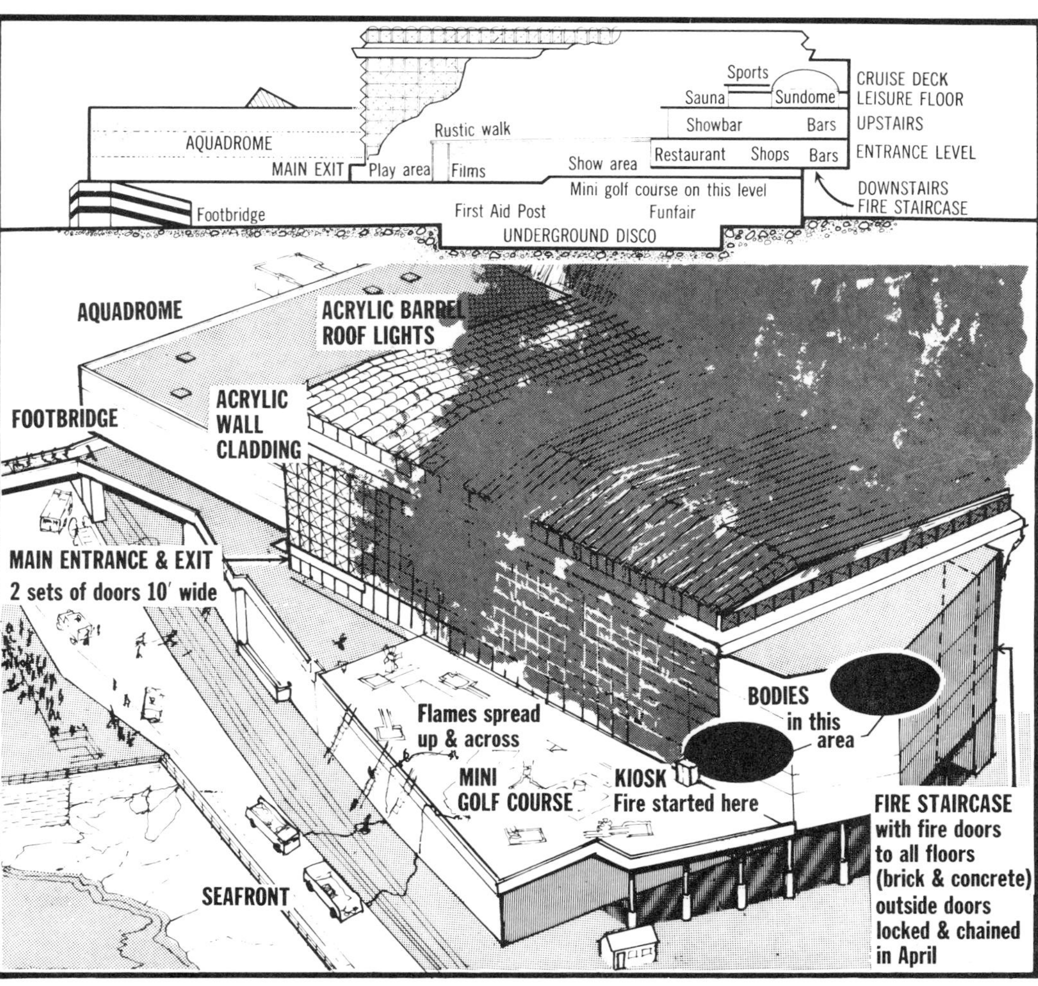

the fire disaster at Britain's Summerland entertainment centre. There were again many photographs but they could not, even cumulatively, match either the drama or lucidity of Peter Sullivan's two-part diagram. He depended a great deal, of course, on information gathered by reporters.

Photography is not allowed in British courts. The fact graphic by Arthur Horner comes to the rescue with numerals to explain who's who.

Marching against the Mafia

The role of the artist

If information graphics are neglected, unadorned drawing is the greatest untapped source of enlightenment, fun and inspiration in modern printed journalism. Van Gogh once wrote: 'If their lordships, the managers, would consent to rank scenes from the daily life of the people under current events, I should gladly try my best to make them.' He did not in the end submit his drawings of popular life in the Hague to a magazine because he was too shy. There is less encouragement today. Turn back the pages of *Illustrated London News, Graphic* magazine or the *Daily Graphic* in London; *Harper*'s or *New York World* in the United States, or one of the French magazines such as *La Vie Moderne* or *Le Figaro Illustré* and compare the visual richness with today's standard photographic fare. Or look simply at the pictures in the entertaining paperback, *The Artist as Reporter* by Paul Hogarth.

There have been revivals, notably in *Fortune, Sports Illustrated* and the *New York Times* under Louis Silverstein. But there is almost no reporting by drawing on the spot and even news illustration languishes. There are problems—fundamentally reconciling the subjectivity of the artist with our need in the press for literal description. Mike Rand at *The Sunday Times*, who wants to revive drawing in the press, says: 'I'm not interested in anything that is just dec-

OBSERVER REVIEW

23 SEPTEMBER 1973

Montevideo at 9.45 a.m. on 8 January 1971: Artist Michael Heslop's reconstruction of the kidnap. Jackson, in the back of the embassy Daimler, had two unarmed guards in a following Cortina to protect him, but they were helpless in the crowded down-town street to prevent his capture. About 50 Tupamaros took part in the ambush, and in clearing nearby streets for the getaway.

KIDNAP

GEOFFREY JACKSON, British Ambassador in Uruguay, was snatched from his car by Tupamaro guerrillas in 1971, and held in underground prisons for nearly nine months. Here, for the first time, he tells the full, dramatic story of his violent abduction.

JAMES BOND says somewhere that 'Once is happenstance, twice is coincidence, and three times is enemy action.' When, after a relatively quiet life, nocturnal telephone calls proliferate; when pleasant, solitary walks along beaches and in pine forests bristle with horizon-marching silhouettes, and there are sudden encounters with the courting young in unlikely trio formation; when your golf game is regularly intercepted by casual youthful spectators on remote fairways; when for the third time your path is crossed by professional violence—this is the moment you grasp that, however much the world around you may be changing, your own private world is changing still more.

Early in 1970 urban guerrilla kidnappings had taken a disastrous turn with the abduction and subsequent murder of Count von Spreti, the German Ambassador to Guatemala. In Brazil there were the successive kidnappings of the United States, German and Swiss Ambassadors, who were traded at an escalating exchange rate for political prisoners.

Then, in Uruguay itself, a terrorist commando kidnapped the Second Secretary of the US Embassy. This young diplomat escaped by a remarkable feat of gymnastics: though wrapped up like a side of bacon he contrived a back-flip over the tail-gate of the open truck in which he was being carried off. He was picked up unhurt; but Dan Mitrione, an American police official, kidnapped the same morning, was found murdered a week later.

From this moment on I was to have little peace of mind. The sense of being spied upon intensified and became at last regularly identifiable. At times I felt that my watchers had lost all sense of clandestinity, even of discretion. It became quite normal for me, and my staff, to recognise the same motor-scooter, with the same number-plate though perhaps a change of crew, skirmishing round the vicinity of the residence, then showing up as my official car was parked by the chancery offices.

We experimented with routes, and the timing of journeys to, and especially from, my office. I had always believed that I was most exposed out of the centre of Montevideo, owing to the narrow streets of the old down-town business centre. Such a setting seemed to favour neither attack nor getaway. Between the down-town and my home lay the Rambla—a beautiful drive, but disconcertingly lonely and deserted outside the morning, noon and evening rush hours. So only down-town did I feel safe, heaving a sigh of relief each morning as I reached its crowded seclusion, and feeling restive when I left it for the Rambla and, particularly, the network of thinly trafficked roads and avenues through the parks which were the only approach to my home. There was where I believed my danger to lie.

I said goodbye to my wife rather more hastily than usual on the morning of 8 January 1971. I had an appointment with a

This is the first of three extracts

finish her bath, I would keep him waiting. So I dashed into our bathroom and kissed her—I remember that her lips were wet —and told her that I would have the office ring her when I left to come home for lunch.

It was a beautiful morning, and the way we took to the Rambla was very quiet; the President had just left on a seaside holiday, taking with him many of the usual security forces. As always, I was relieved when we turned

see for a long time. Two of the team gave me the impression of having mouths so full of teeth as to have too many, until I realised that this appearance was a rictus, a grimace of sheer tension. The blond youngster badgering me with his pistol—for which I was afterwards told he was disciplined—was very young, little more than a sixth-form schoolboy, and so over-excited that I wondered if he was not drugged.

hands, having been taken sick, and was being moved to hospital. I decided that to exploit the cover offered by one nice old lady would do her no good, and me still less, and heard the van-doors slam to with resignation.

Even so, and so soon as this, I was already able to inject some relative relief into my resignation. I started on what was to be a long, continuous and constantly updated process of inward accountancy. On the credit side I

imminent extinction, which led me to volunteer that all this was a gross blunder; we British did not pay ransom or trade hostages —remember my colleague Jasper Cross. Again came the answer 'Quiet!' with its routine accompaniment of a butt-end on the nape of my neck, while the butterfly tightened and tightened over my crossed wrists till they lost all sensation. One wrist was to remain completely paralysed for three months, but then became as good as new again, I can only suppose through the body's marvellous capacity to regenerate a severed nerve by some sort of a by-pass growth.

Until our unprogrammed pause for the more stabilised insertion of hypodermic needles I had not really had leisure to try to keep track of time, though I should estimate that barely five minutes had elapsed before my change of vehicle, and not much more till the next pause to avoid undue bouncing. From this point to my final destination did not, I think, take more than another 10 minutes. I was able to keep some track of time by counting on the 'one-and-two and three' system, and am reasonably sure of my accuracy despite the fact that one or the other of the drugs that had been administered to me was beginning to take effect with that unmistakable head-swimming I recall from my occasional experiences of surgery.

For some time the road had been quite rough, and suddenly, with barely a reduction of speed, our vehicle turned off over what felt like a pronounced gully at the edge of the road into what,

a garage-door swung to behind us. After the tumult of the last 20 minutes or so, the quiet was oppressive, almost sinister. I was hoisted by my arms and legs and deposited on not too hard a floor.

The kerchief across my eyes was removed, and around me was a circle of shoes. A pair of quite beautifully cut, brown grain slip-ons broke the relative if still hard-breathing silence with the words '*Ay, pobrecito*—poor man —what a pistol-whipping he's had—bring me a cloth and some alcohol.' The voice, in a particularly soft, almost lilting Spanish, seemed and still seems strangely familiar; I am convinced I knew it from before. It contained a quality of mirth yet, at the same time, of great evil, though the hand which removed the blood from my brow was gentle, even skilled.

From the foetal position in which I lay, I straightened out. When my feet hit solid substance before my knees had fully unbent I turned my head and looked. By the light of a not too powerful electric bulb I could see at eye-level an expanse of smooth concrete with, above, a conglomerate of rough stone and cement. To my right was a square mesh of strong steel pig-wire, and a timber upright or two. I paused, looked again, and laughed, I like to believe with no hysteria and in pure irony.

With equal amusement, and perhaps even a touch of mock-resentment, the gentle voice inquired, 'And what, Ambassador, do you find to laugh at in this your present situation?' 'At what looks so like a newspaper

orative. It must have some informative value. I don't want to put anything on the page that just looks pretty.' That is right, but many artists have met the need and enriched journalism without losing their souls. One thinks of Feliks Topolski, Edgar Ainsworth, James Boswell, Ronald Searle, Paul Hogarth, Ben Shahn, Renato Guttuso, Milton Glaser, Peter Blake, Julian Allen, Roger Law, Arthur Horner, Adrian George and others.

The drawings at the top of p. 295 and above are by Gerald Scarfe, from the scene, and a reconstruction by Michael Heslop. Scarfe went for *The Sunday Times* to watch the protest march through the Mafia country of Western Sicily, led by Danilo Dolci. (Dolci wrote a message on the drawing.) Compare that with the typical agency photograph of the same event.

Heslop's drawing for the *Observer* shows what happened when Geoffrey Jackson, British Ambassador in Uruguay, was snatched by guerrillas from his Daimler in down-town Montevideo. Heslop talked with Jackson on Tuesday and finished the artwork by Friday noon for an 8-column presentation.

Finally, there is Harry Hants' drawing of an unphotographed scene in the House of Commons—where cameras are not allowed—when an Opposition spokesman, in a furious row, seized the Mace.

SUNDAY TIMES weekly review

OCTOBER 27 1974

29

Drawing by John Thirsk

BREAKDOWN

A nervous breakdown is no rarity in our society; one in six of all women and one in nine of all men will spend some part of their lives in a psychiatric hospital. But it is much less usual for a Professor of Psychology to suffer a severe mental crisis and be able to chronicle each step of his treatment. This is the story of one man who was able to see the whole process from both sides of the fence

ABOUT TWO YEARS AGO, in my mid-forties, I had a sudden and severe mental breakdown. There was nothing unusual about the breakdown nor about the events in my own life that led up to it. The only unusual feature of the case was that I am myself a psychologist and was able to view the events from both sides of the fence. Although one in six women and one in nine men spend some part of their lives as an in-patient in a psychiatric hospital, there is still a formidable degree of ignorance and prejudice surrounding mental illness and its treatment. In what follows, I treat the topic of mental illness in the context of my own case in the hope of clarifying some of the contentious issues involved.

The immediate cause of my breakdown lay in an event of too personal a nature to enter into here. It seems in retrospect that, given my psychological make-up, it was tailor-made to cause me the maximum possible hurt. Within a period of twenty-four hours, my life disintegrated and I changed from being cheerful, outgoing and continually active into someone who was a prey to the most tortured thoughts and self-recriminations with neither interest in nor ability to cope with the outside world. It is possible that my previous style of life had led up to the breakdown: for years I had never given myself time to reflect and had unquestioningly devoted myself to pursuing my own research in psychology, to teaching, and to organising work within the subject. I lived in a whirlpool of ceaseless activity and loathed the thought of relaxing.

The onset of my neurosis was marked by levels of physical anxiety that I would not have believed possible. If you are almost involved in a road accident, there is a moment's delay and then the pit of your stomach seems to fall out and your legs go like jelly. It was this feeling multiplied a hundredfold that seized me at all times of the day and night. My dreams were often pleasant, but as soon as I awoke panic set in and it would take a few moments to work out what the panic was about. The realisation brought anguish: an irrevocable and cataclysmic event had occurred from which I could not imagine recovering. I got so little sleep at night, that I would sometimes doze off in the daytime, but I would get only a few seconds of forgetfulness before waking again in terror.

My thoughts were so obsessive that I lost all ability to concentrate. For five months I was virtually unable to read even the daily paper. I tried to force myself to study but the effort was hopeless and there was one book on psychology that I must have started several hundred times, but I never succeeded in getting past the first page and even that I was unable to understand. One of the consequences of being unable to read or to follow a film or play was the most extreme boredom. There was nothing to look forward to except fitful bouts of sleep and I lived in a hell of anxiety and boredom. There were two activities—driving a car and doing the Times crossword—which were mildly therapeutic: in my normal state, I would have condemned both of them as being a waste of valuable time.

After spending about a week in this condition, I sought help from a GP. He referred me to a psychoanalyst. My own experience as a psychologist had made me sceptical about the value of analysis, but in my desperation anything seemed worth trying and against my better judgment, I agreed to go. The analyst lived in a quiet suburban house. He was a tall, thin, slightly shy and gentle man in his forties. He warned me that he charged seven guineas a session which was really a London price but he always had more patients than he could cope with. He allowed me to ramble on rather incoherently about my problems and my background

formed part of my obsessive thoughts, and I arrived in a state of terror. He occupied a small flat permeated by the smell of cooking. He was late and his wife showed me into a squalid consulting room where I lay down on a

father. If I had ever entertained any such feeling, I had long since forgotten it, but I found the suggestion most upsetting. Indeed around this time, I read, in a lucid moment, a clinical case about someone who exactly fitted my picture of myself. He suffered from tormenting obsessions similar to my own, and had been under analysis for twenty years without showing any signs of improvement. He was diagnosed as a repressed passive homosexual. There seemed no hope for me. I should of course have realised that according to Freudian doctrine the only men who are not repressed passive homosexuals are unrepressed passive homosexuals.

This analyst further undermined my few remaining shreds of self-respect by interpreting what I had supposed to be virtues as vices: for example, decency became weakness. Since my condition continued to deteriorate, I decided to have done with the second analyst and went to the GP to tell him that

"I had to pass buildings associated with some of the events that formed part of my obsessive thoughts, and I arrived in a state of terror"

conscious drives and their etiology.

Numerous studies have been undertaken of the curative effects of dynamic therapy including psychoanalysis. The usual finding is that the recovery rate from neuroses is exactly the same after such therapy as after other forms of therapy or no therapy at all, though a few studies suggest that analysis benefits some patients and about the same number suggest it tends to make patients worse. It may be wondered why there are still so many ardent practitioners of psychoanalysis. It seems likely that a well-established psychological mechanism is at work: analysis is an expensive, time consuming and painful experience. For anyone who has been through a training analysis to admit to himself that the whole procedure is useless, he must be prepared to acknowledge having made a major mistake in the way he has spent his resources. Moreover, there is experimental evidence to show that patients unconsciously provide psychoanalysts with the sort of material they wish to hear: when a patient starts talking about topics the analyst thinks are important or begins to make himself the sort of interpretations the analyst believes are fruitful, the analyst will reward the patient by expressing interest and approval. Such is the human desire for approval, that it is little wonder that patients quickly catch on to what the analyst wishes to hear and produce just that material which fits in with his ways of thinking, thus confirming his faith in his own dogmas. Moreover, since many patients recover anyway, all analysts will have some patients who get better. Those who do not recover will eventually drop out of analysis (if only because they can no longer afford it) and the analyst can close his case notes by writing "terminated analysis prematurely." When I challenged my own analysts with figures on recovery rates, they both made the same reply. One said, "For every shrink in the south of England making people better, there are six elsewhere

Continued on next page

These are examples of the rich opportunities for using artists in print journalism. They can report, illustrate or comment with refreshing vivacity. There are physical limitations. For newspapers, the work must be in line (not wash); on time; and the illustrator has to think.

Breakdown: John Thirsk was commissioned to produce a big single drawing for a feature in which a professor of psychology described his own nervous breakdown. The author wanted to remain anonymous, so identifying photographs or drawings were out. Thirsk focused on an incident where the author wrote: 'I had to pass buildings associated with some of the events that formed part of my obsessive thought and I arrived in a state of terror'. The distinctive background of Charing Cross was chosen.

£ sign: The ambulatory sterling-sign-cum-city-gent was published during a currency crisis, one of the entrants in a *Sunday Times* contest to find artists who could illustrate Britain at work and in business.

Portrait: Familiar faces become hackneyed by routine portraiture. Drawing is the answer—caricature for comment; or cooler, recognisable portraits with a dash of vinegar for

ordinary news. In Arthur Horner's drawing of the newspaper magnate, Lord Beaverbrook, the facial tone is the small print of a newspaper.

The Potato: The story was that the humble spud had become a celebrity, scarce and soaring in value. Peter Brookes' comment works well at small scale. A bag of best King Edwards to the photographer who can match it for effectiveness.

The human pyramid: A remarkable example of the capacity of an intelligent artist to express a complex idea. Two Oxford economists argued that Britain was in difficulties because there were too few people in productive industry making goods that were sold. Too many had drifted into the public sector where they did not produce marketable goods but made claims on those produced by the diminished productive sector. There was a good graphic idea for this series—photographing people on the bus to work and labelling each with their occupation. It was published but it did not disentangle the story as neatly.

Strip Cartoon: This example by Nick Faure is about housebreaking but there is hardly any sequential story or instructional feature which is not capable of rendition in strip cartoon.

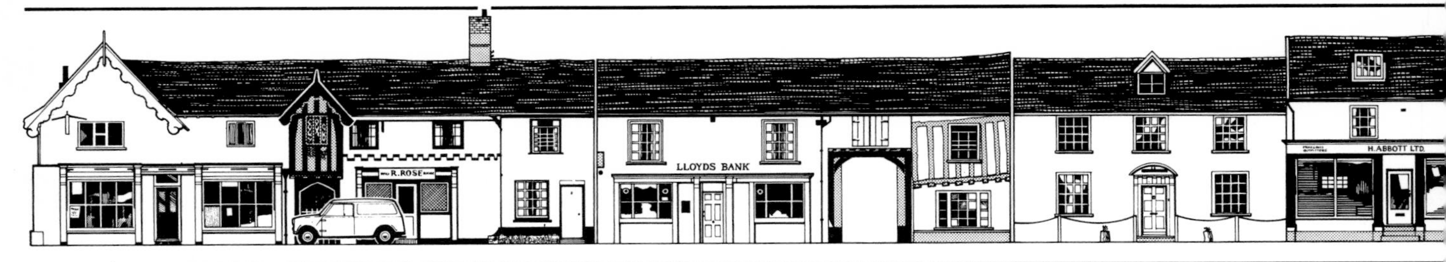

Peter Sullivan

Bloomsbury was once delightful terraces, in human scale of the kind drawn above. London University's new intrusion into Russell Square (below) now dwarfs its old neighbours

Three lessons of the Bloomsbury sacrifice

By IAN NAIRN

BYE-BYE Bloomsbury — at least, that part of it owned by London University. The photograph here is of the University's Institute of Education and Law in Russell Square, courtesy of Denys Lasdun, architect of the National Theatre and one of Britain's best. It has replaced a spiky mock-Gothic church and stock brick terraces of a kind drawn above.

It has been designed with care and panache and, with one enormous reservation, would be a handsome building—somewhere else. In Bloomsbury it is a disaster.

Analytical drawing is most valuable for the economical detail it offers and the control of perspective. Birds, bees, butterflies, flowers, buildings, . . . you can go through ten alphabets for the subjects that are ideal, especially for newspapers where line reproduces well on coarse newsprint. The village terrace (*top*) would be hard to photograph without apparent distortion and only drawing can give the clear description required of individual features.

The rest of the two pages is a study of a problem in journalism where drawing and photography worked together. Bloomsbury, London, used to be one of the visually most congenial areas of the capital, terraced Georgian family houses forming adjacent squares with small areas of trees and park. London University has spoiled much of it and Ian Nairn wrote an attack on a culminating bit of development, the replacement of a spiky mock-Gothic church and terrace with a tall glass and concrete building, intimidatingly out of human scale and character with the surroundings. The new building was photographed from every angle by Bryan Wharton in a valiant attempt to relate its bland bullying style to the decorative detail and intimacy of the remaining period houses. It could not be done. It proved impossible to show both the older terrace and the new central feature of the new building, its abandonment of a first floor to concrete piers and staircase. Photographing the two separately did not work either. Even in good light photographs did not do justice to the terrace and to take it frontally affected the perspective (see photograph right).

Peter Sullivan was therefore asked to draw and at short notice produced the admirable drawing which is the main illustration here. This was run as a 4-column lead to the feature with a photograph of the intrusive new building adjacent (*above left*).

San Francisco Examiner
Monarch of the Dailies
VOL. CIX MONDAY SAN FRANCISCO, NOVEMBER 11, 1918—SIXTEEN PAGES MONDAY CC ✱ NO. 134

"PEACE ON EARTH"

GERMANY SURRENDERS

(By Universal Service)

WASHINGTON, November 11.---The armistice terms have been signed by Germany, the State Department announced at 2:45 this morning.

The armistice was signed at 5 a. m. today, Paris time, and hostilities will cease at 11 a. m., Paris time.

The armistice will not be made public before 8 o'clock this morning.

KAISER, PRINCE AND ARMY STAFF FLEE TO HOLLAND

LONDON, November 11 (Monday). — The Dutch

Austrian Rulers Reach Switzerland In Wild Flight Before Red Mob

BATTLE RAGES IN BERLIN; WOUNDED FILL HOSPITALS

LONDON, November 10.—Berlin is in the hands

City Is Ablaze At Midnight; Rolph Proclaims Today Holiday

WASHINGTON, November 11.—The terms of the armistice, it was announced, will not be made public until later. Military men here, however, regard it as certain that they include:

Immediate retirement of the German military forces from France, Belgium and

Flavour graphics

British newspapers, led initially by the *Daily Express*, the *Evening Standard*, the *Observer* and *The Sunday Times*, have set new standards for flavour graphics. One would say they invented them and they did, in their sophisticated modern style, for a variety of purposes. But the idea had been around for some time, witness the American eagle celebrating the end of the First World War for the *San Francisco Examiner*. It is crude, jingoistic, over-sized, but marvellously exuberant and colourful on the grey page of text. Flavour graphics are today virtually unknown in newspapers outside Britain, yet they are excellent as signallers and co-ordinators. When they are used in this latter way for big feature presentations the words and pictures, as Ken Baynes has put it, 'form a unit on the page which acts as a cross between an advertisement and a book jacket'. The graphics give the symbolic flavour and, stretched across the whole text, knit together words and display heading. The examples here are all successful in different ways.

Empire Games: A simple label by Bert Hackett for the *Birmingham Post*, the runner's head neatly breaking the title. It is capable of considerable reduction.

SUNDAY TIMES weekly review

12 JANUARY 1969

49

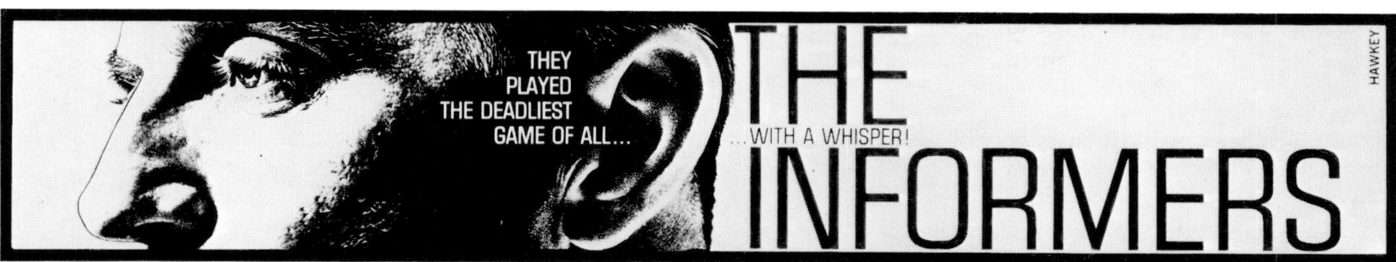

Conway Stewart: The famous fountain pen company had run into financial difficulties. This flavour graphic headed a long feature article. It was ingenious of Peter Brookes to use a Conway Stewart pen to write the title of the article and for the ink to run out (to have the pen shaking at the time was, perhaps, a little excessive).

Russia: There was little illustration material for this feature, but Edwin Taylor overcame the difficulties by allusive typography and a severely bordered photograph of Russian people cropped to suggest crowding—a fragment of a vast population. On the turn-page this large flavour graphic could be reduced to a double or even single column and still be clear enough as a signal.

The Informers: A Ray Hawkey projection for a *Daily Express* fiction serial. The small type running into a large ear and between the main caps heading really does seem to whisper.

Merger Mania: A business article in the *Observer* on a rash of take-overs and mergers attracted this wry flavour graphic of city types flowing into each other and into the main heading. Economical and more fun than other graphic efforts based on the idea of an octopus.

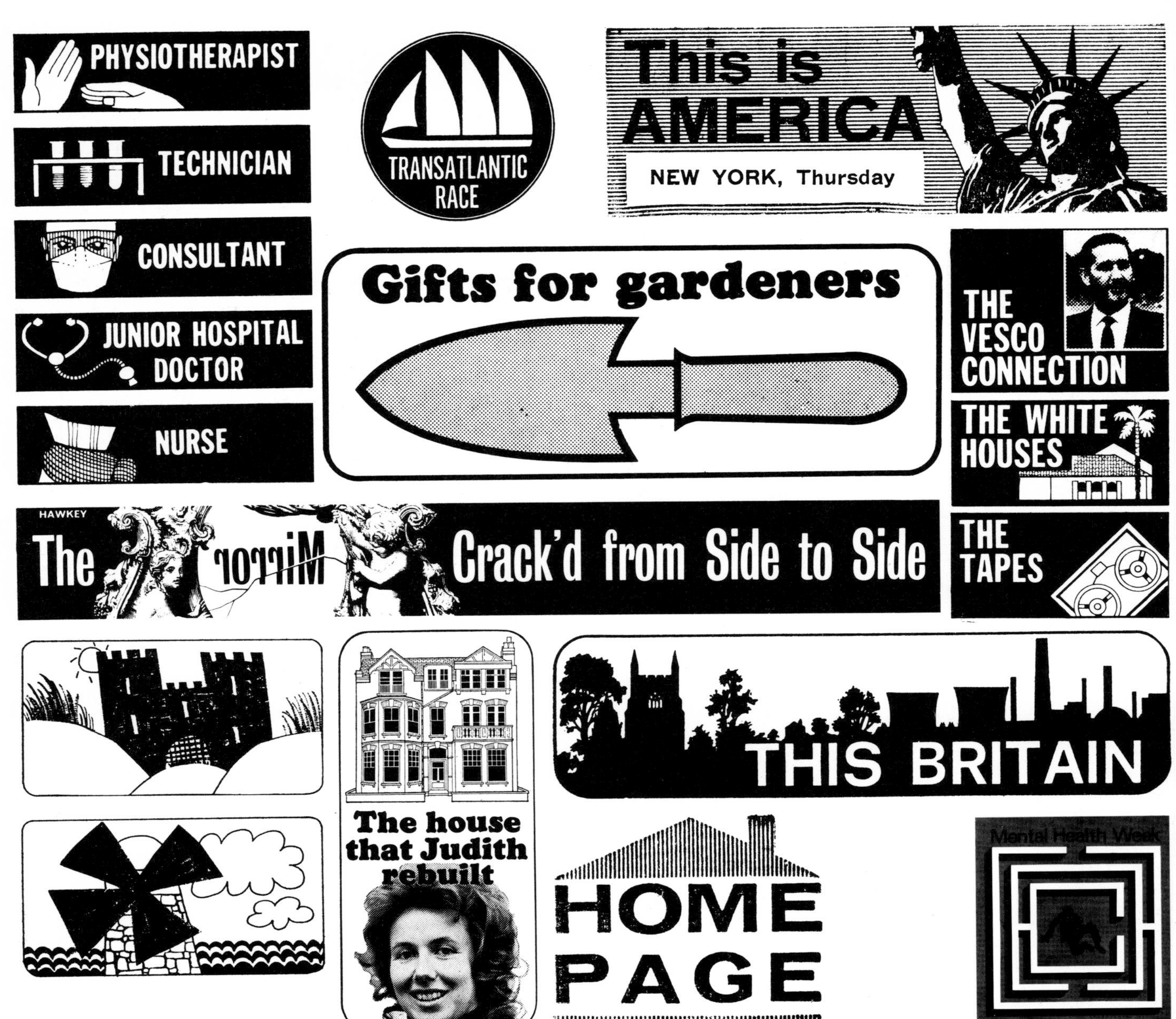

The smaller flavour graphics are examples of the versatility of the form. These simple flags must not be much bigger, if at all, than the display type that would have otherwise have to be used. They are a sauce which must not be diluted: Gifts for gardeners is too big.

Regular features: Letters, gardening, city, sport, and the like are usefully flagged with a flavour graphic: Home Page (*Northern Echo*), This Britain (*Sunday Times*), and This is America (*Daily Express*). The problem is to devise a recognisable symbol which is not hackneyed.

Graphics for themes: Some long articles divide naturally into sections, usually divided by side-headings. A flavour graphic can provide the breaker when colour is otherwise limited on the page. Two examples are the groups headed Physiotherapist in a feature on the health service and (*right*) The Vesco Connection, The White Houses and The Tapes, breakers devised for an article on Watergate.

Serials: The House that Judith Rebuilt flagged a short serial and The Mirror a fiction serial. The severity of the lettering emphasises, against the baroque figures, the finality of the crack in the mirror.

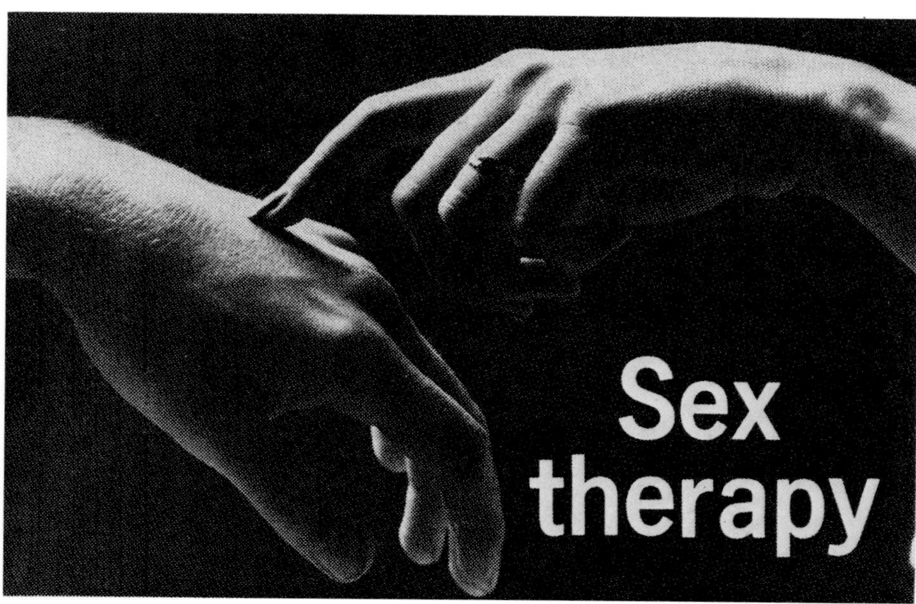

Column breaks: The jolly castle and windmill were part of a group dividing an article on holidays.

Campaigns: A flavour graphic can be a campaign in itself. Bert Hackett devised a series for the *Birmingham Post* which pressed the dangers of drinking and driving and often ran without text. Mental Health Week is another from *The Post,* and very compelling it is. *The Sunday Times*—which invented the word 'juggernaut' for the extra-large lorries—used a flavour graphic which showed the juggernaut in scale with a Mini.

Certain graphic symbols rapidly became overworked—the torn wedding picture for divorce, broken lettering for mental health or alcoholism. But ingenuity is always breaking through. Sex Therapy had its difficulties (straightforward photographic illustration either too dull or too interesting) and the close-up of male-female hands with reverse lettering made the point concisely and chastely.

The other flavour graphics make feature presentations out of little—Georges Simenon against a montage of his thrillers; Kipling stuck down in a photograph album with Pabst type which is appropriately quirky; and computer tape for Johnny Miller's scientific approach to his golf.

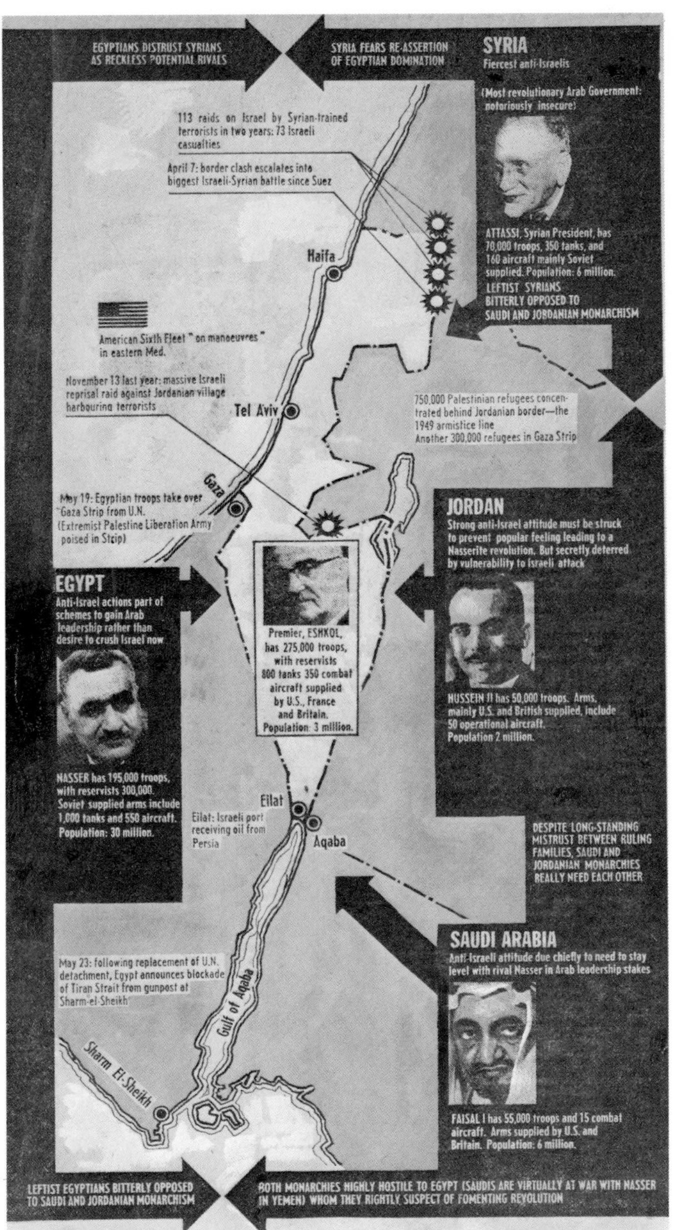

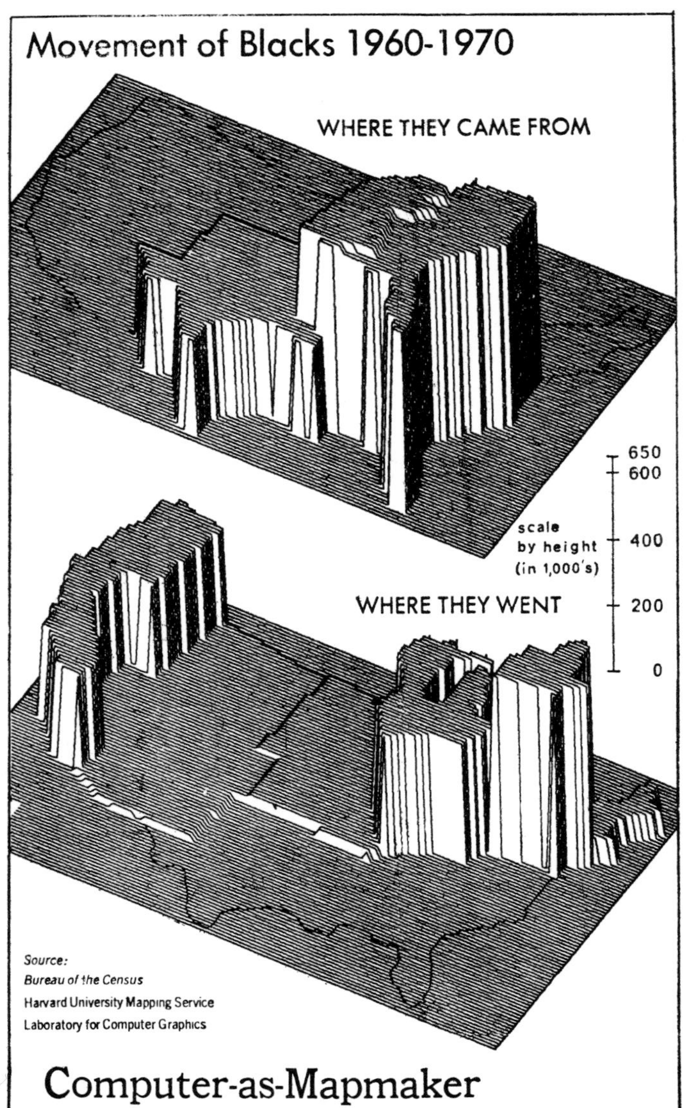

Making the most of maps

News is no respecter of borders or of our rudimentary ideas of places. Where is Ujiji? That was the question in 1872 (Stanley met Livingstone). Where are Seveso and Peachville and Kuneitra? Simple location maps are well within the capacity of any newspaper, though a remarkable number play blind man's bluff with the reader. The conventional flat map will always be good graphics, but there are stories where the map grid can be stretched to indicate other than physical relationships and to plot sequences.

At the start of the Six-day war in the Middle East the map at left diagnosed the different relationships. This combination of drawing, type and photographs, with the conflict emphasised by strong black arrows, showed in one block the combatant states, their leaders, philosophies and the flashpoints of the fighting.

If large scale graphics like this are to make sense, editorial executive and artist must together be alert to two failings: squeezing in so much information that confusion is produced; and, in attempting this, making the type in the graphics too small. Artwork is generally designed to be reduced by one third. The editorial executive must always satisfy himself that, when reduced, the type is at least 9pt, especially in the more condensed

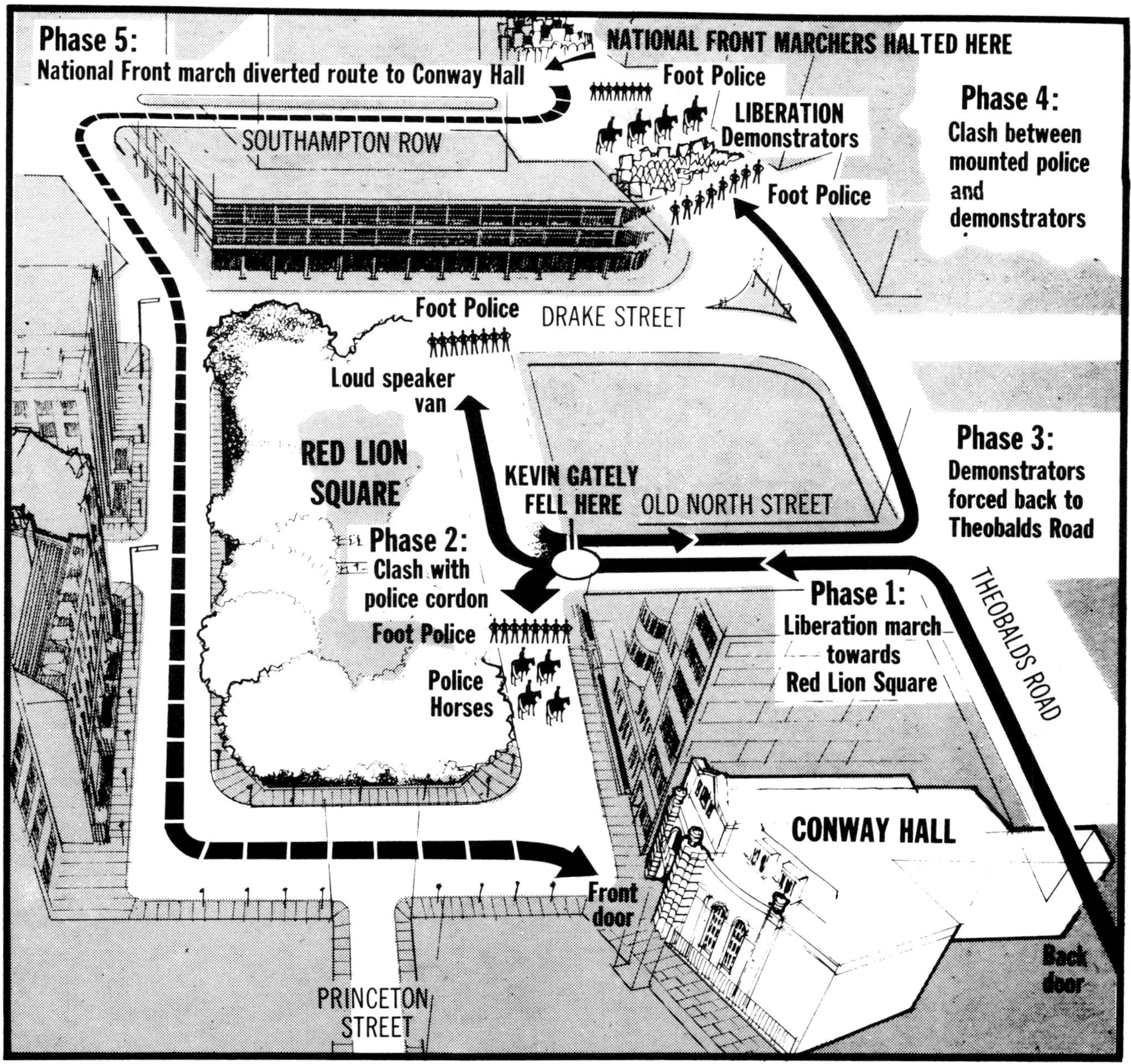

sans serif faces. Of course even 7pt is readable in text, but a bigger size is needed for graphics and it is better to err on the big side. The words should be fastidiously edited.

It is arguable whether the Middle East map has gone too far—it is included to show the possibilities—but there is no doubt about the success of the street map (*above*) where police tried to keep apart two rival groups of demonstrators and a man died. Five phases of action are delineated by text and broken and continuous lines. The type is big and clear, the meeting hall and square picked out in white with tone for the rest of the buildings. The designer depended on information from reporters. Where were the police? What happened next?

The human skills behind this map cannot be replaced but computer graphics are developing. A computer drew three-dimensional maps of the movement of blacks on a two-dimensional service for Harvard University Mapping Service and it was run in the *New York Times* (*left*). It has a weakness in specific information: it is difficult, for instance, in the second map to compare black population density in the West with that in the Middle Eastern states. But the practical advantage is in its dramatic summary of the trends hidden in vast amounts of information.

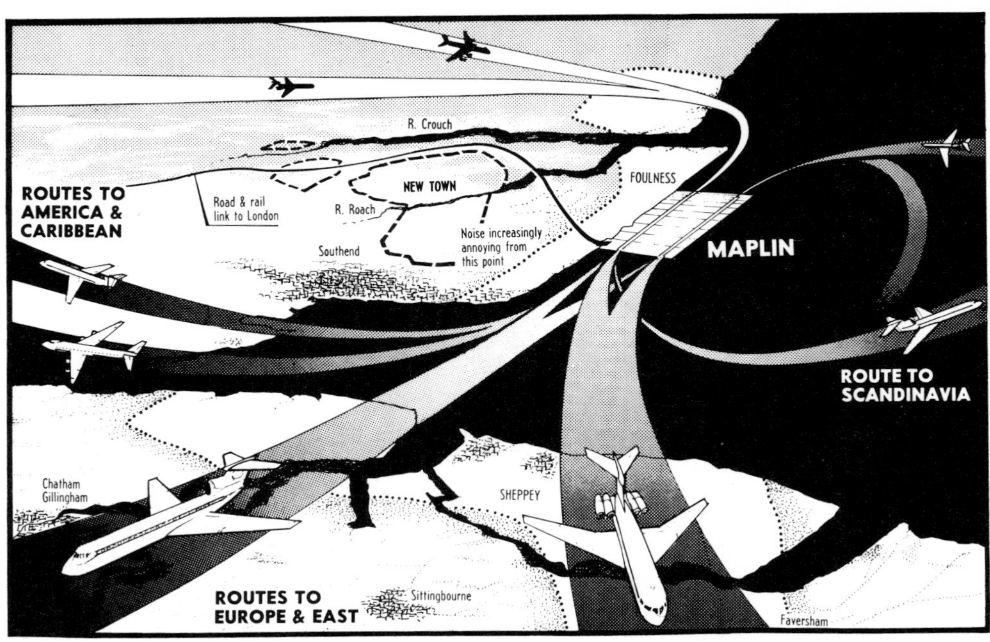

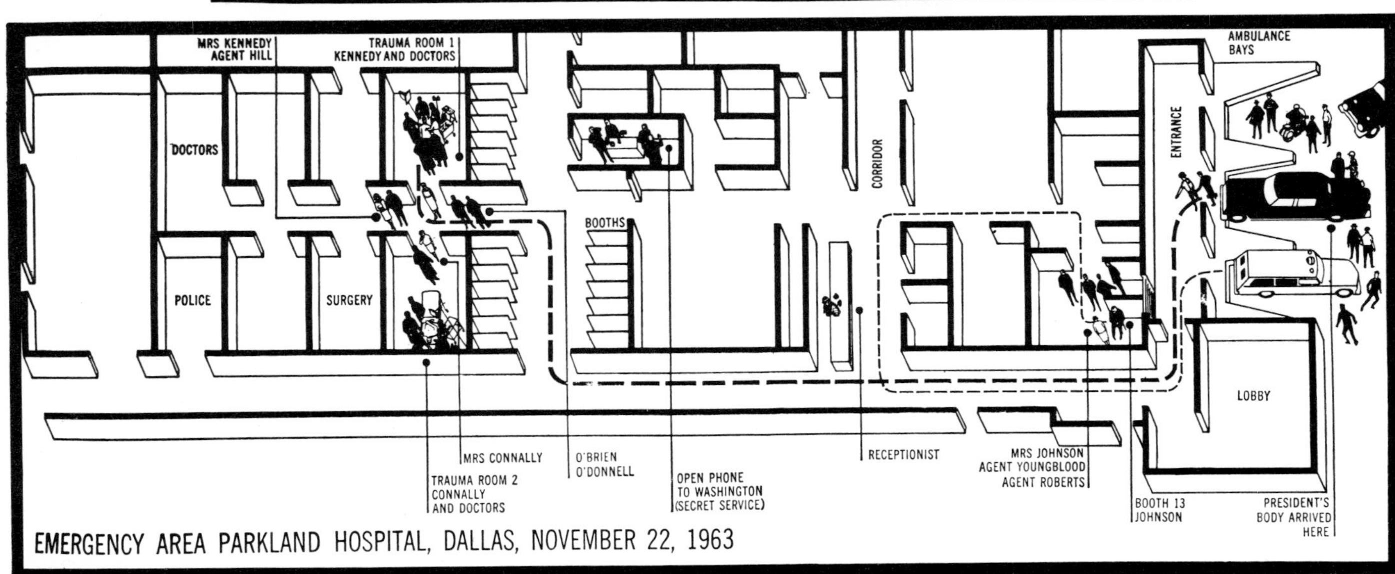

Does it work? That is the first question for the stretched map. Ernest Hoch, when chairman of the Icograda Commission on Standardisation, made the point: 'So long as we treat graphic design as an expression in aesthetic self-expression we are falling short of requirements'. There may be quarrels about refinements on the very different maps here but they all work—and do things that words and photographs cannot do. They can stand on their own; but of course in publication they all benefited by captions and accompanying text.

Maplin: This was the proposed site of a controversial new airport which was to be built into the sea over mud flats. Everybody wanted to know how they would be affected by noise, and for this they had to be given some idea of the pattern of flights and volume. This the map does, showing towns in relation to approach and take-off points for different destinations. The temptation to include more places was strong and resisted; it remains a short cut to understanding immediately.

Dallas Hospital: A map by Roy Castle of the interior of the Dallas hospital where President Kennedy was taken after being shot. All the key characters are located, economically symbolised (see, for instance, Mrs. Kennedy) and neatly identified. The rooms and the route of the President's

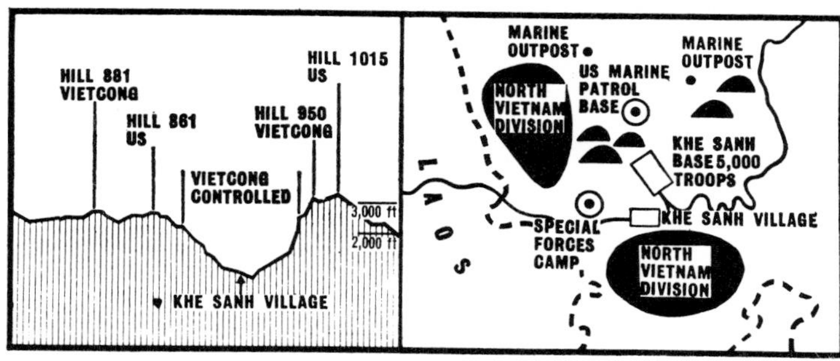

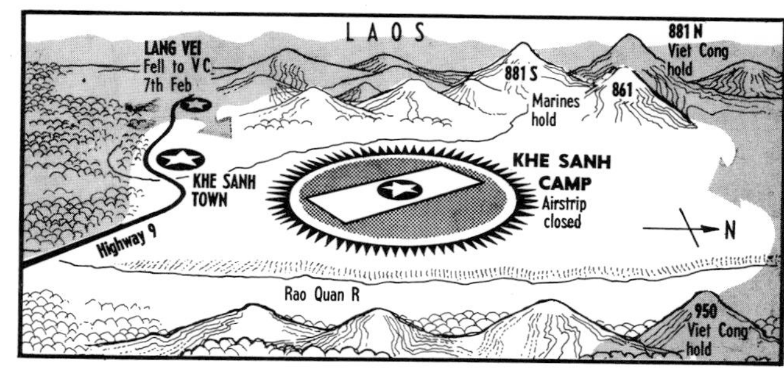

stretcher are also clearly labelled. This map was an essential accompaniment for the narrative; but by itself it told several stories. The original dimension was $15\frac{1}{2}''$ by $6\frac{1}{2}''$ but the type was perhaps slightly on the thin side.

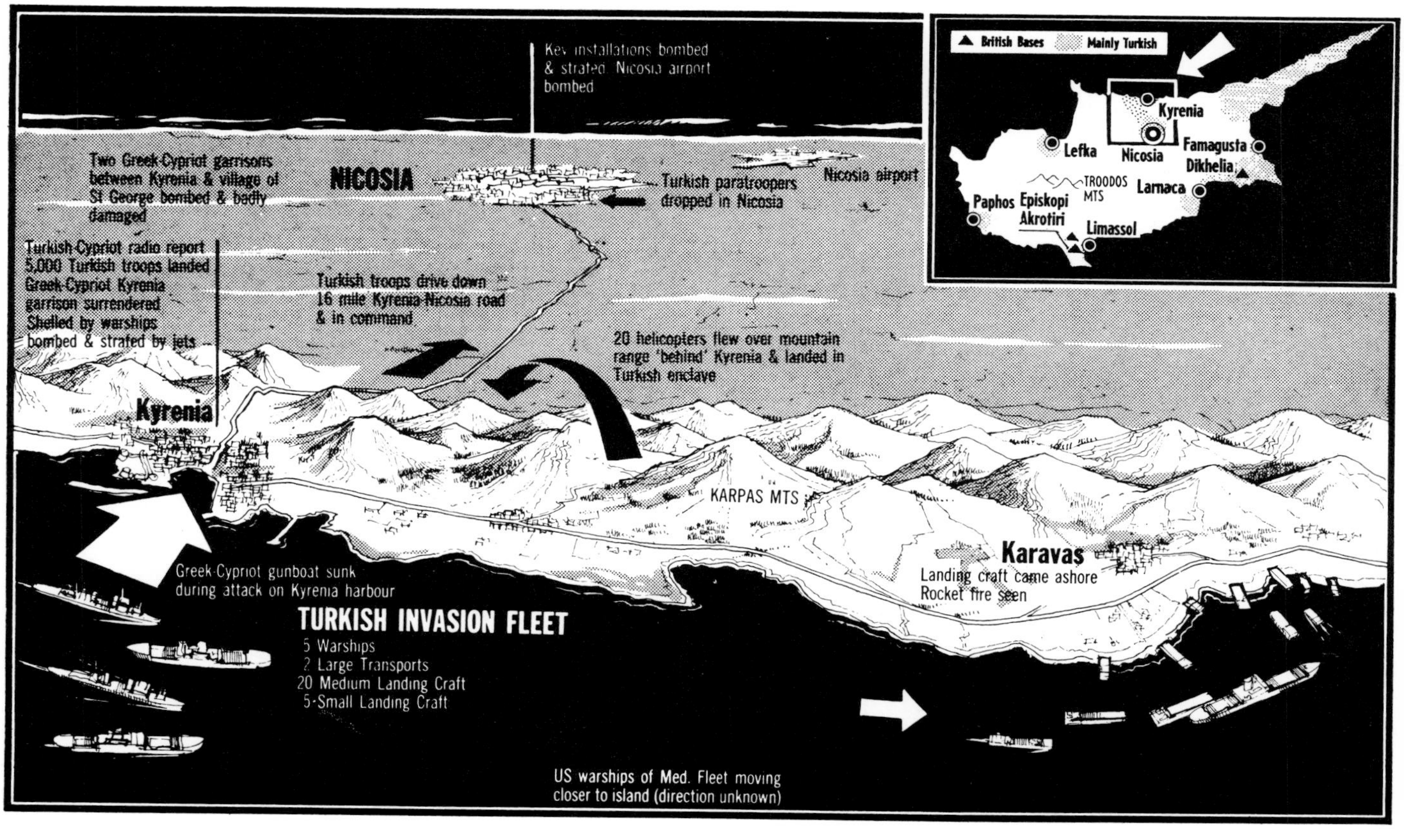

Khe Sanh: Five thousand US Marines were trapped in Khe Sanh in Vietnam encircled by 20,000 enemy in the surrounding hills. A traditional flat map of that area gives no indication of the nature of their predicament and the importance of the hills which were being contested, so at the top left a side-elevation accompanied the flat map. But the best solution (short of a relief model) is a facts graphic which gives some feeling of the third dimension. Some artistic licence has to be permitted but a truer feel is presented (*top right*).

Cyprus: This map showing the Turkish invasion of Cyprus was produced during the Saturday as information came in from the war front. A squat fat arrow pinpoints the major assault by sea, a curving arrow shows the path of 20 helicopters over the mountains to a Turkish enclave. The sea is black, tone marks the inland areas and white is used for the mountains and Nicosia. A small locator map places the action on the island. The type was, again, a bit thin (original dimension $9'' \times 5''$) but this newsy map was well worth its position on the front page.

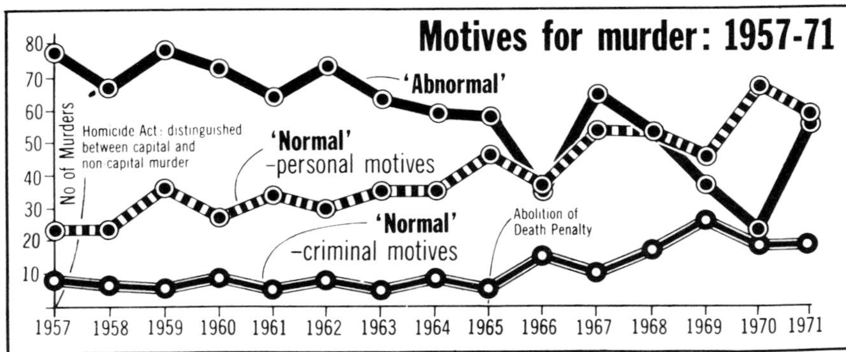

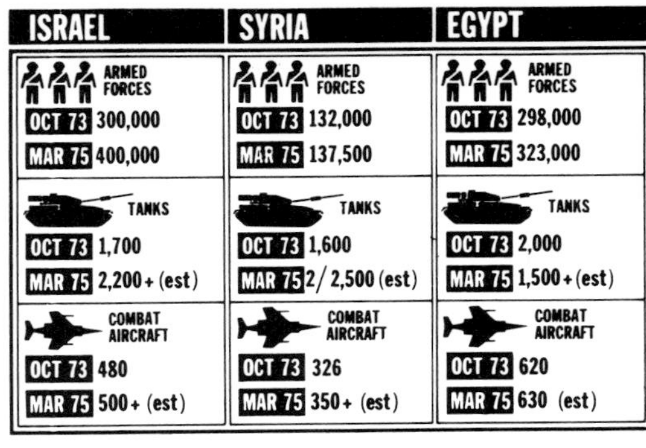

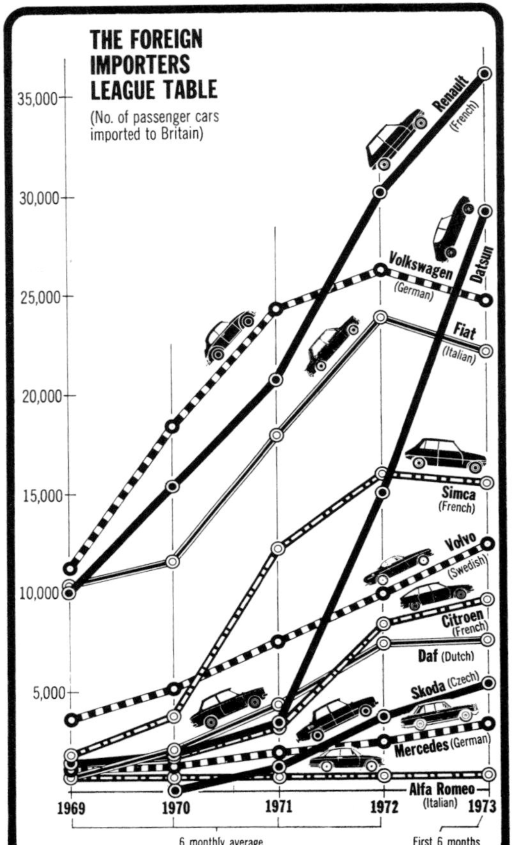

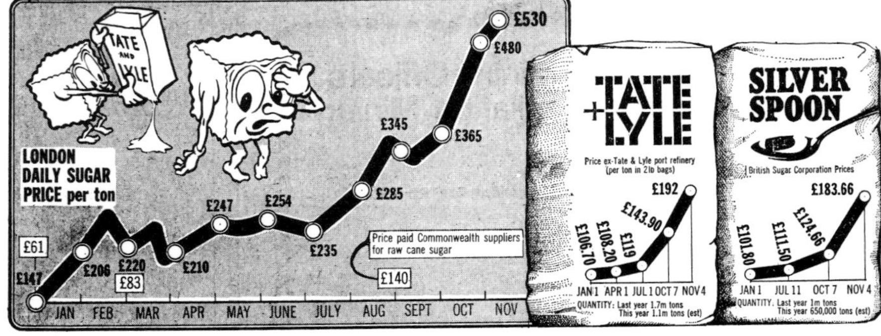

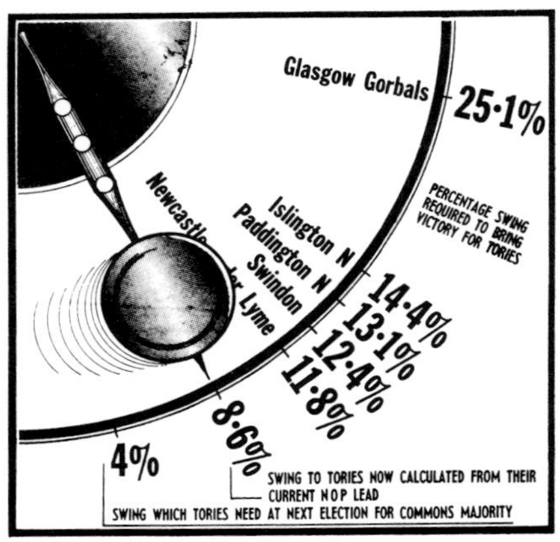

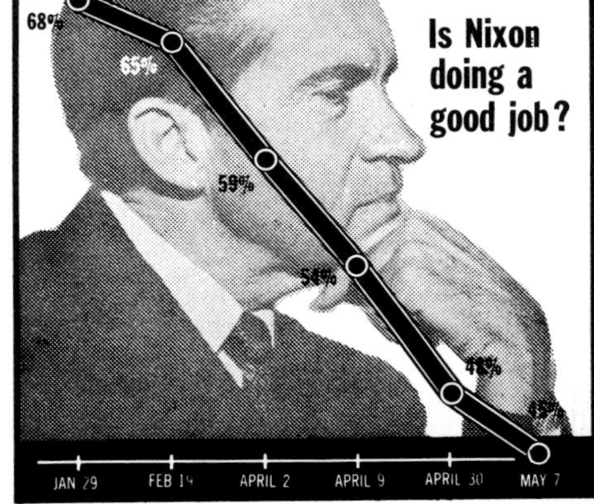

Charts that tell at a glance

Merely to turn words into diagrams, charts and tabulations does not guarantee good graphics and better communication. As Robert Waterhouse wrote in surveying the work of *The Sunday Times* and *Observer*: 'Like anything else there has to be a come-on; a boring drawing is not better than a boring story.' The drawing has to appear interesting; it has, in this, not to distort the facts. But a good analytical chart does something more: it explains itself at once. We read it for confirmation, not for explanation. It should always be possible to grasp—at first glance—at least three-quarters of the story. Charts and diagrams which are crowded or very complicated may hinder rather than aid perception.

The test is particularly well met on three of the charts on these pages—Nixon, industrial production, and growing children. The graphic of Nixon's falling popularity is superimposed on a faded picture of Nixon looking thoughtful. An even apter choice of photograph inspired the presentation of the index of industrial production, the graph running between the outstretched hands of the then Minister for Industry. The scale of the graph had to be adjusted to fit the photograph but there is no distortion. It takes more space than a simple

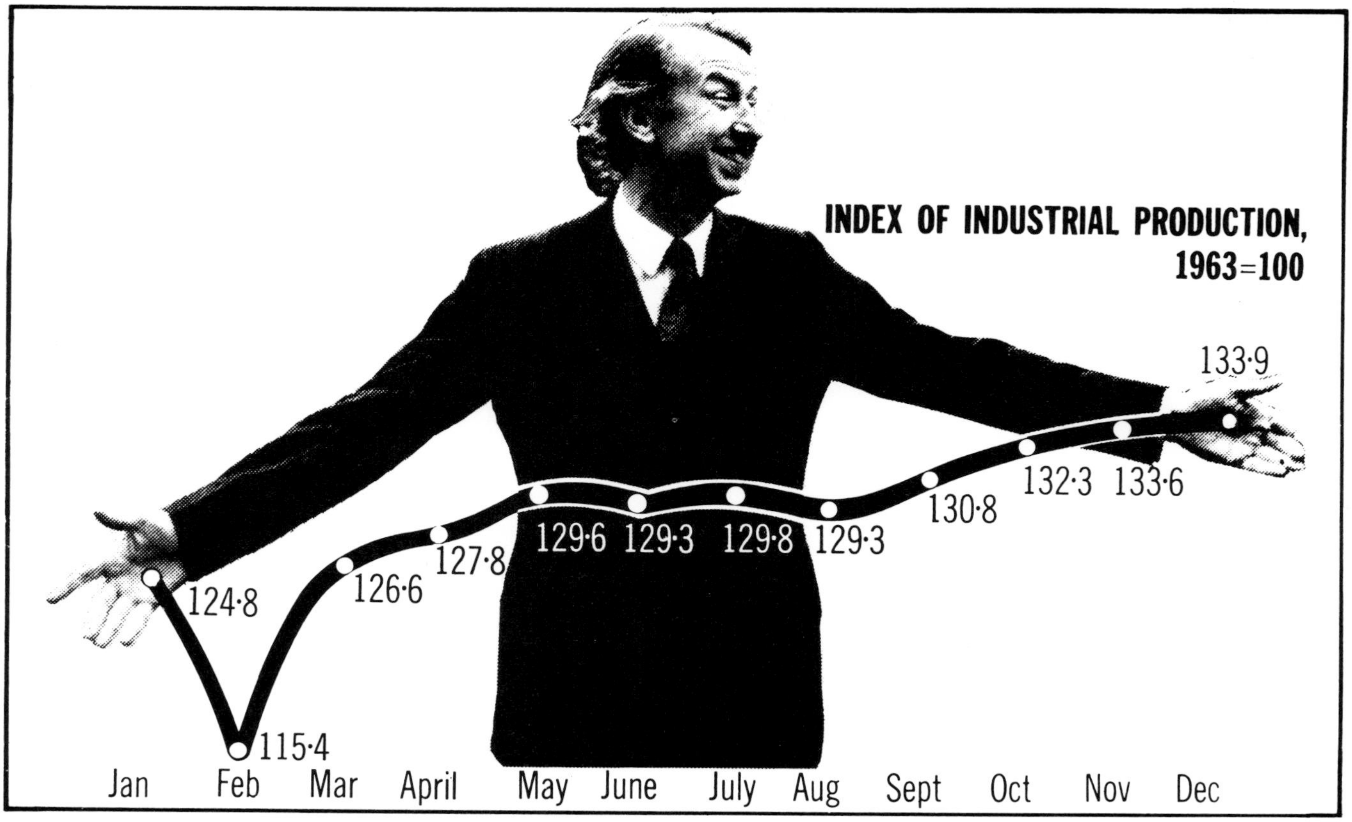

INDEX OF INDUSTRIAL PRODUCTION,
1963=100
124·8
115·4
126·6
127·8
129·6
129·3
129·8
129·3
130·8
132·3
133·6
133·9
Jan
Feb
Mar
April
May
June
July
Aug
Sept
Oct
Nov
Dec

HT.
(Inches)
60
50
40
30
20
10
0
1905
1965
1905
1965
1905
1965
Five years
Nine years
Eleven years

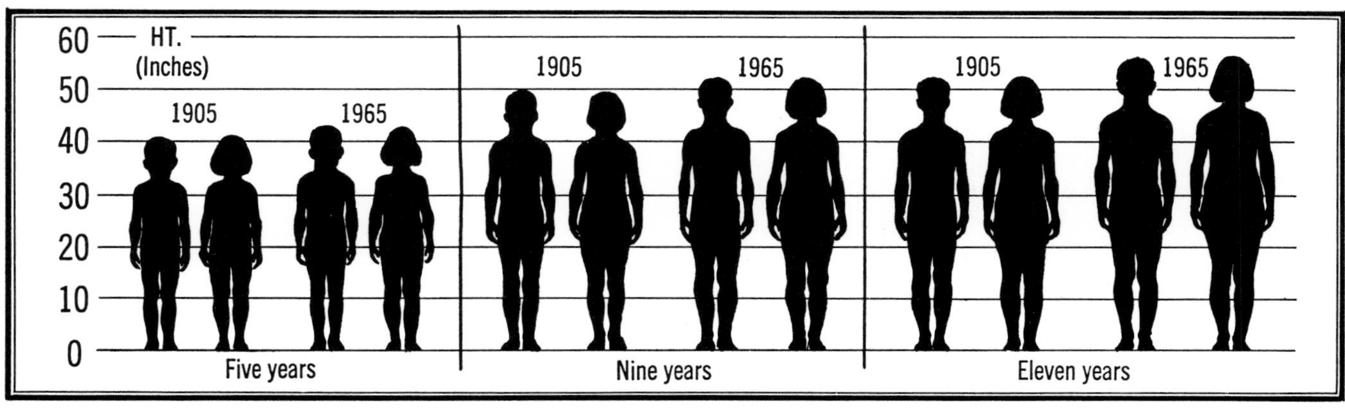

table of the information, but it provides at the same time an illustration sufficient to carry a page. The simplicity and clean workmanship of this chart is similar to that in the children's chart. A Government report had given statistics showing how boys and girls of 1965, aged five, nine and eleven, were bigger than boys and girls of 1905. Again, the graphic presentation takes more space but one learns the scale of the development and gets a sense of seeing the children grow.

The comparative weaponry of Israel, Syria and Egypt would be a simple enough table in figures; the graphics here are for colour. The virtues of the car chart and Motives for Murder, however, is that they present comparisons instantly which would, in a table of figures, take some pondering. The car chart is noteworthy for comparing eleven different manufacturers' figures with only four styles of drawn lines.

Sugar: The visually sparse subject of sugar prices has been enlivened by a comic drawing of Mr. Cube, again, with its tone background, enough to be a main illustration.

Voting swings: A shuddering pendulum indicates the effect of different swings of voting preference.

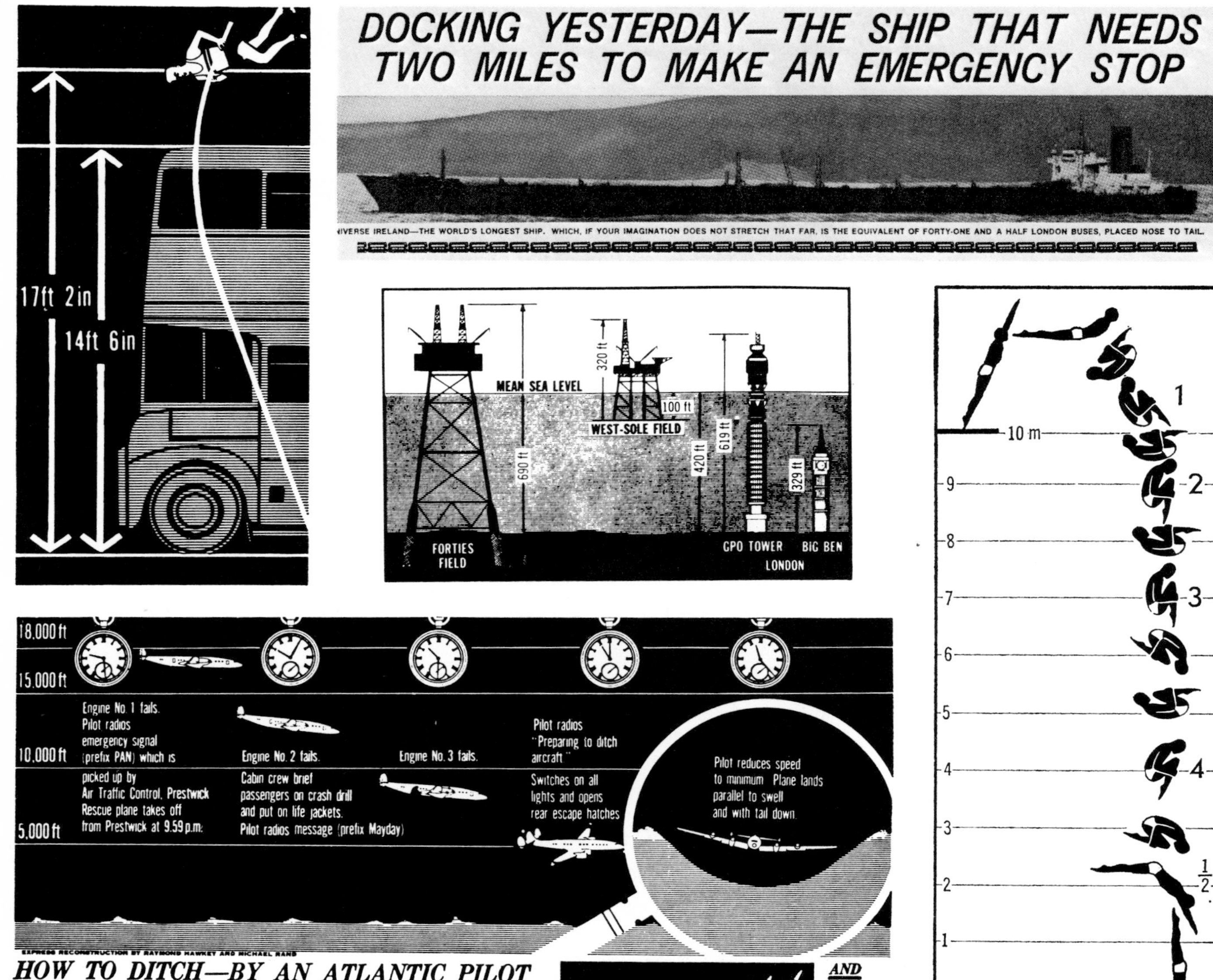

Dramatic scale and sequence

Graphics can convey an arresting idea or scale or analyse sequence in very small amounts of space.

The world's longest ship: This could not have more than 12 inches in width in the photograph in the *Sun*; but the newspaper gave its readers a vivid idea by comparing a line of buses.

The vaulter: This time the familiar size of the bus is used by Roy Castle to make us gasp at the height of a pole vault. The ruthless economy of this graphic is to be commended: nothing gets in the way of the message.

The oil rigs: Two symbols familiar to Britons—Big Ben, buried beneath the sea, at 329 ft, and the GPO tower. Three essential points about scale symbols: They must be familiar, recognisable in barest outline, and drawn simply.

Sequence

The diver graphic, stripped of inessentials or mannerism, explains itself, but behind the plane crash is a testimony to teamwork. The Super Constellation had come down over the Atlantic without loss of the 76 passengers. The *Daily Express* set to work to dramatise the sequence. A transatlantic pilot told a reporter what a pilot would try to do if his plane ditched into the ocean. Based on this, work started at 5pm on a theoretical

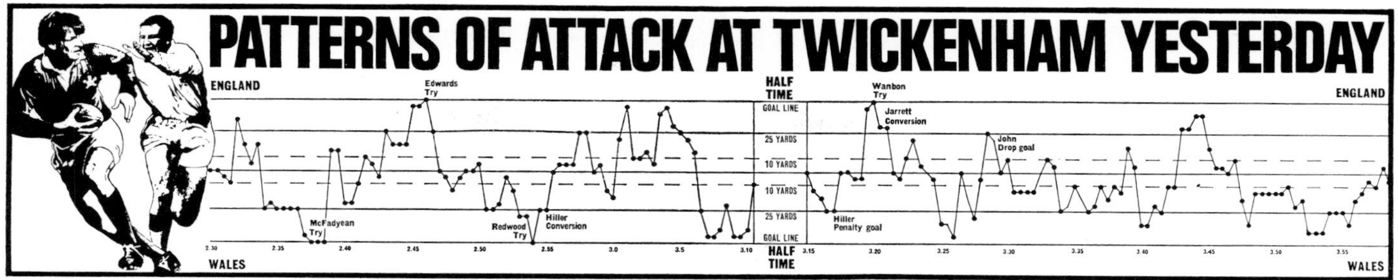

The graph, plotting the ball's movements every 30 seconds, shows Wales's better use of fewer chances. They scored two tries from only four spells of a minute or more in the England '25.' England scored twice in seven periods of pressure.

GEOFFREY NICHOLSON reports on the match

ONE OF the most promising internationals between these two coun-

bered for his prodigious 19 points against England at Cardiff last season, succeeded with only one kick at goal.

True, two of his failures led to Welsh tries, but that was through England's handling errors. Generally, Wales were lucky to get back to Paddington with a single championship point.

The English selectors, on the whole, were proved right to change and rejuvenate the side It had enough life and energy to have captured the game,

ENGLAND 11 pts WALES 11

Jarrett missed with the long, angled penalty kick, but this did the Welsh cause little harm, since McFadyean knocked on in front of his posts.

Two scrums later, Edwards broke on the blind side, dummied a pass out to his left and as the English defence went with the swing of his Watkins's hands. The big Welsh right wing, bending out of one pair of English hands and breaking through a second tackle, seemed almost certain to score.

But when finally he was brought down almost on the England line, he must have tried to shuffle the ball

ibly steadying as the English were just as noticeably beginning to lose their edge. Yet England came back upfield to force a five-yard scrum, only to throw their chance away when Redwood put the ball in askew. And it looked long odds on Wales managing to draw level.

Outplayed

But then, after 15 minutes of the half, Wales had one of their rare successes in the line-out, and crucially

COMMENT by CLEM THOMAS

LIKE MOST drawn contests,

mains that Wales were lucky to obtain their fifth drawn game at Twickenham since the war.

The key to the match lay in the 75 lines-out, of which England won 34, Wales 18, and 23 were inconclusive. England won most of theirs decisively whereas the Welsh possession was ineffectual. England, however, frittered away much of the marvellous possession obtained by West and Gay in the long line and Parsons and Larter in the

again looked a player of tremendous class.

In comparison, the English halves were far more unsettled. I would say that the fault lay with Finlan, who was indecisive and always appeared to waste that valuable split second making up his mind what to do. Redwood served him well and was, as expected, the most positive scrum-half who has played for England since Jeeps.

As a result, the English three-

illustration into which the real facts were married as the news flashes were received. Mike Rand worked on the main drawing, Roy Castle on the magnifying glass, John Hill on the watches. Ray Hawkey co-ordinated the finished work with the type and captions, and the facts with the reporters. The brilliantly effective sequence was finished by 7pm.

Twickenham: Photographs can capture a pivotal point in a match or an exciting sequence. Graphics can analyse some sporting encounters in a way which is meaningful for the general reader and totally absorbing for the fan. This is a relatively unexplored area for graphics. An easy practical graphic is to draw the 18 holes of a golf championship, each one no bigger than elongated postage stamps, and plot on each the strokes the winner took. The example from rugby is more ambitious. The *Observer* graph plotted the position of the ball every thirty seconds between the England half and the Welsh half. The England half of the ground, in the first half, is at the top; and the Welsh at the bottom. A very clear idea is obtained of how Wales made better use of fewer chances. This was published across a full page in the *Observer*.

Table tennis: Graphics can cope, and do, with anything from 'how to make a cake' to 'five steps to nuclear power'.

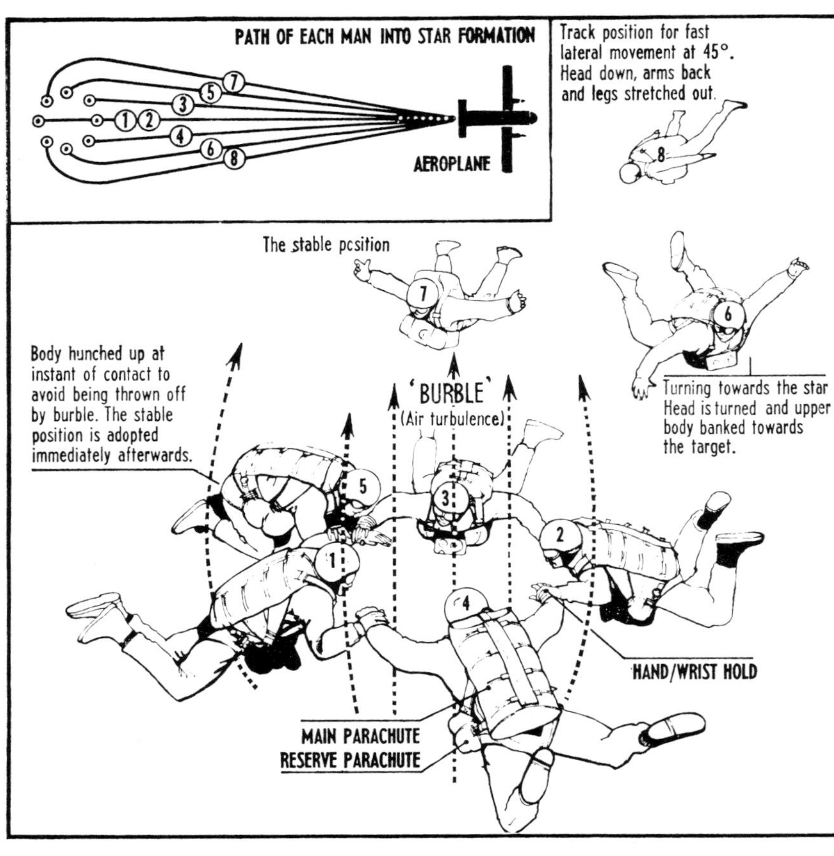

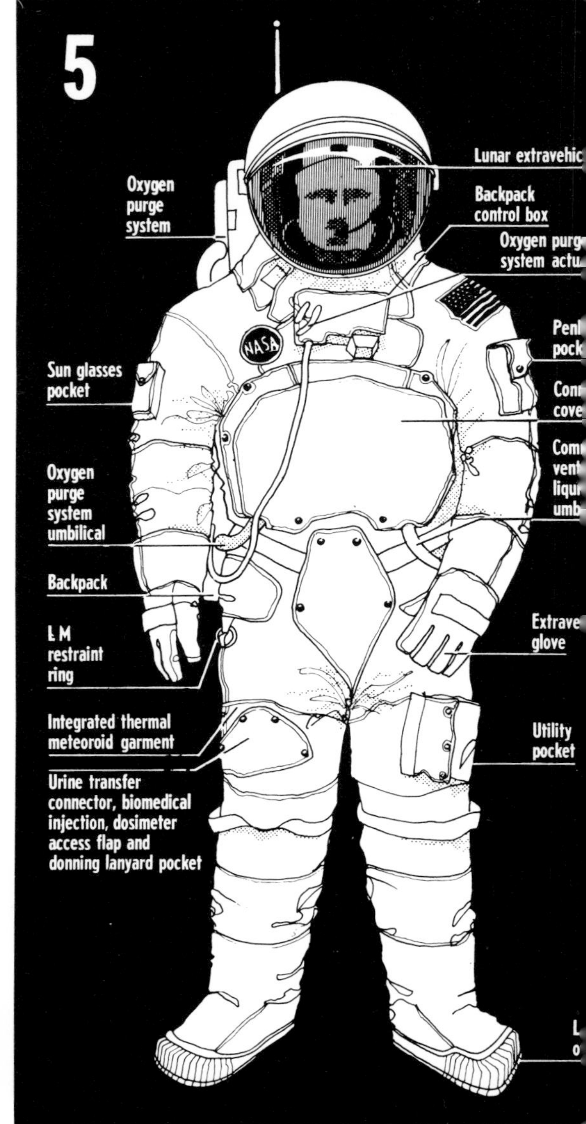

Parachuting: Television news one night showed an astonishing fragment of film of eight men falling through the air with unopened parachutes, hands and wrists linked in a star formation. It was, said the news announcer, a European record and he moved on to other items. This is a classic example of how newspapers, with graphics, can respond to the interest aroused by television. How do eight men get in that position? How do they link up when they jump separately out of a moving aircraft and fall at 200 miles an hour? Even with split-second sequence jumping, by the time the last man of eight comes to jump he is 300 ft above and 470 ft beyond the first jumper. The answers are in the fact graphic (above). The parachutists treat the body like an aircraft. The first man can slow his fall to 120 mph by adopting a spread-eagled stable position; the others can move in his direction by flying the body like an aircraft, tilting and tipping. As the group links up it creates an air turbulence 'burble' which is a problem for later arrivals, but that, too, is demonstrated in the drawing. Words enrich the accompanying story with elaboration and anecdote.

The graphic works but it could have been improved. Tint for the sky, leaving the jumpers white, would have picked them out more vividly. The

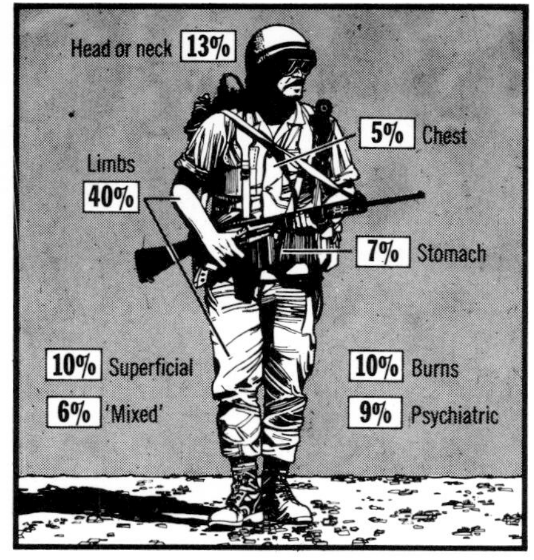

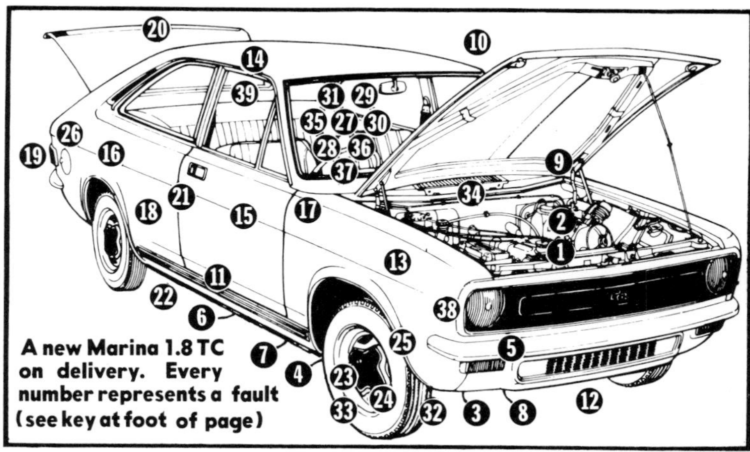

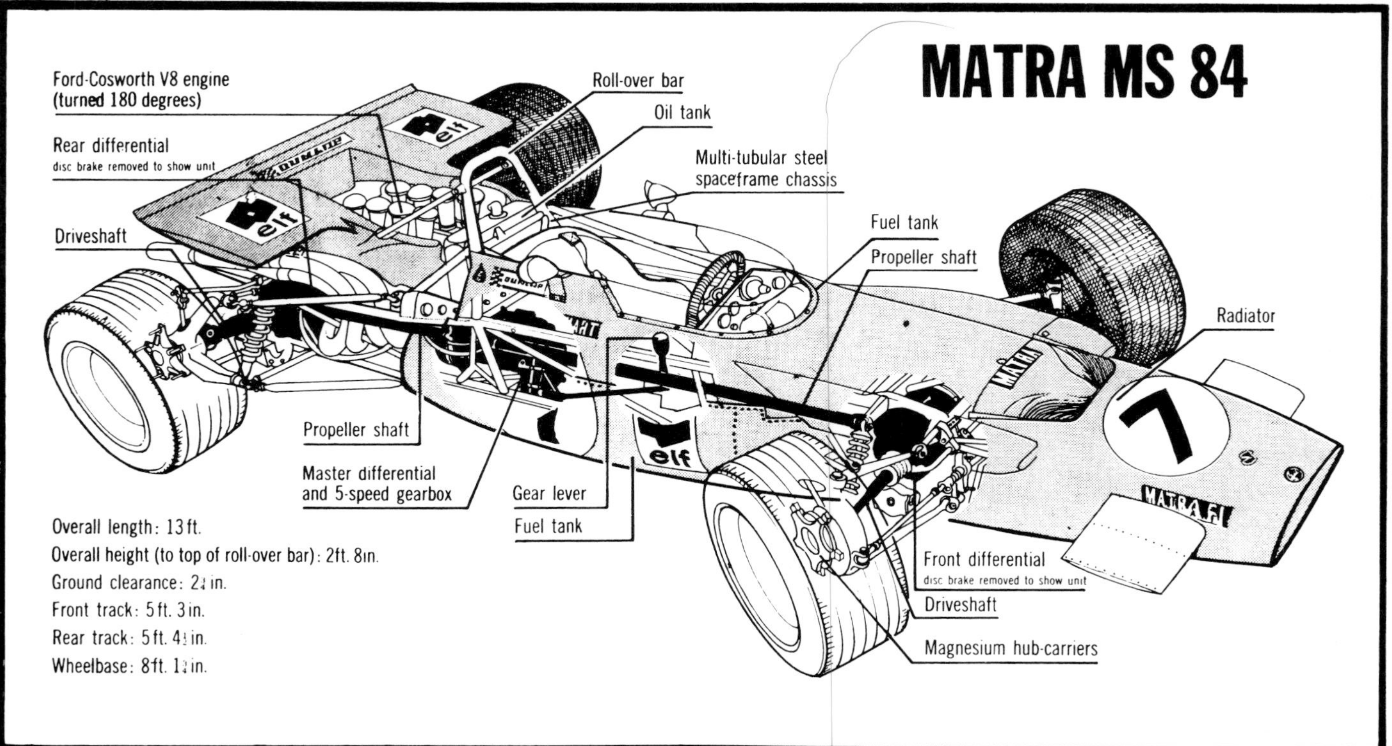

condensed type is not the easiest when there are too many words in one group (*middle left*). The inset box of the formation squeezes down on the action. These are refinements on a graphic which succeeds in saying something worthwhile. The **football** graphic makes a simple movement hard to comprehend.

Moon man: Black background projects the figure and the text stands out clearly. But—and it cannot be repeated too often—the type must be big and clear. Sans faces, provided they are not too condensed, are best.

Infantryman: A top left headline saying 'Risk Areas' (space created by moving 'head or neck' to right) would have made this explain itself as an analysis of where soldiers could most expect injury. But the percentage in white against tone and the perspective are excellent.

The cars: Two forms of labelling. The numbers on the saloon car are for two reasons. To write words against the 39 information points identified would overload the drawing. Secondly, a stock of numbers on artpaper can be kept readily available and be stuck down on a completed drawing without waiting for art-proofed type. The racing car, with only 16 reference points, benefited by the more precise labelling along identifying lines.

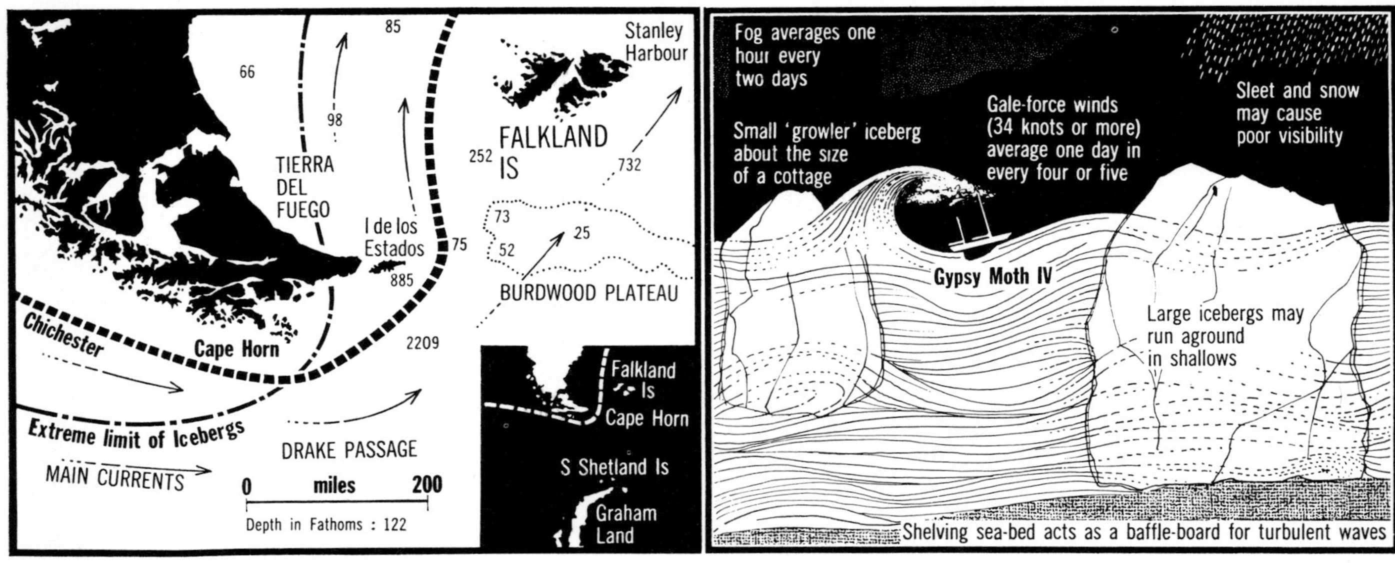

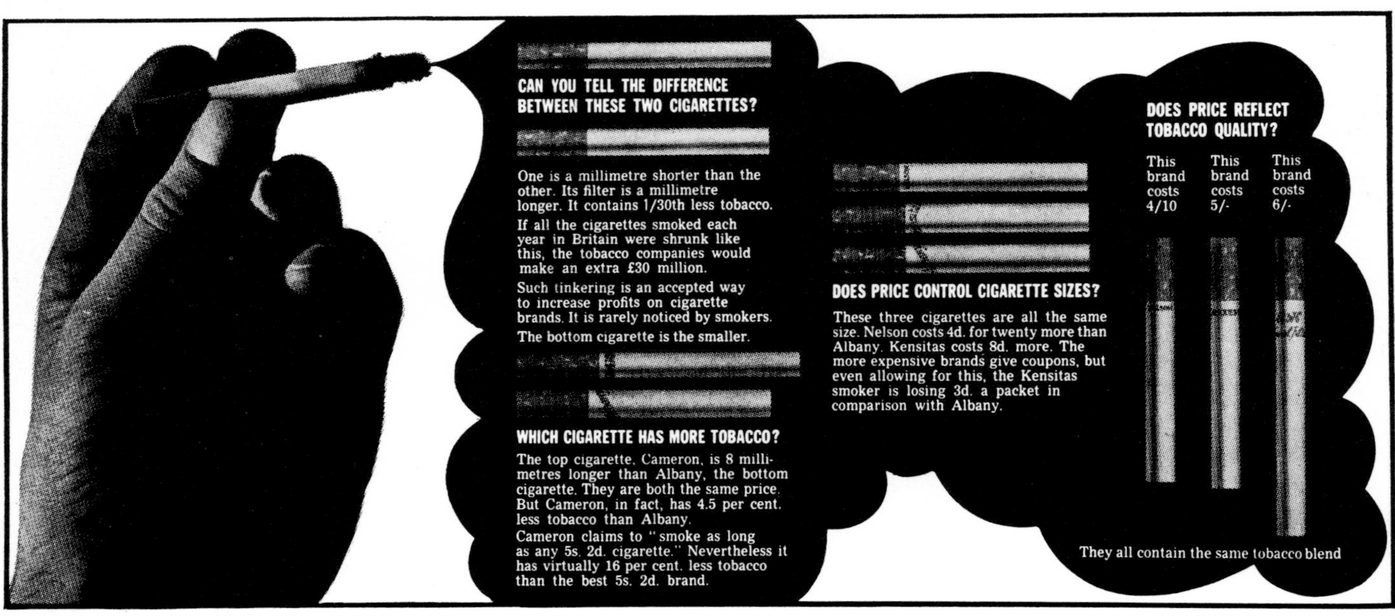

Combining fact and flavour

The marriage between fact and flavour is notably successful in these examples.

Chichester map (*top*): The effect of this combination of graphics, by Peter Sullivan, is that of the television camera which first shows the scene whole and them zooms in on a close-up. The first map, with inset to scale, is the route Francis Chichester was expected to take in sailing single handed round Cape Horn in *Gypsy Moth IV*. Then in the next drawing the perils of the route are analysed and projected. Immediately one is impressed by the frailty of the vessel.

Cigarettes: The design by Edwin Taylor has information and colour in equal measure. The text described the ways cigarette companies minutely reduce the amount of tobacco in their products without disturbing the smoker's confidence that he is getting value for his money. The text was detailed and precise and the graphics had to be clinical, too, while dramatising the idea of something going up in smoke. The starting point of the graphics was that cigarettes are white, so this meant there had to be a black background. The next point was that the cigarettes should be portrayed in actual size, since the varying size of

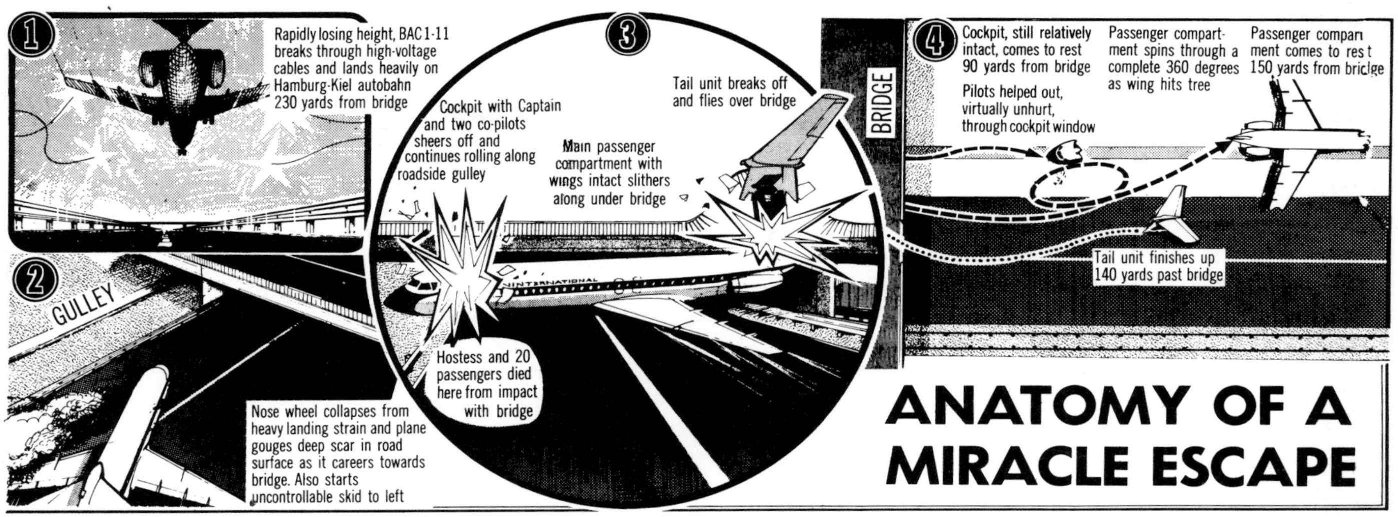

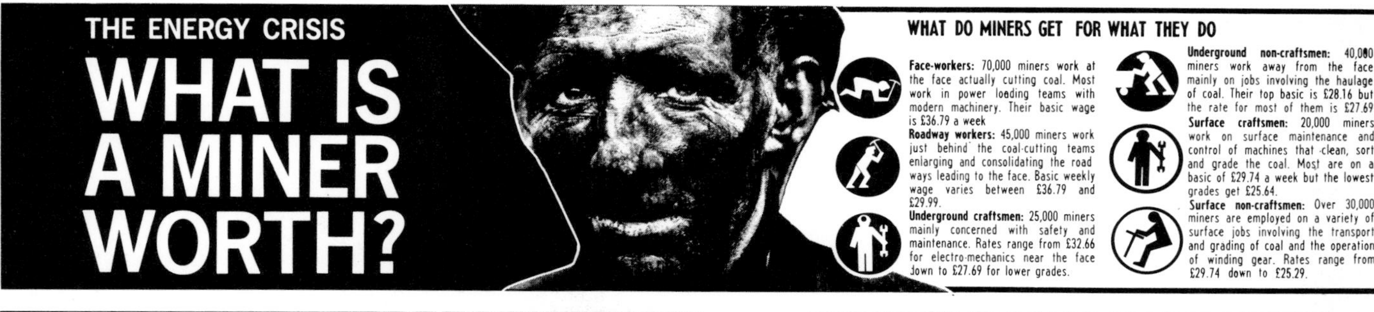

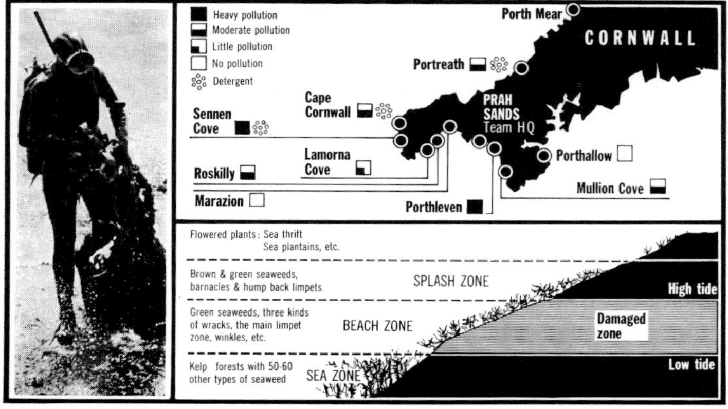

cigarettes was the central theme of the article. The graphics fastidiously compared sizes of cigarettes and tobacco content and united this information in black smoke clouds.

Anatomy of escape: Quick team work between artists and reporters produced a dramatised digest of what happened when an airliner hit high voltage cables just above the Hamburg-Kiel autobahn.

What is a miner worth? Flavour from a splendid miner's face emerging from blackness matched with facts of the wages of different groups in a white panel. Each wage grouping is introduced by a clear symbol.

Oil spill and Moon: The ability of graphics to demonstrate several dimensions of a scene. In the oil spill (*left*) the top map shows the area and scale of pollution in the south-west of England between different resorts after the huge *Torrey Canyon* oil tanker had been wrecked. The bottom diagram reports on the damage to life on an individual beach at different tide levels. A half tone of a frogman adds flavour. In the Moon graphic we get three perspectives: the Moon map locating the area of exploration, a side elevation on the geology, and a flavour drawing of men on the spot with their equipment.

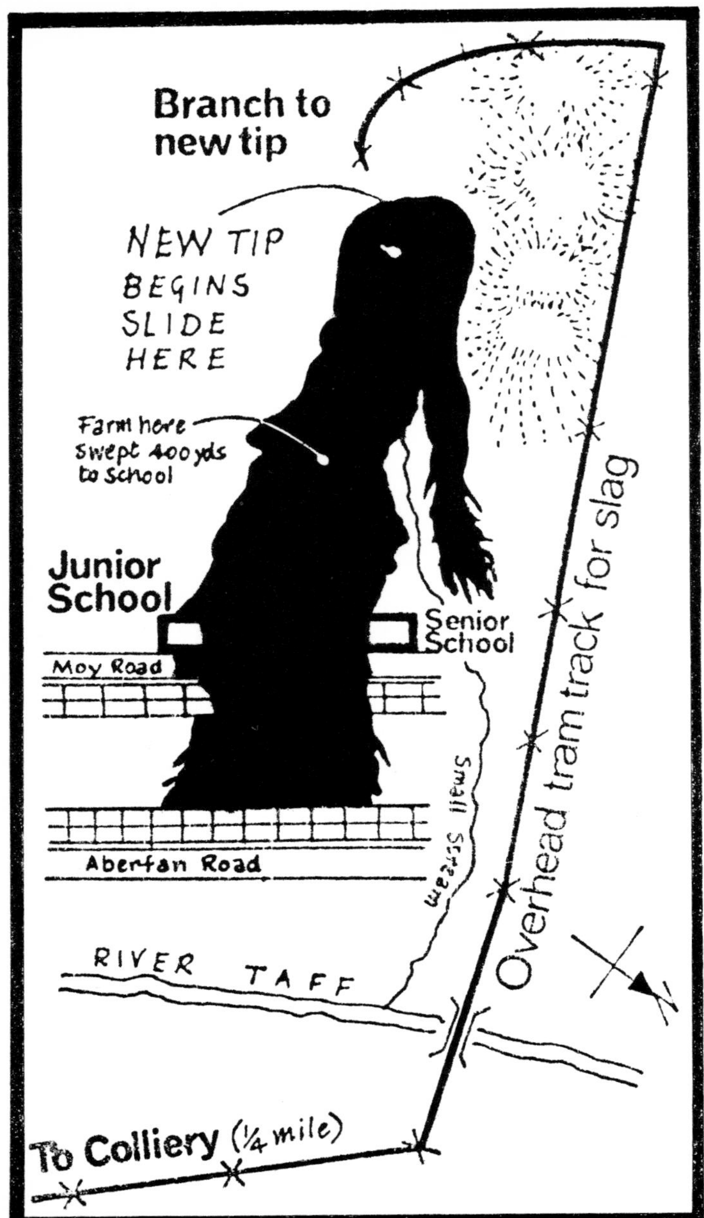

THE SUNDAY TIMES

No. 7482 23 October 1966 Ninepence

A rope ladder to freedom after filing cell bars

Double spy Blake escapes from gaol

By Dan van der Vat

Under the mud lies Aberfan's future: now against hope, the rescuers toil to save it

Why did it happen? 7 questions remain

Public inquiry into Aberfan disaster

By Sunday Times Staff

A MOTHER:

It's a terrible thing, but he wouldn't get up, so I went up to his bedroom and I clouted him and I pulled him out of bed and I said you'll get no breakfast this morning. He went off crying and that's the last I saw of him. What can I do? I can't tell him it was just because I got a headache.

A POLICEMAN:

They don't look frightened. When we brush the muck off their faces they look quite tranquil.

'This is dreadful'

Drawn in Aberfan by Peter Sullivan yesterday, this map shows where the new tip was being built, not far from the five old tips and above the school. A section 60 yards long and 40 yards deep has simply slid downhill, leaving a sheer cliff of slag over which the tipper rails now hang

Sunday Times inquiry—How did it happen, p 4; the day of death p 5

HARRODS for winter cruising

Tanker reported sunk at sea

Live news

Paul Revere depicted British Redcoats shooting down Boston citizenry in an engraving in the *Boston Gazette* of 1770. The long tradition of the artist as reporter has unhappily been broken, as I remarked earlier (page 295), but there is one new development of promise which is for the graphic designer, rather than the illustrator, to act as reporter. This effectively began in 1966 when Peter Sullivan was despatched from London to produce diagrams on the spot of the disaster at Aberfan, South Wales, where a huge coal tip collapsed, engulfing the village school and houses and killing 200, many of them children. In less than 24 hours of difficult on-the-spot observation and drawing, Sullivan produced what amounted to a sketch plan of a tragedy. His work analysed the tragedy in two dimensions: two drawings explained the general scene, one a revealing side elevation of the avalanche, and one a map; and then a third map focused on the details of the buried school. It identified rooms and the locations of individual deaths and survivors. The information was inscribed on the drawing in neat handwriting. There was no time for type, titillation or flavour; and it would have lessened the urgency of the work. Collectively—and all three had to be

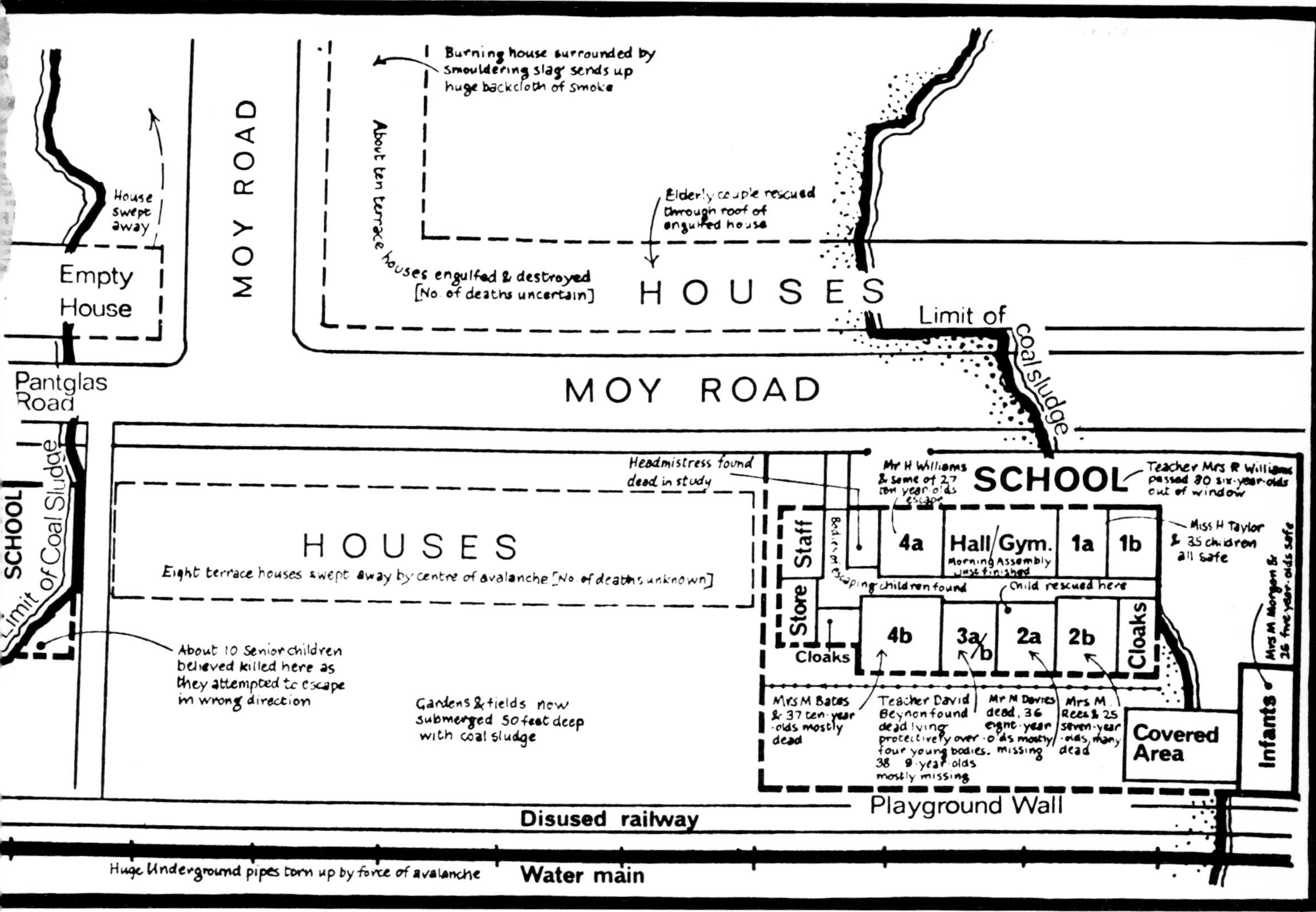

used—these three graphics gave the reader a fuller understanding of what had happened than was remotely possible in words and pictures either still or moving.

Sullivan went out again as a reporter when Mount Etna volcano erupted in 1971 and sent molten lava towards the villages of Fornazzo, St. Alfio and Macchia. The world had watched in awe all week as television cameras relayed pictures of the 50ft. wall of red lava advancing on farmland and houses. But it was impossible to understand what was happening. Sullivan remedied this with diagrams and drawings. From material he was able to obtain locally and his observations, he produced a big relief map which showed the volcano, the coastal capital of Catania, the high villages and the fissures; a flat sketch map depicting the configurations which mattered, especially the dried-up river bed which the lava was following; and finally, a small diagram which used London's River Thames and a London bus (of course) to demonstrate the scale of things. The flow was 'roughly the width of the River Thames from St. Paul's to Greenwich and about twice the height of a double decker bus'.

In 1972, Sullivan visually reported the Munich Olympic Games seizure of hostages and the succeeding shoot-out at the airport. He took his camera and co-operated with three Insight reporters. Horner contributed illustrative drawings. The Sullivan overview of the scene gave clear analysis but naturally lacked the impact of a close-up of the action. This was provided by the Horner visualisations.

In 1977 the graphic artist John Grimwade went to Cologne to reconstruct the ambush of Hans Schleyer with help of reporters. This new journalism is different from the work of the old 'news illustrators' who imagined scenes from news clipping because the emphasis is on analysis and accuracy, rather than on adding excitement and colour.

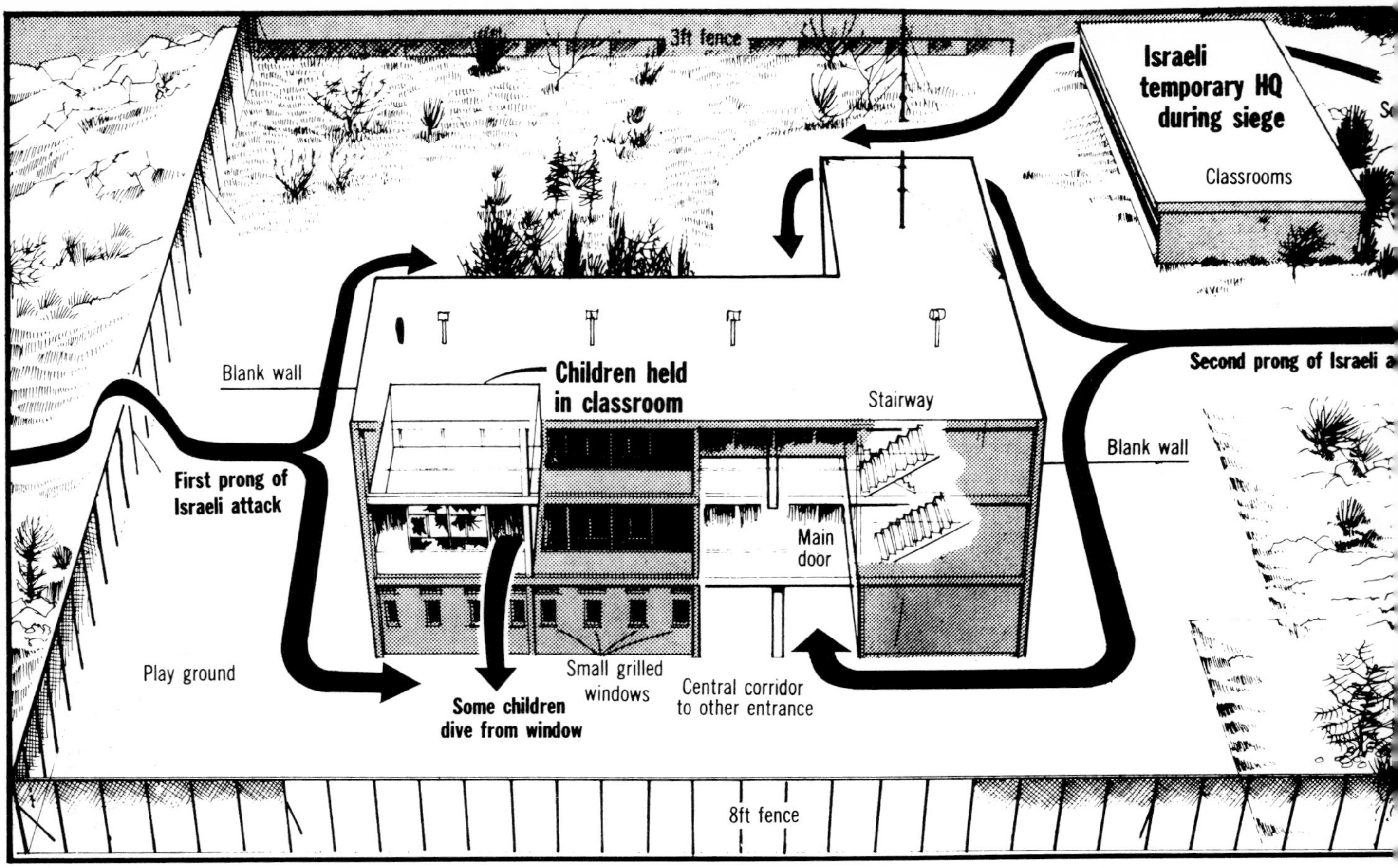

3ft fence
Israeli temporary HQ during siege
Classrooms
Second prong of Israeli a
Blank wall
Children held in classroom
Stairway
Blank wall
First prong of Israeli attack
Main door
Play ground
Small grilled windows
Central corridor to other entrance
Some children dive from window
8ft fence

START
CAMBRIDGE
Craven Steps
Mile Post
Hammersmith Bridge
Chiswick Steps
Barnes Bridge
FINISH
0
2.27
4.21½
7.49
12.26
16.49
20.22
OXFORD ¾ length
1 length
1 length
1½ lengths
3½ lengths
3½ lengths

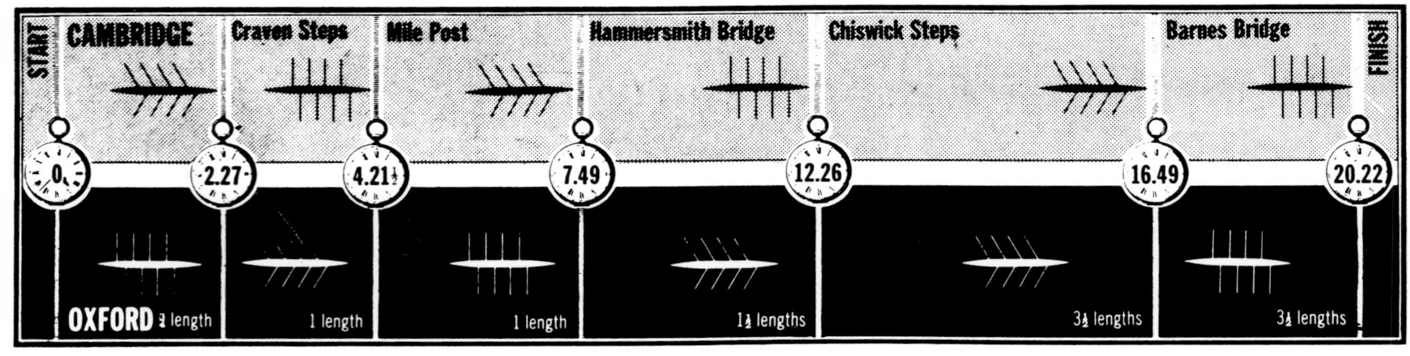

These are quick responses to news in fact graphics and drawing. The action map (*top*) demonstrates Israeli tactics in storming the school at Ma'Lot where Palestinian terrorists held 100 schoolchildren hostage. This graphic is easier on the eye than a reconstruction (*far right*) of events in Londonderry, Northern Ireland, on January 30th (Bloody Sunday) 1972 when the graphic was attempting to cope with a series of complicated and passionately disputed incidents. In the space of 20 minutes, a company of paratroopers killed 13 Catholics and wounded 14, in response, it was claimed, to gunmen who had used the demonstration crowds as cover for their attack. There was not one incident, as at Ma'Lot, but many, and each of them might in other circumstances have required a separate diagram or drawing. The map simplifies buildings into blocks (unlike Red Lion Square page 306, where less was happening), with three symbols for dead, wounded and IRA fire. The published size was 13″ by 8″.

The boat race graphic (*above*) was ready for publication not much more than an hour after the Oxford and Cambridge boat race. The format was prepared in advance. All that had to be done was stick down the pre-drawn boats and the time and distance numerals.

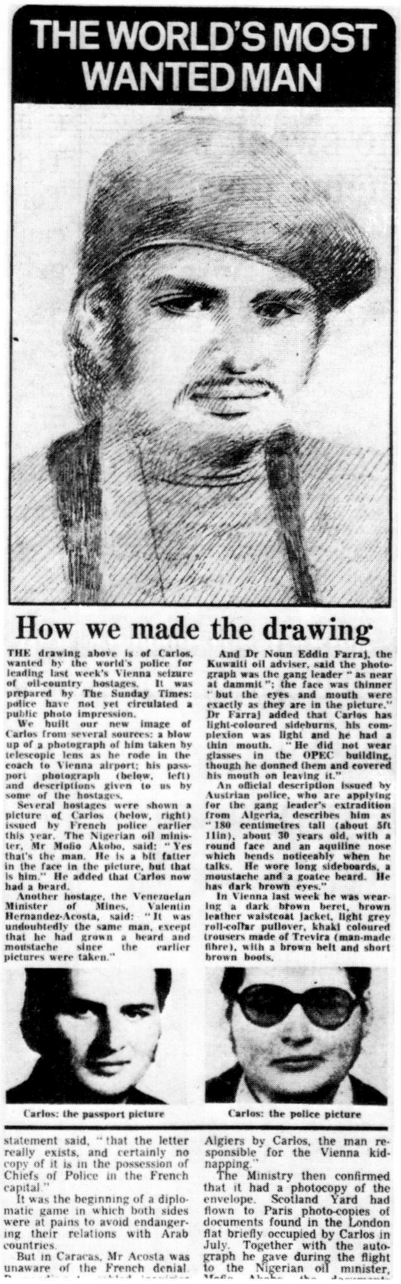

THE WORLD'S MOST WANTED MAN

How we made the drawing

THE drawing above is of Carlos, wanted by the world's police for leading last week's Vienna seizure of oil-country hostages. It was prepared by The Sunday Times: police have not yet circulated a public photo impression.

We built our new image of Carlos from several sources: a blow up of a photograph of him taken by telescopic lens as he rode in the coach to Vienna airport; his passport photograph (below, left) and descriptions given to us by some of the hostages.

Several hostages were shown a picture of Carlos (below, right) issued by French police earlier this year. The Nigerian oil minister, Mr Mofio Akobo, said: "Yes that's the man. He is a bit fatter in the face in the picture, but that is him." He added that Carlos now had a beard.

Another hostage, the Venezuelan Minister of Mines, Valentin Hernandez-Acosta, said: "It was undoubtedly the same man, except that he had grown a beard and moustache since the earlier pictures were taken."

And Dr Noun Eddin Farraj, the Kuwaiti oil adviser, said the photograph was the gang leader "as near at dammit"; the face was thinner "but the eyes and mouth were exactly as they are in the picture." Dr Farraj added that Carlos has light-coloured sideburns, his complexion was light and he had a thin mouth. "He did not wear glasses in the OPEC building, though he donned them and covered his mouth on leaving it."

An official description issued by Austrian police, who are applying for the gang leader's extradition from Algeria, describes him as "180 centimetres tall (about 5ft 11in), about 30 years old, with a round face and an aquiline nose which bends noticeably when he talks. He wore long sideboards, a moustache and a goatee beard. He has dark brown eyes."

In Vienna last week he was wearing a dark brown beret, brown leather waistcoat jacket, light grey roll-collar pullover, khaki coloured trousers made of Trevira (man-made fibre), with a brown belt and short brown boots.

Carlos: the passport picture

Carlos: the police picture

statement said, "that the letter really exists, and certainly no copy of it is in the possession of Chiefs of Police in the French capital."

It was the beginning of a diplomatic game in which both sides were at pains to avoid endangering their relations with Arab countries.

But in Caracas, Mr Acosta was unaware of the French denial.

Algiers by Carlos, the man responsible for the Vienna kidnapping."

The Ministry then confirmed that it had a photocopy of the envelope. Scotland Yard had flown to Paris photo-copies of documents found in the London flat briefly occupied by Carlos in July. Together with the autograph he gave during the flight to the Nigerian oil minister,

Wanted man: All the newspapers and television had been using two old photographs of the terrorist, Carlos, who led the kidnapping of the oil-country hostages in Vienna. On release, the hostages testified that he had acquired a new disguise—a beard, moustache and light sideburns. *The Sunday Times* collected a corroborated description of as many features as possible of the new Carlos and Sheila Ware then drew an impression.

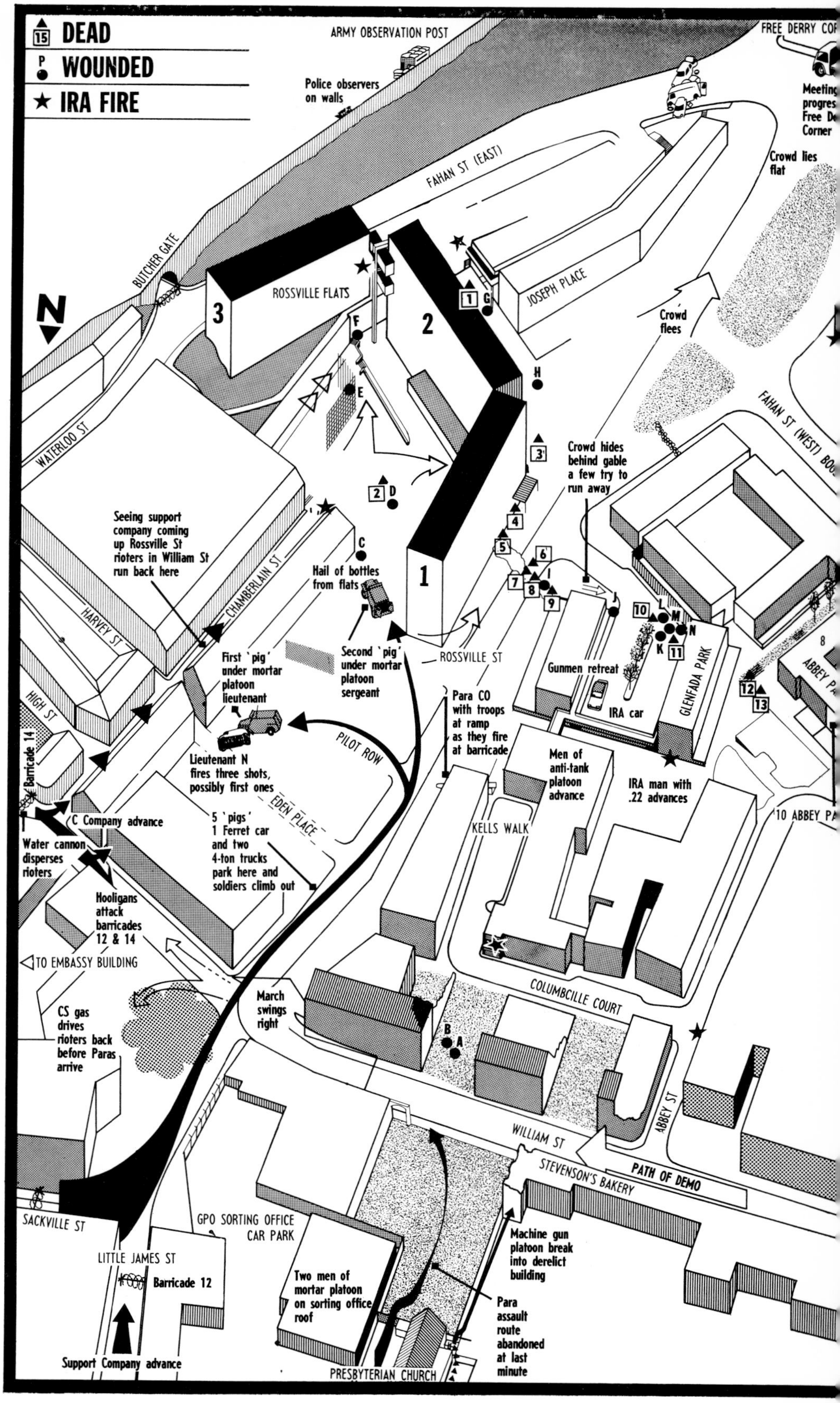

15 DEAD
P WOUNDED
★ IRA FIRE
ARMY OBSERVATION POST
FREE DERRY COR
Police observers on walls
Meeting progres Free De Corner
FAHAN ST (EAST)
Crowd lies flat
BUTCHER GATE
ROSSVILLE FLATS
JOSEPH PLACE
Crowd flees
N
WATERLOO ST
FAHAN ST (WEST) BOG
Crowd hides behind gable a few try to run away
Seeing support company coming up Rossville St rioters in William St run back here
Hail of bottles from flats
CHAMBERLAIN ST
HARVEY ST
HIGH ST
First 'pig' under mortar platoon lieutenant
Second 'pig' under mortar platoon sergeant
ROSSVILLE ST
Para CO with troops at ramp as they fire at barricade
Gunmen retreat
IRA car
GLENFADA PARK
ABBEY PA
PILOT ROW
Lieutenant N fires three shots, possibly first ones
Men of anti-tank platoon advance
IRA man with .22 advances
Barricade 14
C Company advance
EDEN PLACE
10 ABBEY PA
KELLS WALK
Water cannon disperses rioters
5 'pigs' 1 Ferret car and two 4-ton trucks park here and soldiers climb out
Hooligans attack barricades 12 & 14
TO EMBASSY BUILDING
March swings right
COLUMBCILLE COURT
CS gas drives rioters back before Paras arrive
WILLIAM ST
ABBEY ST
STEVENSON'S BAKERY
PATH OF DEMO
SACKVILLE ST
GPO SORTING OFFICE CAR PARK
Machine gun platoon break into derelict building
LITTLE JAMES ST
Barricade 12
Two men of mortar platoon on sorting office roof
Para assault route abandoned at last minute
Support Company advance
PRESBYTERIAN CHURCH

Teamwork

Here, finally, are two news spectaculars to emphasise the theme of what can be achieved with close liaison between the reporters and the designers, and how vital it is to have a proper visual reference library.

Space rocket (*far right*): The news during the week was that Apollo 13 astronauts Lovell, Swigert and Haise were in danger because something had gone wrong with the rocket returning them from the moon. The design department of *The Sunday Times* hoped that it could produce a graphic that would enable readers to follow the news sensibly and characterise the plight of the astronauts. It was fed with pre-launch literature and news reports and Peter Sullivan bought and assembled a model of the rocket. This combined effort enabled them in the end to do more than show the spatial relationships and the tiny area where the spacemen were trapped. The quality of the information assembled enabled them to reach careful visual conclusions about the mishap and predict that there had been no explosion. The graphic was published at 14″ deep and nearly 6″ wide, a decisive recognition of its value, dramatic in shape and scale but concentrating on what mattered.

Rescue at Entebbe: The graphic here was published over nearly the entire top half of *The Sunday Times Review* front, 12½″ wide by 8½″ deep. It was a bold attempt to show, on incomplete information, what it was like when the Israeli commando force landed on the night of 3rd July 1976 to rescue 104 hijacked hostages guarded by some 100 Ugandan troops and 10 terrorists.

There were plenty of fairy stories around. Collecting the facts was more difficult. The basic references needed for accurate drawing, for instance, included: a Hercules C130 transport with Israeli markings; the hijacked Air France airbus; Entebbe airport and control tower (there was a new and old tower and acquiring a photograph of the right one took several days). The narrative needed even more investigation. Insight reporters in Israel, Paris, East Africa and London tried to reconstruct the whole story from interviews but had a special brief to obtain and corroborate details of the scene—how many troops and planes? Where did the fighting occur? Where was the airbus parked? Reporters, artist and art director collaborated on agreeing the

53 MINUTES

TWENTY-SIX hours before Israel's "mission impossible," President Idi Amin Dada was in splendid spirits. Dressed in his light blue field marshal's uniform, his chest brimming with medals, he was attending, as outgoing chairman, an evening celebration at the 13th summit meeting of the Organisation of African Unity in Mauritius. Israel, it seemed, was about to release the Palestinian prisoners well before the Sunday morning deadline for the execution of the 105 Jewish hostages at Entebbe airport, and Amin was telling anyone who cared to listen how brilliantly he had handled everything. He had even taken care to disarm half the Ugandan troops at the airport: he had just appointed himself President for life and there was always, his sophisticated listeners would understand, the problem of armed insurrection.

Amin's recital of his achievements fell on more than normally attentive ears. Israel had an informant at the OAU and within minutes his self-indulgent revelations were passed on to Tel Aviv. All week, against the clock, Israel had been putting together bits and pieces of information, assessing the chances of a rescue. It had been like making a jigsaw in the dark, but Amin turned the light on to the last few pieces. At 7.30 am on Saturday, July 3rd, Israel's Prime Minister Yitzhak Rabin made up his mind: the odds had shortened. The military knew enough to risk the raid.

ISRAEL had considered a military intervention from the beginning. Only hours after the Air France plane with its 253 hostages landed at Entebbe, General Mordechai Gur, Chief of Staff of the Israeli Defence Forces and the Defence Minister, Shimon Peres, met in the Defence Ministry in Tel Aviv to consider a commando raid. But on Monday evening when Peres and Gur attended a tense Cabinet meeting in Jerusalem Gur had a bleak response to Rabin's question "Do we have a military option?" The military was willing, troops were on alert, but they had too many questions, too few answers and too little time to get them before the Thursday noon deadline. The Cabinet had no alternative but to vote for negotiation—while urging the military to devise some less than wholly reckless plan which would not sacrifice the hostages (only half of them at this stage Israelis).

Gur's multi-dimensional riddle was this: How could a large Israeli force fly 2,200 miles to Entebbe and back when no aircraft could

Entebbe, midnight July 3. Four Israeli Hercules have landed—two of them off to the right. A Boe

ing force against both the invaders and the hostages in seconds?

General Gur had learned from bitter experience that delay spells

in the Six-Day war—but in 1974 he had been criticised by an Israeli commission of inquiry into the massacre at Maalot where three

gence from the beginnin the Ugandan airport, engineers had after all he build the new runway and

ENTEBBE

ane circles the airport. Drawing: Peter Sullivan

of negotiation. its position to it to Ambassador Kampala, Renard

murder in exchange for some of the hostages. That Thursday morning Amin invited Bar Lev to Uganda and the Israelis pre-

a child. I was not surprised."

ON THE ground at Entebbe Amin's role was less ambiguous.

facts in the graphic, a perspective was selected (some foreshortening was inevitable) and the caption content was tightly edited in a numbered sequence. A major effort and worth it; but perhaps next time they will give us all a photo call.

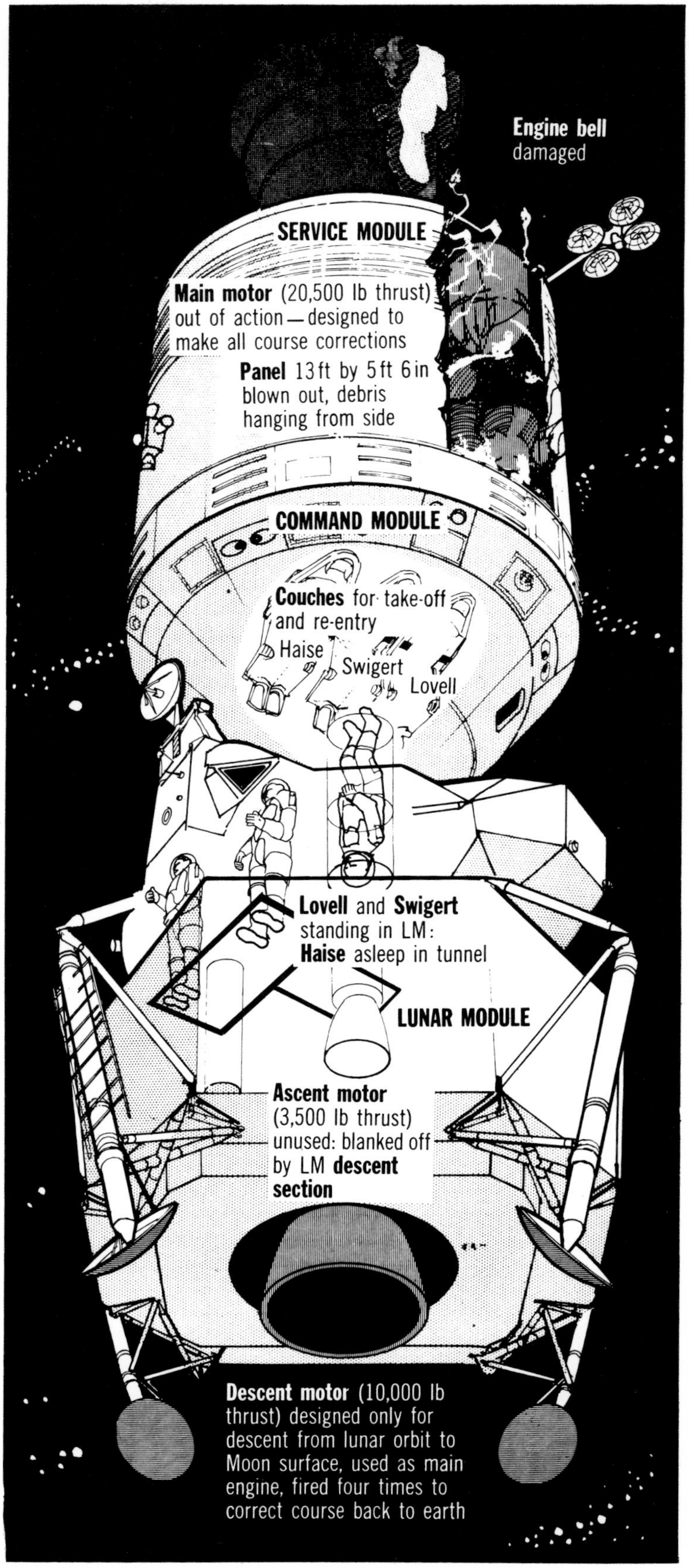

How to find a Picture

With the assistance of Doris Bryen

Picture researchers have days of routine but always the chance of happily stubbing a toe on buried treasure. The picture which opens this short section (*facing page*) is the world's earliest known live news photograph, certainly the first of a crowd; and it has not been published in a book before. It came to light only in 1977 in the Queen's archives in Windsor during research for a BBC programme. It is a daguerrotype by W. E. Kilburn recording 20,000 Chartists assembling in an anxious London in 1848 to press their demands for Parliamentary reform. Until its discovery the Duke of Wellington's funeral in 1852 was thought to be the first time an attempt had been made to photograph a public ceremony and 1854 the first success at Crystal Palace. The earliest surviving news picture, strictly speaking, is, Carl Stelzner's Hamburg fire daguerrotype in 1842, six years before the Chartists, but it was taken after the fire; it is a picture of ruins. It is, of course, a precious historic record, and there is a lesson for us in that. More than 40 daguerrotypes were made of the Hamburg ruins by Stelzner and Hermann Biow. Only three Stelzners remain—two found recently by Ann Turner of the BBC. All the others have been lost by neglect and even today newspapers and magazines have been discarding big complete collections of irreplaceable negatives. In Britain, history, art and journalism are now served by a *Directory of British Photographic Collections* compiled by Dr. J. W. Wall and listing 1,580 collections on behalf of the Royal Photographic Society.

But how do you find a picture? In one day the picture researcher may be asked to come up with prints and copyright clearance of the new Miss World, Scott Fitzgerald with Sheila Graham, the defeated Governor of Mississippi, Jane Russell in the Howard Hughes cantilever bra, 'an exciting picture of an ocean-going yacht over on its side in heavy spray', and 'that picture by whatisname of all those black recruits in Biafra'. It helps, as Doris Bryen has remarked, to have an insatiable interest in events from before Christ until the day after tomorrow, but there are practical steps for visual sleuths.

Research divides into specific and non-specific pictures.

Specific pictures

The usual sources are the publication, an agency or the photographer. Most publications give tiny credit lines alongside the photograph; in books there is generally a separate list of credits: it should be a universal rule that all pictures carry credits. It is fairer to the originator and helpful to researchers. When you order a print from any of these sources, send a photostat and also specify date, page number, and give a brief description. Some sources charge for a print, but it is essential to stress that a reproduction fee is payable only on publication.

Sometimes there is no credit and the publication has lost the print. Or the search is for a picture remembered but not retained in published form. Try:

1 The specialised photographers and specialised agencies. *The Picture Researcher's Handbook* (*see bibliography*) is essential and I append some more useful names.

2 The subject of the picture if it is a person.

3 The companies in that area or their public relations officers if it is a product.

4 The writer of the accompanying text or writer interested in the subject sought.

5 University departments, specialised institutions and Government agencies (such as the American Bureau of Indian Affairs).

For pictures of current news interest, the news agencies of United Press International and Associated Press are indispensable. The picture editor may not be content with what has been wired already. He may want the latest picture. The picture researcher then asks the picture editor of the agency to contact his agent in the appropriate country and ascertain if anything can be wired to his central office, and collected by hand.

Non-specific pictures

A publication's own library is a starting point. You may be asked for a photograph of a girl skier, say, and have never heard of anyone in the sport. Begin with the clippings, collect some names, and then go to the picture library. A good picture researcher will get to know the publication's own library well, but visit also, as often as allowable, the libraries of outside agencies and other publications. Specialist publications may be the best source on architecture, science, sport, motoring, fishing and so on. These possibilities are often overlooked. You want a photograph of a stolen Rembrandt? The Mansell Collection owned by Miss Louise Boutroy is renowned for its coverage of famous paintings and social and news pictures up to the thirties. Naval subjects? The National Maritime Museum has a print room on all naval subjects. Theatre? Try the Raymond Mander and Joe Mitchenson collection.

The bigger picture libraries can

324A A new discovery is the world's earliest known live news photograph, 1848

only be tasted. The Radio Times Hulton Picture Library has some six million prints and photographs carefully filed and captioned. It includes the Topical Agency which holds news subjects dating from the early 1900's to 1950's and all the *Picture Post* photographs taken by Hulton staff photographers. Three other great agencies are Time-Life (marvellously card-indexed in New York), AP and UPI (see below).

Book libraries, museums and art galleries are prime sources for ideas and pointers to locations of original prints. In Britain the London Library houses one of the world's finest collections of rare and modern books. In New York the New York Public Library has a strong section on historical pictures.

A reader's ticket should be obtained for the British Museum's reading room, print room, and students room department of MSS. The reading room ticket covers the newspaper library at Colindale. A catalogue of the National Portrait Gallery is useful, giving dates of the sitters and the artists. Municipal authorities have archives and so do some historical associations.

In all this, utmost care has to be taken on copyright which in law varies according to a number of factors. When in doubt seek expert advice. Agency pictures can generally be published without special permission, provided the appropriate fee is paid on publication. There are some photographers, however, who have to be approached and the fee arranged.

No picture researcher can stir without a copy of *The Picture Researcher's Handbook* and also *Willings Press Guide* in Britain (listing all newspapers and foreign magazines and papers as well). In the United States the *Editor and Publisher Year Book*, published by The Editor and Publishers Co. Inc., and *Literary Market Place*, published by R. R. Bowker Co., which is the business directory of American book publishing, are essential.

Finally, there are personal aids. Build up a big address book of photographers and their specialities. Keep a scrap book of pictures which might be useful and especially cartoons. Always put the date of publication and the title: good line prints can be reproduced, once copyright is cleared, without acquiring the original. Go to art shows and buy a catalogue. Acquire books with illustrations, especially political and satirical cartoons.

Ideas will come naturally to the picture researcher who gets absorbed in the business. Seek exactly what is requested—and present them in a labelled folder—but ask for a proof of the article and a better idea may occur. Where do you begin to illustrate a discussion of the effect of war on religion? Doris Bryen came up from somewhere with a marvellous photograph of an enormous crucifix flung on the floor of a bombed church. Nobody had seen it before. Layouts had, satisfyingly, to be changed.

On the following page, is a brief guide to some useful picture sources.

Picture Sources

NEWS AGENCIES

ACME NEWSPICTURES, 220 East 42nd Street, New York, U.S.A. Picture library for United Press International, black and white mostly.

ASSOCIATED PRESS LTD., 85 Farringdon Street, London E.C.4. Radio pictures from most parts of the world. Head office New York.

BELFAST NEWS LETTER, 7 Rathmore Crescent, Belfast, Ireland.

BELFAST TELEGRAPH, 124 Royal Avenue, Belfast, BT1 1EB. Good coverage on the Ulster scene—can wire pictures to London.

CAMERA PRESS LTD., Russell Court, Coram Street, London W.C.1. British and foreign royal portraits. Literary and political personalities. Agents for many well-known photographers.

CATHOLIC HERALD, 63 Charterhouse Street, London E.C.1. Religious portraits, mostly Roman Catholic, but willing to lend pictures not their copyright, many foreign priests.

CENTRAL PRESS, 2 Gough Street, London E.C.4. General news, sports and portraits (have a few pre-war pictures).

DEVON NEWS, Exeter, Devon.

EXPRESS FEATURES, Oldbourne Hall, Shoe Lane, London E.C.4. (*Daily Express*).

FINANCIAL TIMES, Bracken House, Cannon Street, London E.C.4. Good for photographs of business men.

GLOBE PHOTOS INC., 67 West 44th Street, New York, U.S.A. They say they have everything, but they are most well known for pictures of personalities, particularly in the entertainment world.

JOHN FROST, NEWSPAPER HISTORIAN, 8 Monk's Avenue, New Barnet, Herts. Papers and magazines from pre-Great War, kept in good condition. Pictures from them can be copied.

JOHN HILLELSON, 145 Fleet Street, London E.C.4.

KEYSTONE PRESS AGENCY LTD., Bath House, 52–62 Holborn Viaduct, London E.C.1.

LONDON NEWS SERVICE, 68 Exmouth Market, London E.C.1.

MONITOR PRESS, 17 Old Street, London E.C.1.

PACEMAKER, 20 Lower Windsor Avenue, Belfast. This agency can radio pictures to London.

PHOTO NEWS SERVICE, 250 Boulevarde General Wahis, Brussels, Belgium. E.E.C. personalities.

PICTORIAL PRESS, Woodbridge House, 1 Woodbridge Street, Clerkenwell Green, London E.1.

PRESS ASSOCIATION, Salisbury Court, Fleet Street, London E.C.4. Mostly British news pictures—some foreign.

REX FEATURES, 8–9 East Harding Street, London E.C.4.

TOPIX, Greater London House, Hampstead Road, London N.W.1. Agents for *The Sunday Times* pictures and other Thomson papers.

UNITED PRESS INTERNATIONAL, 8 Bouverie Street, London E.C.4. Main offices New York and Brussels. Excellent contact for Common Market. E.E.C. Has subsidiary agency, Popperfoto, 24 Bridge Lane, E.C.4., which holds Paul Popper's negatives on diverse subjects.

UNIVERSAL PICTORIAL PRESS, 30 New Bridge Street, London E.C.4. Mostly British political portraits, some foreign.

U.S.A. MAGNUM PHOTOS INC., 1156 Sixth Avenue, New York, U.S.A. Deals only with the top American photographers. Has office in Paris.

TIME-LIFE, Time Life Building, Rockefeller Center, New York, N.Y. 10020, U.S.A.

WIDE WORLD PHOTOS, 50 Rockefeller Plaza, New York, U.S.A. Represents Associated Press.

ANIMALS, INSECTS, FLOWERS, WILD LIFE

A–Z BOTANICAL COLLECTION, 54 The Grove, London W.5. Colour only.

BRUCE COLEMAN LTD., 16a–17a Windsor Street, Uxbridge, Middlesex. (Colour and black and white).

CAMERA PRESS, Russell Court, Coram Street, London W.C.1. (Represent many naturalist photographers).

DOUGLAS WILSON, MARINE BIOLOGICAL SOCIETY, The Citadel, Plymouth, Devon. (Fish, colour and mono).

ERIC HOSKING, 20 Crouch Hall Road, London N.8. Superb collection of birds.

KEW GARDENS, Richmond, Surrey, England.

AMERICAN MUSEUM OF NATURAL HISTORY, Central Park West, 79th Street, New York, N.Y. 10024, U.S.A.

NATURAL HISTORY MUSEUM, Cromwell Road, London S.W.7.

ZOOLOGICAL SOCIETY OF LONDON, Regents Park Gardens, London N.W.1. Mono and colour and good reference library. (Zoos in Europe e.g. Berlin and Amsterdam also can help with pictures).

ARTS, ARCHITECTURE, ARCHAEOLOGY, MUSEUMS

ASHMOLEAN MUSEUM, Oxford. Can supply colour and black and white pictures from their collection.

ARCHITECTURAL PRESS, 9 Queen Anne's Gate, London S.W.1.

ARTS COUNCIL OF GREAT BRITAIN, 105 Piccadilly, London W.1. Mostly modern paintings, etc., but can advise where pictures are.

BBC PUBLICITY, 10–12 Cavendish Place, London W.1.

BIBLIOTHEQUE NATIONALE, 58 Rue de Richelieu, Paris, France. Very co-operative and helpful, especially if you can get there and do your own research. You can get help by correspondence but it takes time.

DEPARTMENT OF THE ENVIRONMENT, Room 401, Hannibal House, Elephant and Castle, London SE1. Ancient monuments, historic buildings, public statues, memorials, palaces, embassies, military buildings, Royal parks.

COURTAULD INSTITUTE, 20 Portman Square, London W.1. Reference library for the world's most famous paintings.

FITZWILLIAM MUSEUM, Cambridge.

GIRAUDON, 9 Rue des Beaux Arts, Paris, France. Large collection of paintings in colour and black and white.

THE LORD CHAMBERLAIN'S OFFICE, St. James's Palace, London S.W.1. Colour and black and white prints of Royal collection. Apply here for permission to photograph or publish H.M. The Queen's pictures.

MANSELL COLLECTION, 42 Linden Gardens, London W.2. Especially black and white of paintings in foreign galleries.

NATIONAL MARITIME MUSEUM, Greenwich, London S.E.10. Royal Navy and Merchant Navy from early times.

NATIONAL PORTRAIT GALLERY, St. Martin's Place, London W.C.2. British portraits.

PITT-RIVERS MUSEUM, Oxford. (Archaeology).

RADIO TIMES HULTON PICTURE LIBRARY, 35 Marylebone High Street, London W.1.

READING MUSEUM OF RURAL LIFE, Reading, Berkshire, England. Agriculture, early farm tools, but takes time to get prints.

ROYAL INSTITUTE OF BRITISH ARCHITECTS, Portland Place, London W.1. Good for portraits of architects as well as buildings.

ROGER VIOLLET, 6 Rue de Seine, Paris, France. Mostly paintings.

HISTORY

THE BETTMAN ARCHIVES, 136 East 57th Street, New York, N.Y. 10022, U.S.A. Historic and medical subjects.

BROWN BROTHERS, Sterling, Pennsylvania, U.S.A. Mostly historic black and white pictures.

CHARLES BROWN, 14 Longfellow Road, Worcester Park, Surrey, England.

THE GUILDHALL, LIBRARY AND ART GALLERY, London E.C.2. Historical and archaeological pictures of London.

RAYMOND MANDER AND JOE MITCHENSON, 5 Venner Road, London S.E.26. Historical theatre collection.

WAR

BILDERDIENST ULLSTEIN, 100 Berlin 42, Tempelhof Mariendorfe Dam. War pictures.

IMPERIAL WAR MUSEUM, Lambeth Road, London S.E.1. War photographs and paintings of World War I and II.

ENTERTAINMENT

B.B.C. PUBLICITY, 10 Cavendish Place, London W.1. Television and radio.

BRISTOL OLD VIC, King Street, Bristol.

BRITISH FILM INSTITUTE, Stills Library, 81 Dean Street, London W.1. Information and Reference Book Library 127–132 Charing Cross Road, London W.C.2.

CINEMA BOOKSHOP, 13 Great Russell Street, London W.C.1. Library of film stills, can get pictures quickly.

CONTEMPORARY FILMS, 55 Greek Street, London W.1.

COWBOYS WILD WEST PICTURE AGENCY, Brentwood, Essex.

DANCING TIMES, 18 Hand Court, London W.C.1.

DOUGLAS JEFFREY, Garden Flat, 5 Englands Lane, London N.W.3. Theatre.

EMI PUBLICITY, 20 Manchester Square, London W.1.

ERIC AUERBACH COLLECTION, 29 Abercorn Place, London N.W.8. Music personalities.

JOHN KOBAL, 38 Drayton Court, Drayton Gardens, London S.W.10. Cinema.

JOHN VICKERS, 54 Kenway Road, London S.W.5. Theatre.

ROGER CLIFFORD, 17 Clifford Street, London W.1. Public relations for theatre.

ROGER WOOD, 293 Liverpool Road, London N.1. Ballet.

VICTOR HOCKHAUSER, 4 Holland Park Avenue, London W.11. Music classic.

SPORT, TRAVEL, MISCELLANEOUS

AEROFILMS, Elstree Way, Boreham Wood, Herts. World wide coverage of air photographs; also have interesting old photographs from abroad.

BARRATTS PHOTO AGENCY, 68 Exmouth Market, London E.C.1. Incorporated with Sport and General and other agencies—racing, football, golf, police court and trial pictures.

BEKEN OF COWES LTD., Cowes, Isle of Wight. Yachting pictures.

BERTRAND ET FILS, 3 Avenue Joffre, Chantilly, France. Race horses.

BRITISH TRAVEL, 64 St. James's Street, London S.W.1. All British travel subjects.

J. ALLAN CASH COLLECTION, 23 Martaban Road, London, N.16. Travel (all J. Allan Cash negatives). World coverage.

CENTREHURST LTD., Africa House, Kingsway, London W.C.2. Travel pictures, colour and black and white (Spain and Ireland chiefly).

COLORIFIC, 16 Spring Street, London W.2. Agents for *Life* pictures.

COLORSPORT, (Stewart Frazer), 44 St. Peter's Street, London N.1. Football, colour and black and white.

GOLF INTERNATIONAL, Askew Road, London W.12.

IAN ALLEN, Terminal House, Station Approach, Shepperton, Middlesex. Publishes histories on railways. Has some prints and gives good advice on where to get pictures of trains.

PROVINCIAL PRESS, Southport, Lancashire. For north country racing (Grand National etc.)

SYNDICATION INTERNATIONAL LTD, 40 Northampton Road, London E.C.1. (*Daily Mirror*). Sport generally.

INTERNATIONAL AGENCIES

AFRICA MAGAZINE, 38 King Street, London W.C.2. African political figures, also will advise other sources.

ARNOLDO MONDADORI, Via Bianca di Savoia, Milan.

GAMMA, 4 Rue Auguste Vacquerie, Paris 16, France.

NOVOSTI PICTURE AGENCY, 3 Rosary Gardens, London S.W.7. They act solely for U.S.S.R. pictures and can, given time, contact Moscow for material.

PAUL ALMASY, 2 Villa des Peupliers, 92 Neuilly-sur-Seine, France.

SCALA, Via Gioberti 34, Florence, Italy.

Bibliography

PHOTOJOURNALISM

ASSOCIATED PRESS. *The Instant It Happened*. New York: Associated Press, 1972. Great news photographs selected by AP editors, with commentary.

BAYNES, Ken. *Scoop Scandal and Strife*. London: Lund Humphries.

BORGES, Jaques, and VIASNOFF, Nicholas. *L'Aristocratie du Reportage Photographique*. Paris: Balland, 1974. Book of pictures of scoops.

FABER, John. *Great Moments in News Photography*. London: Thomas Nelson and Sons, 1960.

HICKS, Wilson. *Words and Pictures*. New York: Arno Press, 1952. Essential reading in history of photojournalism. The late Mr. Hicks was picture editor of *Life* from 1937–45 and executive editor until 1950.

HODGSON, David. *All About Action Photography*. London: Pelham Books, 1976. Good short primer.

HOPKINSON, Tom. *Picture Post 1938–50*. London: Allen Lane the Penguin Press, 1970.

HURLEY, Gerald D. and McDOUGALL, Angus. *Visual Impact in Print*. Chicago: Visual Impact Inc., 1971. Well-illustrated advice on sizing, cropping, retouching, with good examples of picture pages and excellent bibliography.

KEYSTONE. *Weltsensationen im Bild*. Dortmund. Schropp Verlag: 1972. Riveting collection of news pictures from archives of Keystone Hamburg, London, New York, Paris and Tokio.

KNIGHTLEY, Phillip. *The First Casualty*. London: André Deutsch, 1975. Fascinating study of the war correspondent.

MacDOUGALL, Curtis. *News Pictures Fit to Print*. Oklahoma: Journalistic Services, Box 761, Stillwater, 1971. Thoughtful and entertaining discussion of ethics at Northwestern.

McLEAN, Ruari. *Magazine Design*. London: Oxford University Press, 1969.

ROTHSTEIN, Arthur. *Photojournalism*, New York: American Photographic Book Publishing Co. Inc., 1965. Second edition. Comprehensive text book by former technical director of *Look* Magazine.

SZARKOWSKI, John. *From the Picture Press*. New York: Museum of Modern Art, 1973. Fascinating brief collection of news pictures in paperback, with essay.

TIME-LIFE Library of Photography. Time-Life International. Nederland N. V. *Photojournalism*, 1971, is most relevant but others in beautifully presented series are *Documentary Photography, Great Photographers, The Print, The Art of Photography*, and *Techniques of Photography*.

INDIVIDUAL PHOTOGRAPHERS

ANGEL, Heather. *Nature Photography: Its Art and Techniques*. London: Fountain Press, 1972.

ARNOLD, Eve. *The Unretouched Woman*. New York: Alfred Knopf. London: Cape, 1976–7.

BISCHOF, Werner. New York: Grossman, 1974. One of series of monographs by International Center of Photography, New York (ICP), 1130 Fifth Avenue, New York 10028.

BRANDT, Bill. *Shadow of Light*. New York: Viking, 1966. London: Gordon Fraser, 1977.

BRASSAI. *Camera in Paris*. London: Focal Press, 1949.

CAPA, Robert. *Images of War*. New York: Grossman, 1964. *Slightly Out of Focus*, Henry Holt, 1947.

DANZIGER, James and BARNABY, Conrad III. *Interviews with Master Photographers*. New York, London: Paddington Press, 1977.

ELLIOTT, Erwitt. *The Private Experience: Personal Insight of a Professional Photographer*. Alskog Book. London: Thames and Hudson.

FENTON, Roger. London: Gordon Fraser, Arts Council. No. 3 in series.

FUSCO, Paul. With McBRIDE, Will. *The Photo Essay*, Alskog Book. London: Thames and Hudson.

HARDY, Bert. Gordon Fraser Monographics, London, in association with the Arts Council.

HINE, Lewis W. 1874–94: *Two Perspectives* London: Studio Vista, 1975.

LANGE, Dorothea. New York: Museum of Modern Art and Doubleday, 1966.

LIMPKIN, Clive. *The Battle of Bogside*. London: Penguin Books, 1972. Vivid news pictures.

MARK, Mary Ellen and LEIBOVITZ, Annia. *Photojournalism: The Woman's Perspective*. Alskog Book. London: Thames and Hudson.

McCULLIN, Don. *The Destruction Business*. London: Open Gate Book with Macmillan. Under the title *Is Anyone Taking Any Notice?* Cambridge, Mass, 1971. Photographs and comments by brave and gifted McCullin.

NEWMAN, Arnold. *One Mind's Eye*. Boston: David R. Godine, 1974. Collection of work of master of environmental portrait.

RODGER, George. London: Gordon Fraser, Arts Council.

SMITH, W. Eugene and Aileen M. *Minamata*. London: Chatto and Windus. New York: Holt Rinehart and Winston, an Alskog-Sensoriom Book, 1975.

SNOWDON. *Assignments*. London: Weidenfeld and Nicolson, 1972. Nearly twenty years of Snowdon's journalistic work, including some from his social essays on loneliness, mental illness, etc.

STEICHEN, Edward. *A Life in Photography*. New York: Doubleday, 1963.

WEINER, Dan. New York: Grossman, 1974. One of the series in ICP Library.

ZIMMERMAN, John. *Photographing Sport*, with Mark Kauffman and Neil Leifer. Alskog Book. London: Thames and Hudson, 1975.

HISTORY

BEATON, Cecil and BUCKLAND, Gail. *The Magic Image*. London: Weidenfeld and Nicolson, 1975. Invaluable study of photographers from 1839 to present day.

GERNSHEIM, Helmut, *Creative Photography*. New York: Bonanza Books, 1974.

GERNSHEIM, Helmut and Alison. *The History of Photography*. London: Thames and Hudson, 1969. Massive study, especially interesting for photojournalists are news photography (chapter 22), portraits (chapter 26), movement (chapter 34), documentation (chapter 35), press photography (chapter 36).

GIDAL, Tim N. *Modern Photojournalism, Origin and Evolution, 1910–1933*. New York: Collier, Macmillan, 1972. A short scholarly account.

HENDRICKS, Gordon. *Eadweard Muybridge*. London: Secker and Warburg, 1975. General bibliography with selection of Muybridge's motion pictures.

MUYBRIDGE, Eadweard. *The Human Figure in Motion*. London: Chapman and Hall, 7th imp. 1931. The famous report with 250 pages of photographs. *The Stanford Years 1827–1882*. Stanford University, 1972. History of Muybridge's work at Palo Alto Farm.

NEWHALL, Beaumont. *The History of Photography*. New York: Museum of Modern Art, Doubleday, 1964. See especially chapter 9; documentary (chapter 10); instant vision (chapter 11); and for the printed page (chapter 13).

GENERAL WORKS

BERGER, John. *Ways of Seeing*. London: Pelican, BBC and Penguin Books, 1972. Provocative and stimulating.

BETHERS, Ray. *Composition in Pictures*. New York, London: Pitman, 1949. Analysis of paintings but also suggestive about photography.

CAPA, Cornell. *The Concerned Photographer*. New York: Grossman. London: Thames and Hudson, 1972. Introduction to work of Marc Riboud, Roman Vishniac, Bruce Davidson, Gordon Parks, Ernest Haas, Hiroshi Hamaya, Donald McCullin, W. Eugene Smith.

EVANS, Hilary and Mary and NELKI, Andra. *The Picture Researcher's Handbook*. Newton Abbot, London, Vancouver: David and Charles.

FEININGER, Andreas. *Total Picture Control*. New York: Amphoto, 1972. See also *The Complete Photographer*. New Jersey: Prentice Hall, 1965. *Principles of Composition*. New York: Amphoto, 1973. *The Perfect Photograph. Photographic Seeing*. New Jersey: Prentice Hall, 1973. London. Thames and Hudson 1974. Mr. Feininger is prolific and professional on camera techniques.

LYONS, Nathan. *Photographers on Photography*. New Jersey: Prentice Hall, George Eastman House, Rochester, 1966. Brilliantly edited, thought-provoking selections from 23 photographers, including Eugene Smith, Cartier-Bresson, Edward Steichen, Paul Strand, Alfred Stieglitz, Minor White. No illustrations.

MARÉ, Eric de. *Photography*. London: Penguin Books, 1972. Good general introduction but Part 1, History and Purpose, may be read with profit by photojournalists.

SCHUNEMAN, R. Smith. *Photographic Communication*. London: Focal Press. Miami University, 1972. Mr. Smith, professor of journalism and mass communication at the University of Minnesota, summarises 15 years of contributions to Wilson Hicks International conferences on photo-communication.

STERN, Bert. *How to Turn Ideas into Images*. Alskog Book. London: Thames and Hudson. Paperback in series Masters of Contemporary Photography.

SZARKOWSKI, John. *Looking at Photographs*. New York: Museum of Modern Art, 1973. Commentary on 100 pictures from the collection. *The Photographer's Eye*. New York: Museum of Modern Art, Doubleday, 1966.

WALL, Dr. J. *Directory of British Photographic Collections*. London: Heinemann, 1977. Invaluable reference compiled on behalf of the Royal Photographic Society.

CARTIER-BRESSON, Henri. *The Decisive Moment*. New York: Simon and Schuster, 1952. Out of print but see also *The World of Cartier-Bresson*, Viking Press, 1968.

GRAPHICS AND PRODUCTION

CRAIG, James. *Production for the Graphic Designer*. London: Pitman. New York: Watson-Guptill, 1974.

CROY, Otto R. *Graphic Effects by Photography*. New York: Hastings House, 1973. Professor Croy's book translated from German. Professional level.

FLETCHER, A. FORBES, C., GILL, B. *Graphic Design : Visual Comparisons*. London: Studio Vista, 1963. New York: Reinhold, 1974.

DE SAUSMAREZ, Maurice. *Basic Design, The Dynamics of Visual Form*. London: Studio Vista, 1968.

DE VRIES, Leonard. *History as Hot News 1865–1897*. London: John Murray, 1973. Contemporary text and illustrations from *The Illustrated London News* and *The Graphics*. Shows us what we are missing by monopoly of the photograph.

HOGARTH, Paul. *The Artist as Reporter*. London: Studio Vista, 1967. New York: Reinhold Publishing Corpn.

LOCKWOOD, Arthur. *Diagrams*. London: Studio Vista. New York: Watson-Guptill, 1969.

MAGAZINES

AMATEUR PHOTOGRAPHER, Surrey House, 1 Throwley Way, Sutton, Surrey.

BRITISH JOURNAL OF PHOTOGRAPHY, 24 Wellington Street, London, W.C.2.

CAMERA, C. J. Bucher, Lucerne, Switzerland.

CAMERAWORK, Half Moon Photography Workshop, 27 Alie Street, London E.1.

COLUMBIA JOURNALISM REVIEW, Graduate School of Journalism, Columbia, New York, 10027.

CREATIVE CAMERA, 19 Doughty Street, London W.C.1.

DESIGN MAGAZINE, Design Council, 28 Haymarket, London, S.W.1.

THE IMAGE, Baroque Press, 38 James Street, London W.1.

MODERN PHOTOGRAPHY, Seymour Press, 334 Brixton Rd, London S.W.9.

NATIONAL PRESS PHOTOGRAPHER, Fargo, North Dakota, U.S.A.

NEWS PHOTOGRAPHER, 170 West End Ave. New York 10023, U.S.A.

PHOTO, 63 Champs-Elysées, Paris 8.

PHOTOGRAPHIC JOURNAL, 14 South Audley Street, London. W.1.

PHOTOGRAPHY MAGAZINE, Argus Press Distributors, 12–18 Paul Street, London E.C.2.

PHOTO-TECHNIQUE, Penblade Publishers, 50–60 Wigmore St. London W.1.

POPULAR PHOTOGRAPHY, Ziff-Davis, 1 Park Avenue, New York 10016.

PRACTICAL PHOTOGRAPHY, East Midland Allied Press.

SLR, Haymarket Publishing Ltd., Craven House, 34 Foubert's Place, London. W.1.

UK PRESS GAZETTE, Bouverie Publishing, Fetter Lane, London E.C.4.

Press Photo Awards

World Press Photo contest—World Press Photo, Holland Foundation, PO Box 3084, Koninginneweg 24, Amsterdam, Holland. Probably the most widely regarded.

Press Photographer of the Year: Organised by the Institute of Incorporated Photographers and the Midland Bank.

Sports Photographer of the Year: Organised by the Royal Photographic Society and the Sports Council (rules from RPS, 14 South Audley Street, London W1Y 5DP).

British Press Pictures Awards contest, organised by Mirror Group Newspapers Ltd., Holborn Circus, London EC3.

Nikon Photographic Award organised by Rank Audio Visual Ltd., PO Box 70 Great West Road, Brentford, Middlesex TW8 9HR.

Ilford £1000 Print Awards, organised by Ilford. Photojournalism and commercial categories.

The Pulitzer Prizes—Office of the Pulitzer Prize Committee, 702 Journalism, Columbia University, New York, N.Y. 10027, U.S.A. One for news photography and one for feature photography.

Pictures of the Year—Co-sponsored by the National Press Photographers Association, the University of Missouri School of Journalism and Nikon Inc. Address: Pictures of the Year Awards, School of Journalism, University of Missouri, Columbia, Missouri, 65201, U.S.A.

The Sigma Delta Chi Award for News Photography—Society of Professional Journalists, Sigma Delta Chi Award, 35 East Wacker Drive, Chicago, Illinois 6061, U.S.A.

The Robert Capa Award for Photography—Given by the Overseas Press Club, The Biltmore Hotel, 55 East 43rd Street, New York, N.Y. 10017, U.S.A.

The George Polk Award for Photography—Given by Long Island University, Brooklyn Centre, Brooklyn, New York 1120, U.S.A.

The Heywood Broun Award for Pictures That Help Right a Wrong—Given by the Newspaper Guild, 1125 15th Street N.W., Washington D.C. 20005, U.S.A.

The Royal Photographic Society (14 South Audley Street, London WIY 5DP) is open to all who are interested in photography. It takes a special interest in photojournalism with lectures, visits, publications and exhibitions, and has reorganised its regulations so that it can award distinctions of Fellowship and Associateship to visual journalists.

The Photographers Gallery. 8 Great Newport Street, London W.C.2. Rendezvous, exhibitions, books.

Credits

The author and publishers thank most warmly all the photographers, their agents and companies who generously assisted with this publication. Every attempt has been made to trace and acknowledge all the photographs. If there are any oversights, they are regretted. The author will be glad to hear if any of the 'photographer unknown' prints can be identified.

For the help given in preparation of this book, the author is additionally grateful to the following:

George W. Ashton, Ilford; Lord Barnetson, United Newspapers; Bruce Bernard, *Sunday Times Magazine*; Stewart J. Boyd, picture editor of the *Scotsman*; Kelvin Brodie, *Sunday Times*; Camera Press; Central Press; *The Daily Mail*; *The Daily Mirror*; Sue Davies, The Photographers' Gallery, London; *Detroit News*; John Dodge, formerly of National Council for the Training of Journalists; Bob Edwards, *Sunday Mirror*; Don Evans, *Northern Echo*; Arthur Firth as Northern editor of the *Daily Express*; Colin Ford, National Portrait Gallery; Yvonne Freund, Time Life Picture Agency; Bertram Garai of Keystone; David A. Gouldon, Essex County Newspapers; *The Guardian*; D. W. Hackett; Jack Hallam; John Hillelson, Magnum; Imperial War Museum; L. H. Jones, Express Newspapers; H. G. Kersting, as executive director of World Press Photo, Holland; The Kobal Collection; Derek S. Langdon, U.P.I.; T. Legoubin, Colorific Photo Library; Library of Congress; Stefan Lorant; Ted Majeski, U.P.I.; W. D. Matthews, Associated Newspapers; Henry Mecinski of Associated Press; Midland Bank; Mirror Group Newspapers; John Morris as picture editor of the *New York Times*; Marjorie Morris, as editor of *News Photographer* (U.S.); Museum of Modern Art, New York City; Bernard Neighbour; *New York Daily News*; A. C. Noble, of Argus South African Newspapers; Novosti Press Agency; Richard O'Regan, Associated Press; Geoffrey Pinnington, *The People*; Popper; Lynda Poley; Eric Pothecary, Press Association; Radio Times Hulton Picture Library; Mike Rand, *Sunday Times Magazine*; The Rank Organisation; Jim Spencer, U.P.I.; Frank Spooner, Gamma; Roy Strong, Victoria and Albert Museum; *Sunday Times* Darkroom; the *Sun*; *The Times*; Topix; J. W. Vickers, Ilford; Kenneth Warr, Royal Photographic Society; Charles Westberg, *Northern Echo*; Al Whalen, U.P.I.

Picture credits

1A	Topix
1B	Associated Press
2A	Edmund Hillary / *The Times*
3A	John Gilpin / Australian Consolidated Press, Sydney
4A	Army / Navy Taskforce / Associated Press
5A	Eddie Adams / Associated Press
6A	Bob Jackson / Camera Press
6B	*New York Herald Tribune*
7A	Kyoichi Sawada / United Press International
7B	Malcolm W. Browne / Associated Press
7C	Kent Gavin / *Daily Mirror* / Rank Award
8A	Nguyen Kong (Nick) Ut. / World Press Photo Award / Associated Press
8B	F.C.I. / *The People*
9A	James Jimmy Sime / Central Press
10A	Unknown
11A	Kelvin Brodie / *Sunday Times*
11B	Bert Hardy / Radio Times Hulton Picture Library
12A	United Press International
12B	Camera Press
12C	Leon Herschitt / Camera Press
12D	Planet News (Now United Press International)
12E	Associated Press
12F	Alfred Harris / Topix
12G	Topix
13A	Gordon Rule / Scotsman Publications / Rank Award
14A	Frank Herrmann / *Sunday Times*
14B	Imperial War Museum
14C	Arthur Rothstein
15A	Stanley Devon / *Sunday Times*
16A	Chris Smith / *The Sun* / Rank Award
17A	*The Times*
17B	*The Guardian*
18A	Ford Jenkins
18B	Feininger Photographic Society / United Press International
19A	Victoria and Albert Museum

20A	Gary Kagan / *New York Daily News*
21ABC	Bert Hardy / Radio Times Hulton Picture Library
22A	Bert Hardy / Radio Times Hulton Picture Library
23A	Cor Out / A & P / World Press Photo Award
23B	*New York Daily News*
24A	Sally Soames / *Sunday Times*
24B	Courtesy Mercedes-Benz
25A	R. Smithies / *The Guardian*
26A	Stanley Devon / *Sunday Times*
26B	Jill Freedman
26C	John Randle / *Birmingham Evening Mail* / Midland Bank Award
26D	David Cairns / *Daily Express* / Midland Bank Award
27A	Bryan Wharton / *Sunday Times*
27B	Mike Taylor / *Sunday Times*
28A	Mike Taylor / *Sunday Times*
28B	Alan Ballard / *Sunday Times*
28C	John Hopkins / *Sunday Times*
29A	Malcolm Aird / *Sunday Times*
29B	Paul Hopkins / *Sunday Times*
29C	*Daily Express*
30A	Mike Taylor / *Sunday Times*
30B	David Beal / *Sunday Times*
31A	Associated Press
32AB	Associated Press
33A	Bert Hardy / Radio Times Hulton Picture Library
35A	*The Northern Echo*
36ABC	Frank Herrmann / *Sunday Times*
37A	Nico Koster / *De Telegraaf* / World Press Photo Award
37B	John Randle / *Birmingham Evening Mail* / Midland Bank Award
37C	Ron Ernst / *Detroit News*
38A	Ben Steffen / World Press Photo Award
38B	Bob Coon / *Detroit News*
38C	United Press International
39A	Thurston Hopkins
40ABC	Frank Herrmann / *Sunday Times*
41AB	Frank Herrmann / *Sunday Times*
42AB	Ralph Morse / Time Life
42C	Nat Fein / *New York Herald Tribune*
43A	Bryan Wharton / *Sunday Times*
43B	Kelvin Brodie / *Sunday Times*
44A	Ian Tyas / Keystone / Midland Bank Award
45A	Ian Tyas / Keystone / Midland Bank Award
46A	Ian Tyas / Keystone / Midland Bank Award
48A	Charles Westberg / *The Northern Echo*
49A	Ossie Stamford / *The Northern Echo*
50A	Clive Limpkin / *Sunday Express* / Rank Award
50B	Alfred Markey
50C	Tony Spina / *Detroit Free Press*
51A	Peter McGrath / *Essex County Standard*
51B	*The Northern Echo*
52A	John Milne / *Daily Express*
53A	*The Northern Echo*
53B	*The Northern Echo*
54A	*The Northern Echo*
55A	David Cooksey / *Daily Express*
56A	Chris Thornton / *Sunday Times*
57A	*The Sun*
57C	Ian Wright / *The Northern Echo*
58A	Walker Evans / Library of Congress
58B	Michael Brennan / *Sun*, Manchester / Rank Award
59A	*The Northern Echo*
60A	*The Northern Echo*
61BCD	Ian Wright / *Sunday Times*
62A	Roger Scruton
63A	Dorothea Lange / Library of Congress
64A	Neal Slavin
65AB	Stanley Devon / *Sunday Times*
66AB	Stanley Devon / *Sunday Times*
67A	Stanley Devon / *Sunday Times*
68A	Eadweard Muybridge / Dover Publications
69A	Mark Seymour / Press Association
70A	*Yorkshire Evening Press*
71A	Colin Theakston / *The Northern Echo*
71B	Kent Gavin / *Daily Mirror* / Rank Award
71C	Olle Seijbold / *Dagens Nyheter* / World Press Photo Award
72A	Tommy Collins / *Irish Times* / Ilford Award
72B	Harold Evans
73A	*Sunday Times* / Topix
73B	*Sunday Times* / Topix
74A	*Sunday Times* / Topix
74B	P. A. Reuter
75A	E. D. Lacey / Ilford Award
76A	Sven Erik Sjoberg / *Dagens Nyheter* / World Press Photo Award
77AB	Michael Ward / *Sunday Times*
78D	Man Ray
79A	Co Rentmeester / *Life* / World Press Photo Award
79B	Chris Smith / *The Sun* / Rank Award
79C	E. D. Lacey
80A	Chris Smith / *The Sun* / Rank Award
80B	E. D. Lacey
81A	Frank Herrmann / *Sunday Times*
82AB	Frank Herrmann / *Sunday Times*
83A	A. W. Brownscombe
83B	Lyle Wachovsky
84A	Robert Capa / Magnum Print Courtesy I,C.P.
85A	Michael Ward / *Sunday Times*
86A	Terence McNally / *Sunday Times*
86B	Esther Bubley
86C	Michael Ward / *Sunday Times*
87B	*Sunday Times*
88A	Peter Kemp / *Associated Press*
88B	Clive Limpkin / *The Sun* / Ilford Award
89A	Murray Becker / Associated Press
90A	Murray Becker / Associated Press
90B	Philadelphia Public Ledger
91A	Alfred Gescheidt
92A	*Esquire*
93A	Chris Smith / *The Sun* / Rank Award
94A	Colin Theakston / *The Northern Echo*
95A	Stewart Fraser / Colorsport
95B	*Paris Match*
95C	Unknown
95D	George Tames / Associated Press
96A	Lord Snowdon
97A	Associated Press
98A	Arnold Newman
98B	Stanley Devon / *Sunday Times*
99A	Fred Hansen / Associated Press
100AB	Stanley Devon / *Sunday Times*
101A	Marion Kaplan / Camera Press
101B	Romano Cagnoni
101C	Stanley Devon / *Sunday Times*
103ABC	Michael Daines / Anglia Press Agency
105A	Horst Faas / World Press Photo
107A	Stanley Forman / *Boston Herald American*
108A	Associated Newspapers
108B	Yasushi Nagao / United Press International
108C	Joseph Stallino / Associated Press
109A	Frank Hudson / *Daily Mail*
110A	Bob Schutz / Associated Press
110B	Bert Hardy / Radio Times Hulton Picture Library
110C	Ray Gora / *Chicago Tribune*
11A	Steve Starr / Associated Press
111B	John T. Daniels / Associated Press
111C	Associated Press
112A	*Oxford Daily Mail*
112B	Jack Bradley / *Peoria Journal Star* / Courtesy Associated Press
113A	John Sadovy
114ABC	John Sadovy
115A	Planet News / United Press International
115B	Associated Press
116A	Mark Kauffman / Sports Illustrated / Time Inc.
117A	Don McCullin / *Sunday Times*
119A	Robert Capa / Magnum / Courtesy I.C.P.
119B	Harry Benson / Time Life / U.S. National Press Photographers Associated Award
120A	Bert Hardy / Radio Times Hulton Picture Library
120B	Eve Arnold
121A	Dan Weiner / Courtesy I.C.P.
121B	Keystone
122A	Ron Haeberle / *Life Magazine* © 1969 Time Inc.
123A	W. Eugene Smith
125A	Cartier-Bresson / Magnum
127A	Robert Capa / Magnum / Courtesy I.C.P.
128ABC	Photographer unknown / *New York Times*
129A	Photographer unknown / *New York Times*
131AB	Associated Press
132A	Stuart Heydinger / *The Observer*
133ABC and 134A	Alan Aaronson / *New York Daily News*
135AB	Walter Frentz / Associated Press
136A	Jime Domke / *San Francisco Examiner*
136B	Sal Veder / Associated Press / Pulitzer Award

137ABC	Colin Theakston / *The Northern Echo*
138ABCDE	United Press International
139A	Press Association
140A	M. Ludford / United Press International
142A	United Press International
142B	Roger Ansong
142C	United Press International
142D	Nguyen Kong (Nick) Ut / Associated Press / World Press Photo Award
143A–I	Ian Bradshaw / *Sunday Mirror* / Midland Bank Award
144A	Ian Bradshaw / *Sunday Mirror* / Midland Bank Award
145AB	Joe Rosenthal / Associated Press
146AB	Joe Rosenthal / Associated Press
147B	Joe Rosenthal / Associated Press
148A	Joe Rosenthal / Associated Press
149A	Associated Press
150A	Eddie Adams / *Time* / World Press Photo Award
151A	James Pickerell / Camera Press
151B	Popper
151C	James Pickerell / Camera Press
151DE	Associated Press
151F	Popper
152A	James Pickerell / Camera Press
152B	Keystone
152C	Associated Press
152D	Popper
152E	Frank Herrmann / *Sunday Times*
153A	Kelvin Brodie / *Sunday Times*
154A	Kelvin Brodie / *Sunday Times*
155AB	Fay Godwin
156ABCD	Fay Godwin
157AB	Eva Sereny / *Sunday Times*
158AB	Eva Sereny / *Sunday Times*
159AB	Keystone
160A	Ernst Haas / Courtesy I.C.P.
161A	Bert Stern (Alskog)
162A–F	Lord Snowdon
163A	Camera Press
163B	*New York Times*
163CD	*Time*
164A	Rank Film Distributors Ltd.
164B	*Sunday Times*
164C	Kelvin Brodie / *Sunday Times*
164D	Penny Tweedie
164E	Marion Kaplan / Camera Press
164F	Alain Mingam
164GH	Ralph Crane / Camera Press
165A	Kelvin Brodie / *Sunday Times*
165B	Vsevolod Tarasewich / Novosti Press Agency / World Press Photo Award
165C	Alfred Markey / World Press Photo Award
166A	Lord Snowdon
167A	Bill Brandt
168ABC	Bill Brandt
169A	Associated Press
170A	Associated Press
170B	Mark Shaw
171A	M. C. Meyboom
172A	W. F. Leyns
173ABCD	Hurst Ossinger / United Press International / World Press Photo Award
173EFG	J. Parke Randall / Associated Press
175ABC	Malcolm Browne / Associated Press
175DEFG	Bob Coon / *Detroit News*
177A–F	Michael Brennan / *Sun*, Manchester / Rank Award
179AB	Bryan Wharton / *Sunday Times*
180ABC	Bryan Wharton / *Sunday Times*
181AB	Norman Midgley / *Daily Express*
182A	Norman Midgley / *Daily Express*
183A	Press Association
184AB	Rex Features Ltd / Sipa Press
185A	Unknown
185B	Associated Press
186A	Stefan Tihor / Bulgarian Telegraph Agency / World Press Photo Award
186BC	United Press International
186D	Kyoichi Sawada / United Press International
187A	Associated Press
188A	James Thomson / *Glasgow Herald*
189A	Kip Rano / Rex Features
191A	Aubrey Hart / *Evening Standard* / Midland Bank Award
193A	Planet News—United Press International
195A	Press Association
196A	A.N.P.
197A	Henri Dauman / *New York Times*
198A	United Press International
199A	Terence Fincher / *Daily Express* / Rank Award
201A	Pat Burns / *New York Times*
203A	Jenao Olivares / Associated Press
205A	Associated Press
207AB	United Press International
208AB	United Press International
209AB	United Press International
210AB	United Press International
211A	Neil Libbert / *Sunday Times*
212A	United Press International
213A	Stanley Devon / *Sunday Times*
213C	Popper
213D	Associated Press
214AB	Associated Press
217A	Photographer unknown / Associated Press
218C	Photographer unknown / Associated Press
218A	United Press International
220A	Melville Parry / Topix
223A	Associated Press
225A	P. Jones Griffiths / Magnum
226A	Ray News / *Argos-Leader*, Sioux Falls / Courtesy Associated Press
226B	John Lindsay / Associated Press
228A	Colin Theakston / *The Northern Echo*
229A	Max Desfor / Associated Press
229B	Don McCullin / Magnum
230A	Murray Sayle / *Sunday Times* / Topix
230B	Beverley Goodway / *The Times*
231A	John Filo / Courtesy Associated Press
233A	Keystone
235A	John Lindsay / Associated Press
237A	N.A.S.A.
238A	United Press International
239A	Garbo / Kobal Collection
239B	David Barnes / *Sunday Times*
239C	Karsh of Ottawa
239D	Colin Davey / Camera Press
239E	Stephanie Simmonds / Oxfam
239F	Kelvin Brodie / *Sunday Times*
239G	United Press International
240A	Central Press
240B	Photographer unknown / *Sunday Times* archives
240C	Alfred Harris / Topix
240D	*Daily Express*
240E	David Kilpatrick
241A	*Sunday Times* Archives
242A	Photographer unknown / Courtesy Alexander Berners
243A	Peter Mitchel / World Press Photo Award
243BC	Wil Hofland / World Press Photo Award
244A	*Daily Mirror*
245A	Robert Freson / *Sunday Times Magazine*
247AB	Felix Man / *Weekly Illustrated* / Courtesy Stefan Lorant
248A	Stefan Lorant / *Weekly Illustrated*
249A–K	Eddie Adams / Associated Press
256B	Leonid Bergoltsev / World Press Photo Award
259A	Bert Mason / *Daily Mail*
263A	Associated Press
266A	Leonardo Henrickson
267A	Keystone
272A	Frank Herrmann / *Sunday Times*
273A	Adrian Williams
273B	Frank Herrmann / *Sunday Times*
275B–G	Adrian Williams
277A	Harold Evans
277B	Kelvin Brodie / *Sunday Times*
277C	Michael Ward / *Sunday Times*
278A	Hugues Vassal / Gamma
279ABCD	Eva Sereny
279E	Headliners (U.K.)
281B	Peter Dunne / *Sunday Times*
283A	Kelvin Brodie / *Sunday Times*
283BCD	Murray Sayle / *Sunday Times* / Join up by Jack Hallam
284DEFG	Peter Dunne / *Sunday Times* / Join up by Jack Hallam
285A	Kobal Collection
285C	*The Northern Echo*
286B	Army Air Forces / Print courtesy *Life*
324A	W. E. Kilburn. Reproduced by gracious permission of Her Majesty the Queen Elizabeth II.

Graphics

In the section of graphics, I am indebted to the following artists, designers and editors.

Peter Brooke; David Case; Roy Castle; Bob Christopher of *Newsweek*; *Daily Express*; *Daily Mail*; Nick Faure; John Grimwade; Bert Hackett of *The Birmingham Post*; Ray Hawkey; Harry Hoffman; Horner; Ford Jenkins, the photographer; Don MacKay of *Newsweek*; Duncan Mil; *New York Times*; *Observer*; Michael Rand; Gerald Scarfe; John Sewell; Edwin Taylor; John Thirsk; Sheila Ware.

Index

Figures in *italics* refer to illustration numbers